Reconfiguring the Portrait

Technicities

Published
Lyotard and the Inhuman Condition: Reflections on Nihilism, Information and Art
Ashley Woodward

Critical Luxury Studies: Art, Design, Media
Edited by John Armitage and Joanne Roberts

Cold War Legacies: Systems, Theory, Aesthetics
Edited by John Beck and Ryan Bishop

Fashion and Materialism
Ulrich Lehmann

Queering Digital India: Activisms, Identities, Subjectivities
Edited by Rohit K. Dasgupta and Debanuj DasGupta

Zero Degree Seeing: Barthes/Burgin and Political Aesthetics
Edited by Ryan Bishop and Sunil Manghani

Rhythm and Critique: Technics, Modalities, Practices
Edited by Paola Crespi and Sunil Manghani

Photography Off the Scale: Technologies and Theories of the Mass Image
Edited by Tomáš Dvořák and Jussi Parikka

The Informational Logic of Human Rights: Network Imaginaries in the Cybernetic Age
Josh Bowsher

Art and Technology in Maurice Blanchot
Holly Langstaff

China and the Wireless Undertow: Media as Wave Philosophy
Anna Greenspan

Reconfiguring the Portrait
Edited by Abraham Geil and Tomáš Jirsa

www.edinburghuniversitypress.com/series/TECH

Reconfiguring the Portrait

Edited by Abraham Geil and Tomáš Jirsa

EDINBURGH
University Press

Edinburgh University Press is one of the leading university presses in the UK. We publish academic books and journals in our selected subject areas across the humanities and social sciences, combining cutting-edge scholarship with high editorial and production values to produce academic works of lasting importance. For more information visit our website: edinburghuniversitypress.com

Edinburgh University Press Ltd
13 Infirmary Street,
Edinburgh, EH1 1LT

First published in hardback by Edinburgh University Press 2023

Typeset in 11/13 Adobe Sabon by
IDSUK (DataConnection) Ltd

A CIP record for this book is available from the British Library

ISBN 978 1 3995 2507 7 (hardback)
ISBN 978 1 3995 2508 4 (paperback)
ISBN 978 1 3995 2509 1 (webready PDF)
ISBN 978 1 3995 2510 7 (epub)

Contents

Figures

Contributors

Elisa Aaltola is a philosopher who has specialised in animal and environmental ethics and moral psychology. Aaltola has written around forty peer-reviewed articles on themes such as the moral status of non-human animals, the role of emotions in understanding climate change, the moral psychology of anthropocentrism, and the relevance of propositional language in making sense of animality, together with a number of Finnish monographs and edited volumes. In English, she has published *Animal Suffering: Philosophy and Culture* (Palgrave, 2012) and *Varieties of Empathy: Moral Psychology and Animal Ethics* (Rowman and Littlefield, 2018), and she co-edited the volume *Animal Ethics and Philosophy: Questioning the Orthodoxy* (Rowman and Littlefield, 2014) with John Hadley.

Pietro Conte is Associate Professor of Aesthetics at the State University of Milan. Before taking on his current position, he worked at the University of Lisbon (2015–18) and at Ca' Foscari University of Venice (2018–22). His research focuses on illusion, hyperrealism, immersive (virtual) environments, and the multifarious practices of unframing, a thematic cluster he first explored in the monographs *Unframing Aesthetics* (2019) and *In carne e cera. Estetica e fenomenologia dell'iperrealismo* (*Flesh and Wax: Aesthetics and Phenomenology of Hyperrealism*, 2014). He is a team member of the ERC project 'An-Iconology: History, Theory, and Practices of Environmental Images', where he is carrying out research on digital immortality and contemporary developments in thanatology.

Sudeep Dasgupta is Associate Professor in Media Studies, University of Amsterdam. His research interests and publications focus on aesthetics and politics in the fields of visual culture, globalisation and migration, gender and queer studies, and postcolonial studies. His book publications include the edited volume *What's Queer about Europe?* (with M. Rosello; Fordham University Press, 2014) and

Constellations of the Transnational: Modernity, Culture, Critique (2007). Recent publications include 'Disidentification, Intimacy and the Cinematic Figuration of the Postcolonial in Europe', *Mise au Point* (2021), 'The Aesthetics of Displacement: Dissonance and Dissensus in Adorno and Rancière', in *Distributions of the Sensible: Rancière, between Aesthetics and Politics* (2019), and 'The Aesthetics of Indirection: Intermittent Adjacencies and Subaltern Presences at the Borders of Europe', *Cinéma & Cie* (2017).

Georges Didi-Huberman is a philosopher and art historian; he teaches at the École des Hautes Études en Sciences Sociales (Paris) and has held fellowships from such institutions as l'Académie de France, Harvard University Center for Italian Renaissance Studies, the Warburg Institute in London, and the Getty Research Institute in Los Angeles. He has also been a Visiting Professor at Johns Hopkins, Northwestern, Berkeley, Courtauld Institute, Freie Universität (Berlin), Basel, and Tokyo, among others. He has curated several exhibitions, such as *L'Empreinte* (Centre Georges Pompidou, Paris, 1997), *Atlas* (Museo nacional Centro de Arte Reina Sofía, Madrid, 2010), and *Nouvelles histoires de fantômes* (Tourcoing, Rio de Janeiro, Beirut, Paris). He has published about fifty books on the history and theory of images, some of them translated into English, such as *Fra Angelico: Dissemblance and Figuration* (University of Chicago Press, 1995), *Invention of Hysteria: Charcot and the Photographic Iconography of Salpêtrière* (MIT Press, 2003), *Confronting Images: Questioning the Ends of a Certain History of Art* (Pennsylvania State University Press, 2005), and *Images in Spite of All: Four Photographs from Auschwitz* (University of Chicago Press, 2008).

Abraham Geil is Senior Lecturer of Film Studies in the Media Studies Department at the University of Amsterdam, where he directs the MA Programme in Film Studies, and a Research Fellow at the Amsterdam School of Cultural Analysis (ASCA). He holds a PhD in Literature from Duke University. He has taught previously at the University of Iowa and the New School for Social Research, and was a recipient of the Andrew W. Mellon/American Council of Learned Societies Dissertation Fellowship. His research and teaching lie at the intersection of critical theory, aesthetics, and film studies, with a focus on the history of film theory. He is the co-editor (with Lauren Rabinovitz) of *Memory Bytes: History, Technology, and Digital Culture* (Duke University Press, 2004). His recent articles can be found in journals such as *Novel, Polygraph, World*

Picture, *Paragraph*, and *Screen*, as well as in edited collections on the work of Sergei Eisenstein and Jacques Rancière.

Kaisu Hynnä-Granberg is Postdoctoral Research Fellow in Gender Studies at the University of Turku, Finland. She holds a PhD in Media Studies at the University of Turku. Her research interests include body politics, affect theory, selfies, and social media research. In her PhD, Hynnä-Granberg investigates the body-positive movement in digital media, analysing its affective dimensions and ways of moving the subject. The study focuses on the feeling body and the ways in which the body becomes aware of itself through media practices. Hynnä-Granberg has published in journals such as *Social Media + Society*, *Feminist Media Studies*, and *Fat Studies*.

Tomáš Jirsa is Associate Professor of Literary Studies at Palacký University Olomouc, Czech Republic. His work traces the relations between modern literature and the visual arts, affect studies, media theory, and music video. In 2015 and 2017 he was awarded a junior fellowship from the International Research Institute for Cultural Techniques and Media Philosophy (IKKM) at Bauhaus University, Weimar; in 2019 he was Visiting Scholar at the Amsterdam School for Cultural Analysis (ASCA). Among his recent publications are *Disformations: Affects, Media, Literature* (Bloomsbury, 2021), *Traveling Music Videos* (co-edited with Mathias Bonde Korsgaard; Bloomsbury, 2023), and *How to Do Things with Affects: Affective Triggers in Aesthetic Forms and Cultural Practices* (co-edited with Ernst van Alphen; Brill, 2019). His articles can be found in journals such as *Music, Sound, and the Moving Image, Zeitschrift für Medien- und Kulturforschung, Iluminace*, and *World Literature Studies*.

Roland Meyer is a researcher in media studies at the Collaborative Research Centre *Virtual Lifeworlds* at Ruhr University Bochum. His research focuses on the history and theory of technical images, virtual image archives, and the visual culture of modernity. His publications include *Operative Porträts. Eine Bildgeschichte der Identifizierbarkeit von Lavater bis Facebook* (Konstanz University Press, 2019), *Medien/Architekturen* (special issue of *ZfM – Zeitschrift für Medienwissenschaft*, 2015, co-edited with Christa Kamleithner and Julia Weber), and *Architekturwissen. Grundlagentexte aus den Kulturwissenschaften*, 2 vols (co-edited with Susanne Hauser and Christa Kamleithner, Bielefeld, 2011). In 2016–17 he worked as a curatorial assistant on the special exhibition *The Face: A Search for Clues* at the Deutsches Hygiene-Museum Dresden. In 2017 he led the research group *Das Technische Bild* at the Hermann von Helmholtz Centre for Cultural Techniques of the Humboldt-Universität zu Berlin.

Nicole Erin Morse is an Assistant Professor of Communication and Multimedia Studies and Director of the Center for Women, Gender, and Sexuality Studies at Florida Atlantic University. Their research has been published in *Discourse, Journal of Popular Film and Television, Jump Cut, Feminist Media Studies, Porn Studies, [in]Transition,* and elsewhere. *Selfie Aesthetics: Seeing Trans Feminist Futures in Self Representational Art* (Duke University Press, 2022) examines the political, theoretical, and aesthetic potential of selfies.

Susanna Paasonen is Professor of Media Studies at the University of Turku, Finland. With an interest in studies of sexuality, networked media, and affect, she is the PI of the Strategic Research Council consortium, 'Intimacy in Data-Driven Culture'. Recent publications include *TechnoPharmacology* (with Joshua Neves, Aleena Chia, and Ravi Sundaram; University of Minnesota Press, 2022), *Dependent, Distracted, Bored: Affective Formations in Networked Media* (MIT Press, 2021), *Who's Laughing Now? Feminist Tactics in Social Media* (with Jenny Sundén; MIT Press, 2020) and *Objectification: On the Difference Between Sex and Sexism* (with Feona Attwood, Alan McKee, John Mercer, and Clarissa Smith; Routledge, 2020).

Andrea Pinotti (PhD in Philosophy) is Full Professor of Aesthetics at the Department of Philosophy 'Piero Martinetti' of the State University of Milan, where he runs the ERC Advanced Project 'AN-ICON. An-Iconology: History, Theory, and Practices of Environmental Images', devoted to the interpretation of immersive environments. His main research interests include aesthetics, art theory, art history, the morphological tradition, image theories and visual culture studies, memory studies (monuments and memorials), and empathy theories. In 2018 he was awarded the Wissenschaftspreis der Aby-Warburg-Stiftung in Hamburg. Among his recent publications is *Culture visuelle. Images, regards, médias, dispositifs,* co-authored with Antonio Somaini (Les presses du réel, 2022).

Brian Price is Professor of Visual Studies at the University of Toronto. He is the author of *A Theory of Regret* (Duke University Press, 2017) and *Neither God nor Master: Robert Bresson and Radical Politics*

(University of Minnesota Press, 2011). Price is a founding editor of *World Picture*. He is also series editor, for Northwestern University Press, of *Superimpositions: Philosophy and the Moving Image*.

Kate Rennebohm is currently an SSHRC Postdoctoral Fellow at Concordia University, where she is working on a book manuscript titled *Reviewing the Self-Image: Ethics, Politics, and Moving Image Media*. Recently a visiting faculty member at Harvard University, where she also completed her PhD, her work engages with film and media philosophy and argues for the historical mediation of ethical thought, particularly as concerns media of self-engagement. Her writing has been published in *October*, *Moving Image Review and Art Journal*, *Cinema Scope*, the edited collection *Movies with Stanley Cavell in Mind*, and she co-edited the recent *Screen* issue 'Projecting Cavell: New Contexts, New Questions'. Her essay on 'enforced skepticism' is also forthcoming in *Critical Inquiry*.

Elena Vogman is a scholar of comparative literature and media. She is Principal Investigator of the research project 'Madness, Media, Milieus: Reconfiguring the Humanities in Postwar Europe' at Bauhaus University Weimar and Visiting Fellow at ICI Berlin Institute for Cultural Inquiry. Her current work focuses on the politics of madness and its intersections with decolonial discourse, psychoanalysis, feminism, and institutional psychotherapy. She has published two books, *Sinnliches Denken. Eisensteins exzentrische Methode* (Sensuous Thinking: Eisenstein's Eccentric Method, 2018) and *Dance of Values: Sergei Eisenstein's Capital Project* (2019), and was Visiting Professor at École normale supérieure, Paris and New York University Shanghai. Together with Marie Rebecchi and Till Gathmann she co-curated *Sergei Eisenstein and the Anthropology of Rhythm* (2017) and *Eccentric Values after Eisenstein* (2018).

Sigrid Weigel directed the Research Center for Literature and Culture (ZfL Berlin), which she transformed into a site of radical interdisciplinary work. Prior to that, she taught in Hamburg, Zürich, Berlin, and Princeton, and acted as director of the Einstein Forum. She is the author of numerous books, including *Body- and Image Space: Re-Reading Walter Benjamin* (Routledge, 1996), *Ingeborg Bachmann* (Zsolnay, 1999), *Walter Benjamin, Images, the Creaturely, and the Holy* (Stanford University Press, 2008), and *Grammatologie der Bilder* (Suhrkamp, 2015). She is also editor of a volume of the writings of Aby Warburg, Gershom Scholem, and Susan Taubes, and co-editor of several more, such as *A Neuro-Psychoanalytical Dialogue* *for Bridging Freud and the Neurosciences* (Springer, 2016), *Empathy: Epistemic Problems and Cultural-Historical Perspectives* (Palgrave Macmillan, 2017), and *Testimony / Bearing Witness: Epistemology, Ethics, History and Culture* (Rowman and Littlefield, 2017). She has received several honorary doctorates, and is an honorary member of the MLA. She recently organised an exhibition on 'The Face': *Das Gesicht. Bilder, Medien, Formate* at Deutsches Hygiene-Museum Dresden (2017–18).

Daniël de Zeeuw is an assistant professor in Digital Media Culture at the University of Amsterdam and a FWO junior postdoctoral fellow at the Institute for Media Studies at KU Leuven. He is also an active member of the Open Intelligence Lab (oilab.eu) and the Digital Methods Initiative (digitalmethods.net), co-editor of *Krisis: journal for contemporary philosophy* (krisis.eu) and affiliated with the Institute of Network Cultures (networkcultures.org). His current research and teaching focus on post-truth media epistemologies at the fringes of digital culture, including conspiracy theories, leaking, trolling, and memes.

Series Editors' Preface

Technological transformation has profound and frequently unforeseen influences on art, design and media. At times technology emancipates art and enriches the quality of design. Occasionally it causes acute individual and collective problems of mediated perception. Time after time technological change accomplishes both simultaneously. This new book series explores and reflects philosophically on what new and emerging *technicities* do to our everyday lives and increasingly immaterial technocultural conditions. Moving beyond traditional conceptions of the philosophy of technology and of techne, the series presents new philosophical thinking on how technology constantly alters the essential conditions of beauty, invention and communication. From novel understandings of the world of technicity to new interpretations of aesthetic value, graphics and information, Technicities focuses on the relationships between critical theory and representation, the arts, broadcasting, print, technological genealogies/histories, material culture and digital technologies and our philosophical views of the world of art, design and media.

The series foregrounds contemporary work in art, design and media whilst remaining inclusive, in terms of both philosophical perspectives on technology and interdisciplinary contributions. For a philosophy of technicities is crucial to extant debates over the artistic, inventive and informational aspects of technology. The books in the Technicities series concentrate on present-day and evolving technological advances but visual, design-led and mass mediated questions are emphasised to further our knowledge of their often-combined means of digital transformation.

The editors of Technicities welcome proposals for monographs and well-considered edited collections that establish new paths of investigation.

Ryan Bishop and Jussi Parikka

Acknowledgements

Besides providing riches to read, to live with, and think of even at the least opportune moments, editing a volume of essays also creates an inventory of debt. People we are indebted to for their love and friendship, without which a single page of this volume wouldn't be possible, know who they are. Therefore, we would like to thank out loud those persons and institutions to whom our portrait project owes its inception.

This book was initiated and made possible thanks to the research project 'Between Affects and Technology: The Portrait in the Visual Arts, Literature and Music Video' (JG_2019_007), funded by the Faculty of Arts of Palacký University Olomouc, between 2019 and 2021. For general support we also wish to thank Amsterdam School for Cultural Analysis (ASCA). We are especially grateful to Ryan Bishop and Jussi Parikka, the co-editors of the Technicities series at Edinburgh University Press, for adding our volume to their compelling list of works. Our gratitude goes also to the EUP Commissioning Editor Carol MacDonald, who was of great help during the whole production process.

An inventory of debt and, no doubt, a portrayal of encounters. The co-editors of this book would hardly have met had they not both had the pleasure of knowing Eugenie Brinkema, who – as she always gracefully does, faithful to her generous manner – brought them together in late 2018. In addition to sparking a long-standing collaboration, friendship, and intense encounters between Amsterdam, Olomouc, and Brno, Eugenie has also helped us tremendously with contacting several contributors to this book. As co-editors, our thanks go also to Tomáš Dvořák, Bernd Herzogenrath, and Daniel Nemrava. A special note of thanks to Andrea Průchová Hrůzová and the visual artist Jiří Thýn for allowing us to reproduce his work on the book cover.

Chapter 1 – Introduction

Configurations of Portraiture: Subjectivity, Techniques, Mediality

Abraham Geil and Tomáš Jirsa

The fate of portraiture in art history and theory offers an especially illuminating terrain for thinking the mediations of subjectivity in the post-digital era.[1] As a significant body of art-historical schol-arship has argued in recent decades, the seemingly inextricable link between portraiture and the status of the subject continues to (re)animate the portrait's perpetual resurrection in twentieth- and twenty-first-century art after its various deaths as a pictorial category – even (or especially) as it is carried out under the sign of the 'anti-portrait' (Buchloh 2015; van Alphen 1997; Johnstone and Imber 2020). The 'anti-portrait' has emerged as an umbrella term for a whole host of twentieth- and twenty-first-century artis-tic and curatorial strategies that have sought to radically undo the traditional Western understanding of the portrait inherited from Renaissance painting.[2] In essence, that traditional understanding posited a kind of physiognomic contract between the plenitude of the bourgeois self, on the one hand, and the mimetic model of rep-resentation by which it is portrayed, on the other. Each stood as guarantor of the other.[3]

This is the contract that Picasso was thought to have definitively shredded with his portrait of Gertrude Stein in 1906 and, especially, his 1910 portraits of his dealers Daniel-Henry Kahnweiler, Ambroise Vollard, and Wilhelm Uhde (Bois 1990). Together these paintings have assumed the status of a canonical origin point for the anti-portrait in twentieth-century art (Johnstone and Imber 2020: 8; Brilliant 1991: 149–52). Building on Yve-Alain Bois's famous analysis, Ernst van Alphen describes how these Cubist portraits radically undid the pre-vious contract between subjectivity and representation by shifting from a mimetic model to one of structural difference, splitting the previous semiotic unity between signifier and signified (1997: 241–2). Such dismantling of the traditional portrait at the hands of early twentieth-century avant-garde art movements is, of course, only one way to trace the birth of the anti-portrait.[4]

Rather than marking its demise, as Cubist deconstruction arguably had for other traditional genres in painting such as the nude, the still life, and the landscape, the portrait has been 'continuously re-staged on the ruins of representation' (Buchloh 2015: 474). As evidence, one need only invoke the names of all the significant modern and post-modern artists – Lucien Freud, Francis Bacon, Gerhard Richter, Andy Warhol, Cindy Sherman, Marlene Dumas, to name but a few of the most prominent – whose works carry on and extend the project of portraiture precisely by problematising and even exploding its traditional conception. We can think as well of the way portraiture as a curatorial category seems to provide an inexhaustible resource for organising art exhibitions up to this day. Indeed, the portrait, as Benjamin Buchloh memorably puts it, 'seems to renew itself and rear its heads (like those of the Hydra) almost instantly after their inevitable decapitation' (2015: 473).

The aim of this book is not to forward yet another theory of the portrait that explains this perpetual resurrection in terms of an endless series of movements and counter-movements, with each new iteration of the portrait undone by the next 'anti-portrait' to follow. Rather, our intervention is intended to shift the understanding of portraiture from its existing hermeneutic contexts as a canonical genre of representation to a media-theoretical approach that apprehends it as a diverse set of practices situated in material, technological, and media networks. Reading backwards and forwards in relation to the threshold of (post-) digital systems and aesthetics, this book explores the portrait across a capacious range of media and cultural forms, including literature, drawings, paintings, grave stelae, films, gallery installations, contemporary music videos, deepfakes, social media, video games, and immersive VR interfaces. From nineteenth-century anthropometrics to the operational portraits of AI-read big data, from the ethics of presence in modernist erotic paintings to the Gothic resonances of deepfakes and the cartographic tracings of the movements of neuro-divergent (autistic) children, from the 'avatarisation' of the self online to the loss-of-self portrait in gallery art, from social media profiles of non-human animals to post-mortem visitations of the dead, the individual chapters together make a case for radically expanding the frame of what counts as portraiture. To prepare the ground for this expanded frame, we need to engage in conversation between art history and media theory, a conversation that begins precisely with an attempted murder of its main topic.

Towards a Conversation between Art History and Media Theory

By way of explaining the portrait's unique persistence as something like the *undead* genre of twentieth-century art, Buchloh posits a claim which in many ways sets the terms for the discussion of portraiture from the mid-1990s to the present:[5]

> [W]e can propose that actual correspondences exist between the pictorial and the epistemic, correspondences that attest to a causal nexus between rapidly changing conceptions of the subject, and the equally rapid disintegration and desperate resurrection of the traditional genre of portraiture. (Buchloh 2015: 474–6)

This claim raises the question of how precisely to understand its move from 'correspondences' to causality. What is the directionality, if any, in this 'causal nexus' between mutations in the idea of the subject and the portrait's perpetual death and rebirth? In other words, is this primarily a dynamic internal to the history of art, with portraiture occupying one pictorial category among others in which the strategies of larger movements and counter-movements play out? On this view, older notions of subjectivity are called into question and new pictures of the subject emerge primarily at the level of aesthetic and conceptual innovations in artistic form. Or is it rather that the radical changes in portraiture are 'determined [. . .] more importantly by an epistemic change in the conception of subjectivity' under conditions of image production and circulation that Buchloh does not hesitate to call consumer capitalism's 'regime of total reification' (2015: 474, 486)? In this case, portraiture is compelled to take up a relation to the only models of subjectivity that remain available to it in the wake of the subject's ongoing destruction. Faced with the options of either a reactionary restoration of an outmoded conception of the subject as a unified and unique self (bourgeois interiority) or complicity in the further reification of the subject as pure exchange value (simulacrum), the portrait genre, on this latter view, 'legitimizes itself only by testifying to the historically grotesque claims to provide an adequate representation of the subject' (2015: 487).

In our view, the most fruitful approaches to the portrait are those that keep open this question of the 'causal nexus' between the fate of the subject and its (anti-)representations, taking it not as a site of explanatory closure but rather as the very dialectic driving the proliferation of contemporary portraiture. That is the rich vein of art-historical scholarship that this book seeks to enter into a dialogue with. To begin with, this dialogue must contend with the strong tendency in much of this body of work to make the disappearance of the subject into the dominant (if not the sole) condition of possibility for thinking the portrait today. The ironic pun in the subtitle of Buchloh's seminal essay (the 'Ends of Portraiture') not only conveys the fact that portraiture has never really ended but also signals the presence of a teleology driving its perpetual resurrection: the disappearance of the subject.

'The portrait returns', as van Alphen notes, 'but with a difference, now exemplifying a critique of the bourgeois self instead of its authority; showing a loss of self instead of its consolidation; shaping the subject as a simulacrum instead of as origin' (1997: 242). Indeed, scholars of Western modernism have convincingly demonstrated that the traditional link between visual depiction and interior self is no longer tenable (Woodall 1997), emphasising instead the aesthetics of material surfaces as well as the intersubjective and archival constellations that produce the portrait as a 'social document' (Sousloff 2006: 27) that forms part of the more extensive 'social body' (Sekula 1986: 6). To characterise the way many modernist and contemporary visual artists underscore the removal or deformation of the portrayed faces and bodies, Judith Elizabeth Weiss proposes the term the 'non-depicting portrait', whereby the presence of the portrayed subject 'occurs under the condition of an inerasable difference between the seen and the imagined' (2013: 141). Exploring the recent tendency in figurative art of such artists as David Hockney, Jacques Monory, and Mathilde Hiesse to account for the loss, absence, and disappearance of the human figure, Jean-Luc Nancy argues that the function of what he calls the 'other portrait' is no longer to reproduce a living person but instead to evoke its uncertain identity. Unlike traditional portraiture, which relies on mimetic representation of the sitter's unique subjectivity and whose aim is to render the subject's appearance, the 'other portrait' according to Nancy proceeds from 'an identity that is hardly supposed at all, but rather is evoked in its withdrawal' (2018: 94).

Hans Belting presents the withdrawal of the subject as the end point of a much broader historical teleology in the final chapter of his *Face and Mask* (2017), an impressive work that offers a model for the sort of dialogue between art history and media theory that this book also seeks to foster.[6] Belting traces the cultural history and media archaeology of portraiture from prehistoric death masks to artificially generated identities in the post-digital era. Announcing a new reign of digital faces which rejects any traditional claim of resemblance and likeness of a real human being, Belting argues that we are now immersed in a 'digital masquerade' populated by fully artificial CGI or biotechnically morphed 'cyberfaces' that 'are not faces but rather digital masks with which the production of faces has reached a turning point in the modern media' (2017: 239, 241). On this view, the flood of these synthetic identities and proxies has so inundated the media ecosystem that the portrait can simply no longer be thought in terms of a dialectic of the appearance and withdrawal of 'real' subjects at all. These biotechnological stakes are tackled in many of the present chapters that deal especially with social media identities, such as Iiu Susiraja's subversive Instagram selfies (Kaisu Hynnä-Granberg and Susanna Paasonen), generative AI images (Daniël de Zeeuw and Abraham Geil), VR technologies and environments (Pietro Conte), Jeremy Shaw's gallery installations of moving images (Kate Rennebohm), the cyber proxies of avatars (Andrea Pinotti), and the deepfake videos circulating on YouTube (Nicole Morse). What aligns these chapters is an emphasis on the portrait as a key conceptual figure that allows us to examine the relationship between digital and post-digital systems, politics, and aesthetic forms from within their media settings, operative chains, and circulations.

In other quarters, however, the traditional conception of the portrait devoted precisely to the consolidation of the subject is alive and well. One has only to take a fleeting glance, for instance, at the selection of the Royal Society of Portrait Painters Annual Exhibition 2020 accommodated by the renowned Mall Galleries to get an idea why many modernist painters and contemporary visual artists have either dismantled the grounds of the genre or have discarded it altogether. The exhibited drawings, photographs, and paintings show barely more than a repetitive view of pensive faces, calculated poses and gestures, family gatherings, shy gazes staring sideways. The same predictable pattern holds for the section 'Contemporary Portraits' exhibited by the National Portrait Gallery in London, and even more so for its annual 'BP Portrait Award', which is self-marketed as 'the most prestigious portrait painting competition in the world and represents the very best in contemporary portrait painting'.[7] Faithfully fulfilling all genre aesthetic criteria, the portrait pictures readily comply with the Kantian notion of beauty, the sublime being located on other gallery floors. And when (if at all) it comes to a noticeable backdrop such as a crowded library, an autumn landscape, windows opening on to the garden in blossom, or mirrors reflecting the surrounding faded wallpaper, it turns out that these backdrops are nothing but a *setting* whose main purpose is to underscore the personal story of the model, or, finally, to make the portrayed subject even more conspicuous. In other words, the ground is both ontologically and operatively disconnected from the figure, it is relegated to a secondary role, overshadowed by the portrayed subject's uniqueness, which is simply and 'portraiturely' claimed, depicted, represented.

Against both such triumphal attempts to preserve the traditional portrait *and* the pessimistic tendency to locate its fate in the disappearance of the subject within generalised processes of abstraction and (dis)simulation in the post-digital era, this book takes the very *mediality* of the portrait as the element for rethinking it as a complex network of media operations out of which portrayed subjects substantively emerge as one element in a configuration. Much of the work on portraiture over the last decades thinks it through a single configuration, namely, the subject configuration of the portrait, which it mistakenly takes as the only possible starting point. As such, this discourse tends to reproduce variations of the art-historical narrative about the end of portraiture as an iteration of the disappearance of the subject. The concept of the portrait is not solely the property of art history, and the perpetual transformations, negations, and reconfigurations of portraiture give good reason to open the concept towards its overlooked implications.

The Portrait as Configuration: Mediality and Cultural Techniques

Starting from the premise that a portrait can be conceptualised as a configuration of three interconnected elements – subject, technique, mediality – no one of which constitutes the privileged ground or genre principle of portraiture, what emerges here is rather a kind of *genreless* portrait. A prerequisite for this step is to acknowledge that the portrait is not only nor necessarily a work of art, but a set of cultural techniques for the dynamic performance of subjects (human and otherwise) entangled in specific media environments. These entanglements, connections, and networks – the portrait configurations, that is – are unthinkable without their specific *mediality*, a performative 'structure of the medial' that the media philosopher Dieter Mersch succinctly defines as 'the underlying materialities, dispositives and performances that accompany medial processes' (2013: 210). While this concept of 'mediality' is relatively rare in Anglo-American scholarship (with the important exceptions of Grusin 2010; Sterne 2012; Devine 2019; Ingraham 2020; and Denson 2020), it remains a key term for German media theory and philosophy, employed in relation to law records and bureaucratic practices (Vismann 2008), human and non-human messengers such as viruses, angels, and money (Krämer 2015), media anthropology (Othold and Voss 2015), television 'switching images' (Engell 2021), and aesthetic practices and film philosophy (Herzogenrath, ed. 2020). To think the portrait in its medial capacities and qualities is to consider its two other elements of subjectivity and technique relationally.

A related theoretical approach (likewise borrowed from German media theory) that animates this project is provided by the concept of 'cultural techniques' which, according to one of its main advocates, Bernhard Siegert, seeks to 'reveal the extent to which the human actor has always already been decentered *by* the technical object' (2015: 193).[8] But what actually are cultural techniques and how can this concept help reorient the long-standing and metaphysics-laden debates about portraiture? In his illuminating survey of the concept's history, Geoffrey Winthrop-Young observes that:

> Originally related to the agricultural domain, the notion of cultural techniques was later employed to describe the interactions between humans and media, and, most recently, to account for basic operations and differentiations that give rise to an array of conceptual and ontological entities which are said to constitute culture. (2013: 3)

Among the stunningly promiscuous array of objects that scholars have applied it to, the concept of cultural techniques has been productively brought to bear upon the elementary, age-old practices of writing, reading, drawing, counting, or making music – operations that, as Thomas Macho explains, 'are always older than the concepts that are generated from them' (2003: 179). Developing from this engagement with symbolic technologies that allow for self-referential recursion, the evolution of the concept over the last fifteen years also provides fertile ground for understanding the current media context in the age of algorithms. In this line, Siegert's approach opens up a path by which the portrait can be productively reconsidered as precisely such a technique to be found within the 'chains of operations that link humans, things, media and even animals' (2013: 48). Taken up as a 'cultural technique' in this way, the entire problematic of portraiture is transformed into a matter of myriad configurations and reconfigurations in which the question of the subject (whether in its plenitude or loss) refers to one key element among others rather than the essential touchstone for thinking the portrait.

When Allan Sekula, for instance, examines how photographic portraiture was instrumentalised as part of a broader biopolitical project in the nineteenth century and argues for the portrait as part of a larger operation called 'the archive' – noting that portraiture confronts us with 'a double system: a system of representation capable of functioning both *honorifically* and *repressively*' (1986: 6)– his conceptualisation of the *archive* is poised exactly in the direction of what we are referring to as the portrait as a cultural technique. Sekula's argument hence provides another impulse for our thinking the portrait relationally, as a mutual reconfiguration of subject, medium, and techniques. The notion of cultural techniques is key especially for Roland Meyer and Kate Rennebohm, who, in demonstrating how both analogue and CGI technologies and aesthetic forms absorb and reshape the practices of portraiture from the eighteenth century until today, propose novel concepts that could be useful not the least for art history, media theory, and cultural analysis. While Meyer advances the concept of operative portraits, which stands for elements in chains of operations aimed at assembling, comparing, and connecting vast quantities of images, Rennebohm's term 'loss-of-self portraits' involves portraiture of the media landscapes framing both the finding of the self and the losing of the self.

It needs to be emphasised, however, that to reconfigure the concept of the portrait, as our book attempts to do, is not akin to a critical 'anti-hermeneutic' unmasking of the practices of portraiture that constitute the canonical genre as overly laden with representation and human subjectivity. Instead of 'driving the human out of the humanities' – as the notorious Kittlerian provocation manifested in the title of his 1978 lecture series *Austreibung des Geistes aus den Geisteswissenschaften* suggests (Kittler 1980) – the posthermeneutic frame from which the theory of cultural techniques arises compels us to elaborate upon these representations' performative affordances.[9] Seen in this light, portraiture is continuously reconfiguring itself in terms of its *performativity* – what precisely these portraits do, enact, and generate – and in terms of its *mediality* – where and through which operations the specific portrait's performances come about.

Siegert's notion of cultural techniques is useful not only because it allows for a more dynamic understanding of portraiture in terms of performative configurations, but also because it shows how the traditional, representational, and subject-oriented ground of portraiture can be connected and integrated into a functional media circuit whereby these elements become operational. If '[t]o investigate cultural techniques is to shift the analytic gaze from ontological distinctions to the ontic operations that gave rise to the former in the first place' (Siegert 2013: 48), the chapters in this book contribute precisely to such a shift, arguing for the portrait as a media-theoretical concept and tracing its practices within diverse sets of material, technological, and media networks.

Far from foreclosing the question of the subject in relation to the portrait, this methodological shift seeks to reopen it on a new basis. We will not get very far if we limit our inquiry to what kind of pre-given subject the portrait captures and how that subject is reproduced by the portrait. The more productive questions, which take seriously the performative and media operations of the portrait, are rather: What does the portrait do *with* and *to* its subjects? How does it constitute them as situated in specific spatial and temporal coordinates? Moving between figure and ground, so to speak, we can also then ask how these portrayed subjects are simultaneously constituted *by* and constitutive *of* an entire milieu. In other words, the distinction between the figure and the ground here is not so much ontological as it is operative; there is a radical mediality in the distinction between the portrayed subjects and their 'surroundings'. To examine the portrayed subjects within the 'operative chains they are part of and that configure or constitute them' (Siegert 2013: 58) implies another methodological move: to locate agency as an effect of the entire operation, which includes the subject as one of its elements.[10]

The Structure of the Book

The chapters that follow are organised into four sections: I) 'Genealogies', II) '(Inter)Faces', III) 'Self-Constructions', and IV) 'Afterlives'. Although each section maintains its own thematic focus, they are mutually interconnected and constitute a dialogue that can be read in any order. This collection pursues two simultaneous lines of inquiry shared across its chapters: on the one hand, it considers the operation of various portrait techniques across the diverse range of artworks, media, and cultural techniques that these chapters explore; on the other, it unpacks how all these examples situate the mediation of the subject – human and otherwise – within wider media, technological, and social ensembles. Together these lines of inquiry seek to transform, reconfigure, and redefine the very notion of the portrait – and why it matters to the contemporary study of media and the arts.

The first section opens with two chapters that trace the instrumentalisation of the photographic portrait from its pre-history in eighteenth-century physiognomic uses of the silhouette to twenty-first-century AI-generated images. Together these chapters chart a dual history of photographic portraiture as simultaneously a technological operation (from analogue to computational photography) and a mechanism for discipline and governance (from anthropometrics to algorithmic facial recognition).

Indeed, one of the questions that resonates with the contemporary political stakes of the entire collection is posed by Roland Meyer in the first chapter on the operative portrait: 'How did our faces become big data?' In his exploration of this question, Meyer develops a concept of the 'operative portrait' by focusing on four exemplary episodes from a more than 200-year-long history of technically produced portraits: Johann Caspar Lavater's Physiognomics in the 1770s; Alphonse Bertillon's police identification protocols from the 1880s; the radical redefinitions of the portrait's social function in the Soviet avant-garde of the 1920s; and the media performances of identity in Andy Warhol's Factory of the 1960s. Thus Meyer offers a set of detailed snapshots that together reveal the ways in which the traditional claim of the portrait to represent an autonomous individual has been gradually supplemented, even replaced, by the promise of operativity.

Along a parallel line of inquiry, Daniël de Zeeuw and Abraham Geil compare two salient moments in the operationalisation of portrait photography: Francis Galton's 'composite portraits' of social 'types' in the last quarter of the nineteenth century and AI-generated portraits of non-existent individuals from the first quarter of this century. In both cases, the figure portrayed, whether a type or an individual, does not refer to any empirically existing person. Rather, de Zeeuw and Geil argue, these portraits refer to operations of abstraction that belong to two distinct but related biopolitical epistemes – the nineteenth-century statistical and the twenty-first-century algorithmic, respectively. Their contribution attempts to trace both the continuities and epistemological breaks between these two logics as they are instantiated in two pivotal moments in the history of portrait photography's instrumentalisation.

Finally, Sigrid Weigel's contribution rounds off this first section of the book by tracing an 'artefactual genealogy' across an even longer *durée* stretching from anthropomorphic grave stelae in the Arabian Peninsula dating from the fifth and fourth millennia BCE through silent film of the early twentieth century up to the present of online avatars. Through this sweeping history, Weigel develops a radically denaturalising approach to the human face, taken as the privileged figure of the human, by tracing its historical production and trajectory as an artefact across a range of cultural and technological dispositifs.

The second section, '(Inter)Faces', focuses squarely on the site that is perhaps the ground zero for discussions of portraiture – the face. But in keeping with the theoretical aims of the book as a whole, the contributions to this section seek in various ways to decentre the face as origin by elucidating the conditions of possibility by which it has come to stand as a privileged threshold experience in and with media. According to the approach pursued here, the face in portraiture is always already an *inter*face on to a medium.

In turning to the medium of the contemporary music video, Tomáš Jirsa's chapter attends to the sonic as well as visual dimensions of the portrait interface, reading the affordances of music videos for the ways they 'desubjectify' the face in order to amplify the affective work of audiovisual forms and their performative mechanisms. Putting two videos from the current hip-hop and trip-hop scene, Earl Sweatshirt's *Chum* (2012) directed by Hiro Murai and Massive Attack's *The Spoils* (2016) directed by John Hillcoat, into dialogue with Jean-Luc Nancy's concept of the non-representational portrait (2018) read through the lens of media philosophy, Jirsa's chapter argues for the displacement of the human facial image from its traditional function of expressing interiority to a thematisation of form and technicity in a contemporary audiovisual medium.

Elena Vogman's chapter pursues a rather different instance of what Nancy elucidates as the desubjectifying effects of the non-representational portrait in Fernand Deligny's work with neurodiverse ('autistic') children in the Cévennes (1967–96). Through cartographic drawings that he called 'wander lines' as well as his innovative uses of film, Vogman argues that Deligny's educational practice and theory sought to trace the 'minor gestures' of these children in order to produce what were in effect 'relation portraits' of the medium, body, and milieu. By considering the ways that Deligny's practice was nourished by theories of milieu that emerged at the beginning of the twentieth century in the disciplines of biology, ethology, psychology, and ethnography, Vogman seeks to reactivate an under-explored critical path in the history of portraiture and its value for research and experimental practice.

Nicole Morse's contribution meanwhile opens up a surprising medial interface or constellation between nineteenth-century Anglo-American Gothic literature and twenty-first-century AI imaging technology by reading the prevailing discourse around today's 'deepfakes' as a kind of neo-Gothic horror fiction with its dark fantasies about portraiture's relationship to bodies, gender, sexuality, and control. Morse seeks to critique the misogyny that underpins not only the production of deepfakes but also, and more insidiously, the very rhetoric intended to warn against their cultural dangers. In their inventive reading of works by Nathaniel Hawthorne, Robert Browning, Edgar Allan Poe, Oscar Wilde, and others, Morse argues that Gothic stories about lifelike portraiture provide a genre-based model of immanent critique that illuminates the violent misogyny of the deepfake without reinforcing or reproducing it.

Elisa Aaltola's contribution rounds off this section of the book by extending the problematic of portraiture and the mediation of the face beyond the human. Interrogating the ethics of situating non-human animals in the all-too-human milieu of social media, Aaltola takes up the case study of 'Esther', a pig whose profile has reached celebrity status on Facebook, and questions the violence that such anthropomorphic portraiture does to non-human subjects in their particularity. Eschewing a purely critical reading, however, Aaltola also explores the possibility of a more redemptive dimension in this case study by considering how the online phenomenon of 'Esther' might also occasion a different kind of interface or encounter between human and non-human animals beyond the prevailing modes of instrumentalisation and anthropomorphism.

The third section, 'Self-Constructions', explores the transformative effects that various cultural techniques of portraiture have on the relationality of self to other as well as of the 'I' to itself. Sudeep Dasgupta's contribution opens this section with a far-reaching discussion of the framing of race, gender, and sexuality through critical readings of a remarkable range of historical and contemporary portraits in painting and photography as well as the curatorial and theoretical discourses through which they have been apprehended. Against theorisations by Leo Bersani and others that valorise 'formlessness' in their critiques of portraiture's representation of subjectivity, Dasgupta calls for a reframing of subjects by citing and critically restaging their confinement within discourses that normalise identity. In doing so, he argues that the portrait pictures the subject's emergence in the image through aesthetic opacity, deploying an unresolved play of forms to register the conflictual psychic, social, and historical relations which reverberate through race, gender, and sexuality.

Andrea Pinotti's chapter takes up a significant technological transformation in the practices of self-portrayal by analysing what he calls the 'avatarisation' of the self in an array of virtual worlds online. Engaging with the uncanny practice of the avatar as at once old and new, Pinotti traces its theological background as the incarnation of the god in various world religions as well as its historical analogues in a series of figures such as the 'double', the 'alter ego' and the 'doppelgänger'. On the side of the 'new', Pinotti examines the avatar as a digital proxy for the self in recent digital visualisation technologies such as infographics and holograms. The pragmatic and symbolic spectrum of the avatar's rhetorical potential, he argues, is very flexible, spanning from the revelation of the 'authentic' self to the disguising deceit of the mask, and including all intermediate possibilities between these two extremes, in principle allowing its user to negotiate a quasi-infinite variation of selfhood.

The other two chapters in this section consider how contemporary artists have probed and experimented with transformations in the technicity of self-portraiture. Kaisu Hynnä-Granberg and Susanna Paasonen redeem the much-maligned Instagram 'selfie' as a mode of creative practice in the work of the Finnish artist Iiu Susiraja, known especially for her self-portraiture making use of mundane objects such as appliances and foodstuffs in domestic spaces, and the foregrounding of her own body with its carnal thickness. Rather than interpreting Susiraja's work as a critical commentary on selfie culture within the realm of high art, Hynnä-Granberg and Paasonen explore it as a ludic visual practice that broadens understandings of what self-shooting is and can be.

In her philosophically rich reading of the Canadian visual artist Jeremy Shaw's 'Quantification Trilogy' films (2014–18), Kate Rennebohm discovers a new genre that she dubs the 'loss-of-self' portrait. Bringing Michel Foucault's conception of 'technologies of the self' as well as the claims of different media theorists into conjunction with the Quantification Trilogy films, Rennebohm contends that the self-portrait, broadly conceived, plays an essential and as yet under-theorised role in these technologies of the self, with their processes of self-focused and self-building work. Reading Shaw's films as a unique kind of portrait, the 'loss-of-self' portrait, Rennebohm finds revealed in the very endeavour of individuals to escape themselves the inescapability of a media landscape that cannot be transcended.

The fourth and final section, 'Afterlives', makes an explicitly temporal and existential turn. If all portrait-making can be understood as an attempt to bring some absence into presence, then putting the dead back into contact with the living is perhaps the limit case of portraiture as such. In his contribution, Brian Price takes up the most traditional medium for portraiture – painting – and locates within it a radically transgressive operation that oscillates between the scandal of the flesh and the eternalness of stone. Price's chapter argues that what is truly transgressive about the controversial erotic portraits of the French painter Balthus is found not in the sexualisation of their young subjects but in the way that they 'steal from time so as to exist in and across time'.

The two remaining contributions explore the ways that portraiture performs and transcends the threshold between life and death in media as different as 'speech scrolls' and virtual reality within a diverse range of cultural contexts. Georges Didi-Huberman turns to Mexican funeral photographs and 'speech scrolls' to meditate on the question of how the dead can 'speak' to us through mute images and words. The volume concludes with Pietro Conte's wide-ranging exploration of the claims made for the capacity of VR technology to achieve the portrait's dream of bringing the dead back to life. Conte takes up the recent example of a 'reunion' between a South Korean mother and her dead daughter through VR simulation as an instance of how the technological fantasy of closing the gap between life and death at best results in an intensification of the oscillation between proximity and distance, immediateness and hyper-mediation.

Notes

1. This chapter is an outcome of the research project 'Between Affects and Technology: The Portrait in the Visual Arts, Literature and Music Video' (JG_2019_007), funded by the Faculty of Arts of Palacký University Olomouc.
2. For an especially illuminating survey of the 'anti-portrait' in artistic and curatorial practice as well as an emergent theoretical rubric, see Johnstone and Imber 2020.
3. Ernst van Alphen (1997: 241) puts the matter concisely: in its traditional form 'the portrait embodies a dual project: it gives authority to the portrayed as well as to mimetic representation'. In a similar vein, Allan Sekula (1986: 6) suggests that the traditional function of portraiture, 'which can be said to have taken its early modern form in the seventeenth century, is that of providing for the ceremonial presentation of the bourgeois self'.
4. The invention of photography is another. This narrative finds a recent iteration as a curatorial strategy in the 2004 exhibition at the Hayward Gallery in London entitled *About Face: Photography and the Death of the Portrait* (see Johnston and Imber 2020: 11).
5. Johnstone and Imber (2020: 9) note that Buchloh's 'Residual Resemblance' essay is 'exemplary of the way in which debates about the "ends of portraiture" or "the death of the portrait" intensify in the final decade of the twentieth century, in both academic discourse and curatorial practice'. As Judith Elisabeth Weiss (2013: 139) notes, however, the cultural diagnosis of the portrait's end was made already at the turn of the nineteenth century by the prominent art historian Jacob Burckhardt in his lecture given in Basel in 1885, 'Die Anfänge der neueren Porträtmalerei' (The Beginnings of New Portraiture), when he stated: 'We are essentially already looking at portraiture as a historically completed whole.'
6. For a recent project that engages with Belting's work via Bernhard Siegert and Thomas Macho's conceptualisations of 'cultural techniques', see Soncul 2019.

7. https://www.npg.org.uk/whatson/bp-portrait-award-2018/exhibition/ (last accessed 16 February 2022).
8. For a detailed discussion of the concept of cultural techniques, its genealogy, and contextual background, see Geoghegan 2013 and Winthrop-Young 2013.
9. On the difficulties of translating Kittler's famous phrase, see Weber (2018: 70), who renders it as 'Exorcising spirit from the humanities'. According to Siegert (2015: 3–6), who situates the post-hermeneutic phase of German media theory between the end of 1990s and today, a decisive feature of the post-hermeneutic turn is its interest in 'the exteriority/materiality of the signifier' and the non-essentialist view of media: 'There is no subject area, no ontologically identifiable domain that could be called "media".'
10. For a similar argument, see Winthrop-Young (2013: 9, 11): 'If ideas, concepts and in some cases the objects themselves emerge from basic operations, then it is only logical to assume that this also applies to the agent performing these operations [. . .] cultural techniques refer to processing operations that frequently coalesce into entities which are subsequently viewed as the agents or sources running these operations.'

References

Alphen, Ernst van (1997), 'The Portrait's Dispersal: Concepts of Representation and Subjectivity in Contemporary Portraiture', in Joanna Woodall (ed.), *Portraiture: Facing the Subject*, Manchester: Manchester University Press, pp. 239–56.

Belting, Hans (2017 [2013]), *Face and Mask: A Double History*, trans. Thomas S. Hansen and Abby J. Hansen, Princeton, NJ: Princeton University Press.

Bois, Yve-Alain (1990), 'Kahnweiler's Lesson', in Yve-Alain Bois, *Painting as Model*, Cambridge, MA: MIT Press, pp. 65–100.

Brilliant, Richard (1991), *Portraiture*, London: Reaktion.

Buchloh, Benjamin H. D. (2015 [1994]), 'Residual Resemblance: Three Notes on the Ends of Portraiture', in Benjamin H. D. Buchloh, *Formalism and Historicity: Models and Methods in Twentieth-Century Art*, Cambridge, MA: MIT Press, pp. 471–508.

Denson, Shane (2020), *Discorrelated Images*, Durham, NC: Duke University Press.

Devine, Kyle (2019), *Decomposed: The Political Ecology of Music*, Cambridge, MA: MIT Press.

Engell, Lorenz (2021), *The Switch Image: Television Philosophy*, New York: Bloomsbury.

Geoghegan, Bernard Dionysius (2013), 'After Kittler: On the Cultural Techniques of Recent German Media Theory', *Theory, Culture & Society*, 30(6): 66–82.

Grusin, Richard (2010), *Premediation: Affect and Mediality after 9/11*, New York: Palgrave Macmillan.

Herzogenrath, Bernd (ed.) (2020), *Practical Aesthetics*, New York: Bloomsbury.

Ingraham, Chris (2020), *Gestures of Concern*, Durham, NC: Duke University Press.

Johnstone, Fiona, and Kirstie Imber (2020), 'Introducing the Anti-Portrait', in Fiona Johnstone and Kirstie Imber (eds), *Anti-Portraiture: Challenging the Limits of the Portrait*, London: Bloomsbury, pp. 1–24.

Kittler, Friedrich (ed.) (1980), *Austreibung des Geistes aus den Geisteswissenschaften. Programme des Poststrukturalismus*, Paderborn: Schöningh.

Krämer, Sybille (2015 [2008]), *Medium, Messenger, Transmission: An Approach to Media Philosophy*, trans. Anthony Enns, Amsterdam: Amsterdam University Press.

Macho, Thomas (2003), 'Second-Order Animals: Cultural Techniques of Identity and Identification', *Theory, Culture & Society*, 30(6): 30–47.

Mersch, Dieter (2013 [2008]), 'Tertium Datur', *MATRIZes*, 7(1): 207–22.

Nancy, Jean-Luc (2018), *The Portrait*, trans. Sarah Clift and Simon Sparks, New York: Fordham University Press.

Othold, Tim, and Christiane Voss (2015), 'From Media Anthropology to Anthropomediality', *Anthropological Notebooks*, 21(3): 75–82.

Rodchenko, Alexander (1989 [1928]), 'Against the Synthetic Portrait, For the Snapshot', in Christopher Phillips (ed.), *Photography in the Modern Era: European Documents and Critical Writings, 1913–1940*, New York: Metropolitan Museum/Aperture, pp. 238–42.

Sekula, Allan (1986), 'The Body and the Archive', *October*, 39: 3–64.

Siegert, Bernhard (2013), 'Cultural Techniques: Or the End of the Intellectual Postwar Era in German Media Theory', *Theory, Culture & Society*, 30(6): 48–65.

Siegert, Bernhard (2015), *Cultural Techniques: Grids, Filters, Doors, and Other Articulations of the Real*, trans. Geoffrey Winthrop-Young, New York: Fordham University Press.

Soncul, Sukru Yigit (2019), 'Facial Politics of Images and Media: Mask, Body, Immunity', PhD thesis, University of Southampton.

Sousloff, Catherine (2006), *The Subject in Art: Portraiture and the Birth of the Modern*, Durham, NC: Duke University Press.

Sterne, Jonathan (2012), *MP3: The Meaning of a Format*, Durham, NC: Duke University Press, 2012.

Visman, Cornelia (2008), *Files: Law and Media Technology*, trans. Geoffrey Winthrop-Young, Stanford, CA: Stanford University Press.

Weber, Samuel (2018), *The Technological Introject: Friedrich Kittler between Implematation and the Incalculable*, New York: Fordham University Press.

Weiss, Judith Elisabeth (2013), 'Before and After the Portrait: Faces between Hidden Likeness and Anti-Portrait', in Mona Körte, Ruben Rebmann,

Judith Elisabeth Weiss, and Stefan Weppelmann (eds), *Inventing Faces: Rhetorics of Portraiture between Renaissance and Modernism*, Berlin: Deutscher Kunstverlag, pp. 133–46.

Winthrop-Young, Geoffrey (2013), 'Cultural Techniques: Preliminary Remarks', *Theory, Culture & Society*, 30(6): 3–19.

Woodall, Joanna (ed.) (1997), *Portraiture: Facing the Subject*, Manchester: Manchester University Press.

1 Genealogies

Chapter 2

Operative Portraits, or How Our Faces Became Big Data

Roland Meyer

In January 2020 a previously obscure IT company made worldwide headlines. Clearview AI had collected billions of facial images from social networks and other online sources without the knowledge or consent of the people depicted in them, fed them into a huge database, and now promised its customers, security agencies as well as private individuals, that it could identify almost anyone anywhere in mere seconds. With its software, a single photo taken with an ordinary smartphone often seems to be enough to find out the name of an unknown person as well as their online profiles – something early Clearview AI investors are said to have tried out enthusiastically at parties (Hill 2020a; 2020b).

As this recent example made shockingly clear, in the last decade our faces have become just another form of big data: myriad digital portraits captured by ubiquitous smartphones, circulating online in extensive digital networks and automatically processed by sophisticated algorithms, are now a valuable resource for tech companies and government agencies alike. Facial recognition has transformed our living faces into digital anchors that allow scattered personal data to be tracked, traced, and linked together into ever-growing profiles. Under conditions of networked image production and distribution, each identifiable face can now serve as a link between previously unconnected images. What's more, because our faces are visible online as well as offline, they have become the interface between the physical world we inhabit with our bodies and the platforms that manage our digital identities. After all, it is the same face captured by a surveillance camera in a football stadium that is accessible through our Instagram accounts. This, as I want to argue in this chapter, fundamentally changes the function of pictorial representations of individual faces. The images we take of ourselves no longer merely represent us – they have become *operative portraits* (Meyer 2019), elements in chains of operations aimed at assembling, comparing, and connecting vast quantities of images.

From the Representative to the Operative Portrait

This notion of operative portraits is based on Harun Farocki's concept of 'operative images' (sometimes also translated as 'operational images'). In his film essays and writings from the early 2000s, Farocki analysed a new type of technical image: images that, in his now classic formulation, 'do not represent an object but are part of an operation' (2004: 17). In other words, these images are not made to depict the world, but to intervene directly in it – for example, by controlling so-called 'intelligent' weapons systems, operating self-driving vehicles, or monitoring automated assembly lines. What all operative images have in common is that they do not stand on their own as stable, singular, and autonomous artefacts, but have become standardised serial elements of technical processes into which they are supposed to seamlessly integrate. To the extent that these processes become fully automated, operative images can even become invisible to the human eye and be treated as mere digital data captured by optical sensors and analysed by algorithmic processes: 'The computer', as Volker Pantenburg reminds us, 'does not need the image' (2017: 49). In many cases, however, facial recognition being a prime example, images are still needed to teach computers to 'see'. Most of today's machine vision algorithms, as Kate Crawford (2021) and others have shown, have been trained and tested using vast amounts of images available online, made by humans for other humans.

Nevertheless, speaking of 'operative portraits' almost seems like a self-contradiction, at least if one considers the classical art-historical notion of what a portrait is. Traditionally, the portrait has been the paradigmatic case of pictorial *re-presentation*, an image striving to make virtually present what, or rather who, is physically absent. At least since the early Renaissance, the individual portrait could thus function in European visual culture as a kind of proxy or double of the body. As Hans Belting (2014: 62–83) has shown, the singular, autonomous painted portrait, as it was invented in the Netherlands around 1400, documented and affirmed the equally singular and autonomous individuality of the person depicted, with the material body of the framed and mobile easel painting standing in for the absent body of the subject. Since the pictorial portrait itself acted as a kind of quasi-individual, it also addressed exclusively an individual beholder, as Gottfried Boehm (1985) has pointed out. Returning the viewer's gaze, the portrait aims to establish a relationship of mutual recognition between the individual in the picture and the one in front of it.

However, this classical idea of pictorial representation can hardly account for the new functions that digital images of faces have recently acquired, where huge amounts of visual data are scanned in automated processes and analysed by machines that are unable to return the gaze of the depicted and are uninterested in their autonomous individuality. The term operative portraits is therefore an attempt to grasp a fundamental change in the portrait's function: rather than representing an individual whose autonomous individuality precedes the act of representation, the billions of digital images of faces circulating in social networks have become operative images, fuelling the ongoing production of digital identities. And rather than synthesising the various aspects of an individual into a single and permanent representative image, such operative portraits are exchangeable elements in ongoing series of visual documents, destined to be compared and combined with unlimited masses of other data.

This contemporary situation, while unprecedented in its scale and impact, has, as I would like to argue, a long pre-history in modern visual culture. Since the beginnings of technical image production, the traditional claim of the portrait to represent an autonomous individual has been gradually supplemented, even replaced, by the promise of operativity. Underlying the modern history of the portrait is thus a history of an ongoing functional transformation from the representative to the operative portrait that can be traced, a gradual move from the single image towards the endless image series, from the purely visual image to complex assemblages of visual and non-visual information, and from the representation of an autonomous individual to standardised records capturing the performance of bodies in confrontation with technical media.[1] In the following, I want to highlight four scenes from this history: the new forms of image analysis emerging with Johann Caspar Lavater's Physiognomics in the 1770s; Alphonse Bertillon's police identification protocols from the 1880s, which transformed photographic images into comparable datasets; the radical redefinitions of the portrait's social function in the Soviet avant-garde of the 1920s; and the media performances of identity in Andy Warhol's Factory of the 1960s. Finally, and in conclusion, I would like to ask again what constitutes the historical specificity of the present situation in this ongoing history of the reconfiguration of the portrait.

1775 – Lavater: The Instrumentalisation of the Portrait

The first of these historical scenes takes us back to the late 1700s. The Swiss pastor Johann Caspar Lavater, who made physiognomic character interpretation a popular fashion throughout Europe in the 1770s, was not only the author of a highly questionable theory; he also, as I would like to argue, invented a new practice of using images that would prove to be even more consequential than his ideas about physiognomy. As stated again and again throughout his work, Lavater deeply mistrusted the portrait artists of his time, and the art of draughtsmanship in general (Althaus 2010: 145–9). Artistic portraits, he felt, rarely fixed the defining features he was looking for in an individual face. While he nevertheless employed several notable artists for his richly illustrated *Physiognomic Fragments* (1775–78), he famously favoured an early mechanical method of image production: the silhouette, which reduced the face to nothing but a shadow, isolating from all its features only one single, two-dimensional but stable line, the outline of the profile (Stoichita 1997: 157–67). This shadow image was, according to Lavater, the 'weakest and emptiest', but at the same time the 'truest and most faithful' image of a human being conceivable – faithful, that is, if the source of light, the face, and a screen were installed exactly parallel and at a correct distance from each other (Lavater 1776: 90) (Figure 2.1).

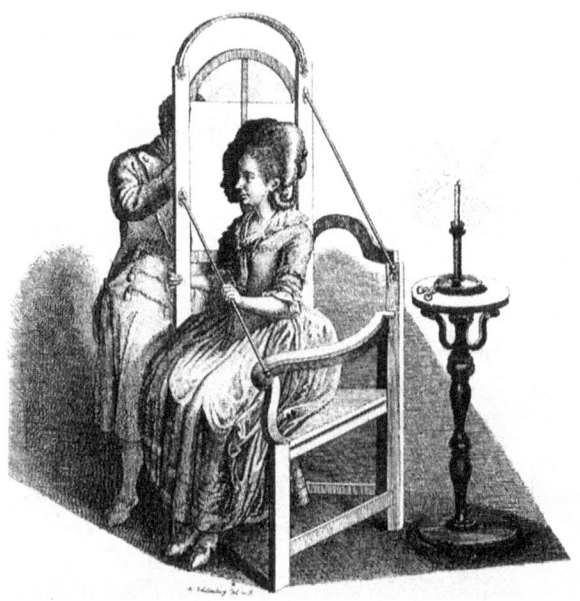

Figure 2.1 Johann Rudolf Schellenberg, Lavater's Silhouette Machine, c. 1775

A technical means to guarantee these regulated conditions of image production was the silhouette machine, which became fashionable at the end of the eighteenth century (Frieß 1993: 133). The silhouette, after being mechanically captured by such early media apparatuses, could then be used for subsequent image operations: the segmentation into distinct and measurable sections or the isolation of comparable forms, such as the characteristic linear shape of diverse eyes, ears, or foreheads (Figure 2.2). Thus, for Lavater, the human face only became truly legible through the construction of a spatial dispositif that defined a new format for technical images, the standardised profile, which would subsequently be translated into geometrical forms, discrete measurements, and readable signs. 'Physiognomy', as Barbara Stafford (1991: 84) put it, 'was body criticism', an anatomical dissection with elaborate graphical methods.

Although a human gaze was still needed to interpret the silhouette and its significant details, it was precisely the imperfection of this human gaze that made the whole technical effort necessary in the first place. For according to Lavater's imagination, the true physiognomic genius would need a visual acuity that only angels and immortal souls could fully attain. Since these heavenly beings are not bound by the limitations of the earthly body, they have infinitely higher vision

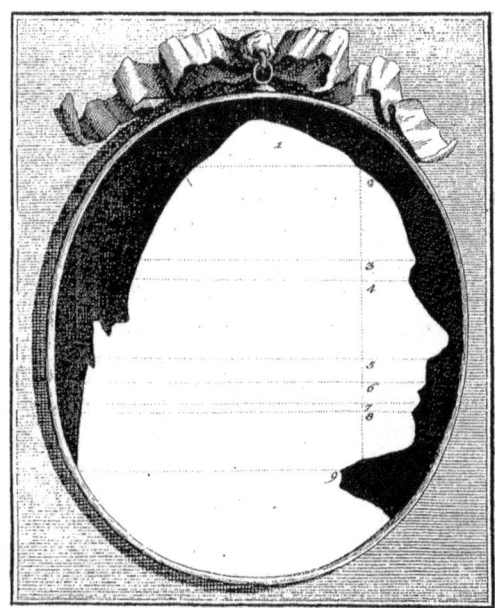

Figure 2.2 'Segments of the Profile', from *Physiognomic Fragments*, vol. II, 1776

and are able, as Lavater says (2001: 287), to see 'even the most distant object in every clarity' – for example, each individual drop of water in a waterfall. Thus they succeed in what human adepts of physiognomy could only accomplish with technical means: to grasp the whole human being immediately in its visible totality, and at the same time to break this totality down into discrete signs that can be read like the letters of a text (2001: 451). For such an angelic vision there is no difference between seeing, reading, and measuring: every visible being becomes immediately interpretable. Lavater thus measured his own physiognomic method against the ideal of a disembodied, non-human vision, a gaze of angels and immortal souls infinitely faster and more precise than the human gaze.

Now, why does this non-human gaze, detached from all bodily limitations, become conceivable, even desirable, in the late eighteenth century? Lavater's physiognomy, I would like to argue, must be understood not least as a reaction to a major shift in the logistics of images, the emergence of new modes of pictorial production and the mobilisation of images through new networks of image distribution. The visual culture of the second half of the eighteenth century witnessed a boom in portrait production, which ultimately changed the social function of the portrait (Kanz 1993). Especially with the silhouette, images of individuals now could not only be produced quickly and rather inexpensively, but also be easily reproduced, stored, and passed on in intimate networks. They were collected in albums and scrapbooks, attached to letters, and sent as gifts to friends, and it also became customary to make a silhouette as a souvenir of guests travelling on (Althaus 2010: 33–75). Thanks to a well-developed postal system,[2] drawings, prints, and silhouettes now circulated over long distances (Gutbrodt 2003: 123–30). And for the first time, what was practically realised only with the invention of photography in the nineteenth century became at least conceivable: a 'democratisation' of the portrait, the representation of almost anybody regardless of social status.

This new, deregulated economy of representation is evident in Lavater's own collection of art, his 'Kunstkabinett', which at his death in 1801 comprised more than 20,000 pictures. During Lavater's lifetime, this collection was in constant flux: he repeatedly gave away, exchanged, and sold individual sheets; Karin Althaus (2010: 18) estimates that a total of around 30,000 drawings, prints, and silhouettes passed through his hands. Like Lavater's *Physiognomic Fragments*, which comprised four thick volumes and never reached a systematic conclusion, his art cabinet was subject to a logic of boundlessness, not least because it largely suspended any conventional hierarchy of representation (Swoboba 1999). For him, every individual was worthy of a portrait. Lavater's collection therefore contained faces of peasants, bourgeois, scholars, and aristocrats, of men, women, and children alike. But while he opened up the means of representation to potentially include every individual, these portraits were no longer treated as individual representations. They became documents to be compared, evaluated, and analysed. Gottfried Boehm (2003) has pointed out the sharp contrast between the tradition of the bourgeois portrait and Lavater's pictorial operations. The images Lavater collected were not treated as representative doubles of autonomous individuals but as a means to classify and compare people. He did not want to enter into an exchange of gazes – rather, his cold and dissecting gaze refused to recognise the portrayed as an equal counterpart. For Lavater, the individual portrait was no longer a self-contained, autonomous representation; it was an element in endless streams of images circulating through postal networks and waiting to be processed by a disembodied gaze. In response to the proliferation, mobilisation, and universalisation of image production in the eighteenth century, his protocols for image analysis used images as operative surfaces that could be broken down into their elements to extract stable, legible, and, above all, comparable data.

1885 – Bertillon: The Datafication of the Portrait

Such a dissecting and filtering way of looking at the human face, as Lavater already envisioned and described it, was, however, formalised, codified, and actually institutionalised only about a hundred years later. Where Lavater in his *Fragments* ultimately failed – and perhaps never even intended – to establish a strict set of rules for reading faces, the French police officer Alphonse Bertillon turned the analytical dissection of bodies and faces into a learnable system of police identification. One part of his system was the so-called *portrait parlé*, or 'spoken portrait': around 1900, policemen at the Paris prefecture were trained by Bertillon to disassemble the features of a photographed face in order to memorise them for the purpose of finding wanted criminals (Figure 2.3).

Bertillon was convinced that natural languages, while offering enough adjectives for extreme cases, were generally lacking in differentiations for describing the ordinary. His answer was a multiplication of designations, which should correspond to the statistical distribution of anatomical variations. Bertillon's police students were to learn the subtle differences in facial features from serial photographs that

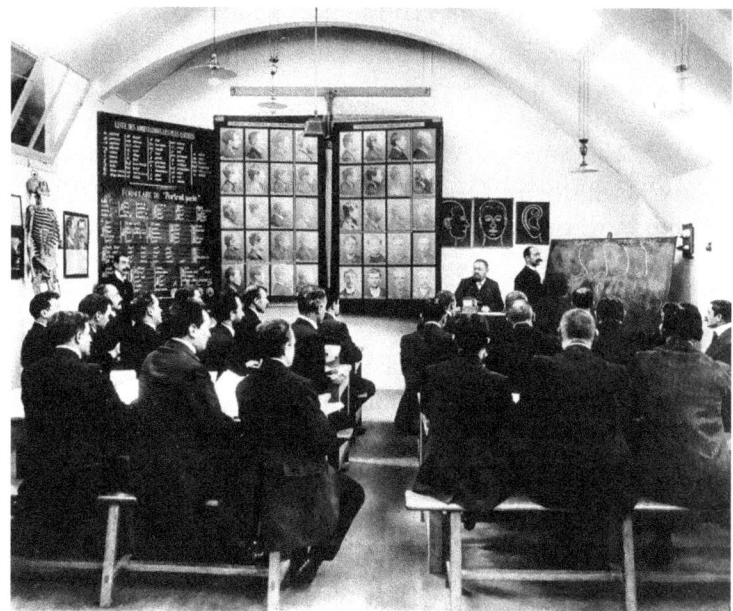

Figure 2.3 Policemen learning the *portrait parlé* at the Paris police prefecture, c. 1900

bore some similarity to Lavater's catalogues of ears, eyes, and fore-heads. But while Lavater's dissection of the profile was ultimately rooted in the idea of an indivisible 'total character' that revealed itself in even the smallest detail, Bertillon's training of the gaze was based on a different semiotic model. The features that his police students were supposed to memorise were not characteristic details that contained the whole, but randomly distributed, statistical differences. Only their improbable combination would make a single face distinguishable from any other face – beyond this system of interchangeable elements and their structural recombinations, facial features for him were nothing more than meaningless data – data, though, that could be symbolically coded, written down as discrete signs, telegraphed, and compared across spatial and temporal distances (Gunning 1995: 32–3; Ellenbogen 2012: 15–16).

Speaking in today's terms, Bertillon understood image production and image analysis as forms of data processing. The *portrait parlé* was only one part of a comprehensive system of data acquisition that, under the name of anthropometrics, became the worldwide standard for the identification of criminal suspects for a few decades, only to be superseded by fingerprinting in the early twentieth century (Cole 2001). Bertillon's system was a reaction to a media logistical

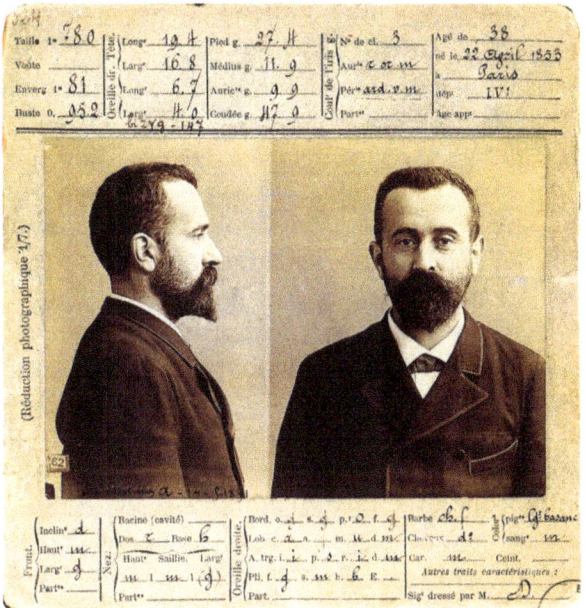

Figure 2.4 Anthropometric fiche of Alphonse Bertillon, 1891

crisis at the Paris Police Prefecture, which in the 1880s struggled with photographic overproduction, as it was precisely the vast number of pictures now taken by the police identification service on a daily basis that rendered them basically useless. To find out the true name of a suspect, one would need a photograph for comparison, but to find the photograph in the registers, which were sorted alphabetically, one would first need to have the name (Phéline 1985: 34). Bertillon's anthropometric system of identification, or 'Bertillonage' as it was called later, was developed in the 1880s in response to this bureaucratic problem of information retrieval. Its central element was not the photograph but the anthropometric file card or *fiche*, a hybrid storage format that combined photographic and written records, integrated visual data into numerical datasets, and made pictures as data retrievable using bodily measurements as metadata (Figure 2.4). By measuring an anonymous body and comparing its data to the statistical mean (this was Bertillon's basic idea), one could calculate a stable and unforgeable code of identity, supposedly much more reliable than a name or a face. Used as metadata, bodily measurement thus allocated to every single body, that is, its photograph and the file card it was mounted on, a discrete address within a predefined data structure. With Bertillon, as Allan Sekula (1986) famously analysed, the photograph becomes but one element in a larger bureaucratic system: the archive.

Not unlike Lavater, Bertillon harboured a deep mistrust of portraiture, and even of images in general. Conventional portrait photography with its changing styles, aesthetic effects, and expressive poses seemed to him completely unsuitable for police purposes. Nevertheless, he did not dispense with photography altogether, but wanted to tame it through new and strict formatting standards. These standards were marked by their unconditional will to standardise the conditions of capture as completely as possible. To this end, Bertillon designed a complex technological apparatus, meticulously arranging bodies and cameras, chairs and instruments, places, directions, and distances (Figure 2.5). As Bertillon stated, this photographic dispositif was intended to force the *operateur* into 'uniformity' and 'precision', namely through the 'material impossibility' of deviating from the standardised picture format (quoted in Phéline 1985: 13).

With his combination of archival data capture and standardised image production, Bertillon established a new format for recording individual differences that was not limited to suspect identities and deviant subjects. On the contrary, as far as Bertillon was concerned, his system was a way of making all bodies comparable and thus providing

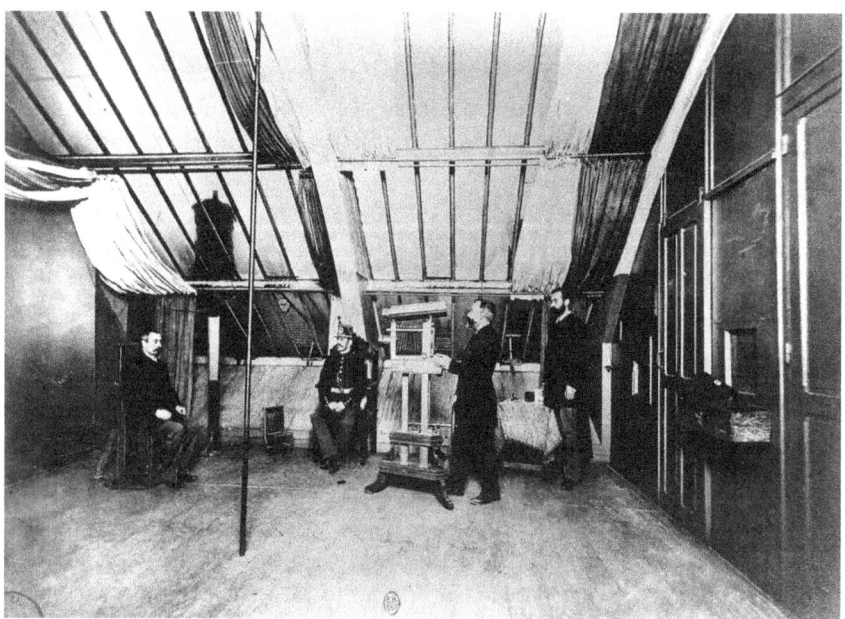

Figure 2.5 Photo studio of the identification service of the Paris police, c. 1900

each and every person with a uniquely defined and scientifically determined identity (Bertillon 1890). Perhaps the most notable example of this is Bertillon's portrait of Émile Zola, which was created in 1896 as part of a comprehensive medical-psychological examination of the author (Hagner 2004: 192–3). Under the direction of the psychiatrist Edouard Toulouse, a team of scientists subjected Zola to a series of psychometric tests, prepared graphological and hereditary reports, and examined his fingerprints as well as his urine. Bertillon was responsible for recording Zola's anatomy and physiognomy and comparing them to the statistical norm. Somewhat disappointingly, given the extraordinary significance of his subject, he concluded his report by stating that the anatomical characteristics of Zola 'do not exceed the limits of normal variation' (Toulouse 1896: 142).

Rather than only making recidivist criminals identifiable, Bertillon's system aimed to make all individuals comparable to each other, by recording their deviations from the mean and locating them in a distribution of differences. Within this system, the photographic portrait ceased to function as the representative double of a unique individual; instead, it became a serialised document of the always repeatable confrontation of a random subject with an anonymous apparatus of data acquisition. This serial logic of the archive, as I would like to show in the following two historical scenes, ultimately extended beyond the sphere of institutional image practice. After 1900, what applied to criminal identification also became valid for artistic as well as everyday image practice: the single portrait now no longer stood for itself, but became an element of ongoing and practically unlimited series of images and data.

1928 – Brik and Rodchenko: The Networked Portrait

Long before they began to determine our digital everyday experience, media formats of continuous recording and systematic archiving of quotidian appearances and expressions were anticipated in the debates about photography and portraiture in the Soviet avant-garde of the 1920s. The common concern of constructivist critics and artists such as Osip Brik, Alexander Rodchenko, and others was to prove the superiority of photography over painting, namely a documentary photography that freed itself from all traditional pictorial values of what they called 'easel art'. For them, the struggle against painting was also the struggle against a false consciousness. In his essay 'From the Painting to the Photograph' (1928), Brik argues that the painter, unlike the photographic apparatus, is unable to simultaneously capture all elements of a given situation in their actual relationships. That is why the staged painterly portrait shows only atomised individuals, isolated and detached from their actions and environments. For Brik, this was not only a technical but also an ideological matter: the painterly portrait necessarily reproduced the bourgeois ideology of the autonomous individual. Only photography, which instantly records all the details of a given situation, could capture the individual as an element of a complex social environment.

Thus, for Brik, the photojournalist's candid snapshot of a people's commissar in the midst of the masses was superior to any studio portrait. For those people who were seen in the same picture with the commissar are by no means incidental to the understanding of the commissar's role: 'To the contemporary consciousness, an individual person can be understood and assessed only in connection with all the other people – with those who used to be regarded by the pre-Revolutionary consciousness as background' (Brik 1989: 231) Brik, who was influenced by Ferdinand de Saussure's structuralism (see Kurchanova 2010: 58), understood identity, not unlike Bertillon, as being defined within a system of relations. But while Bertillon aimed to map anatomical differences on to a bureaucratic data structure in order to identify individuals, Brik was striving for a structural understanding of society as a whole: 'That is why we pay attention not to the individual characters as such, but to the social movements and connections that define their particular positions' (Brik 1989: 231).

For Alexander Rodchenko, too, the painterly portrait corresponded to a bygone epoch that still believed in stable identities and unchanging truths. In his eyes, only snapshot photography could keep up with the dynamics of the present. His oft-cited, manifesto-like appeal 'Against the Synthetic Portrait, For the Snapshot' (1928), published three months after Brik's essay, culminates in the call: 'Crystallize man not by a single "synthetic" portrait, but by a whole lot of snapshots taken at different times and in different conditions' (Rodchenko 1989: 242). For Rodchenko, the victory of photography over the traditional arts was evident in the failed attempts to create a true portrait of Lenin. There was, he argued, a whole plethora of snapshots of Lenin taken during his lifetime and collected in a 'large file of photographs' that anyone could consult. And while since his death many traditional artists had tried to depict the revolutionary leader in paintings and sculptures, often enough with the help of those very photos, none had succeeded in showing 'the real V.I. Lenin' (Rodchenko 1989: 220) – and that would not happen in the future either. Measured against the abundance of existing documents, any traditional work of art could only represent a one-sided attempt at synthesis: 'It should be stated firmly that with the appearance of photographs, there can be no question of a single, immutable portrait. Moreover, man is not just one sum total; he is many, and sometimes they are quite opposed' (Rodchenko 1989: 241).

For Rodchenko, a truly authentic Lenin memorial therefore would consist of an even more extensive photo file, supplemented by 'archives of his books, writing pads, notebooks, shorthand reports, films, phonograph records' (Rodchenko 1989: 241). What Rodchenko thus proposed instead of a single, immutable artistic portrait was a collectively created dossier fed by anonymous sources – a personalised profile 'constructed from discrete data sets', as Sven Spieker (2008: 132) writes, and 'structurally open', since it could be continuously supplemented by new images and data. With Rodchenko, the photographic archive, which for Bertillon was a mere tool of identification, becomes the basis of a monumental portrait, as bureaucratic recording, filing, and indexing take the place of previous artistic means of representation – at least in theory, as Rodchenko's ambitious plans were never realised.

Under the impact of a double revolution, namely a political one that aimed to abolish all hierarchies of representation and a media logistical one that made technologies of visual recording such as portable cameras accessible to the masses, the Soviet avant-garde conceived of a new relationship between representation and the represented that radically broke with the tradition of the individual portrait. Synthetic representation was to be replaced by collective archival documentation of all aspects of reality. This meant a far-reaching dissolution of the subject of the portrait. No longer just 'characteristic' features, but all visible manifestations of a person's life, and no longer just isolated individuals, but all forms of social interaction could now become the subject of a portrait. However, this was by no means connected with a naive belief in photography's claim to truth, as is sometimes attributed to the Soviet avant-garde (see, for example, Groys 1992: 29).

For Rodchenko, Brik, and other like-minded authors (for example, Sergei Tretyakov), the 'photographic image', as Benjamin Buchloh has pointed out, 'was defined as dynamic, contextual, and contingent, and the serial structuring of visual information emphasized open form and a potential infinity' (1994: 56). In a way, these authors heralded a new idea of networked images that can only be technically realised under today's digital conditions: images no longer appeared as autonomous artefacts but as interconnectable documents, contingent traces of life that only acquired their documentary status as elements of larger structures, series, and sequences. Produced by an infinite number of distributed actors and assembled and combined in endlessly expandable structures, they would enter into the collective large-scale project of a continuous recording of reality.

1964 – Warhol: Competitive Performances

While the representative portrait was based on the idea of the singularity of an individual visibly manifesting itself in an equally singular image, the photographic archive gave rise to new media formats of comparability preceding every single act of image production. The autonomous image, which was supposed to capture the uniqueness of an autonomous subject, could now be superseded by endless series of anonymous records and standardised documents. While the significance of this new state of affairs for artistic production had first been theoretically debated within the circles of the Soviet avant-garde, hardly any artist of the twentieth century has placed it so consistently at the centre of their artistic production as Andy Warhol. For Warhol, the act of portrait production was no longer about the artist's ability to create a unique representation of an individual, but about the ability of the portrayed to meet the demands of a standardised recording situation, as well as the potential of the resulting images to gain recognition in the circuits of media circulation (see Breitz 1999; Weingart 2010; Foster 2012: 109–72).

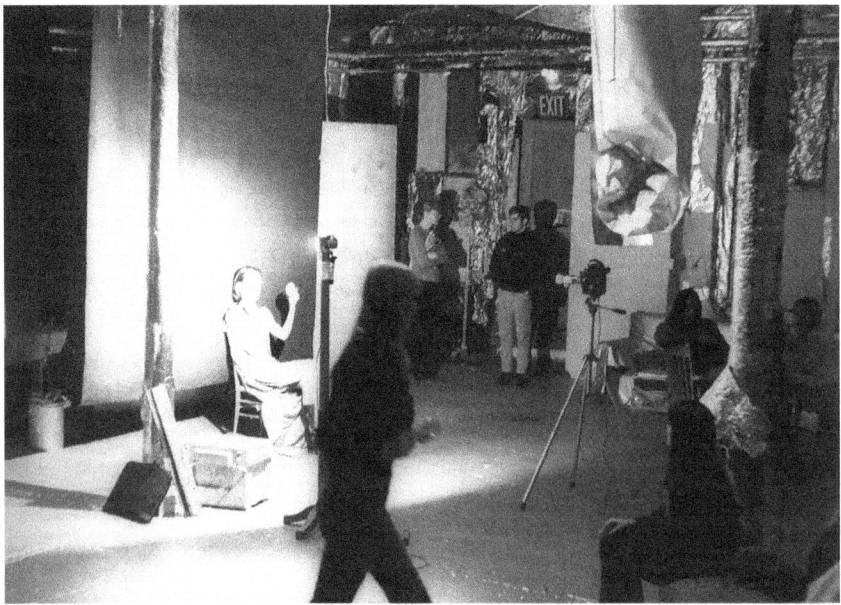

Figure 2.6 Billy Name, *Ivy Nicholson prepares for her Screen Test at the Factory*, 1966

This reconfiguration of the portrait can be seen is his early photobooth portraits as well as in his celebrity paintings, but probably no other series of Warhol's works illustrates it as vividly as those short films that have become known as *Screen Tests* (see James 1989: 58–84; Angell 2006; Murphy 2011; Crimp 2012). Between 1964 and 1966, almost anyone who visited the Silver Factory was invited to take their place in front of Warhol's camera, resulting in no fewer than 472 *Screen Tests* in total (Figure 2.6). The *Screen Tests* thus form an unprecedented collection of cinematic portraits that include not only most of the members of Warhol's entourage, but also countless models, gallery owners, artists, critics, and celebrities. Regardless of social differences, they were all indiscriminately subjected to the same recording format, which was as strict in form as it was indeterminate in content: a face in close-up, silent, black and white, filmed with a still camera. The running time of each film corresponds to the length of a 100-foot film reel, about four minutes at a playback speed of sixteen frames per second. There is no editing, let alone a plot or script. The minimal setting of *Screen Tests* was designed to combine repressive moments with moments of playful freedom. For example, spotlights were often deliberately used to irritate the actors, while at the same time they were instructed to look directly into the camera, not to move, not even to blink. It remained open, however, whether compliance with the instructions or precisely a break with them was expected. 'After turning on the camera', Warhol Superstar Mary Woronov remembers, 'everybody left me there, alone. They just turned around and walked away, leaving me with a running camera pointed at my face. Next to the muzzle of a gun, the black hole of the camera is one of the coldest things in the world' (quoted in Murphy 2011: 2).

'[T]o preserve one's humanity in the face of the apparatus' is what film production, according to Walter Benjamin (2010: 22), imposes on the actors: 'Film makes test performances capable of being exhibited, by turning the exhibitability of the performance itself into a test.' That Warhol's *Screen Tests* play out this testing character of the cinematographic apparatus, reduced to its basic parameters, has been noted repeatedly, most recently by Hal Foster (2012: 167–72), who also marks an important difference: Warhol can be located historically right between the psychotechnical aptitude tests of Taylorism that Benjamin had in mind and the demands of our present, with its flexibilised work biographies constantly pushing us to develop a distinctive personal profile. However, what above all distinguishes the cinematic apparatus described by Benjamin from the *Screen Tests* is its economic and social structure: for Benjamin, 'apparatus' means not only the technical recording process, but the entire filmic production and distribution apparatus organised according to the division of labour. Accordingly, for him it is a 'body of experts' that evaluates, fragments, and reassembles the actor's performance in front of the camera in order to produce a marketable product for a mass audience (Benjamin 2010: 22). In Warhol's Factory, on the other hand, there are neither expert panels nor mass audiences; rather, audiences and actors are more or less identical and evaluate each other. Thus, the *Screen Tests* have less to do with the structure of Hollywood than with today's social media: instead of addressing an anonymous audience, images become a medium of interaction, competition, and peer-review between loosely connected social networks.

While in front of Warhol's camera social barriers were largely suspended and penniless dropouts could become superstars just as much as millionaires' daughters, this does not mean that the *Screen Tests* would showcase the equality of all people. Instead, relative differences between individual performances became all the more important. In Warhol's world, individuality is not something that escapes general comparability, but it is only produced performatively in a system of universal competition. At the regular screenings at the Factory, it became a social game to evaluate the performances, to understand them as 'tests of the soul' (Murphy 2011: 2). Questions of ranking, inclusion, and exclusion thus were present in the production of the *Screen Tests* from the very beginning. The very first filmic portraits were intended for two compilations entitled *Thirteen Most Beautiful Boys* and *Thirteen Most Beautiful Women*, respectively. Significantly, however, the final ranking was never fixed: for both the 'Boys' and their female counterparts, there existed a pool of over forty film roles, so that compilations could be rearranged for each screening, depending on who was expected. If, for example, the wife of a collector was to visit a screening at the factory, Warhol and his crew could make sure that she was included in the selection (Angell 2006: 190, 243).

As early as the 1960s Warhol's Factory experimentally staged a new way of life now very familiar to us, informed as it was by the question of what it means to become one's own image (see Graw 2009). 'Cameras were as natural to us as mirrors', Warhol's close collaborator Billy Name remembers. 'It was almost as if the Factory became a big box camera – you'd walk into it, expose yourself, and develop yourself' (Name 1997: 18). Being part of Warhol's Factory meant living under the conditions of ubiquitous recording devices, permanent surveillance, social media, and an all-encompassing logic of competition and ranking. The multimedia image production of the

Factory, which also included Warhol's extensive use of photobooths, polaroids, and tape recorders, thus went a decisive step beyond the model of the archive: its aim was not only the continuous document- ing of reality, as in Rodchenko's imaginary archival project, but rather the production of a new form of performative individuality. Confronting the black holes of Warhol's diverse cameras and other recording devices, the inhabitants of his world faced never-ending testing situations in which they had to prove their individuality again and again, without ever knowing the final results.

Conclusion: Ubiquitous Operativity and the Visibility of Images

Admittedly, these four historical vignettes hardly add up to an over- arching, coherent narrative. But what I hope to have achieved is at least to indicate a series of fundamental transformations in the way portraits have been seen, used, and theorised; transformations which, taken together, amount to a veritable reconfiguration of the portrait. In each of these episodes, as different as they may be, the traditional representational function of the portrait is questioned, even abandoned, in favour of new affordances: technical images of faces becoming measuring instruments and operative surfaces of data extraction (Lavater), series of standardised archival inscriptions made searchable via metadata (Bertillon), networked elements in ongoing processes of profiling (Rodchenko), and records of individual perfor- mance within a system of ranking and competition (Warhol).

Obviously, all these aspects resonate strongly with contempo- rary digital visual culture. With YouTube and Instagram, the perfor- mance of individuality in confrontation with recording media and social systems of evaluation and ranking, as it was still being playfully experimented with in Warhol's Factory, has become a billion-dollar business. The personalised profiles created of each and every one of us by platforms such as Google and Facebook, documenting our most mundane everyday activities and mapping the interconnected complexity of our social relationships as an algorithmically analys- able 'social graph', far exceed anything Brik and Rodchenko could have imagined. Meanwhile, the fusion of image production and data acquisition in order to manage ever-expanding image collections, as it seemed possible for the first time with Bertillon's archive, has moved beyond the sphere of bureaucratic institutions and become the stan- dard setting for all our mobile digital gadgets. And finally, Lavater's dream of a non-human vision, which could decipher the visible world as a text made of discrete signs, has found its technical realisation in today's machine vision and pattern recognition algorithms.

While the operative use of images used to be limited to definable tasks and confined social spaces, now every image we take of ourselves and share online can be scanned, analysed, and compared, becoming an element in endless streams of data. The technical effort of formatting once needed to make the world accessible to a quantifying, non-human gaze has sunk into our media infrastructure. It is embedded in the devices with which we surround ourselves, the networks, services, and platforms that we use on a daily basis, and it also shapes the social practices that we have developed in dealing with digital images. But while we have accustomed ourselves to gazing into the small black hole that constantly points at us from our laptops and smartphones, the processes of pattern recognition that our images undergo once we upload them to the cloud are hidden more than ever from our view. Behind every black hole, there is now a black box, or even several of them.

This new ubiquitous operativity of images has led to discussions about the invisibility of operative images (see Paglen 2016). Indeed, thinking of operative images as mere visual data automatically captured by ubiquitous sensors and algorithmically analysed without human intervention raises the question of whether they are still images at all (Broeckmann 2016: 127–8). But as the example of Clearview shows, images visible to human eyes still play a major role even in automated processes of facial recognition. It is our digital culture, with its networked visuality, its endless number of selfies and snapshots scattered across online platforms, that drives most of today's machine vision: both as training data for machine learning and as a resource for automated surveillance (see Meyer 2021).

Operative portraits are therefore still *images* – and not mere datasets – because and insofar as they are not fully integrated into automated chains of operations. Their visibility to human eyes is not merely incidental. Images matter because they matter to the people who are producing, sharing, evaluating, annotating, and commenting on them *en masse*, and this mostly invisible human labour is what essentially drives automated vision. Without human eyes today's algorithms would still be blind. Images, because they mean more and different things to human viewers than mere datasets, have now become interfaces between the visible and the invisible, interfaces that ensure the connection between visual culture and automated processes, linking human vision and algorithmic image processing.

Notes

1. For a more nuanced account of this history, see Meyer 2019, on which this chapter is based.
2. For a media-archaeological account of Central Europe's postal system, see Siegert's (1999) classical study.

References

Althaus, Karin (2010), '"Die Physiognomik ist ein neues Auge". Zum Porträt in der Sammlung Lavater', PhD dissertation, Basel University, http://archiv.ub.uni-heidelberg.de/artdok/volltexte/2010/1201 (last accessed 30 April 2022).

Angell, Callie (2006), *Andy Warhol Screen Tests: The Films of Andy Warhol Catalogue Raisonné*, vol. 1, New York: Abrams.

Belting, Hans (2014), *An Anthropology of Images: Picture, Medium, Body*, Princeton, NJ: Princeton University Press.

Benjamin, Walter (2010 [1935]), 'The Work of Art in the Age of Its Technological Reproducibility', trans. Michael W. Jennings, *Grey Room*, 39: 11–38.

Bertillon, Alphonse (1890), *Das anthropometrische Signalement: Neue Methode zu Identitäts-Feststellungen, Vortrag am internationalen Congresse für Straf- und Gefängnisswesen zu Rom*, Berlin: Fischer's Medicinische Buchhandlung.

Boehm, Gottfried (1985), *Bildnis und Individuum. Über den Ursprung der Porträtmalerei in der italienischen Renaissance*, Munich: Prestel.

Boehm, Gottfried (2003), '"Mit durchdringendem Blick". Die Porträtkunst und Lavaters Physiognomik', in Ulrich Stadler and Karl Pestalozzi (eds), *Im Lichte Lavaters: Lektüren zum 200. Todestag*, Zürich: NZZ Libro, pp. 21–40.

Breitz, Candice (1999), 'The Warhol Portrait: From Art to Business and Back Again', in *Andy Warhol Photography*, Hamburg: Kunsthalle; Pittsburgh: Andy Warhol Museum, pp. 193–9.

Brik, Ossip (1989 [1928]), 'From the Painting to the Photograph', in Christopher Phillips (ed.), *Photography in the Modern Era. European Documents and Critical Writings, 1913–1940*, New York: Metropolitan Museum/Aperture, pp. 227–33.

Broeckmann, Andreas (2016), *Machine Art in the Twentieth Century*, Cambridge, MA: MIT Press.

Buchloh, Benjamin H. D. (1994), 'Residual Resemblance. Three Notes on the Ends of Portraiture', in Melissa E. Feldman (ed.), *Face-Off. The Portrait in Recent Art*, Philadelphia: Institute of Contemporary Art, University of Pennsylvania, pp. 53–69.

Cole, Simon A. (2001), *Suspect Identities: A History of Fingerprinting and Criminal Identification*, Cambridge, MA: Harvard University Press.

Crawford, Kate (2021), *Atlas of AI: Power, Politics and the Planetary Costs of Artificial Intelligence*, New Haven, CT: Yale University Press.

Crimp, Douglas (2012), *'Our Kind of Movie': The Films of Andy Warhol*, Cambridge, MA: MIT Press.

Ellenbogen, Josh (2012), *Reasoned and Unreasoned Images: The Photography of Bertillon, Galton, and Marey*, University Park, PA: Pennsylvania State University Press.

Farocki, Harun (2004), 'Phantom Images', *Public*, 29: 12–22, https://public.journals.yorku.ca/index.php/public/article/view/30354 (last accessed 30 April 2022).

Foster, Hal (2012), *The First Pop Age: Painting and Subjectivity in the Art of Hamilton, Lichtenstein, Warhol, Richter, and Ruscha*, Princeton, NJ: Princeton University Press.

Frieß, Peter (1993), *Kunst und Maschine. 500 Jahre Maschinenlinien in Bild und Skulptur*, Munich: Deutscher Kunstverlag.

Graw, Isabelle (2009), 'When Life Goes to Work: Andy Warhol', *October*, 132: 99–113.

Groys, Boris (1992), *The Total Art of Stalinism: Avant-Garde, Aesthetic Dictatorship, and Beyond*, Princeton, NJ: Princeton University Press.

Gunning, Tom (1995), 'Tracing the Individual Body: Photography, Detectives, and Early Cinema', in Leo Charney and Vanessa R. Schwartz (eds), *Cinema and the Invention of Modern Life*, Berkeley: University of California Press, pp. 15–45.

Gutbrodt, Fritz (2003), 'Physiognomik, Predigt, Okkultismus. Lavater und die Medien der Kommunikation im 18. Jahrhundert', in Ulrich Stadler and Karl Pestalozzi (eds), *Im Lichte Lavaters: Lektüren zum 200. Todestag*, Zürich: NZZ Libro, pp. 117–40.

Hagner, Michael (2004), *Geniale Gehirne. Zur Geschichte der Elitegehirnforschung*, Göttingen: Wallstein.

Hill, Kashmir (2020a), 'The Secretive Company that Might End Privacy as We Know It', *New York Times*, 18 January 2020, https://www.nytimes.com/2020/01/18/technology/clearview-privacy-facial-recognition.html (last accessed 30 April 2022).

Hill, Kashmir (2020b), 'Before Clearview Became a Police Tool, It Was a Secret Plaything of the Rich', *New York Times*, 6 March 2020, www.nytimes.com/2020/03/05/technology/clearview-investors.html (last accessed 30 April 2022).

James, David E. (1989), *Allegories of Cinema: American Film in the Sixties*, Princeton, NJ: Princeton University Press.

Kanz, Roland (1993), *Dichter und Denker im Porträt. Spurengänge zur deutschen Porträtkultur des 18. Jahrhunderts*, Munich: Deutscher Kunstverlag.

Kurchanova, Natasha (2010), 'Osip Brik and the Politics of the Avantgarde', *October*, 134: 53–73.

Lavater, Johann Caspar (1776), *Physiognomische Fragmente, zur Beförderung der Menschenkenntnis und Menschenliebe. Zweyter Versuch. Mit vielen Kupfertafeln*, Leipzig, Winterthur: Weidmanns Erben und Reich.

Lavater, Johann Caspar (2001), 'Aussichten in die Ewigkeit, In Briefen an Herrn Joh. Georg Zimmermann, königl. Großbrittanischen Leibarzt in Hannover', in Ursula Caflisch-Schnetzler (ed.), *Johann Caspar Lavater: Ausgewählte Werke in historisch-kritischer Ausgabe*, vol. II, Zürich: NZZ Libro.

Meyer, Roland (2019), *Operative Porträts. Eine Bildgeschichte der Identifizierbarkeit von Lavater bis Facebook*, Konstanz: Konstanz University Press.

Meyer, Roland (2021), *Gesichtserkennung (Digitale Bildkulturen)*, Berlin: Wagenbach.

Murphy, J. J. (2011), *The Black Hole of the Camera: The Films of Andy Warhol*, Berkeley: University of California Press.

Name, Billy/Schorr, Collier (1997), 'A Talk with Billy Name', in Matthew Slotover (ed.), *All Tomorrow's Parties: Billy Name's Photographs of Andy Warhol's Factory*, London: Frieze, pp. 17–29.

Paglen, Trevor (2016), 'Invisible Images (Your Pictures Are Looking at You)', *The New Inquiry*, 8 December, https://thenewinquiry.com/invisible-images-your-pictures-are-looking-at-you/ (last accessed 30 April 2022).

Pantenburg, Volker (2017), 'Working Images: Harun Farocki and the Operational Image', in Jens Eder and Charlotte Klonk (eds), *Image Operations: Visual Media and Political Conflict*, Manchester: Manchester University Press, pp. 49–62.

Phéline, Christian (1985), *L'image acusatrice*, Paris: Les Cahiers de la Photographie.

Rodchenko, Alexander (1989 [1928]), 'Against the Synthetic Portrait, For the Snapshot', in Christopher Phillips (ed.), *Photography in the Modern Era: European Documents and Critical Writings, 1913–1940*, New York: Metropolitan Museum/Aperture, pp. 238–42.

Sekula, Allan (1986), 'The Body and the Archive', *October*, 39: 3–64.

Siegert, Bernhard (1999), *Relays: Literature as an Epoch of the Postal System*, Redwood City, CA: Stanford University Press.

Spieker, Sven (2008), *The Big Archive: Art from Bureaucracy*, Cambridge, MA: MIT Press.

Stafford, Barbara (1991): *Body Criticism: Imagining the Unseen in Enlightenment Art and Medicine*, Cambridge, MA: MIT Press.

Stoichita, Victor I. (1997), *A Short History of the Shadow*, London: Reaktion.

Swoboda, Gudrun (1999), 'Die Sammlung Johann Caspar Lavater in Wien. Herkunft – Struktur – Funktion', in Gerda Mraz and Uwe Schögl (eds), *Das Kunstkabinett des Johann Caspar Lavater*, Vienna: Böhlau, pp. 74–95.

Toulouse, [Édouard] (1896), *Enquête médico-psychologique sur la supériorité intellectuelle: Émile Zola*, Paris: Societé d' Editions scientifique.

Weingart, Brigitte (2010), '"That Screen Magnetism": Warhol's Glamour', *October*, 132: 43–70.

Chapter 3

'This Person Does Not Exist': From Real Generalisation to Algorithmic Abstraction in Photographic Portraiture

Daniël de Zeeuw and Abraham Geil

This Person Does Not Exist (TPDNE) is an online project launched in 2019 by a former Uber software engineer to call attention to the latest innovations in the emerging field of AI photography and video. With each visit to the project's webpage a new photorealistic portrait is displayed (Figure 3.1). These portraits, which are seemingly indistinguishable from photos of actual persons, are generated by advanced deep-learning algorithms called Generative Adversarial Networks (GANs). Announcing the presence of 'this person' whose existence is simultaneously denied, the title of the project is a performative contradiction that plays upon the most basic expectation regarding a photographic portrait: that it refers to an empirically real person (whether living or dead) outside of the portrait. Thus the site is designed to enact the very epistemological crisis – the inability to distinguish between real and fake, true and false – through which developments in 'synthetic media' are typically framed.[1] With this rhetorical strategy the site partakes in the broader discourse around 'deepfakes' and fake news (Warzel 2018; Cover et al. 2022) and associated media panics around a coming 'Infocalypse' (Schick 2020) or 'Information Dark Age' (Hannah 2021).[2]

As with many such projects, TPDNE wavers between indulging in a fetishistic fascination with the technology showcased and sounding the alarm about its dangers.[3] A small text box on the site tells the user 'Don't panic' (the surest sign that there is something to panic about), counselling us instead to 'Learn how it works' and linking to several YouTube tutorials that provide introductory (but still quite

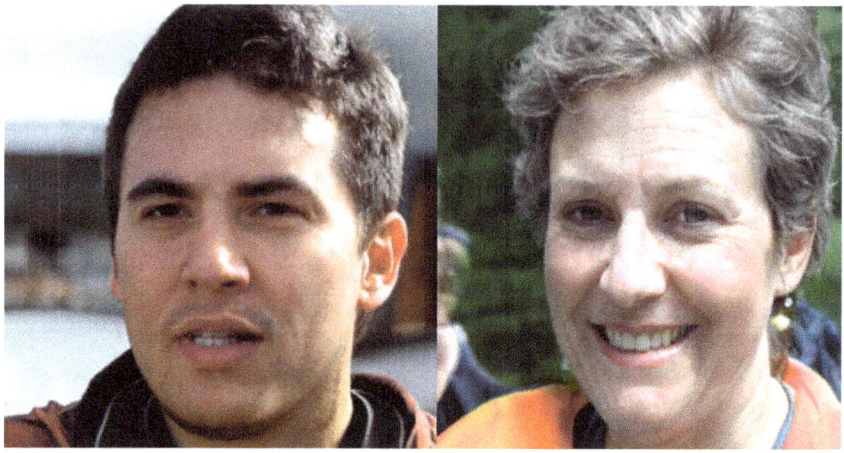

Figure 3.1 Two randomly generated computational portraits obtained by visiting and refreshing the page www.thispersondoesnotexist.com, 6 April 2022

technical) explanations of GANs. In this way, the project aims to facilitate a kind of technical media literacy adequate to the age of AI, opening the black box of its technological process to a broader public and providing forensic training in how to spot the visual artefacts that (for now) give away the fakes. Viewed in the light of portraiture's modern history, the warning sounded by the rhetorical framing of TPDNE and the forensic education it seeks to spur can be seen as an attempt to protect the portrait's referential function – what Hans-Georg Gadamer (2004) influentially dubbed 'occasionality', the intentional relation between the portrait and the 'being' of the person portrayed (see van Alphen 1997: 240–1; Johnstone and Imber 2020: 3). The prominent art historian Richard Brilliant places this notion of occasionality at the heart not just of portraiture's generic definition but of an entire social imaginary: 'This vital relationship between the portrait and its object of representation directly reflects the social dimension of human life as a field of action among persons' (1991: 8). Indeed, this statement could easily stand as an overarching articulation of what is thought to be at stake in much of the contemporary discourse around the social and political dangers of 'deepfake' technology.

But it is worth pausing to ask what gets assumed in this framing of the AI portraits of TPDNE in terms of the epistemological crisis of our supposedly 'post-truth' age. To begin with, the threat to which a 'forensic education' in state-of-the-art technology is posited as the obvious defence would seem to presume a very traditional notion of the portrait, one that has already been under threat for a long time and that in many quarters has ceased to exist at all, from contemporary art galleries to the proliferation of the online simulacra of 'cyberfaces' (Belting 2017) without human referents. From this perspective, the rhetorical framing of TPDNE begins to appear more like an effort to restore what Benjamin Buchloh describes as the 'foundational promise' of portraiture, which persists as 'a latent argument found in every traditional photographic portrait of the twentieth century' – that is, the promise to 'the spectator of the continuing validity of essentialist and biologistic concepts of identity formation' (2015: 477). This framing presupposition about what is threatened by TPDNE's AI portraits also leads to the conflation of the dangers they pose with the dangers of the deepfake. Such a conflation overlooks a deceptively simple distinction: whereas the latter are fake images of real people, the former are real images, as it were, of fake people. Both arguably play upon the presumed occasionality of the portrait – whether cast in Gadamer's humanist vision or Buchloh's critical recasting of it – but deepfakes work by in effect preserving occasionality in order to appropriate and redirect it towards deceptive and often violent ends.[4] In the AI portraits of TPDNE, by contrast, there is no link to an individual empirical person to begin with, and 'occasionality' as such is evacuated from their technical genesis even as it can be deployed after the fact as a fictional effect.

To what, then, do these AI portraits refer? And in what sense are they still portraits? One way to approach these questions can be found in Roland Meyer's (2019; see also his chapter in this volume) recent concept of the 'operative portrait', which builds upon Harun Farocki's category of 'operative images' – defined as images that 'do not represent an object but are part of an operation' (2004: 17). To what sort of operation do the TPDNE portraits belong? That question is at once technological, historical, and political; in order to begin to answer it, we contend, it is necessary to first shift the point of comparison away from both images of 'actually existing' people as well as 'deepfake' portraits. Rather, the more illuminating comparison lies between AI portraiture and the photographic portraits of an older but equally non-existent person, namely the 'average man' – that chimera of mid-nineteenth-century statistics that the Victorian eugenicist Francis Galton sought to visualise in his famous technique of composite photography (Figure 3.2).

If this comparison seems counterintuitive, it is perhaps less because these two instances of the 'operative portrait' reside at an historical distance of a century and a half from one another and involve radically different technical means of production, than it is

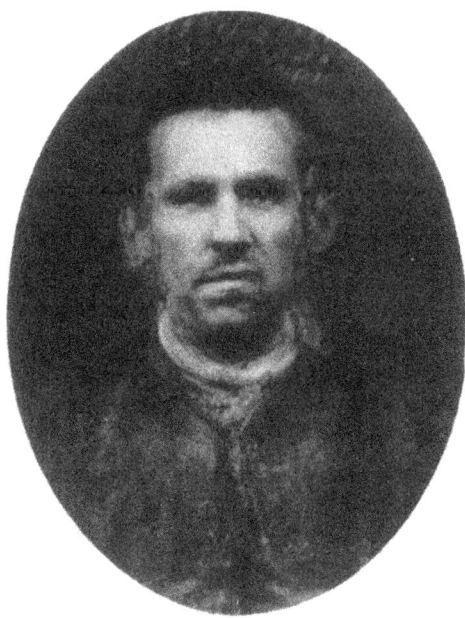

Figure 3.2 Francis Galton, 'Composite Portrait of a Criminal Type', 1897

due to the fact that, as portraits of the individual and the type respectively, they occupy opposite poles in a dialectic of particular and general. Whereas from the perspective of type, the human face captured by the camera represents an immeasurable and excessive, because singular, phenomenon, from the perspective of photography, type represents an aberration from its essential nature as a technological medium. But just as the photographic type is haunted by the singular as its material condition of appearance, the photographic portrait of the individual is also haunted by type as its immanent possibility (the rounded shape of this nostril can be computed as a deviation from a statistical norm). The portrayal of the type and the portrayal of the individual cannot be thought in isolation from one another in the operationalisation of photography that we seek to trace here.

What gets missed by framing the AI portraits of TPDNE as yet another instance of visual fakery undermining trust in the veracity of photographic images as symptomatic of our digital 'post-truth' predicament, we argue, is their participation in a longer technological and political history of the instrumentalisation of photography, including its connection to statistics, the archive, and the search for what Galton refers to as 'real generalisations'. This historical lineage turns less on questions of truth and falsity than on the operationalisation of photography for mapping, surveilling, and manipulating social and biological life. In shifting the way we critically read synthetic media projects such as TPDNE, we hope to show that what the project itself presents as an epistemological crisis actually appears, from another perspective, as a kind of solution (resolution or outcome) of an older epistemological problem: the nineteenth-century dream of merging the optical empiricism of photography with the abstract precision of statistics.

Composite Photography and the Quest for Real Generalisations

In his first paper on composite photography, published in *Nature* in 1878, Galton proclaimed that his new technique

> enables us to obtain with mechanical precision a generalised picture; one that represents no man in particular, but portrays an imaginary figure, possessing the average features of any given group of men. These ideal faces have a surprising air of reality. Nobody who glanced at one of them for the first time, would doubt its being the likeness of a living person. Yet, as I have said, it is no such thing; *it is the portrait of a type, and not of an individual.* (Galton 1878: 97; emphasis added)

What sort of figure is conjured here in this squaring of the circle between statistical generalisation and the mechanical precision of photography – an 'ideal' face imparted with a concrete impression of living 'reality'? To begin with, this figure's epistemological ground had already been established by the codification of social statistics during the first half of the nineteenth century. In the context of this positivist episteme, the 'reality' of the type to be portrayed was secured by the category of the 'average man', elaborated most prominently by the Belgian statistician Adolphe Quetelet in his 1835 treatise *Sur l'homme* (see Sekula 1986: 19–24). Rather than asking *who* or *what* this purely statistical apparition of the 'average man' was supposed to be, Sekula shifts our attention to the means or methodology of its constitution. The question then becomes '*how* was the average man?' (Sekula 1986: 20). And to what ends was 'he' put? The answers to those questions are to be found in the complex history of the rise of social statistics in the middle of the nineteenth century in conjunction with biopolitical regimes of state and colonial power.

For our purposes in this chapter, the question of means and ends is directed at how Galton's 'portrait of a type' is qua photographic portrait. How is this figure *figured*? For Galton, this meant achieving through the technique of composite photography a new form of the portrait as 'pictorial statistics' (1879: 166). This aspiration to merge the optical empiricism of photography with the abstraction of statistics 'was fundamental', Sekula argues, 'to a broader integration of the discourses of visual representation and those of the social sciences in the nineteenth century' (1986: 19).[5] In their book *Objectivity*, Lorraine Daston and Peter Galison situate Galton's project squarely in relation to the emergence of a new mechanical ideal of objectivity in mid-nineteenth-century scientific practice. In the rhetorical construction of that ideal, the mechanical automism of the photographic image elevated it to the status of an 'emblem for all aspects of non-interventionist objectivity' (Daston and Galison 2007: 187). In his method for producing composite portraits, Galton sought to devise a procedural formalism that would match the mechanical automism of photography in its removal of fallible human perception and judgement.

This procedure was quite straightforward in itself, requiring only about half a page of description in Galton's inaugural paper on composite portraits. Having selected the sample photographs of the type in question (mugshots of 'male criminals', for example), the first step would be to puncture each of them with twin pinholes in order to 'hang them up one in front of the other, like a pack of cards [. . .] in such a way that the eyes of all the portraits shall be as nearly as possible superimposed' (1878: 97). Once the photographs were aligned in this way, Galton would then expose them in succession to a camera with a single sensitive plate. The exposure times were derived fractionally by dividing the total exposure time for a given composite by the total number of individual portraits. In his example, applying a total exposure of eighty seconds to eight individual portraits would require a ten-second exposure each. The resulting 'composite photograph', Galton avers, 'represents the picture that would rise before the mind's eye of a man who had the gift of pictorial imagination in an exalted degree' (1878: 97). Of course, no such person exists, he hastens to add, as the 'imaginative power of even the highest artists is far from precise, and is so apt to be biased by special cases that may have struck their fancies, that no two artists can agree in any of their typical forms' (1878: 97).

In fact, the human capacity that Galton's composite portraits claimed to perfect and thus supersede was not merely the 'pictorial imagination' of artists but the faculty of generalisation as such. In an article published the following year entitled 'Generic Images', Galton remarks that 'the human mind is [. . .] a most imperfect apparatus for the elaboration of general ideas' (1879: 169) due its propensity for exaggeration. First analogising his technique to the empiricist model of the mind's generation of abstract ideas from the particularities of sense perception, Galton then argues that composite photography achieves the mechanical perfection of this process with the quantitative precision and consistency of statistics precisely by evacuating human intervention all together. His technique was thus designed to shift 'the epistemic burden of generalizing from the observer to the camera' (Ambrosio 2016: 554). Ultimately, Galton's overarching claim that his composite photographs visualised the type as a 'real generalisation' can be seen as the result of adopting a reified conception of eighteenth-century Lockean empiricism at the service of his very contemporary project of splicing the biopositivism of social statistics with emerging ideals of mechanical objectivity.

The governing logic of this project precedes Galton's empirical procedure and determines how its results are read. Galton unwittingly gives the game away in his statistical interpretation of the characteristic blurring around the periphery of the composite portraits. 'The blur of their outlines, which is never great in truly generic composites, except in unimportant details, measures the tendency of individuals to deviate from the central type' (Galton 1879: 166). In this way the empirical traces of the individual are at once retained as evidence of statistical deviation and subordinated to the presumed stability of the average type concretised in the centre of the composite. This interpretation of the visual data ignores the fact that blurring is actually spread over the entirety of the image even if it is more conspicuous at the periphery of the face than its centre. 'Only an imagination that wanted to see a visual analogue of the binomial curve would make this mistake' as Sekula (1986: 48) observes. Galton's interpretation of the pictorial evidence in his composite portraits produces an 'extraordinary hypostatization': the 'symmetrical bell curve now wore a human face' (Sekula 1986: 48). The solidified features at the centre of the face represented the statistical average measured at the apex of the y-axis and centre of the x-axis, while the blurred outlines registered the deviations flattening out on the left and right sides.

The more encompassing name for what Galton saw in the 'real generalisations' of his composite portraits was the apparatus of late nineteenth-century power/knowledge that Sekula famously dubbed 'the archive'. In Sekula's elaboration, the archive describes a larger system of abstract procedure and statistical knowledge in which both the photographic camera and the older model of optical empiricism that it promised to perfect were at once instrumentalised and decentred. Sekula reads Galton's will to see in the face an immanent expression of the Gaussian curve as his attempt to 'embed' the epistemic authority of the archive in a single photographic image. At the same time, it was an attempt to preserve the older authority of optical empiricism in the new name of mechanical objectivity under the tremendous pressure of an 'historical context in which abstract, statistical procedures seemed to offer the high road to social truth and social control' (Sekula 1986: 55).

Deep-Learning Algorithms, GANs, and AI Portraiture

At what juncture do Galton's composite portraits of types and the AI portraits of TPDNE intersect, if at all? Is there a clear historical or paradigmatic continuity between these two forms of artificial portraiture – the interfacing between statistics and photography being a common denominator – or are they rather the *relata* of an epistemological break, from the mechanical and linear causality of the nineteenth century to the cybernetic rationality of the twenty-first century?

Little research has been done on this lineage from the real generalisations of composite photography to the algorithmic abstractions of synthetic media, and even then the focus is typically on the way deepfake videos dynamically map one face on to another. Situating the latter in the history of photographic composites, Dondero writes:

> Unlike with Galton's portraits of types, the relevant process [here] is that of accumulating images of the same person so as to make him or her into the type of him or herself, so to speak. And then make the type applicable onto another person. (2021: 448)

While many of the underlying processes of TPDNE are identical to those used to generate deepfakes, there are also key differences. Most importantly, instead of replacing one face with another, the GAN used for TPDNE is trained on images containing objects of a certain type (e.g., faces, chairs, or artistic styles) that it learns to recognise and create new singular instances of. So if these portraits are no longer *of* a particular person, nor creating a type of a person him- or herself, they can still be said to obliquely represent the thousands of faces used as training data. In contrast to Galton's method of composite photography, the AI portraits of TPDNE involve many complex steps and layers of processing, prediction, and abstraction. The project uses the styleGAN2 algorithm, which is one among many GANs developed for different purposes. GANs can be trained not only on faces but on all kinds of objects and visual styles, and can be equally applied to other digital media formats such as audio, video, or text (Karras et al. 2020).[6] The first GANs were developed by Ian Goodfellow in 2014 and further developed by NVIDIA as a show-case for their state-of-the-art graphical processing units (GPUs) that do the heavy computational lifting required by GANs.

A GAN works with training data comprising thousands of images of a specific type – faces, sunrises, Van Gogh paintings – that progres-sively iterate through thousands of training cycles, effectively teach-ing itself to produce images that are impossible to distinguish from the images in the training dataset. Said by Goodfellow to be inspired by game theory and its application in market economics, a GAN consists of two deep neural networks pitted against each other in a zero-sum game (meaning that if one party wins the other loses).[7] A GAN is designed so that each neural net is assigned the role of either Discriminator or Generator. What makes the resulting network 'adversarial' is that the goal of each is to minimise the other's success in favour of its own, and it achieves this by constantly testing and receiving feedback from the other, issuing in 'a self-contained arms race of information generation and discrimination' (Fletcher 2018: 459). Whereas the aim of the Generator is to produce an image that the Discriminator cannot tell apart from any image in the original training data (for example, photographic portraits of real persons), the Discriminator is set up to maximise the ability to tell real and fake apart. Put simply, this cat-and-mouse game ends when the Discrimi-nator, instructed to rate the likelihood of an image being authentic or generated, always returns a probability score of 0.5, meaning the chance of the image's being either is equal, that is, it cannot tell the difference (the technical term for this is 'Nash equilibrium'). Game theory offers a way of formalising the paradoxical logic of collabo-ration through competition, where the adversarial relation between actors induces a process of self-learning optimisation on the level of the system as a whole. When the optimal state is reached, the Gen-erator has learned the capacity to produce photorealistic images on its own.

The analogy often used to explain GANs is that of a cunning art forger (the Generator) and a police officer tasked with identi-fying potential forgeries (the Discriminator). And here too a logic of optimisation through competition based on the cybernetic prin-ciple of 'positive feedback' occurs: because, despite the officer's goal of reducing the number of forgeries passing as real artworks, by responding to the very act of judging these works to be real or fake, the forger will slowly but steadily learn how to produce better fakes.

Moreover, if the art forger identifies certain strategies that increase the probability of passing the test of authenticity, it will dynamically reallocate cognitive resources to maximise those strategies, just as the forensic agent will optimise those strategies that she finds yield a higher chance of detecting fakes. What makes this learning 'deep' is that instead of using brute computational force, deep neural nets use forms of path- and pattern-finding that resemble human cognition (for example, when we are learning a foreign grammar and notice that we are not doing well on conjugations, we will pay more attention to those cases).

In light of the lineage we are tracing here, it is notable that this common explanation resorts to forensic metaphors that also pervade the nineteenth-century biopolitical imaginary that Galton, Bertillon, and others partake in. As Boltanski (2014) notes, sociology as a scientific discipline co-emerged with the popular literary genre of the detective and spy novel. Both the scientist and the detective navigate a world of objective forces in search of cues of deviance; and both are obsessed with an incessant but hidden criminality – whether expressed in typical facial features or by leaving fingerprints at the crime scene. While TPDNE and similar applications of GANs do not have this forensic purpose of identifying or screening individual persons through facial recognition systems that use similar designs, the analogy shows how the technical make-up of GANs incorporates key elements of the larger forensic history and biopolitical lineage in which both photography and statistics are tied up in various shifting constellations.

On a more theoretical level, a deep neural net operates by statistical abstraction: if the goal is to recognise chairs in images, for example, it will establish an abstract representation or 'statistical profile' that exists as a vector space containing all probable instances of chairs, similar to how empiricist philosophers of mind going back to John Locke would claim we arrive at a general idea of 'chair' based on our past experiences of chairs of different sizes and shapes, and from different viewing angles. Although based more in Kantian schematism than the empiricist's *tabula rasa* mind, the American philosopher Charles Sanders Peirce refers to such empirical syntheses as 'generalized percepts' (quoted in Ambrosio 2016: 561). Interestingly, Peirce uses Galton's method of composite photography as a metaphor for how the mind generates ideas by abstracting from particulars, and Galton himself plays with this idea as well (Ambrosio 2016: 549, 554). A predicate such as yellow, Peirce writes, 'conveys its signification by exciting in the mind some image, or, as it were, a *composite photograph* of images' (cited in Hookway 2002: 29, emphasis added). In a way, then, the vectorial profiles created by GANs are a more advanced version of Galton's composite photographs, another attempt to arrive at real generalisations building on advances in statistics and computer science. Rather than the mechanical character of the camera eliminating human agency and thus securing the 'objectivity' of the generalisations, here it is the *unsupervised* learning capacities of deep neural nets that perform a similar function, even when the stated goal of scientific validity is displaced to more practical computational concerns.

Beyond recognising chairs in images, GANs can also generate new chairs by remixing in so-called 'nuisance parameters' (features of a chair specific to that particular one) subtracted but retained in the process, just as Galton's composite photographs retain the individual facial data that compose them, rather than merely representing the average, thus lending 'visual evidence to the material content of our generalizations' (Ambrosio 2016: 556).[8] To make each generated portrait unique, two inputs are used to secure variation: noise vectors and a randomised latent vector. As Liu explains, whereas the first creates 'stochastic variations such as exact placement of hair or frickles [sic] within a face image', the second 'determines more global features in images such the shape of the head' (2019: 1). Moreover, latent vectors can be recombined using simple arithmetic (addition and subtraction). For example, when you subtract the vector 'man' from the statistical profile of 'man with sunglasses' and you add the vector 'woman', this will generate photorealistic portraits of women wearing sunglasses.[9]

The computational portraits of TPDNE are thus composites, but in a different way than Galton's: rather than overlaying photographed faces at equal exposure times, a portrait is algorithmically assembled – and in this sense is more akin to montage than composite. Rather than a single average face, GANs produce an average single face: each time completely different and seemingly unique, a random singular instance of what all the faces in the dataset taught the AI a face can be. Accordingly, these portraits do not aspire to represent the average face of a typical social figure, group, or class. Yet they are 'typical' in the sense that, as the product of the combinations (or rather 'inspirations') of the thousands of faces on which the deep-learning algorithm (GAN) is trained, they will naturally tend to incorporate the facial characteristics 'typical' for the dataset in question. Moreover, the type is generated 'in between' the training on photos of actual persons and the generation of newly non-existing persons, in the form of a vectorial profile that can be recombined at will with other latent vectors in a logical space potentially containing hundreds of dimensions.

The Algorithmic Abstractions of AI Portraits

What do we face in the face of a person who does not exist? Linda Nochlin (1974: 29) famously defined the specificity of the portrait as the only genre that 'demands the meeting of two subjectivities', the artist and the sitter, each placed in the position of watching and judging the other. What then do we make of a portrait from which this intersubjective encounter is absent? Or rather, if there is a confrontation between two subjectivities in the AI portraits of TPDNE, they are the inhuman subjectivities of the two neural networks, the Generator and the Discriminator, locked in the generative competition of their zero-sum game. What then becomes of the sitter? Is there still some remnant of Gadamer's notion of the portrait's 'occasionality' to be found in the traces of the thousands of faces that went into its algorithmic composition, a communication or communion from beyond this face? In concluding we want to suggest that, despite its title, what is uncanny about TPDNE is not that the person depicted does not exist, but that it reveals how the individual is always already mediated and 'grounded' by something that exceeds it, in the form of the typical, the average, or the general. Rather than only thinking the movement from particular to general as a process of abstraction, the individual can be thought as a concretisation of the various transindividual forces that compose it. In a way, then, TPDNE shows that we, too, do not exist, at least not in the way that the traditional portrait as an intersubjective encounter seeks to establish by performing a coherent personal identity.

This displacement of the subject to its general environmental conditions can be illustrated through a scene from Robert Musil's unfinished literary masterpiece *The Man Without Qualities* (1930–43), whose protagonist Ulrich at some point comes to experience himself as a composite of systemic realities that encapsulate and exceed him. A mathematician with a keen eye for the law of large numbers, Ulrich comes to view and feel himself to be an insignificant variable in a larger ensemble of impersonal forces, a random point on the bell-shaped curve of a Gaussian distribution where 'our personal motion to right or to left, this way or that is of no consequence to the average value' (Sypher 1979: 28). Consequently, his own thoughts and feelings seem to belong not to him personally but to 'a great complex of events robbing them of any essence by which they might be called his' (Sypher 1979: 10). Living a surrogate existence, his identity has become that of *anyone*, as 'he lives not only in the scientist but in the businessman, in the administrator, in the sportsman, in the technician' (Sypher 1979: 11). Or, in the terminology of the

AI-generated portrait, rather than being *this* or *that* particular person, Ulrich feels himself partaking in the transindividual realm where such individual-types are probabilistically prefigured.

Whereas conventional experience takes the visibly concrete as the ground of empirical reality that drives subsequent generalisations – the latter of which are thereby ontologically reduced to existing abstractly, 'as if' and/or 'merely in thought' – for Ulrich, only the statistical mechanisms that govern the natural and social world possess any purchase on reality, while the particular and concrete become incidental, insignificant combinations of an abstract space of possibility, mere empty points on a line. The immutable statistical laws that rule over the physical and social world now assume existential primacy, overcoding empirical reality, and extending to his sense of self. Indeed, the ingenuity of this scene in the book hinges on the fact that this primacy is somehow concretely experienced by Ulrich as the (impossible) subjective perspective on a perspectiveless, brutally objective world. Ultimately, however, Ulrich's experience of the domination of the general over the particular is as one-sided as the naive empiricist claim that generalisation is nominal to sense impression. There is, in other words, a dialectic of the abstract and the concrete, general and particular, type and individual.

Similarly, TPDNE shows how singular faces can be generated through algorithmic abstraction, and by so doing tempts us to view their ontological predicament as our own, in that we too are composite beings, 'real abstractions' forever caught between these two extreme vantage points. This is especially true in the context of the global apparatuses of digital capture that take the form of big data. The latter transforms unique personal characteristics into classifiable features that are generally available, comparable, and – as is the case with synthetic media – virtually recombined into new faces. As Roland Meyer writes in the case of automated facial recognition databases:

> As probable or improbable differentiators, these [facial] features always exist outside of the individuals whom they make recognizable. They represent repetitions or deviations within statistically normalized multitudes [. . .] The statistical disenchantment of the person locates these differences within pre-recorded sets of comparative data, and its most impersonal element is not the biological body but rather the masses of other bodies with which the latter is compared. (2016: 109)

At this point, and in conclusion, we might reframe the question we started with in the following way: if the nineteenth-century obsession with racial and criminal types drives the 'real generalisations' of Galton's composite photographs, what drives the 'algorithmic abstractions' of synthetic media in the case of TPDNE and other synthetic media? Although we can only gesture towards an answer here, it seems that while Galton's project is firmly embedded in the nineteenth-century biopolitical imaginary of objective types, the abstractions of synthetic media are oriented towards the frictionless manipulation and recombination of human and non-human materials into ever new plastic forms and arrangements. Rather than cutting up the social into types, synthetic media exploit these materials as sites of identity, value, and exchange, ultimately encapsulating the 'language of life' itself (Asgari and Mofrad 2015).

Increasingly, synthetic media play a role in the realm of production and the automation of labour by AI. The GANs used in TPDNE are already used to generate synthetic fashion models that can be used to showcase clothing in online fashion stores such as Zalando, and the website Generated Photos promises copyright-free production of stock models for marketing and PR that still require human labour, including a Face Generator where you can freely tweak race, gender, age, etc. (Figure 3.3).[10] More than a mass surveillance or privacy threat or the epistemic crisis of deepfakes, for us these instances of synthetic media signify a new stage in photography's historical entanglement with statistics, relocated from the biopolitics of racial and criminal types to the flexible, scalable, and automated production of visual identity cues for digital capitalism.

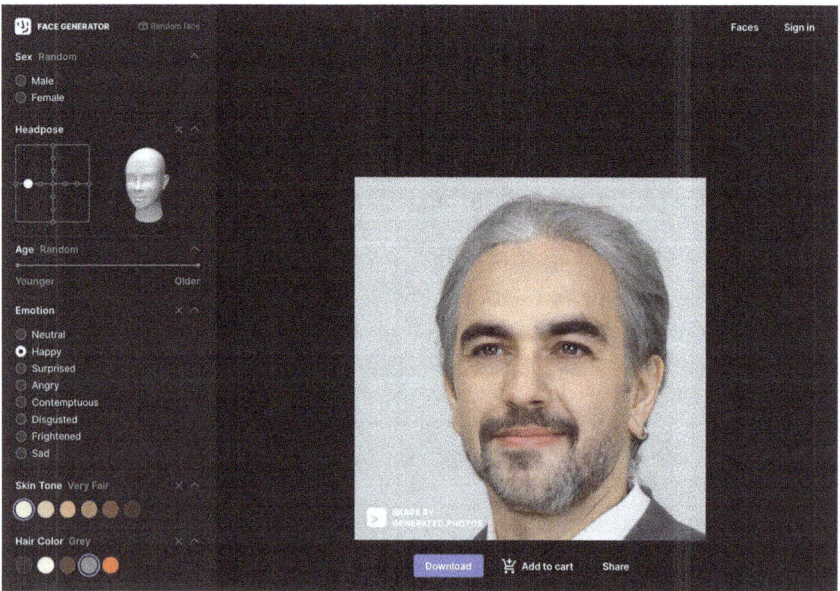

Figure 3.3 Example face with adjustable parameters generated by a GAN on Generated Photos (https://generated.photos)

Notes

1. As Nina Schick (2020) notes, the terminology around these new technologies has not yet stabilised. While algorithmically manipulated video is now commonly known as 'deepfake' – a term coined by the Reddit user u/deepfakes in November 2017 – the larger field is sometimes referred to as computational photography, synthetic media, or generative media. In this chapter we use the term AI portraiture for the algorithmic generation of photorealistic images of non-existing persons generated by GANs.

2. As the CEO of the cybersecurity firm Deeptrace, which has a vested commercial interest in such panics, writes in the preface to one of its reports: 'The rise of synthetic media and deepfakes is forcing us towards an important and unsettling realization: our historical belief that video and audio are reliable records of reality is no longer tenable.'

3. As if to showcase the sheer multiplicative power of this fetishistic dimension, the website this x does not exist collects the proliferating sites inspired by TPDNE to generate an astonishing variety of fake things with GANs: for example, 'this cat does not exist', 'this snack does not exist', 'this butterfly does not exist', and so on.

4. Besides issues of evidence and authenticity, one of the threats of deepfakes is the proliferation 'non-consensual deepfake pornography', which it is claimed comprise 96% of all deepfake videos found online; for a more detailed and critical account of this new form of pornography, see van der Nagel 2020.

5. Not insignificantly, Galton opens his inaugural paper on composite photography by crediting a conversation with Herbert Spencer, the founding figure of social Darwinism, as the genesis of his idea for the method (1878: 97).

6. For an overview of current applications of GANs, see the card game 'Collective Vision of Synthetic Reality' designed by Lenka Hamosova, https://shop.hamosova.com/Collective-Vision-of-Synthetic-Reality-Digital-Card-Deck-p273478629 (last accessed 2 March 2023).

7. The use of deep neural nets (sometimes called Artificial Neural Nets (ANN) or Deep Convolutional Neural Networks (DCNN)) is what distinguishes so-called deep learning from earlier developments in machine learning (of which deep neural nets are still considered an instance). What makes these computational forms of learning from data 'deep' is that they seem to more closely mimic the complexly layered, multi-dimensional, and non-linear workings of cognitive processes in the human brain (Buckner 2018).

8. For a more detailed explanation of this process of 'transformational abstraction', see Buckner 2018.

9. This technique was first developed in the domain of natural language processing (NLP), also known as Word2Vec. Example: the vector of king – man + woman = queen. For an explanation, see https://kawine.github.io/blog/nlp/2019/06/21/word-analogies.html (last accessed 2 March 2023).

The same process of vectorisation (based on learning from patterns to generate new instances) could in principle be applied to biological life as well, with far-reaching consequences (Asgari and Mofrad 2015).

10. Recently the company ClearviewAI stirred controversy and came under scrutiny for using the profile pictures of millions of social media users to train its AI models in an illicit use of publicly available data (Hill 2020). Meanwhile Google showcased an advanced version of its text-to-image GAN called Imagen, which creates photorealistic images of textual descriptions, while excluding humans due to fears over its tendency to reproduce all-too-human gender and racist stereotypes.

References

Ambrosio, Chiara (2016), 'Composite Photographs and the Quest for Generality: Themes from Peirce and Galton', *Critical Inquiry*, 42(3): 547–79.

Asgari, Ehsaneddin, and Mohammad Mofrad (2015), 'Continuous Distributed Representation of Biological Sequences for Deep Proteomics and Genomics', *PloS one*, 10(11), https://doi.org/10.1371/journal.pone.0141287 (last accessed 5 May 2022).

Belting, Hans (2017), *Face and Mask: A Double History*, trans. Thomas S. Hansen and Abby J. Hansen, Princeton, NJ: Princeton University Press.

Boltanski, Luc (2014), *Mysteries and Conspiracies*, Cambridge: Polity.

Brilliant, Richard (1991), *Portraiture*, London: Reaktion.

Buchloh, Benjamin H. D. (2015 [1994]), 'Residual Resemblance: Three Notes on the Ends of Portraiture', in Benjamin H. D. Buchloh, *Formalism and Historicity: Models and Methods in Twentieth-Century Art*, Cambridge, MA: MIT Press, pp. 471–508.

Buckner, Cameron (2018), 'Empiricism without Magic: Transformational Abstraction in Deep Convolutional Neural Networks', *Synthese*, 195(12): 5339–72.

Cover, Robert M., Ashleigh Haw, and Jay Daniel Thompson (2022), *Fake News in Digital Cultures: Technology, Populism and Digital Misinformation*, Bingley: Emerald Publishing.

Daston, Lorraine, and Peter Galison (2007), *Objectivity*, New York: Zone Books.

Dondero, Maria Giulia (2021), 'Composition and Decomposition in Artistic Portraits, Scientific Photography, and Deep Fake Videos', *Lexia. Rivista di Semiotica*, 37–8: 439–54.

Farocki, Harun (2004), 'Phantom Images', *Public*, 29: 12–22, https://public.journals.yorku.ca/index.php/public/article/view/30354 (last accessed 15 May 2022).

Fletcher, John (2018), 'Deepfakes, Artificial Intelligence, and Some Kind of Dystopia: The New Faces of Online Post-Fact Performance', *Theatre Journal*, 70(4): 455–71.

Gadamer, Hans-Georg (2004), *Truth and Method*, trans. J. Weinsheimer and Donald G. Marshall, London: Continuum.

Galton, Francis (1878), 'Composite Portraits, Made by Combining Those of Many Different Persons into a Single Resultant Figure', *Nature*, 18 (May): 97–100.

Galton, Francis (1879), 'Generic Images', *Notices of the Proceedings at the Meetings of the Members of the Royal Institution of Great Britain*, 9: 166.

Gates, Kelly (2011), *Our Biometric Future: Facial Recognition Technology and Our Culture of Surveillance*, New York: New York University Press.

Hannah, Matthew (2021), 'QAnon and the Information Dark Age', *First Monday*, 26(2), https://doi.org/10.5210/fm.v26i2.10868 (last accessed 15 May 2022).

Hill, Kashmir (2020), 'The Secretive Company that Might End Privacy as We Know It', *New York Times*, 18 January 2020, https://www.nytimes.com/2020/01/18/technology/clearview-privacy-facial-recognition.html (last accessed 30 May 2022).

Hookway, Christopher (2002), '". . .A Sort of Composite Photograph": Pragmatism, Ideas, and Schematism', *Transactions of the Charles S. Peirce Society*, 38(1/2): 29–45.

Johnstone, Fiona, and Kirstie Imber (2020), 'Introducing the Anti-Portrait', in Fiona Johnstone and Kirstie Imber (eds), *Anti-Portraiture: Challenging the Limits of the Portrait*, London: Bloomsbury Visual Arts, pp. 1–24.

Karras, Tero, Samuli Laine, Miika Aittala, Janne Hellsten, Jaakko Lehtinen, and Timo Aila (2020), 'Analyzing and Improving the Image Quality of StyleGAN', https://doi.org/10.48550/arXiv.1912.04958 (last accessed 30 May 2022).

Liu, Yifei (2019), 'Controlled Modification of Generated (Style)GAN Latent Vectors', *Computer Science*, https://www.semanticscholar.org/paper/Controlled-Modification-of-Generated-(Style)GAN-Liu/b84e90c-9d16a1cc1ba6153f351b08611d1077d30 (last accessed 30 May 2022).

Meyer, Roland (2016), 'Augmented Crowds: Identity Management, Face Recognition, and Crowd Monitoring', in Inge Baxmann, Timon Beyes, and Claus Pias (eds), *Social Media—New Masses*, Chicago: University of Chicago Press, pp. 101–6.

Meyer, Roland (2019), *Operative Porträts. Eine Bildgeschichte der Identifizierbarkeit von Lavater bis Facebook*, Konstanz: Konstanz University Press.

Nochlin, Linda (1974), 'Some Women Realists: Painters of the Figure', *Arts Magazine*, 48(8): 29–33.

Schick, Nina (2020), *Deepfakes: The Coming Infocalypse*, New York: Twelve.

Sekula, Allan (1986), 'The Body and the Archive', *October*, 39 (winter): 3–64.

Sypher, Wylie (1979), *Loss of the Self in Modern Literature and Art*, Westport, CT: Greenwood Press.

van Alphen, Ernst (1997), 'The Portrait's Dispersal: Concepts of Representation and Subjectivity in Contemporary Portraiture', in Joanna Woodall (ed.), *Portraiture: Facing the Subject*, Manchester: Manchester University Press, pp. 239–56.

van der Nagel, Emily (2020), 'Verifying Images: Deepfakes, Control, and Consent', *Porn Studies*, 7(4): 424–29.

Warzel, Charlie (2018), 'Believable: The Terrifying Future of Fake News', *BuzzFeed News*, 12 February, https://www.buzzfeednews.com/article/charliewarzel/the-terrifying-future-of-fake-news (last accessed 30 May 2022).

Westerlund, Mika (2019), 'The Emergence of Deepfake Technology: A Review', *Technology Innovation Management Review*, 9(11): 40–53.

Chapter 4

The Face as Artefact: Towards an Artefactual Genealogy of the Portrait

Sigrid Weigel

> The most we can do is weave a legend around this man Kafka. It is as if he had spent his entire life wondering what he looked like, without ever discovering that there are such things as mirrors. (Benjamin 1999: 495)

We do not know what the faces of people who lived in earlier eras looked like.[1] We have no idea with what kind of facial expressions they addressed themselves to their contemporaries and what their smile, their sadness, their fear, or their anger might have looked like. And we cannot be certain whether we would consider the faces of the people living in the past to be beautiful and pleasant or whether we would rather turn away. We know their features only through pictorial re/presentations:[2] from sculptures, whose stony eye sockets look at us as if they were blind; from grave masks with their 'dead gazes', which appear strange or mysterious to us; or from paintings, the art from which portrait emerged.[3] The latter, standing for the idea of a faithful picture of a person with individual facial features, has become the ideal of the likeness: the portrait as similar image of a living model, in which the face is captured as a seemingly natural expression of his or her character. Our image of the human being is based not insignificantly on the history of images.

While the genre of portraiture in painting is the ideal image of the human face, it is also an exception within a vast manifold of facial images: faces that have been handed down to us from times before the age of pictorial portraiture, faces from the history of science and medicine, media faces, surveillance pictures, and deconstructions in modern art. We are familiar with faces mainly in the form of pictorial artefacts.

The Human Face – Artefact and Image of the *Humanum*

Human faces never stand for themselves alone; they receive their meaning through a *vis-à-vis*, the interplay between seeing and being seen, that is, the constellation between one's own face and the face of the Other – or even the mirror image. The double semantics of face in German, *Gesicht* as sight (*Sicht*) and visage (*Angesicht*, literally 'being seen'), corresponds to this reciprocity of the gaze. A face that is not looked at by anyone loses its meaning as a *visage*; it is merely that part of the head that is concerned with sensory perception, food intake, and speech production. It is only through looking back that the front of the head becomes a visage – a human face. Yet this description should not be confused with the idea of a natural face; it does not presume any necessary opposition between natural face and artefact. When, according to a developmental perspective (Lemche 2002; Adamson and Frick 2003; Weigel 2017b), the intersubjective exchange of glances and expressions forms the primal facial experience of the infant and its development into an empathic creature, this primal scene of the human face is later superimposed by facial patterns of different social contexts and images from the cultural history of re/presentations.

Today, the image that looks at me from the mirror and the features of the Other are part of an endless loop with countless re/presentations from news, photos, film, and art, from the internet and advertising pictures in public spaces. How many faces might you see every day? How many of them are perceived involuntarily and only fleetingly, and how many are actually looked at? The latter are undoubtedly the smallest part: those persons with whom looks or even words are exchanged. The way we perceive and interpret these faces is essentially shaped by artefacts. Our knowledge of the meaning of complex facial expressions and often ambiguous countenances is generated by pictures from all kinds of material images, analogue and digital likenesses, and by the wealth of textual descriptions of the human face; and this implicit, largely non-conscious knowledge gets projected on to the physiological appearance of today's people. In European cultural history, the face – as the external image of a creature with affects or feelings – has become the condensed image of the *humanum*, and yet it is at the same time a composite image of countless pictorial traditions, of descriptions and the features of contemporaries. Facial expressions handed down through artefacts, those seen in real time, and one's own features and expressive gestures are difficult to distinguish from one another.

Etymology and the history of concepts reveal a fascinating field of interrelationships and tensions. While the idea of the person, for example, is derived from the mask in ancient Greek, the distinction between mask and face was still unknown to the Greek *prósopon*, which literally means 'that which is *vis-à-vis* the eyes (of another)'. In ancient times, face was 'simply that side of the head that you were looking at'. No distinction was made 'between the natural face and the artificial face' (Weihe 2004: 35, 27). In contrast, the Latin equivalent distinguished *persona* (mask) from *facies* (face) and *vultus* (facial expression). The meaning of the face in history travels between the idea of the face as the most important part of the human body, the placeholder for the person, and an object of cultic practices as well as artistic, medical, and everyday shaping. In the age of plastic surgery and morphing, of digital face recognition and the robotic simulation of facial expression patterns, the face's recognisability has become the object of (de-)composition techniques for everyone. The present dominance of artificial faces sheds light on manufacturing and framing processes in the past as well, on codes of expression and cultural techniques of readability (see Weigel 2022). A purely *natural history of the face* does not exist,[4] for the face, together with the body, is subject to numerous cultural techniques and semiotic practices, and it is itself the medium of habituated gestures and techniques of self-fashioning (see Greenblatt 1980). It is not only 'social media' that makes us aware of the fact that the face's history is above all a media history: of mediated facial re/presentations as well as the face *as* medium of self-representation, expression, and communication. Recent surgical and digital procedures, meanwhile, render the boundary of the media-theoretical distinction between 'signs-in-the-body' (they concern the language of the body or its excitation) and 'signs-on-the-body' (cultural corporeal practices of appearing, from make-up via training to cosmetic surgery) obsolete (Schmidt 2003).

Despite the growing variety of media- and semio-techniques, the dominant social pattern of interpreting the other's face still refers to the idea that it presents an outward expression of interiority – an enduring impact of the fatal history of physiognomic knowledge, which produced a whole register of pathologising and prejudiced readings of faces (Schmölders 1995; Campe and Schneider 1996; Weigel 2017a). Any face reading according to the model of Lavater's search for character, in which, as Goethe (1960) already noted, 'man is broken down into his elements' in order to 'trace his moral qualities', is based on the myth of an almost natural correspondence between the 'inner' image and the person's outer shape. In the present age of medical feasibility, a similar interpretative pattern comes into play in reverse form, as it were, when the desire for a correction of the facial shape by means of plastic surgery is often motivated by a discrepancy between the 'true personality' and the outer appearance, with plastic surgery then having the task of bringing the body into line with the inner self-image.[5] This inversion is still based on the traditional and amazingly resistant paradigm of *faceism* (see Zebrowitz 1997), according to which the outside appearance is the key to penetrate the inaccessible and invisible inside – both in individual physiognomies and in peoples, if not 'races', as condensed for example in Johann Joachim Winckelmann's dictum that the soul of the Greeks is described 'in the face of the Laocoön' (1995: 20). To chart a way out of the trap of physiognomics is a significant impetus for questioning faces as images of the *humanum* with regard to their genesis as artefacts.

Visagéité – On the Problem of Face Destruction in the 'Post-human' Age

The face as artefact is currently a pre-eminent subject of artistic works. By dissolving, destroying, or deconstructing the unity of the face, by distorting its proportions, and by shifting, displacing, doubling, or removing individual parts – eyes, nose, mouth – from the entirety of the front of the head, by blending different facial features on top of each other, and by creating a bricolage or montage of human features and animal heads or even things, the arts are currently working on an aesthetic that destroys the paradigm of the face as a representative of the *humanum* (Figure 4.1). This development is what Judith Weiss refers to as the *portrait after the portrait* (2012; see also Körte and Weiss 2017). Since many artists cite genre elements of the portrait in order to distort them, contemporary art contradicts the art-historical postulate that 'The faceless portrait does not exist' (Preimesberger 1999: 15). In artistic practice, it seems to be primarily a matter of breaking up the identification of the face and the individual personality in the conventional portrait, as it emerged in the early modern era. Thus, the arts currently radicalise the tendencies of a 'post-human' culture, in whose laboratories such destruction has long been at work, by outdoing existing techniques. In this respect, the prophecy of Gilles Deleuze and Félix Guattari stated four decades ago in *Mille Plateaux* (1980, in the chapter 'Year Zero: Faciality') seems to come true: their statement that the face would have a great future, but only if it is destroyed and dissolved.

Deleuze and Guattari's theory of *visagéité* (*faciality*) has made an enormous impact since its publication, although what one often encounters in the abundance of recent theoretical publications on the face are individual, isolated quotations rather than a real examination

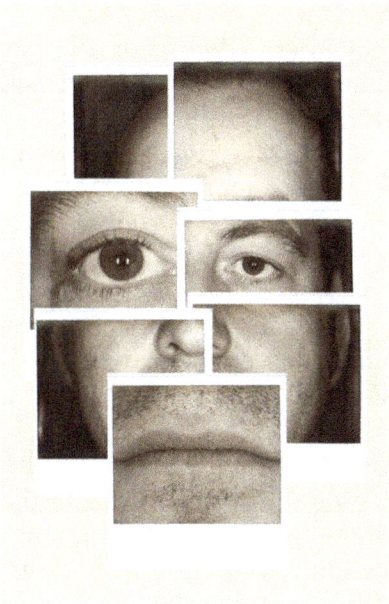

Figure 4.1 David Ayre, *Fractured Faces*, 2011. Public domain

or intense reading of the chapter. Thus, the sentences 'The organization of the face is a strong one' and 'the face is a politics' (1987: 208) can be regarded as the pathos formulas of recent face theory. Most frequently the 'white wall/black hole system' is cited, which was introduced by Deleuze and Guattari as a 'faciality machine' or a 'semiotic machine and regime of signs' (1987: 186, 71, 202). In view of the accelerated development of biomedicine and life sciences, robotic construction, and plastic surgery, in whose laboratories all kinds of face technologies have been developed, a re-evaluation of the much-cited text seems appropriate.

Mille Plateaux shares the gesture of radical de(con)struction with other theories of the zeitgeist of that time, which pursued a struggle against established systems of meaning regarded as the sum of European-Christian culture and interpreted as a system for securing the existing power structure. Deleuze and Guattari use the term 'imperialism' to characterise the power of a new semiotic system – despotic 'assemblages that act through signifiers and act upon souls and subjects' – and place facialisation at its centre: 'You will be pinned to the white wall and stuffed in the black hole. This machine is called the faciality machine because it is the social production of the face' (1987: 200–1). As a consequence of tracing imperialism back to signification, the way out can only be sought on an equally fundamental and abstract level: in *asignificance*, that is a practice that acts against every process of meaning in order to destroy or deconstruct it: 'Only across the wall of the signifier can one run lines of asignificance that void all memory, all return, every possible signification and interpretation' (1987: 209). This counter-movement to signification is connected with a precarious way of dealing with the problem of Eurocentrism, when the face is called 'the typical European', and Deleuze and Guattari state that 'the "Primitives" may have the most human of heads, the most beautiful and spiritual, but they have no face and need none' (1987: 195–6). Such an idealisation of facelessness is symptomatic of a problematic argument in certain critiques of Eurocentrism, when the critique of dominant norms ends up in a normative postulation of exactly reverse concepts.

Now, a real faciality machine has actually been developed since the publication of *Mille Plateaux*, though in the technical form of digital face- and emotion-recognition programs implanted in most social media devices and communication and surveillance systems: a technical machine for formatting the social face and controlling the social body, the most advanced types of which are today produced and used in China. Since these programs are based on a de/coding-system, which reduces the manifold human facial expressions to just six so-called 'basic emotions' (represented in schemata of certain muscle movements appearing like frozen masks rather than faces), the primary task of today would probably be to regain the variety and ambiguity, the diversity and individuality of facial expression rather than idealising facelessness.[6]

But why the face? In *Mille Plateaux*, faciality is emphasised as a special dispositif that emerges as a mixed semiotics at the intersection of signification and subjectivation, namely the system 'white wall/ black hole' (the former stands for signification, the latter for subjectivation). This system receives its cultural-historical signature in *Mille Plateaux* through the eponymous thesis of the year zero, when the authors trace its emergence to the year zero of Christ's birth – with the argument that here the mingling of signification and subjectivation has achieved complete interpenetration. In this way, the face of Christ becomes a metaphor for their entire theory of faciality. It has been repeatedly noted, however, that this thesis is historically untenable. For example, Hans Belting, in his study of the early images of Christ, proves that it is far from the actual historical development 'that this face was produced by Christianity in an hour zero' (Belting 2005: 84). Images of Christ appeared not earlier than in the third and fourth century, at first in the figuration of the youth or *theios aner* (divine teacher) in the tradition of philosophical iconography. Belting assumes that these images originated from a heathen context, while for Christians the question of whether and what image of Christ's face could exist at all was a precarious one that gave rise to the debate about the *vera icon* (Wolf 2002; Wolf et al. 2004). The response to the problem of the 'real image' of Christ is the very likeness that derives from the shroud, in which the traces of Christ's body are visible: 'The authenticity of the shrouds was read off from the facial features, just as these were authenticated by a corporeal trace, connected to the living Christ. Such artifacts were hybrids of image and index' (Wolf 2002: 57). When Belting speaks here of artefacts and characterises the shroud with the imprint as a mixture of contact- and image-medium, this is in line with the perspective of image-theory as a secular approach, while image-theology understands such an image as a contact-relic and Christians of that time as *acheiropoietos*: an image not made by hand.

Before the 'Year Zero' – Genesis of the Likeness from Funeral Cult

It is not only the complicated genesis of Christ's image that contradicts the 'year zero' claim; the pre-Christian history of handed-down human traits is just as instructive. It is a history of a manifold, already fully developed culture of facial re/presentations, mostly imprints, grave masks and other forms of sculptural pictures. This includes not only the developed Roman culture of portraiture, which already followed the claim of true-to-life imaging and produced heads cut into stone as well as the *imagines maiorum*, that is, masks (made of wax or other material) taken from the head of a deceased person. These early types of portrait were used by the Romans both as a political medium and as objects of memorial culture, a cultic worship of ancestors (Flower 1996). Therefore, one can already speak of a 'first heyday of the portrait' for the second and first century BCE, with regard to Rome (Beyer 2002: 21). From Greek antiquity, too, countless portrait statues have survived, although their faces are not (yet) designed according to the principle of similarity, but rather as an *eikon* of idealistic ideas: for example, the statues of statesmen, which are interpreted as 'political topoi' (Beyer 2002: 18), or the retrospective portraits of deceased scholars and authors, which were created in the context of the emerging Hellenistic philology, biography, and museum culture, 'invented faces', which are characterised as 'literary visions of likenesses' (Zanker 1995: 152). In addition, there were the masks of the ancient theatre representing a *typos*, whose forms of expression developed parallel to its representation in sculpture (Weihe 2004).

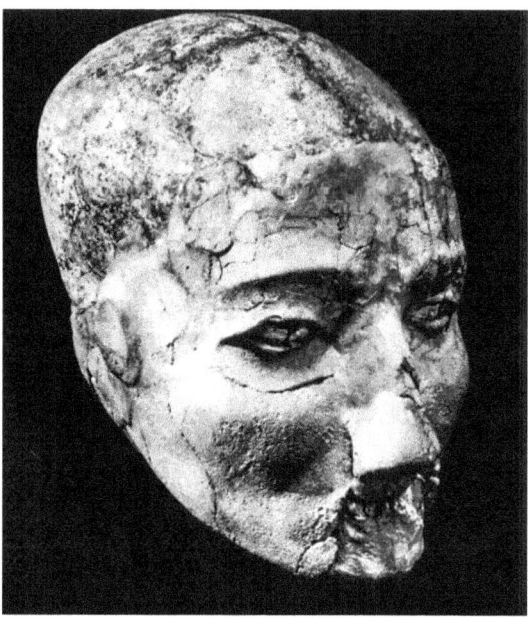

Figure 4.2 Jericho skull (seventh millennium BCE). Kenyon Jericho Archive, UCLA. Public domain

Much further back in history, one comes across numerous archaeological finds from prehistoric and early historical eras, for the most part from burial sites and sanctuaries. They attest to the genesis of the image from the cult of the dead. The appearance of these faces from far away could be more easily associated with the configuration 'white wall/black hole' than the image of Christ can. The best-known are the finds from Jericho from the pre-Christian seventh millennium BCE (Figure 4.2); they point to burial rituals in which the head of the deceased was separated from the buried body, the skull cleaned of decayed flesh and covered with an applied, painted layer of plaster, so that the skulls placed over the buried body bore the imprint-like features of the deceased (Leroi-Gourhan 1967). It is doubtful, however, that the meaning of individuality had been attributed to these skulls and that they already expressed a sense of individuality, tradition, and the continuity of the family (Landau 1989). But they can certainly be regarded as 'head pictures before the image' (Preimersberger 1999: 22), as the primal form or pre-figuration of the likeness and its emergence from the funeral cult. From the viewpoint of image-theory, these objects, a sort of pre-iconic similarity or 'resemblance through contact' (Didi-Huberman 1991: 15; see also Weigel 2022) and a hybrid of imprint and imitation, anticipate that transition from the index to the iconic which would later be associated with the *vera icon*, long before the question of the real picture had even arisen.

From later millennia another kind of image has come down to us, whose schematic re/presentation of the face – eyes/eyebrows, nose, mouth – comes close to the figuration of a mask. When viewed today, one will involuntarily associate these 'abstract' features with the art of classical modernism, which broke with the principle of resemblance of the portrait and borrowed from so-called primitivism. Such facial figurations are found on anthropomorphic grave stelae and 'eye ste-lae' from the Arabian Peninsula, a region which was already covered with sepulchral mounds in the fifth and fourth millennia BCE (these protruded up to two metres above the ground and were marked by stelae as burial and cult sites). Particularly impressive is an 'eye stela' from the fifth to fourth century BCE from the Taymâ region in the form of a 72 cm high rectangular stela made of sandstone; on its front side there is a schematic image of a face, which we today per-ceive as almost abstract: a square with an elongated bar as nose, which at the top merges into two curved eyebrows, under which the two elliptical eye fields are located; a mouth is missing (Figure 4.3). Under the field with this face there is the Aramaic inscription 'Taym, son of Zayd in memory' (André-Salvini et al. 2010: 13).

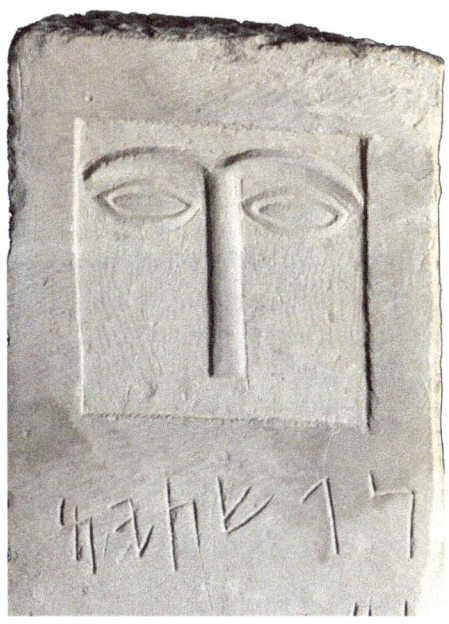

Figure 4.3 Tomb stele from Tamya (Arabian Peninsula), fifth–fourth century BCE. Tamya Museum. Public domain

Concerning the history of images, these representations bear witness to a transition to the (stone) image, in which a schematic reproduction has taken the place of the overmoulding of a skull. In this respect, the image of the face seems to have originated from a type of picture that was later called a mask. If Moshe Barasch (1991) has repeatedly shown that the portrait originated from the mask, these early portraits of the dead can conversely also be regarded as early masks. Mask and portrait are doubtless inseparable in the history of the human face. And the genesis of the portrait from the cult of the dead has left its traces in the memory of the portrait as well. It is no coincidence, according to Andreas Beyer (2002: 116), that skulls appear as an iconographic motif simultaneously with the modern portrait.

Christ's Likeness, Mask, Portrait

In view of the pre-Christian history of face images that are mainly part of the cult of the dead and the phenomenon of an already developed art of likenesses with individualised traits, Christ's face cannot at all stand for a year zero of *visagéité*, although it indeed takes a special position. The 'portrait of Christ' raised problems not just because of the biblical prohibition of images, but also because of the precarious status of the dual nature of its figure: as a deceased human being and the risen Son of God with a missing corpse.[7] His human-like appearance required strong distinctive features to distinguish his holy face from human portraits – and vice versa. In this respect, the format of frontal icon is most striking, as Moshe Barasch (1991: 20–35) has shown; it was reserved almost exclusively for the 'holy face'. The mask-like frontal icon, which in ancient vase paintings was reserved for gods, monsters, and the dead (while mythical figures in action and warriors are shown in profile) and thus not intended to depict mortal creatures, seemed ideally suited for the iconic face of Christ in medieval painting. It was only when monastic Christianity turned into a Christian society and previously supramundane biblical figures became more human-like that the bust portrait took the place of the isolated, bodiless, neckless face.

When the autonomous portrait – that is, the motif of the face isolated from the rest of the body and manufactured 'from life' – evolved in the Renaissance as 'a faithful reflection of individual distinctiveness' (Beyer 2002: 15) and the central object of the 'golden age of similarity' (Didi-Huberman 1994; Kohl 2012), this happened in the midst of a highly developed Christian iconography, with the iconic image of Christ's face having a firm place. Whereas the latter became the model for the autonomous portrait – as recognisable when placing Jan van Eyck's famous *True Face of Christ* (1438) and Dürer's *Self-portrait with Fur Coat* (1500) side by side – the artists invented a different mode to re/present the human face. In an effort to individualise the likeness and to make the portrayed person a counterpart, they developed the three-quarter posture: with the head turned slightly or more strongly to one side, the face looks as if it is directly looking at us. This pictorial format couples similarity and individuality with the reciprocity of the gaze: 'The person in the autonomous portrait, who looks out of the portrait into an "immanent" world of individuals who are capable of images – although not always worthy of being portrayed – demands for its realization a fellow human being, the independent observer, to whom he turns' (Boehm 1985: 9). In addition, there exist many portraits in profile in Renaissance painting, the majority of them of women: there personality and status, here beauty and harmonious proportions. And although the expressive gestures of 'tragic faces' in the Renaissance are largely modelled on those of antique masks (Barasch 1991), they are viewed *en-face* only in exceptional cases. This was reserved for the image of Christ, Mary, and the saints, and, beyond that, royal portraits. The distinction between *en-face* and profile, which Meyer Schapiro (1973) considered to be 'symbolic forms', gained importance after the iconic portraits of Christ had been established in painting and were no longer traced back to the *vera icon*.

In an investigation of the problem of the 'holy face', Georges Didi-Huberman has discussed the *vera icon* topos as a basic image-theoretical question in respect of a fundamental abyss between any likeness and an intricate interweaving of relic and image: 'What immediately springs to mind here is the typology of *relic/icon: relic* refers to what a "Holy Face" is, *icon* expresses *what* it represents (or *that* it represents)' (2012: 57). If the holy face requires a special conception of the image, this problem finds its 'solution' in a certain constellation of proximity and distance. There would be no sacred image, according to Didi-Huberman (2012: 59), that would be able to initiate the dialectical conversion 'of *trace* into *grace*, of the *vestigium* into *visio*' if the proximity inherent in the material process of production (impression, contact) were not represented as distance. Referring to Walter Benjamin's reflection on the aura as a 'strange tissue of space and time: the unique apparition of a distance, however near it may be' (2002: 104), Didi-Huberman emphasises the dialectic of the gaze at work here – 'To experience the aura of an object we look at means to invest it with the ability to look back at us' (Benjamin 2006: 204) – in order to characterise the peculiar image of Christ's face on the shroud: the visual appearance of traces that themselves have the property of disappearing.

A resonance of this auratic charge of the image affects the history of the portrait as well. For in the human likeness there is also a dialectic, albeit different, of presence and absence, of visualisation and disappearance, of exhibition and concealment at work. This does not only concern the survival of the mortal person in the picture, in accordance with the much-cited statement in Leon Battista Alberti's treatise *On Painting* (1435/36): 'Painting contains a divine force which not only makes absent men present [. . .] but moreover makes the dead seem almost alive' (1966: 63). It also concerns the fact that the portrait captures the movements and facial traces of the expressive gestures in the two-dimensional picture, thus re/presenting something fleeting and disappearing in a standstill. And finally, it concerns the impression of being looked at from the picture, the reciprocity between the viewer and the model discussed above.

Admittedly, the history of this genre must be regarded as a closed chapter after the 'criticism of the old concept of the portrait and the individual carried out with the means of painting' (Boehm 1985: 10). Yet the recent boom of large exhibition projects with portraits points to a longing for the lost genre and possibly for 'old faces', especially in the age of proliferating new media faces and multiple modes of post-human facial de(con)structions. At any rate, the genre of portraiture, precisely because of the pictorial scenario of the *mutual* gaze, has played an essential role in cultural work on the image of humans. Recently, evolutionary anthropology has emphasised *Homo sapiens*' ability to recognise in the Other an intentional being similar to the Self (Tomasello 1999), while neuroscience, following the discovery of mirror neurons, has identified the resonance mechanism of a mutual, intersubjective form of 'embodied simulation' (Gallese 2008; see also Lux and Weigel 2017). In this way the natural sciences are discovering insights that are part of the implicit knowledge that traditionally underpinned the cultural history of the face. The work on the human likeness and the portrait has thus considerably contributed to the internalisation of the facial reciprocity which forms the visage (*Angesicht*).

The Face as the Image of the Image
– the Art of Readability

The portrait can also be discussed as the image of the image, because it frequently serves as a paradigm in controversies about the superiority or inferiority of images in relation to language and writing. This position is due to its perception *at a glance*, that is, viewing the face as a unity in an instant, literally in a blink of an eye. According to Lessing, Laocoön's face, the classical sculptural object in the competition of the arts, confronts visual art with the limits of its possibilities, when the expression of pain, passions, and affects is concerned, because its pictorial re/presentation would distort the facial features. Thus, he discusses the problem of a disfiguring ugliness through the example of the veiled face of the father in Timanthes' *Painting of the Sacrifice of Iphigenia* (fourth century BCE) and argues for the principle of a moderating depiction as in an exemplary manner realised in the Laocoön group. On the other hand, the impossibility of describing a beautiful face through language is 'an instance of painting without picture' for him. Taking Ariosto's description of the 'charming Alcina' in *Orlando Furioso* (1516), Lessing addresses a general warning to poets to refrain from such attempts, since 'what is most readily expressed by the painter through lines and colours, is most difficult to express by words' (1853: 142). In Lessing's opposition of the spatial juxtaposition in painting to the temporal succession or seriality of poetry, the face represents *the* paradigm of the pictorial, when he writes that 'it surpasses the power of human imagination to represent to oneself what effect such and such a mouth, nose, and eyes will produce together, unless we can call to mind, from nature or art, a similar composition of like parts' (1853: 138–9). Accordingly, literary descriptions of faces would always be at a disadvantage compared to visual re/presentations.

This judgement refers to the perception of the face as a unit which requires the synthesising gaze. However, the positions of literature and painting swap around as soon as emotions and the fundamental problem of visualising affects are concerned. In *Della Pittura* (1435/36), for example, Alberti already noted 'how difficult it is when attempting to paint a laughing face to avoid making it more weeping than happy', and likewise: 'Who could ever, without the greatest study express faces in which mouth, chin, eyes, cheeks, forehead and eyebrows all accord together to form a laughter or weeping' (1966: 77).[8] This observation about a kind of *antithetical meaning of primal words* in the field of expressive gestures can be found again and again in the discourse on painting.[9] In his *Discourses on Art*, Joshua Reynolds also states of a comparison between the figure of a frenetically laughing bacchanal and the depiction of a grieving Mary: 'It is curious to observe, and it is certainly true, that the extremes of contrary passions are with very little variation expressed by the same action' (1997: 221–2). Against the background of such difficulties, it is no coincidence that deciphering facial expressions primarily runs within the paradigm of *readability*, a reading of facial features trained in the reading of writing, of literal characters. However, the latter always runs the risk of falling into the trap of the physiognomic pattern of interpretation when it is in search of a universal tool for *decoding* emotions through facial expressions, as in the 'Facial Action Coding System' (FACS) (Ekman and Friesen 1975; Ekman et al. 2002), instead of reading the faces of others that are full of ambiguity and require intersubjective experience and sensitivity to decipher their individual and often enigmatic countenances.

While FACS, which is the dominant code system of contemporary empirical psychology, social media devices, and 'affective computing', refers to stereotypical frozen patterns (Weigel 2020),[10] the media history of the twentieth century has introduced a field of advanced and subtle readability of faces through the invention of cinematographic art. With the entry of portraiture into film, the opposition between the advantage of the visual arts in representing the face and the superiority of language to describe and express emotions became obsolete. The film face is the epitome of a simultaneity set in motion, of a temporally stretched gaze, as it were. In film, which has developed the expressive gestures of the face – beyond the physiognomic register – into art, the diverging arts of the Laocoön paradigm are apparently reunified, as are the two sides of the semantics of face, namely seeing and visage (*Angesicht*). As a medium, film benefits from the 'advantages' of images, while at the same time it overcomes the 'weaknesses' of a static art by setting the images – and thus facial movements as well – in motion in two ways: through the gestures and facial expressions of the actors and through the changing perspective of the camera. Therefore, the theorist of early film Béla Balázs stated that 'the whole of mankind is now busy learning' the 'long-forgotten language of gestures and facial expressions' (2010: 10). He interpreted the cinematograph as 'a device at work, giving culture a new turn towards the visual and the human being a new face' (2010: 9). His programmatic sentence, which provided the title for his essay, reads: '*Man will become visible again*' (2010: 10).

Since then multiple techniques, ranging from corporeal techniques such as plastic surgery and Botox treatment to digital techniques such as morphing and the construction of avatars or animated faces, have been invented. These developments more and more blur the line between living faces and artificial faces – up to the production of hybrids, when, for example, by means of digital 'expression transfer' one person's video-portrait gets animated by the facial movements and words of another person. While such computer programs have recently augmented the artefactual history of the face to its extreme and made the representational function of the portrait obsolete, at the same time a new kind of facelessness has emerged, namely a standardisation of digital portraits. Due to the fact that the same facial coding system is implemented into the majority of digital devices and social media, the mimic behaviour of media users obviously more and more assimilates to its stereotypes – as can be seen in the millions of selfies circulating online (see Shin 2014) – and tend to cover and remove the fascinating variety and diversity of individual faces. While the overinterpretation of the old physiognomics and Deleuze and Guattari's 'facelessness' are but two sides of the same coin, with digital portraits a new facelessness of the standardised physiognomy has emerged, which gets mirrored in the living faces of the users. In this way the living human face itself is about to become an artefact.

Notes

1. This chapter is a revised and translated version of Weigel 2013.
2. Re/presentation is used as equivalent for German *Darstellung* in order to emphasise the simultaneity of the process of presentation and that which is represented and thus perceivable. *Darstellung* is the counterpart to *Vorstellung* in the mind, which receives its specific perceivable form only through the *Darstellung*.
3. *Dead Gazes* (*Tote Blicke*) is the original title of Julius von Schlosser's famous work on death masks (2008).
4. As the German translation of Jonathan Cole's 1998 book *About Faces* (*Über das Gesicht. Naturgeschichte des Gesichts und unnatürliche Geschichte derer, die es verloren haben*) suggests.
5. A famous reference case for this kind of 'medical indication' is the so-called Minotaur Syndrome, reported by the Italian surgeon Paolo Morselli in 1993. The case concerned a patient who suffered from the outward appearance of his facial features and a related social discrimination; he believed that his face made him appear aggressive, whereas he regarded himself as gentle by nature. The surgeon undertook plastic surgery on the young man 'to reduce the discrepancy between his true personality and the aggressive morphology' and to achieve a 'more aesthetic and balanced facial profile' by 'softening the facial appearance', which was 'not objectionable in people's judgment' (Morselli 1993: 99–102).
6. For a critique of the epistemic and image-theoretical foundations of 'automatic face recognition', see Weigel 2020.
7. For the empty grave as origin of a proliferating desire for images in the Christian culture, see the chapter on 'Cult Images – Iconoclastic Controversy, the Desire for Images, and the Dialectic of Secularization' in Weigel 2022.
8. Translation modified according to the bilingual edition of Alberti 2002.

9. Sigmund Freud's 'The Antithetical Meaning of Primal Words' (1957) discusses opposite meanings of one and the same word.
10. For the origin of FACS in outdated physiognomic knowledge, see the chapter on faces in Weigel 2022.

References

Adamson, Lauren B., and Janet E. Frick (2003), 'The Still Face: A History of a Shared Experimental Paradigm', *Infancy*, 4: 451–73.

Alberti, Leon Battista (1966 [1435/36]), *On Painting*, trans. John R. Spencer, New Haven, CT: Yale University Press.

Alberti, Leon Battista (2002 [1435/36]), *Della pittura: Über die Malkunst*, trans. Oskar Bätschmann and Sandra Gianfreda, Darmstadt: Wissenschaftliche Buchgesellschaft.

André-Salvini, Béatrice, Carine Juvin, Sophie Makariou, Françoise Demange, and Ali Al Ghabban (2010), *Routes d'Arabie. Archéologie et histoire du royaume d'Arabie saoudite. L'album de l'exposition*, Paris: Musée du Louvre.

Balázs, Béla (2010), *Early Film Theory: Visible Man and the Spirit of Film*, ed. Erica Carter and Rodney Livingstone, New York: Berghahn.

Barasch, Moshe (1991), *Imago hominis: Studies in the Language of Art*, New York: New York University Press.

Belting, Hans (2005), *Das echte Bild. Bildfragen als Glaubensfragen*, Munich: Beck.

Benjamin, Walter (1999 [1931]), 'Franz Kafka: Beim Bau der Chinesischen Mauer', trans. Rodney Livingstone and others, in *Selected Writings, Vol. 2: 1927–1934*, ed. Michael Jennings, Howard Eiland, and Garry Smith, Cambridge, MA: Harvard University Press.

Benjamin, Walter (2002), 'The Work of Art in the Age of Its Technological Reproducibility: Second Version', trans. Edmund Jephcott and Howard Eiland, in *Selected Writings, Vol. 3: 1935–1938*, ed. Howard Eiland and Michael Jennings, Cambridge, MA: Harvard University Press.

Benjamin, Walter (2006), 'On Some Motifs in Baudelaire', trans. Howard Eiland et al., in Michael W. Jennings (ed.), *The Writer of Modern Life: Essays on Charles Baudelaire*, Cambridge, MA: Harvard University Press.

Beyer, Andreas (2002), *Das Porträt in der Malerei*, Munich: Hirmer.

Boehm, Gottfried (1985), *Bildnis und Individuum: Über den Ursprung der Porträtmalerei in der italienischen Renaissance*, Munich: Prestel.

Campe, Rüdiger, and Manfred Schneider (eds) (1996), *Geschichten der Physiognomik: Text, Bild, Wissen*, Freiburg: Rombach.

Cole, Jonathan (1998), *About Faces*, Cambridge, MA: MIT Press.

Cole, Jonathan (1999), *Über das Gesicht. Naturgeschichte des Gesichts und unnatürliche Geschichte derer, die es verloren haben*, trans. Ulrich Blumenbach, Munich: Kunstmann.

Deleuze, Gilles, and Félix Guattari (1987 [1980]), *A Thousand Plateaus: Capitalism and Schizophrenia*, trans. Brian Massumi, London: Continuum.

Didi-Huberman, Georges (1991), 'Le visage et la terre', *Artstudio*, 21: 6–21.

Didi-Huberman, Georges (1994), 'Ressemblance mythifiée et Ressemblance oubliée chez Vasari: la legende du portrait "sur le vif"', *Italie et Méditerranée. Mefrim*, 106(2): 383–432.

Didi-Huberman, Georges (2008), *La ressemblance par contact: archéologie, anachronisme et modernité de l'empreinte*, Paris: Éditions de Minuit.

Didi-Huberman, Georges (2012), 'Near and Distant: The Face, its Imprint, and its Place of Appearance', *Kritische Berichte: Zeitschrift für Kunst- und Kulturwissenchaft*, 40(1): 54–69.

Ekman, Paul, and Wallace V. Friesen (1975), *Unmasking the Face: A Guide to Recognizing Emotions from Facial Clues*, Englewood Cliffs, NJ: Prentice-Hall.

Ekman, Paul, Wallace V. Friesen, and Joseph C. Hager (2002), *Facial Action Coding System: The Manual*, Salt Lake City, UT: Research Nexus. CD-ROM.

Flower, Harriet I. (1996), *Ancestor Masks and Aristocratic Power in Roman Culture*, Oxford: Clarendon Press.

Freud, Sigmund (1957 [1910]), 'The Antithetical Meaning of Primal Words', in *The Standard Edition of the Complete Psychological Works of Sigmund Freud, Vol. 11*, ed. and trans. James Strachey, London: Hogarth Press.

Gallese, Vittorio (2008), 'Empathy, Embodied Simulation, and the Brain', *Journal of the American Psychoanalytic Association*, 56(3): 769–81.

Goethe, Johann Wolfgang (1960 [1811–14]), 'Dichtung und Wahrheit', in *Werke. Hamburger Ausgabe*, vol. 10, ed. Erich Trunz, Hamburg: Wegner.

Greenblatt, Stephen (1980), *Renaissance Self-Fashioning: From More to Shakespeare*, Chicago: University of Chicago Press.

Kohl, Jeanette (2012), '"Vollkommen ähnlich". Der Index als Grundlage des Renaussanceporträts', in Martin Gaier, Jeanette Kohl, and Alberto Saviello (eds), *Similitudo. Konzepte der Ähnlichkeit in Mittelalter und Früher Neuzeit*, Munich: Fink, pp. 181–206.

Körte, Mona, and Judith Elisabeth Weiss (2017), *Randgänge des Gesichts. Kritische Perspektiven auf Sichtbarkeit und Entzug*, Munich: Fink.

Landau, Terry (1989), *About Faces*, New York: Anchor Books.

Lemche, Erwin (2002), *Emotion und frühe Interaktion. Die Emotionsentwicklung innerhalb der frühen Mutter-Kind-Interaktion*, Berlin: Lehmanns Media.

Leroi-Gourhan, André (1967), *The Art of Prehistoric Man in Western Europe*, trans. Norbert Guterman, London: Thames and Hudson.

Lessing, Gotthold Ephraim (1853), *Laocoon: An Essay on the Limits of Painting and Poetry*, trans. E. C. Beasley, London: Longman.

Lux, Venessa, and Sigrid Weigel (eds) (2017), *Empathy: Epistemic Problems and Cultural-Historical Perspectives*, Basingstoke: Palgrave Macmillan.

Morselli, Paolo G. (1993), 'The Minotaur Syndrome: Plastic Surgery of the Facial Skeleton', *Aesthetic Plastic Surgery*, 17: 99–102.

Preimesberger, Rudolf (1999), 'Einleitung', in Hannah Baader and Nicola Suthor (eds), *Porträt*, Berlin: Reimer, pp. 1–25.

Reynolds, Sir Joshua (1997), *Discourses on Art (1769–1791)*, ed. Robert R. Wark, New Haven, CT: Yale University Press.

Schapiro, Meyer (1973), 'Frontal and Profile as Symbolic Form', in Meyer Schapiro, *Words and Pictures: On the Literal and the Symbolic in the Illustration of the Text*, The Hague: Mouton, pp. 37–63.

Schlosser, Julius von (2008), 'History of Portraiture in Wax', in Roberta Panzanelli (ed.), *Ephemeral Bodies: Wax Sculpture and the Human Figure*, trans. James Michael Loughbride, Los Angeles: Getty Research Institute.

Schmidt, Gunnar (2003), *Das Gesicht. Eine Mediengeschichte*, Munich: Fink.

Schmölders, Claudia (1995), *Das Vorurteil im Leibe. Eine Einführung in die Physiognomik*, Berlin: Akademie.

Shin, Nara (2014), 'The Public Profile of an American Girl', https://coolhunting.com/culture/jenna-garrett-public-profile-american-girl/ (last accessed 13 March 2020).

Tomasello, Michael (1999), *The Cultural Origins of Human Cognition*, Cambridge MA: Harvard University Press.

Weigel, Sigrid (2013), 'Das Gesicht als Artefakt. Zu einer Kulturgeschichte des menschlichen Bildnisses', in Sigrid Weigel (ed.), *Gesichter. Kulturgeschichtliche Szenen aus der Arbeit am Bildnis des Menschen*, Munich: Fink, pp. 7–29.

Weigel, Sigrid (2017a), 'Charakter-Köpfe – Kopfform und Körpergestalt als Stigma, physiognomisches Zeichen und Symbol', in Hannes Haberl, Sigrid Weigel, et al., *Schädel Basis Wissen I. Kultur und Geschichte der chirurgischen Korrektur der Schädelform*, Berlin: Kadmos, pp. 91–126.

Weigel, Sigrid (2017b), 'Mimik. Zwischen Face-to-Face und Gefühlscodierung', in Sigrid Weigel (ed.), *Das Gesicht. Bilder, Medien, Formate*, Göttingen: Wallstein, 82–7.

Weigel, Sigrid (2020), 'Der konventionelle Code als buckliger Zwerg im Dienste der Emotion Recognition. Überlegungen zu einer Urgeschichte der digitalen Kultur', *Internationales Jahrbuch für Medienphilosophie*: *Digital/Rational*, 6: 47–79.

Weigel, Sigrid (2022), *Grammatology of Images*, New York: Fordham University Press.

Weihe, Richard (2004), *Die Paradoxie der Maske. Geschichte einer Form*, Munich: Fink.

Weiss, Judith Elisabeth (2012), 'Von Anti bis Meta – Neu-Orientierung der Porträtkunst', *Kunstforum International*, 216: 33–43.

Winckelmann, Johann Joachim (1995 [1756]), *Gedanken über die Nachahmung der griechischen Werke in der Malerei und Bildhauerkunst*, Stuttgart: Reclam.

Wolf, Gerhard (2002), *Schleier und Spiegel. Traditionen des Christusbildes und die Bildkonzepte der Renaissance*, Munich: Fink.

Wolf, Gerhard, Colette Dufour, and Anna Rosa Masetti (eds) (2004), *Mandylion: Intorno al Sacro Volto, da Bisanzio a Genova*, Milan: Skira.

Zanker, Paul (1995), *Die Maske des Sokrates. Das Bild des Intellektuellen in der antiken Kunst*, Munich: Beck.

Zebrowitz, Leslie A. (1997), *Reading Faces: Window to the Soul?*, Boulder, CO: Westview Press.

II (Inter)Faces

Chapter 5

When Face Becomes Interface: Music Video and the Portrait of Mediality

Tomáš Jirsa

It is very likely that anyone who has seen even a few music videos associates them with an image that can hardly be overlooked: the face.[1] Shot and edited with a great variety of angles, lighting, colour, and duration, the facial close-ups in music videos – whether the performer is lip-syncing or just staring into the camera – serve to endorse a song's specific atmosphere. If music video 'killed the radio star' – as the first piece released by MTV in 1981 announced via the Buggles' eponymous song – a perfect assassination of the video star has been committed from within the genre itself.[2] The star is no longer the obvious point, and rather than being revealed in their individuality, the faces and bodies of performers are wired into an audiovisual arrangement through which they are performed and interlinked. Instead of an artist persona, what such videos foreground is the entanglement of performers into an audiovisual arrangement that generates them.

A fleeting glance at some recent experimental productions suffices to show that the most human part of our bodies and the proverbial pathway to the soul has been gleefully dismantled. From the grotesque, weird, and gender-bending heads in Aphex Twins' videos *Come to Daddy* (1997) and *Windowlicker* (1999; both directed by Chris Cunningham) to the racially subversive DIY face-transplant surgery in Tyler, the Creator's *Who dat boy* (dir. Wolf Haley, 2017); from the CGI datamoshing of FKA Twigs's face in *Water Me* (dir. Jesse Kanda, 2013) to Ariana Grande's digitally rendered removal of her own singing face, placed among other masks with her countenance in *No Tears Left to Cry* (dir. Dave Meyers, 2018); from the lo-fi uncanny superimposition of the Clipping rapper's eyes and mouth over the beach passersby in *Summertime* (dir. Carlos López Estrada, 2015) to the surreal multiplication of the protagonist's head crowding and exploding above the Icelandic landscape in Youth Lagoon's *Rotten Human* (dir. Patrick Blades, 2016) – the ubiquitous facial exhibition entails that the more frequently a performer's face appears, the less it reveals about its owner, cutting the ties with any notion of interiority and making the face opaque.

Far from being an exclusive result of contemporary digital aesthetics and computer software, as these examples might imply, the outlined trajectory of the face becoming opaque, deconstructed, and desubjectified has important precedents in the golden age of televisual music video, which spans from the 1980s until around the mid-1990s, also known as the MTV era.[3] In the final extradiegetic sequence of Michael Jackson's legendary video *Black or White*, directed by John Landis in 1991, the facial disconnection from subjectivity is enabled by and reflected through the latest computer technology. Jackson's plea for racial equality, spelled out via the lyrics and enacted by the multicultural dancing scenes across the globe, is further played out by means of CGI processes consisting in visually morphing one face into another. Staging a playful circulation of faces of all kinds of ethnicity, colour, age, and gender that nod to the upbeat rhythm of the half-pop, half-rock 'n' roll song while seamlessly transitioning, the setting also offers a timely meta-commentary on the music video genre in its technological development and collaborative thrust.

In the video's outro, the action takes place within the *mise-en-abyme* space of the recording studio where the previous dominant presence of the singer is taken over by the video crew, cast, and the apparatus, getting the cameras, cables, and computer screens into the spotlight. As a result, the overall scene of production covering both the digital rendering of countless visages through the then highly advanced computational graphics and the studio 'control room' foreshadows the music video faciality that moves past any humanist claim to interiority towards the transformative operation of morphing. By establishing digital technology as a prerequisite of both the visual likeness and visible identity in flux, the video rephrases Friedrich Kittler's famous techno-ontological dictum from 1990, '*Nur was schaltbar ist, ist überhaupt*' (Only what is switchable is at all) (2017: 5), into an epistemological formula proposing that only what is *transformable* is at all. Landis's CGI experiment thus not only pre-echoes the genre of music video as a new media 'laboratory for exploring numerous new possibilities of manipulating photographic images made possible by computer' (Manovich 2001: 311), but also demonstrates that the deconstruction of the face has been present in the genre since its televisual inception. For what those morphing faces indicate and what the following pages will tackle is that in place of representing a pre-established persona – a sort of 'artist on demand' – the music video face performs a task of the *interface* that conducts both the sonic and visual motion while amplifying the interpenetration of sound, moving images, and lyrics.

The Jackson video gives us an important lead, for it privileges the logic of circulation and interconnection over the autonomy of an individual.[4] This opacity of the face raises a couple of questions that will frame the present inquiry: What is the agency of these overexposed, multiplied, and yet desubjectifying faces? And how to think a music video face beyond the boundaries of the classical subject and without the traditional anthropocentric baggage? Putting two videos from the current hip-hop and trip-hop scene, Earl Sweatshirt's *Chum* (2012), directed by Hiro Murai, and Massive Attack's *The Spoils* (2016), directed by John Hillcoat, into dialogue with Jean-Luc Nancy's concept of the non-representational portrait while reading them through the lens of media philosophy, this chapter argues that these works turn the face into a media-affective interface whose main function is to amplify the video's work of audiovisual forms, mediality, and atmosphere.

In so doing these videos open up an avenue for rethinking portraiture as a media operation that undermines the traditional notions of representation, interiority, and subjectivity in favour of unfolding the technological and affective links between sounds, moving images, and lyrics. While the process of desubjectification – ruling out the bind between the face and interiority and hence disputing representation as a prerequisite of portraiture – is a well-known modernist strategy entrenched in the claim for aesthetic autonomy and avant-garde anti-essentialism, thoroughly described in visual arts and film,[5] what distinguishes the selected music videos' take on portraiture is their transformation of the facial image into a media-reflexive relay that operates through and resonates with its sonic and visual environment. This functional use of the face stems from the technicity of both their collaborative production process and their circulation across online platforms. No matter how 'artsy' and experimental the music videos intend to be, their faces are produced as an interface opening on to the nowadays culture – they are made to circulate.

The Face as Loop: *Chum*

How to combine the frenetic pace of Earl Sweatshirt's rap with the existential lyrics about his missing father and dubious friends, an aimless roaming through a hostile city, and the painful plodding on the paths of a languishing psyche? You put them together into a piano loop consisting of two minor chords and hectic staccato drums in the slow 4/4 tempo of 77 bpm. Only rarely does it happen that the chorus of a song is not just referentially – explicitly or symbolically – illustrated, but that, instead, the rap flow penetrates and shapes the whole audiovisual movement of a video, as is the case of the black and white *Chum*, directed by Hiro Murai for Earl Sweatshirt's song from his first studio album *Doris* (2013).

From the intro onwards, the video discloses its strategy of *desubjectification*, showing clearly that were there any meaningful link between the performer and his face, this arises mainly as a question of how the former should disappear behind the latter. Before encountering the rapper, who is both the narrator and key protagonist of the entire nocturnal scene, the viewer is immersed in an ambient background of chirping cicadas and distant traffic, and faced with a frog whose loud croaking punctuates the nocturnal soundscape, in total indifference both to the camera and subsequent events. The darkness, the animal, and the ambient mix of insect and machine sounds thus open up and continue to inform the video's rhythm as well as the mode of its reading. Importantly, the initial dissolve brings Earl Sweatshirt to the fore not frontally, but in a vertiginous, swinging position which is fully coextensive with the chorus and the lyrics' major figure of the pendulum.

> Something sinister to it
> Pendulum swinging slow, a degenerate moving
> Through the city with criminals, stealth, welcome to enemy turf
> Harder than immigrants work, 'Golf' is stitched into my shirt
> Get up off the pavement brush the dirt up off my psyche
> Psyche, psyche

Right after the chorus giving rhythm to the fast cuts on Earl Sweatshirt's revolving face, the pivotal role of the animal is confirmed by a tracking shot into a close-up of the frog's eye – and not the rapper's, as an anthropocentric view would expect – wherein a streetlight is reflected. The contrast of the direct light, flashy reflections, and shadow play complements another anthrodecentric element of the *mise en scène*: whereas the performer is always in both horizontal and vertical motion, the multiplying frogs remain static and grotesquely majestic throughout the video. What reinvigorates the fading glow of the performer's face and the emerging blurring city lights behind it is the continual movement during which Earl Sweatshirt's body floats past a shopping cart with a fire burning inside it, while recounting how his fatherless existence left him in ashes.[6]

As if to imply that memory is only one of many lapsing media, certainly not a reliable archive of the past but more a fuzzy spinoff of the present moment, the camera shortly cuts to a child's toy, the merry-go-round with horses. While this hint to a personal (*qua* subjective and intimate) story lays a trap for one's desire for symbolical reading that always seeks some narrative causality behind the forms, the formal reading I propose avoids the lure of an emotionally charged plot and, instead, probes the counter-movement between what the music video forms *show* and what they actually *do* – and the name of this audiovisual as well as affective operation is the *loop*. In this light, the sequence is governed much less (if at all) by narrative coordinates than by the performative logic of affects involving and combining doubt, confusion, and grief. And since the 'affects take shape in the details of specific visual forms and temporal structures' (Brinkema 2014: 37), instead of being represented and hence used to 'move' the spectator, they are triggered by and further elaborate the formal work of the loop that oscillates and curves within the aural, textual, and visual repetitions. The merry-go-round is hence an iteration and a particular figure of the looping that is both affectively and formally active at every level of the video.

Consider, for instance, the successive shots of the performer–dog–performer–drummer–toy and performer again, which appear at the same staccato pace as the piano tones of Eb minor and G minor and with the hasty cadence equal to the drum strokes. Throughout the video, we simultaneously hear and see the loop that drives the beats, melody, and rap lines while at the same time structuring the drifting *mise en scène*. Enacted by the textual motif of the pendulum and the recurrent piano pattern, the performative operation of this loop frames the overall audiovisual composition. The swaying movement of this loop reaches its climax when the rapper is turned upside down and hangs in the air some three feet above the ground while the rest of the scene remains the same (Figure 5.1). Being literally *suspended* – in both meanings of the word, hoisted bottom-up and pendulous, but also interrupted – the subject is put in suspense and hence in doubt. If the loop is always 'self-contained, enclosed and capable of taking almost any number of fragments within its ouroboros movement' (Bishop 2020: 152), the video's self-devouring and self-generating loop that unfolds in the audiovisual time and space repels the subject from its centre. Yet every loop needs a hook to be tightened around, and in this case it is provided by the moving image that is undoubtedly the most exposed one: the face.

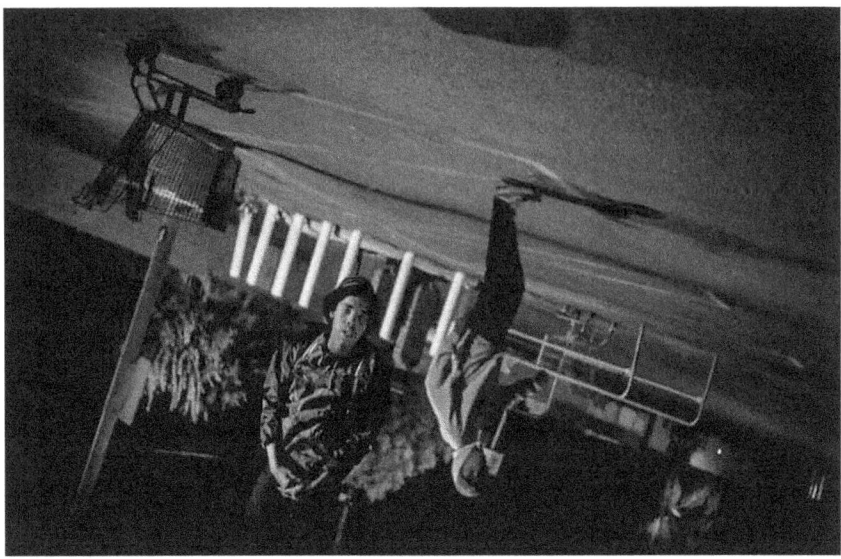

Figure 5.1 Hiro Murai, *Chum*, 2012, Vimeo, screenshot by the author

In fact, there are two kinds of faces, the animal and the human, neither of them belonging exactly to whom they show. In its motionless indifference, the frog face corresponds to the expressionless mask that suddenly appears on the gloomy head of a dog. In the same way that the main protagonist is floating to the beats of the soundtrack, this skeleton-like mask travels throughout the video only to finally land on the back of the drummer. Emphasising its *removability*, the animal face ceases to stand for an animal and becomes a mask which freely switches between the subjects while being continually juxtaposed with and superimposed on the face of the rapper. Having therefore nothing to do with a Deleuze-and-Guattarian 'becoming-animal' (2004: 258–87), the video's take on the face engages in a *short-circuiting* of animal through a cheap Halloween-like mask, ultimately rejecting the romantic essence of otherness in favour of employing the animal's face as a musical element. Instead of expressing some mysterious non- or beyond-human dimension, the video's mute barking and loud croaking, emitted via the animal faces, become a sounding board of the dominant piano loop (Figure 5.2).

If the animal face reifies en route to becoming a replaceable mask, the same direction towards objectification and exteriority is taken up by the human face as well. The position of Earl Sweatshirt's head hanging upside down in the manner of a pendulum is but one in the overall sequence of the mask's transpositions between the dog, the

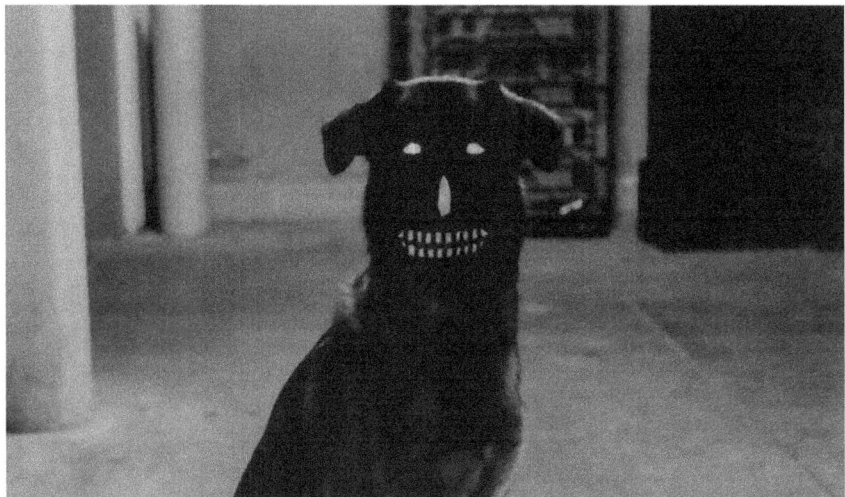

Figure 5.2 Hiro Murai, *Chum*, 2012, Vimeo, screenshot by the author

drummer, and the rapper himself, implying that despite the dominance of the rapper's performing role his face becomes increasingly
removable. These shifts in the faces' positions and roles call for a
reading that would be in line with such spatiotemporal transpositions. Instead of a hermeneutically naive decoding of the emotional,
personal, and symbolic propriety of some inner self residing behind
a transparent and expressive face, the vertiginous movements of the
camera and the face's role of a 'loophole', constantly switching position and light, make the face a 'moveable play of reflections and
angles' (Nancy 2018: 99), revealing absolutely nothing about the
subject's interiority. By no means does this desubjectification mean
that the face loses its importance. Quite the contrary; its sequen-
tial ordering, frequency, and transpositions turn the face into what
Abraham Geil aptly phrases as an 'opaque but nevertheless *readable*
surface[s]' (2017: 67). *Chum* thus transforms the face into a media-
affective *interface* that enhances the video's dark and suspenseful
atmosphere while amplifying the performative work of the audiovisual looping forms. To read this interface is to probe its connectivity,
operationality, and audiovisual movement.

   To make this shift from a conventional transparency to *readable*
opacity, the video boldly unhinges narrative ordering, as is tellingly
summarised by the sign on Earl Sweatshirt's hoodie, which likely
speaks for a viewer's confusion: 'What the Fuck is Really Going On?'
The narrative uncertainty is further underscored by a diegetic inter-
ruption achieved by the interposed views on a nocturnal street that

function more as photographic stills than durational sequences, the only motion belonging either to the camera or to the frogs' throats. What activates these fixed murky images is, again, nothing but the musical structure of the loop, grounded in *repetition* and (inter)facial circularity, by means of and through which the video's dark atmosphere operates. To navigate the non-narrative reading towards the formal work of affects and audiovisual atmosphere is also very close to Murai's own resistance to any storyline synopsis (an omnipresent element, especially in YouTube viewers' discussions), as he put it in an interview: 'Because to me what happens in the video isn't really the point. It's more of a tone thing, or you should just experience it in conjunction with the music' (Klinger 2012).

So there is, after all, a positive answer to the blunt question stitched into the performer's sweatshirt: it's about loop, and it's about face; and these are arguably serious topics – with no less serious conceptual implications – for one short video. Without necessarily clinging to the geometric analogy, the loop resembles the facial *object* on the basis of repetition, and it is due to the capacity of the loop to repeat a sonic event that 'the sound *becomes* an object for the listener' (Steintrager and Chow 2019: 10). Given this objectifying force of repetition – the essential principle of hip-hop sampling – it might be suggested that the face emerges as the audiovisual interface between the sonic and visual loop, an interface that allows the audience to follow the affective force of the video without conflating that force with one of the personal narrative.

The Supplementary Logic of Portraiture

Constituting both the affective and audiovisual centre of music videos, the face acts as a rhythmical membrane that absorbs the song's atmosphere and amplifies it within the audiovisual composition. By the same token, it works as a focal point of the music video's two-way mediality that Mathias Bonde Korsgaard defines as 'a dual synesthetic remediation between sound and image through which music is visualized and vision musicalized' (2017: 86). It is, however, important to note that this media-affective interfaciality could hardly achieve its operational effects without the formal technique of the close-up, a landmark in the history of cinema and its major strategy, which 'embodies the pure fact of presentation, of manifestation, of showing, a "here it is"' (Doane 2003: 91). Building upon Jean Epstein, Béla Balász, and Deleuze's and Guattari's modernist notion of defacialisation, Mary Ann Doane explains how the concept of close-up dismantles the usual view of the face as the 'privileged receptacle of affect' due to its overwhelming scale and proximity, and 'pushes us beyond the realm of individuation, of social role, and of the exchange that underlies intersubjectivity' (2003: 95–6).

But this is also where lies the difference, and why we need to distinguish between the two concepts of film and music video close-ups. While the former accounts for the cinematic face as 'an image rather than a threshold onto a world' (Doane 2003: 91), and relies upon a presumption of aesthetic autonomy, asserting the materiality of the image *qua* image, the latter posits the face in its very threshold position, as a medial interface to the world. Due to the ample scale and close proximity that have not just visual but also musical and sonic qualities, the music video close-up generates the face as both the material and affective link to the surrounding world of which it makes a constitutive part – for the face exceeds its own image on the way to becoming an audiovisual medium. When the camera continually tracks in to a close-up of the rapper's face, this movement exposes that face not so much as a 'sign, a text, a surface that demands to be read' (Doane 2003: 94), but rather as an interface that requires connection.

But how does this interface produce the performer-as-subject which, however desubjectified, is still there? Instead of affirming the conventional understanding of the face as a sign of the subject's singular individuality, Murai's video – assembling masks, animals, and a human face into the sonic and visual looping – emphasises the supplementary nature of the face. The supplement, Jacques Derrida argues, comprises two opposed yet complementary meanings of an addition, 'a surplus, a plenitude enriching another plenitude', and a substitute which fills a void, 'adds only to replace' and whose 'place is assigned in the structure by the mark of an emptiness' (2016 [1967]: 157). In line with the logic of supplement, *Chum* demonstrates that the face that can be added to someone is also the face that replaces and substitutes for someone – it is the face that depersonalises. In order for the face to become an interface that doesn't reveal a self underneath but, instead, connects the performer into a media-affective network, it needs to supplement the subject's identity. And a face that shows while hiding, manifesting its present absence, is another name for a *portrait*.

To make this premise clearer, let us now take a closer look at how Jean-Luc Nancy elaborates the notion of portraiture in both classical and contemporary visual arts. Exploring the position and structure of the subject in relation to the act of looking, Nancy, in his 2000 essay *Le Regard du portrait*, observes a situation of the modernist subject that is no longer 'the self-evidence of an interiority held within itself by the suspension of the world', since this subject threw off 'resemblance and recollection understood in terms of humanism, intentionality, and representation' (2018: 40–1). This non-representational view is then further unpacked in his more recent *L'Autre Portrait* (published in English together with the former essay), where Nancy fleshes out the oft-dismissed etymology of the French verb *portraire*, a composite of the prefix *por-* (for) and the verb *traire* (to draw, e.g. a line). Within the regime of figuration and representation, 'the prefix *por* (originally *pour*) marks an intensification: the line, the outline is applied or carried forth and its intensity sends it in the direction of a substitution of the drawing of the thing drawn' (2018: 47). The gesture of *substitution* – a visual stroke, or a line, surrogating a singular *trait* and hence putting one trace in place of another – that activates the *supplementary* operation of replacing a pre-existing subject while adding a new one is, therefore, an always already present condition of the genre of portraiture, no matter whether those mimetic lines that outline and construct a new figure belong to photography, cinema, fine arts, or music video. The portrait thus fundamentally and always follows the logic of supplement.

Furthermore, Nancy introduces a fitting notion of the 'other portrait', whose aim is no longer to reproduce a living person but instead to present a distanced and uncertain identity that is 'evoked in its withdrawal' (2018: 94). What comes to the fore in such a portrait is always 'the other' – someone who 'withdraws in showing itself' (2018: 49). This other is hence not a new ontological entity, a self-contained person, but the one who dwells in the dynamic of a present absence, emerging *in absentia*, and disappearing while appearing.

Bringing Nancy's notion from painting to the audiovisual field thus allows us to step beyond the received ideas of a purported causality between the faces seen in music videos and the performers' hidden interiority, and, instead, to explore the portrait operations unfolded through the musical, visual, and textual work of forms and affects. In this vein, what Murai's video proposes is a performative (rather than representational) *portrait* that exposes the subject less in its self-contained autonomy than in its withdrawal, in a particular retreat that underscores the subject's *mediality*.[7] Transforming a face into the media-affective interface can thus be understood as the music video's impulse to develop the supplementarity of the portrait within the audiovisual field. That the withdrawal of the subject, present in its absence and absent in its presence, has important ramifications for the amplified mediality of both the sonic and visual forms – and, indeed, for the audiovisual portrait of such mediality – will be discussed in the following section in dialogue with a different video.

A Recursive Portrait of Mediality: *The Spoils*

In line with the trip-hop pioneers Massive Attack's habit of collaborating with acclaimed directors and featuring noted performers from the acting and modelling industry, such as the Kosovo-Albanian actress Arta Dobroshi in *Come Near Me* (dir. Ed Morris, 2016), the fashion model icon Kate Moss in *Ritual Spirit* (dir. Dusan Reljin and Hilde Pettersen Reljin, 2016), and the Oscar-nominated actor John Hawkes in *Take it There* (dir. Hiro Murai, 2016), *The Spoils* (2016), directed by John Hillcoat, features Cate Blanchett, or more precisely, the close-up of her face. Yet instead of acting a role assigned by the video in order to incorporate the musical arrangement and lyrics, Blanchett's face becomes an object of audiovisual transformation. From glitchy close-ups through flickering digital silhouttes to a plaster cast of her head, from a death mask with moving eyes through a monumental Etruscan head to an anthropomorphic porous rock lump – such is the direction of the peculiarly anachronistic metamorphosis and erosion which the actress's head undergoes. While traces of her visage gradually vanish, tearing off any sign of identity, the video presents us with an audiovisual portrait wherein the human face is but one of its constituents. So how is this portrait made, and how do music, sounds, images, and lyrics coalesce to both shape and desubjectify it?

To answer these questions, we first need to unpack the musical and sonic qualities of the song that the video's moving images interact with. 'The Spoils' (released on EP together with the single 'Come Near Me' in 2016) is a slow-paced trip-hop piece in which the gentle synth line, melancholic strings, and mild granulation complement the dreamy lead vocals of the songwriter and lead-singer of Mazzy Star, Hope Sandoval. Written and produced by Massive Attack's Daddy G (aka Grantley Evan Marshall) and the composer Stew Jackson, the musical core of the piece is based on an interplay between the vocal and instrumentalist minimalism, with percussions that clock in ¾ rhythm and 72 bpm with a handclap on every third beat, on the one hand, and rich granular details such as the crackling synths, atmospheric digital sounds, and continual reverberations on the other.[8] While the overall soundscape is driven by the minimal beats, it is the singer's soft voice that regularly rearranges the song's melancholic mood through its inconspicuous changes in tone, loose phrasing, and silent interruptions. This 'multilayered simplicity' is played out in the intro when the strings in C# minor flow in the rhythm of slow waves, orchestrating the arrival of Sandoval's calming voice and the lyrics. Against the backdrop of three chords (Aadd9, B 6/9, C#m/G#) and in a tight range of only two notes (C4 and b), this voice articulates a quietly tormenting interior dialogue whose protagonists are I, you, someone else, and a resulting incertitude: 'I got that feeling / That bad feeling that you don't know / I don't even know her / But I hope that / She comforts you tonight.' To further amplify the troubledness of such a confusing romance, the introspective voice makes a short dramatic pause right before pronouncing 'she' – a pronoun that both outlines and substitutes for an anonymous 'other' that both the lyrics and video make present through its absence.

A formal close reading of *The Spoils* discloses three portrait strategies, each of them employing a specific kind of mediality. While the first is sustained through a polysemantic and intermedial tension between the lyrics, the music, and the moving images, the second involves a visual archaeology of the face. Finally, the third strategy is grounded in a self-reflective mediality to the point that it creates an operative (rather than representational) audiovisual self-portrait. Let's begin with the first portrait strategy that ties the audiovisual elements and discourse into a *disturbing harmony*. While the gentle, slow-pace, trip-hop music, images of the moderately revolving and metamorphosing head shot in long static takes, and a mild phrasing of the lyrics provide a sense of slowness, this serene tempo hovers in a striking contrast with the latter's existential love message, reaching the climax in the following lines: 'But I somehow slowly love you / And wanna keep you the same / Well, I somehow slowly know you / And wanna keep you away.' The chorus thus creates a classic 'fort/ da' movement, uncovering the paradoxical desire to possess and at the same time relinquish the other, while also taming this semantic movement with the restrained vocal range that, in turn, corresponds to a limited angle of the head's motion, opening at 45 degrees and remaining around 10 degrees throughout the video. Unlike Murai's piece where the camera circulates in a pendulum-like motion around the protagonist, in *The Spoils* it is the protagonist's head that appears to slightly revolve around its own axis while undergoing various physical alterations and media metamorphoses.

It would not be difficult to distinguish a few intertextual winks throughout the video, when Blanchett's eyes move in the motionless sculptural bust, as in Jean Cocteau's *Le Sang d'un poèt* (1930), or in the uncanny female mask alluding to Georges Franju's horror film *Les Yeux sans visages* (1960), but the main conceptual thrust of these shots is that they demonstrate the face as an anonymous mouldable matter that dismisses the physiognomic notion of the face as a surface of the inner self. Instead of representing some inner motions of the soul and expressing the subject's emotional depths, which can be read from the facial physiognomic signs, the video provides what Bernhard Siegert dubbed the 'soulless physiognomy', a media operation that leaves the semiotic *reading* of the face in favour of *writing* the face as a surface of 'pure signifiers detached from any affections or psychological causations' (Siegert 2019: 44, 48). For one thing, the face does not belong to the singer whose expressive voice we hear but to a famous actress; and yet it does not function as an index of Blanchett's personal repertoire of film roles but rather evokes 'something generally familiar' (Adorno 2005: 225). For another, the actress's facial expression makes no effort to incorporate the song's mood, and the usual means of correlation between the musical fictional realm and the performer, the lip-syncing, appears very briefly, as if in passing. If the lyrics elaborate the existential meaning of the song's title in its verbal form (to spoil *qua* to ruin) in terms of an injured relationship and flawed trust, and does so against the backdrop of the calmly disturbing music, the visuals, displaying a decaying return to an anthropomorphic rocky matter, track down the semantic layers and etymological inflections of the noun's technical and, indeed, geological meaning, grounded in its Latin root *spoliare* (*OED*, s.v. 'spoil') – a face as an object of archaeological excavation.[9]

What might seem at odds with the current deconstructive practices of the music video face, including all kinds of CGI experiments such as datamoshing, blurring, and digital morphing, is not a naive reconstruction of a 'facial humanity' but rather the face's radical desubjectification. This second strategy takes place through an *anachronistic* descent into the prehistory of the face in terms of an archaeological object, as a purely contingent and anonymous form and matter whose anthropomorphic shape can be covered with any mask whatsoever.[10] The problem of the face's temporality posed by *The Spoils* is one that Georges Didi-Huberman (2002: 55) tackles in relation to the trans-historical survival of images that resist chronological order due to an atemporal resonance and intensity enacted by the anachronistic interplay of continuities and discontinuites through which past and present become entangled in one another.[11] The video can thus be read as a series of visual experiments in the relation between form and matter (without the involvement of any spiritual agency) that uses both the plastic arts but also scientific techniques such as thermal imaging. And this is also where the discursive 'fort/da' movement penetrates the anachronistic trajectory enacting a death drive – the return to matter figured by rough stone.

Importantly, Hillcoat resisted the temptation of the narrative arc that would present the spectator with the actress's face at the end of the video, whereby the entire visual archaeology would gain a purely individualist post-romantic meaning. After a short representational prelude displaying Blanchett's face with slightly open mouth and pensive expression, her personal physical features become gradually anonymised and removed by means of both a multiplication of flickering and glitching effects and through a masquerade when different types of artificial doll-like wigs change on a mannequin's bald head. Following the desubjectifying axis from the protagonist's bust to the kind of anonymous sculpture that is on display in anatomical museums – in the shape of skinned facial bundles of tendons and bare muscles with no space left for any inner motions of the soul – through the shots of a mummy's head, to its physical corruption with the colliding nose, ears, and lips, the video puts to the fore an oval stone head wherein a particular face is but one possibility among an infinite number of other archaic versions thereof. Not only is this stone block reminiscent of burial mounds from ancient funeral rites, but it also claims a founding paradox of any image which consists in the presence of the absence (Belting 2011: 6).[12] Halfway through the video, the presence of the missing subject is further reinforced by the fact that this 'arche-face' appears in a slow lateral movement against the backdrop of the silent strings and the singer's voice pronouncing the word 'away'. Out of this sonic space emerges a face-rock, metamorphosing into a white, coral-like bulk washed ashore, wherein the facial holes and protrusions appear as an elusive reminder of its figurative history before turning into an oval grey stone, absorbed by the visual darkness and waning music (Figure 5.3).

Unhinging the Subject, Connecting the Media

While the song unmistakably develops an ambivalent love pattern, structured around disappointment, generosity, but also a distrust 'spoiling' the relationship, the video's affective work does not take place at the level of representational images but rather throughout its *recursive media operations*. From the intro onwards, the 'still life' moving images show not only a face in transformation but also a self-referential visual noise underscoring its audiovisual mediality, in tune with the sonic texture containing the trembling digital percussion,

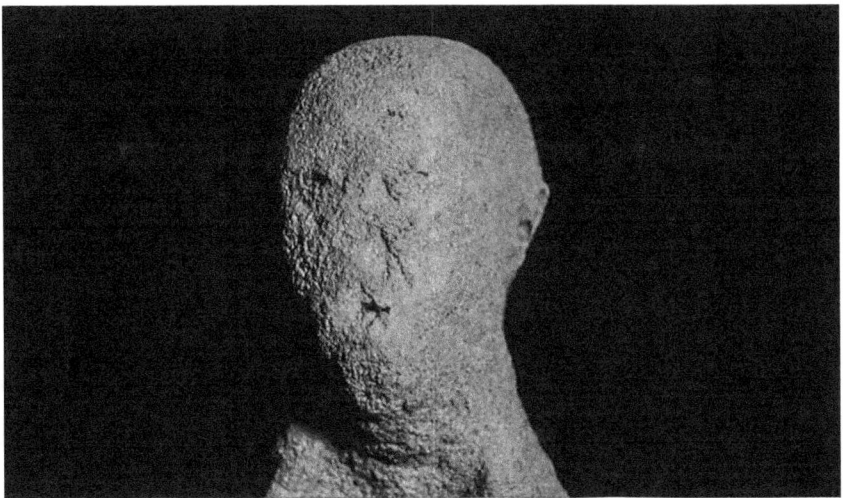

Figure 5.3 John Hillcoat, *The Spoils*, 2016, Vimeo, screenshot by the author

reverberations, and pauses. These media recursions are especially striking not only when the actress's head is warped by the infrared thermography but also before when surrounded by a pale blue halo, evoking a familiar visual artefact of the video glitch, coupled with the flickering red and black and white filters – only to be reinforced by the scattered stripes that appear irregularly across the screen (Figures 5.4–5). For all the temptation to read these self-referential glitches as analogous to the crackling sound of vinyl records, widely used across all kinds of music genres, from hip-hop to acid jazz to pop, in order to achieve the right vibe of 'analogue nostalgia' (Schrey 2014), one should not dismiss the underlying recursive (self-)portrait strategy that conditions such glitches in the first place.[13] The same logic that drives the video's moving images to excavate the face to the point of peeling off any signs of subjectivity is the one that requires us to read these manifold visual rustlings, horizontal streaks, flickerings, and grainy effects *self-reflectively* instead of sentimentally – as an emphasis on the impure materiality of sounds and images whose performative interaction leaves their preinscribed symbolic meanings behind.

Furthermore, the mediality-oriented reading I argue for correlates with both the lyrics and the dominant mood of the song. If a medium becomes visible at the moment of its failure, or, as Sybille Krämer writes, 'only noise, dysfunction and disturbance make the medium itself noticeable' (2015: 31), the same holds true for the contradictory love and erotic relationships as unravelled in the song's chorus.[14] In other words, the couple's relationships understood as

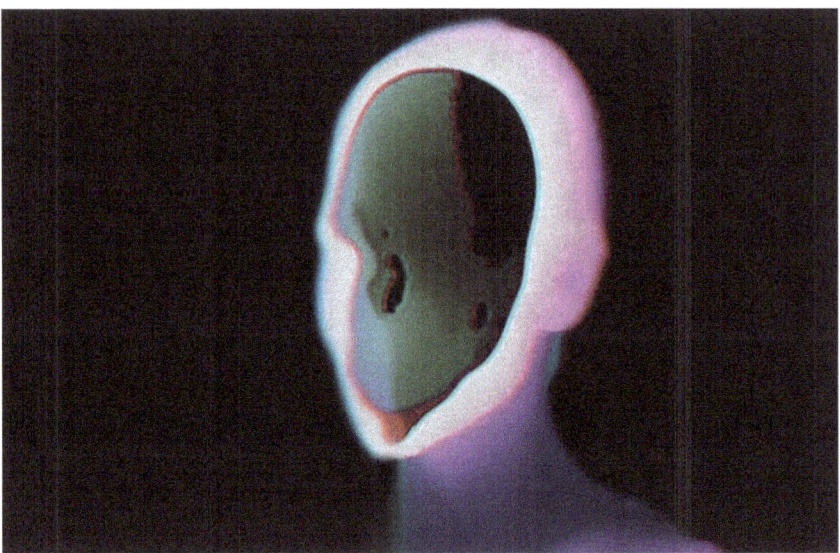

Figure 5.4 John Hillcoat, *The Spoils*, 2016, Vimeo, screenshot by the author

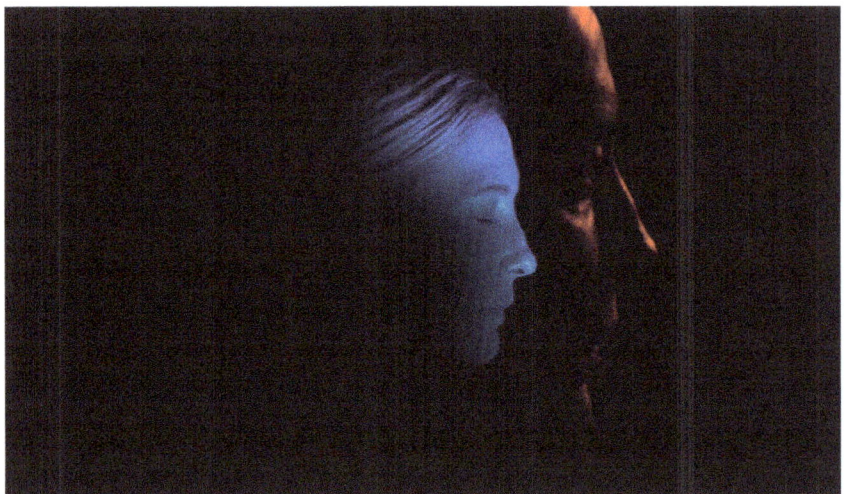

Figure 5.5 John Hillcoat, *The Spoils*, 2016, Vimeo, screenshot by the author

circuits necessitate their *short-circuits* in order to disclose the basic framework upon which they are established – since the very failures, crises, extra-routine clashes and hence 'the spoils' create a relational space for unprecedented steps and gestures that reinvent a circuit of love anew. Now, this medial self-visualisation is *recursive*: it repeats, reflects, and reproduces the video's stratification of the sonic, visual, and discursive layers while laying bare a vital mediation of the audio-visual forms that move away from the grip of subjectivity.

In precisely the same way that two semantic layers of the lyrics – the centripetal ('keep you the same') and the centrifugal ('keep you away') – overlap, so do the optic patterns of moving images, producing a visual *moiré effect*. The latter appears in the first two minutes of the video, first across Blanchett's face in red and blue and then upon the already anonymous bust, being fully fledged during the hesitating pause between the phrases 'keep you' and 'away'. To be sure, by the moiré effect I do not mean an aesthetic experience of *'la moiré'* that Roland Barthes describes in his late lectures on *The Neutral* (1978) in terms of a 'shimmer: that whose aspect, perhaps whose meaning, is subtly modified according to the angle of the subject's gaze' (2005: 51), but rather its original mathematical-physical meaning of the visual distortion seen as a trembling pattern produced by the superimposition of two geometrically regular patterns that *interfere*. It comes as no surprise, then, that such an effect of interference foreshadows a sequence of close-ups of the death mask with the moving eyes, the doll's head with a clumsily attached plastic wig, and, finally, a pixellated digital mask. As a result, the moiré effect – a generative self-reflexive media lapse – not only joins the video's visual archaeology of the face in that it substitutes and, indeed, supplements the subject by an interplay of images, sounds, and lyrics, but it also produces a peculiar *media self-portrait*. And such is the stake of the non-representational yet operative portrait of Hillcoat's music video: to read the face beyond the confines of traditional humanist physiognomy, it needs to be linked to its constitutive mediations and thus become an interface.

Posing the face as a media problem of connection and affective performance, these music videos reinvent the genre of portraiture through their audiovisual means and move it beyond the self. They do so through the act of desubjectification that ties together Murai's aesthetics of facial exteriorisation and Hillcoat's recursive portrait of mediality. This supplementary operation of exposing the subject while removing its subjectivity allows us to rethink the portrait as a media operation undermining traditional notions of representation and identity in favour of unfolding its technological and affective links between sounds, moving images, and lyrics. To understand the always already supplementary gesture of portraiture, separating the face from an inner self, a gesture that finds its extension in the music video trajectory of portraiture, one needs to move past the physiognomic assumption of the face as a semiotic surface towards the face as an operative media assemblage. Instead of reiterating the face as a privileged site of subjectivity and interiority and the proverbial pathway to the soul, both *Chum* and *The Spoils* present the face as a connectable media object – the face as an audiovisual screen that absorbs, intensifies, and gives rhythm to both the moving images and sounds.

As both these examples of the artistic exploration of the facial dispositif show, the self-reflective media portraiture in the music video genre has the capacity to reconfigure the face as both the visual and sonic membrane, a rhythmical centre around which the music and the images revolve, which they take off from and return to. Such rebounds, however, are a far cry from a narcissistic self-exposure of the performer's persona inasmuch as they do not exhibit the face as an embodiment of a unique individual or a performer's ineffable interiority. Instead, the face arises as a conceptually more compelling part of the whole audiovisual network. Neither an idealist face-in-itself, nor a modernist face-for-itself, but rather the media-operational *face in-between* – an interface.

Notes

1. This chapter is an outcome of the research project 'Between Affects and Technology: The Portrait in the Visual Arts, Literature and Music Video' (JG_2019_007), funded by the Faculty of Arts of Palacký University Olomouc.
2. In contrast, see the classic definition of music video, penned by Carol Vernallis (2004: 16) just one year before the global video-sharing website YouTube was launched, claiming that the purpose of the genre is primarily to 'showcase the star, highlight the lyrics, and underscore the music'.
3. Portions of this argument appeared in Jirsa 2019.
4. For the sake of brevity, my discussion brackets what seems to be the main intentional message of the video, rooted in the spirit of North American multiculturalism, which is the face as a site for the universal humanity that can simultaneously accommodate all differences of identity by blending and moving seamlessly between various marked identites of race, ethnicity, gender, and culture. The question remains to what extent the video's purportedly anti-racist logic of inclusion entails the very opposite of that intention. For different readings of colour and race in *Black or White*, see Kinni 2015: 413–16; and a number of chapters in Smit 2016.
5. See esp. van Alphen 2005; Weiss 2013; and Steimatsky 2017.
6. An insightful take on the family background of Earl Sweatshirt (Thebe Neruda Kgositsile) and his relationship to his father, the South African poet Keorapetse Kgositsile (1938–2018), is provided in the *New Yorker* profile by Kelefa Sanneh (2011).

7. By mediality I understand what Dieter Mersch defines as the per-formative 'structure of the medial', that is 'the underlying materialities, dispositives and performances that accompany medial processes' (2013: 210).
8. Among the many reviews of Massive Attack's single, a useful overview of the song's musical qualities is provided by a collective review of the *popmatters* critiques, especially Sutton 2016.
9. Precisely, I'm referring to meaning n. 10 in the *OED* entry *spoil, n.*: 'Earth or refuse material thrown or brought up in excavating, mining, dredging, etc.'
10. For a contrasting futuristic reading of the video, see Stuff 2016.
11. Drawing on Aby Warburg's notion of *Nachleben* – the *survival* of images and motifs throughout history – Didi-Huberman argues for anachronism as a 'temporal way of expressing the exuberance, complexity, and overdetermination of images' (2003: 37). Rather than a fixed representation, any image stands for 'an object of complex, impure temporality: an *extraordinary montage of heterogeneous times forming anachronisms*' (2003: 38).
12. I cannot but refer here to Jean-Pierre Vernant's anthropological research of the *kolossos*, an idol connected to archaic burial rituals in ancient Greece (2006: 321–32).
13. For more on the music video's 'glitch aesthetics' that 'emphasizes the digital presence of images', see Shaviro 2017: 51–75.
14. In her account of the invisibility and disappearance of medium as a condition of its smooth functioning – in what she calls 'aisthetic self-neutralization' (Krämer 2015: 31) – Krämer draws from the negative media theory of Dieter Mersch (2002: 135): 'In the process of its mediatization, the medium conceals itself, remains unrecognizable, disappears as an instrument behind its effects' (quoted in Krämer 2015: 222 n.15). This 'paradox of the medial' then consists in that media 'themselves disappear in their appearance [. . .] their work consists of dissolving themselves in fulfillment of their function' (Mersch 2013: 209, 212).

References

Adorno, Theodor W. (2005 [1963, 1969]), *Critical Models: Interventions and Catchwords*, trans. Henry W. Pickford, New York: Columbia University Press.

Alphen, Ernst van (2005), *Art in Mind: How Contemporary Images Shape Thought*, Chicago: University of Chicago Press.

Barthes, Roland (2005 [1978]), *The Neutral: Lecture Course at the College de France (1977–1978)*, trans. Rosalind Krauss and Denis Hollier, New York: Columbia University Press.

Belting, Hans (2011 [2001]), *An Anthropology of Images: Picture, Medium, Body*, trans. Thomas Dunlap, Princeton, NJ: Princeton University Press.

Belting, Hans (2017 [2013]), *Face and Mask: A Double History*, trans. Thomas S. Hansen and Abby J. Hansen, Princeton, NJ: Princeton University Press.

Bishop, Ryan (2020), 'A Circle of Fragments: Barthes, Burgin, and the Inerruption of Rhetoric', *Theory, Culture & Society*, 37(4): 135–65.

Brinkema, Eugenie (2014), *The Forms of the Affects*, Durham, NC: Duke University Press.

Deleuze, Gilles, and Félix Guattari (2004 [1980]), *A Thousand Plateaus: Capitalism and Schizophrenia*, trans. Brian Massumi, London: Continuum.

Derrida, Jacques (2016 [1967]), *Of Grammatology*, trans. Gayatri Chakravorty Spivak, Baltimore, MD: Johns Hopkins University Press.

Didi-Huberman, Georges (2002), *L'image survivante: Histoire de l'art et temps des fantômes selon Aby Warburg*, Paris: Les Éditions de Minuit.

Didi-Huberman, Georges (2003), 'Before the Image, Before Time: The Sovereignty of Anachronism', trans. Peter Mason, in Claire J. Farrago and Robert Zwijneberg (eds), *Compelling Visuality: The Work of Art in and out of History*, Minneapolis: University of Minnesota Press, pp. 31–44.

Doane, Mary Ann (2003), 'The Close-Up: Scale and Detail in the Cinema', *differences: A Journal of Feminist Cultural Studies*, 14(3): 89–111.

Geil, Abraham (2017), 'Paranoid Critiques, Reparative Reductions: Leys, Sedgwick, and the Productive Opacity of Affect', *Polygraph: An International Journal of Culture & Politics*, 26: 36–64.

Jirsa, Tomáš (2019), 'Faces without Interiority: Music Video's Reinvention of the Portrait', *World Literature Studies*, 4(11): 55–68.

Kinni, Fongot Kini-Yen (2015), *Pan-Africanism: Political Philosophy and Socio-Economic Anthropology for African Liberation and Governance*, Bamenda: Langaa RPCIG.

Kittler, Friedrich (2017 [1990]), 'Real Time Analysis, Time Axis Manipulation', trans. Geoffrey Winthrop-Young, *Cultural Politics*, 13(1): 1–18.

Klinger, Doug (2012), 'Video Chats: Hiro Murai on Chum by Earl Sweatshirt', *IMVDb*, 12 December, https://imvdb.com/blog/2012/12/video-chats-hiro-murai-on-chum-by-earl-sweatshirt (last accessed 16 February 2022).

Korsgaard, Mathias Bonde (2017), *Music Video after MTV: Audiovisual Studies, New Media, and Popular Music*, Abingdon: Routledge.

Krämer, Sybille (2015 [2008]), *Medium, Messenger, Transmission: An Approach to Media Philosophy*, trans. Anthony Enns, Amsterdam: Amsterdam University Press.

Manovich, Lev (2001), *The Language of New Media*, Cambridge, MA: MIT Press.

Mersch, Dieter (2002), 'Wort, Bild, Ton, Zahl: Eine Einleitung in die Medienphilosophie', in Theresa Georgen (ed.), *Kunst und Medium, Gestalt und Diskurs, Vol. 3*, Kiel: Muthesius Hochschule, pp. 131–254.

Mersch, Dieter (2013 [2008]), 'Tertium Datur', *MATRIZes*, 7(1): 207–22.

Nancy, Jean-Luc (2018), *The Portrait*, trans. Sarah Clift and Simon Sparks, New York: Fordham University Press.

Sanneh, Kelefa (2011), 'Where's Earl? Word from the Missing Prodigy of a Hip-hop Group on the Rise', *The New Yorker*, 23 May, https://www.newyorker.com/magazine/2011/05/23/wheres-earl (last accessed 16 February 2022).

Schrey, Dominik (2014), 'Analogue Nostalgia and the Aesthetics of Digital Remediation', in Katharina Niemeyer (ed.), *Media and Nostalgia: Yearning for the Past, Present and Future*, London: Palgrave Macmillan, pp. 27–38.

Shaviro, Steven (2017), *Digital Music Videos*, New Brunswick, NJ: Rutgers University Press.

Siegert, Bernhard (2013), 'Cultural Techniques: Or the End of the Intellectual Postwar Era in German Media Theory', *Theory, Culture & Society*, 30(6): 48–65.

Siegert, Bernhard (2015), *Cultural Techniques: Grids, Filters, Doors, and Other Articulations of the Real*, trans. Geoffrey Winthrop-Young, Amsterdam: Amsterdam University Press.

Siegert, Bernhard (2019), 'Post Mortem Performances: On Duchenne de Boulogne, or Physiognomy in the Age of Technical Media', *World Literature Studies*, 11(4): 42–54.

Smit, Christopher R. (ed.) (2016), *Michael Jackson: Grasping the Spectacle*, Abingdon: Routledge.

Steimatsky, Noa (2017), *The Face on Film*, Oxford: Oxford University Press.

Steintrager, James A., and Rey Chow (2019), 'Sound Objects: An Introduction', in James A. Steintrager and Rey Chow (eds), *Sound Objects*, Durham, NC: Duke University Press, pp. 1–19.

Stuff, Noisey (2016), 'Watch Cate Blanchett's Face Morph and Decompose in Massive Attack's Video for "The Spoils"', *Vice*, 9 August, https://www.vice.com/en/article/xdynya/massive-attack-the-spoils-video-cate-blanchett (last accessed 24 February 2022).

Sutton, William (2016), 'Massive Attack – "The Spoils" Ft. Hope Sandoval (Singles Going Steady)', *Popmatters*, 22 August, https://www.popmatters.com/massive-attack-the-spoils-ft-hope-sandoval-singles-going-steady-2495418953.html (last accessed 5 March 2022).

Vernallis, Carol (2004), *Experiencing Music Video: Aesthetics and Cultural Context*, New York: Columbia University Press.

Vernant, Jean-Pierre (2006 [1965]), 'The Figuration of the Invisible and the Psychological Category of the Double: The Kolossos', in Jean-Pierre

Vernant, *Myth and Thought among the Greeks*, trans. Janet Lloyd and Jeff Fort, New York: Zone Books, pp. 321–32.

Weiss, Judith Elisabeth (2013), 'Before and After the Portrait: Faces between Hidden Likeness and Anti-Portrait', in Mona Körte, Ruben Rebmann, Judith Elisabeth Weiss, and Stefan Weppelmann (eds), *Inventing Faces: Rhetorics of Portraiture between Renaissance and Modernism*, Berlin: Deutscher Kunstverlag, pp. 133–46.

Chapter 6

Tracing Minor Gestures: Relational Portraits with Fernand Deligny

Elena Vogman

Portraiture is a domain in the arts that seems to have been particularly exposed to criticism in the last century. Any positive attitude towards this subject attracts suspicion given its definitive preoccupations with representation, reproduction, and resemblance (Johnstone and Imber 2020). In a beautiful chapter dedicated to 'The Autonomous Portrait', Jean-Luc Nancy highlights this optics: 'The object of the portrait is, in the strictest sense, the *absolute* subject: the subject detached from everything that does not belong to it, withdrawn from all exteriority' (2018: 13). Nancy goes on to analyse the constitution of the subject's autonomy: portraiture becomes synonymous with such precisely organised autonomy, revealing a figure that exists in itself. Nancy then proposes a number of reflections structuring the gaze around the figure which 'must itself be organised around its look – around its vision or its clairvoyance' (2018: 15). This look is what captures or escapes likeness and assigns the portrait subjectivity in its oscillating maze of resemblances and differences. This chapter considers a practice of portraiture that radically evacuates any positive notion of the subject, a method that brings 'portraiture' to the limits of its definition and simultaneously turns the attention towards what it seems to exclude: the body's relations with the environment, its *milieu*. In Nancy's words, this exclusion precisely constitutes the very essence of the portrait's conventional understanding, 'everything that does not belong to it [the subject]', which is its 'exteriority'.

In his collaborations with Jean Oury and Félix Guattari at the psychiatric clinic of La Borde (1965–67), and later in his work with neurodiverse or 'autistic' children in the Cévennes (1967–96), Fernand Deligny dismissed the concept of the (maladjusted and abnormal) subject in favour of a new concept of the milieu. He defines his project as the 'production of a new milieu that allows them [the delinquents] an existence' (Deligny 2007: 1165). This 'milieu' is no longer conceived as a neutral and homogeneous space, an 'exteriority' that exists prior to the relations within it. Rather it is understood as a labile space in which organism and environment can only be apprehended through their dynamic interrelations. The cartographic work that Deligny invented, in collaboration with non-professional educators, the so-called 'close presences', in the Cévennes region in the south of France, implies a tracing of the trajectories of neurodiverse subjects, their *lignes d'erre*. This cartography along with his concept of *moindre geste* – a minor gesture – reveals a critical practice of portraiture. Instead of focusing on representation and resemblance, this practice high-lights the relations between medium, milieu, and body. How do the lines of such tracings or the inscriptions of movement on film produce a milieu? Moving beyond a preoccupation with identi-fication, Deligny's writings and educational practice radically emphasise the intransitive action of both the subject and the line tracing its trajectory. The question is how to inscribe a relation. With *moindre geste* Deligny re-evaluates the incomplete, non-intentional, and 'meaningless' gestures of a neurodiverse child in their immanent force. Such an understanding of minor gesture in the Cevénnes' practice is nourished by theories of milieu that emerged at the beginning of the twentieth century. An engagement with these theories associated with disciplines such as biology, ethology, psychology, and ethnography reactivates an under-explored criti-cal path in the history of portraiture and its use value for research and experimental practice.

Relation and Labyrinth

What does it mean to evacuate the subject from the portrait? And more generally, how is one to get rid of the oscillating paradigms of likeness and strangeness, identity and distance, representation and presentation? Typically associated with the privileged individual subject of Western modernity, the portrait and its preoccupation with likeness is deeply rooted in antiquity (Woodall 1997: 1). However, the heroes of Greek mythology, for instance, acquire their identities not primarily through physiological characteristics but in a confrontation with fate – in a number of psychologically framed situations.

Rejecting representation and identity, Deligny's project consisted in producing relational inscriptions in a particular milieu. He shows how questions of identity and character are rooted in the hero's teleological subordination of space and time. In a significant passage from his 1982 essay *L'Arachnéen* (*The Arachnean*) he uses the motif of the labyrinth to describe this aporetic condition of the antique hero while offering a new understanding of the labyrinth as a milieu of 'endless detours'. *The Arachnean* – a text that is itself composed of detours, repetitions, and associations of a heterogeneous nature – draws on the fields of mythology, anthropology, philosophy, and milieu theory, as well as on personal memories.[1] It is a metaphor for endless complications followed by endless solutions: the path of Icarus on his way through the labyrinth culminating in his tragic flight towards the sun. Crucially, Deligny introduces the labyrinth as an analogy to the main figure of the text – the Arachnean, a spider's web, a network of trajectories of neurodiverse children.

> To admit the persistence of the Arachnean one would require such upheavals in the way the Man-that-we-are [*l'homme-qui-nous-sommes*] has organized ourselves that it is entirely reasonable to think that we will persist on the flight path that has become so ordinary and so powerful that it puts us in orbit, while hoping that what happened to Icarus won't happen to us, Icarus who was so preoccupied with escaping the detours of the labyrinth. And the Arachnean can truly be said to be rich in endless detours. (Deligny 2015: 62)[2]

According to the Greek myth, Icarus and his father Daedalus, the labyrinth's architect, are imprisoned in this maze, located on the island of Crete. In order to escape the labyrinth, Daedalus finds a solution – he fashions two pairs of wings out of wax and feathers for Icarus and himself. However, despite his father's warnings, Icarus cannot resist the temptation and approaches the sun. The wax of his wings melts and he drowns in what is today the Icarian Sea.

For Deligny, the myth serves as a paradigmatic portrait of the humanist project. In other words, Icarus's tragic fate implicitly reflects upon the condition of the 'Man-that-we-are', its finality and its teleology. The labyrinth appears in this parallel as an obstacle, a challenge to be overcome in order to transition to the new level of the thrilling adventure where the hero once again faces his fate. Seduced by the illusion of endless elevation, Icarus rises always higher, but the myth puts an end to this 'Icarian illumination' (Bataille 1988: 38).[3] In opposition to this tragic end, Deligny places the Arachnean – a labyrinth without exit, which, like a spider's web, is a structure 'rich in endless detours'.

But what is an endless detour? What is its logic and its temporality? And how is one to escape the tragic finality of an action, a project, or a goal? To address these questions, I want to explore the possibility of an 'endless detour' as opposed to the teleology of the subject and the paradigm of likeness, following Deligny's conceptualisation of the 'minor gesture' (*moindre geste*) and 'wander lines' (*lignes d'erre*). Referring to the filmic documentation of children's behaviour that gestalt psychologists Kurt Lewin and Max Wertheimer undertook in the late 1920s, my hypothesis addresses less the Icarian myth than a processual dialectics immanent to Deligny's 'endless detours'. I will argue that Deligny's idea of a 'labyrinth' implies a particular situation: a mediation of a milieu in which such detours can emerge, unfold, and be uncovered. Given this specific inscription of the milieu, the process of disclosing endless detours requires work with an optical unconscious, a particular mode of constructing the gaze.

Field Forces, Gestalt, and its Decompositions

Nowhere in his vast body of published work does Deligny mention the Berlin school of gestalt psychology's experimental film practice. Yet despite differences in their approaches and motives for observing children's behaviour, Deligny and the authors of gestalt theory had crucial elements in common. As well as their evident use of the camera for primarily non-aesthetic purposes, they shared a more fundamental concern: the valorisation of the milieu or 'field' of children's action.

Grounded in the assumption that the perceptual field is organised, gestalt psychologists emphasised that organisms perceive entire patterns or configurations rather than isolated elements. Human actions (*Handlungen*) are conditioned by a continuous reorganisation of the field. In order to understand the complexity of behavioural processes, Kurt Lewin and Max Wertheimer were interested in the ontogenetic development of behavioural structure. This is how, in 1929, they came to conduct a series of experiments on their own children. They used the camera to record and examine children's performances in the field, while defining the action as a result of what they called a framework of 'field forces' (*Feldkräfte*).

For instance, in one of their short films we see Hannah, a three-year-old girl who is given the task of sitting down on a stone (Figure 6.1). Hannah is spinning around the obstinate object which she has placed her hands on, as if searching for support. She completes several circles, even trying to conquer the stone with her leg as though she wants to take control of it, but in vain. Lewin explains: 'In order

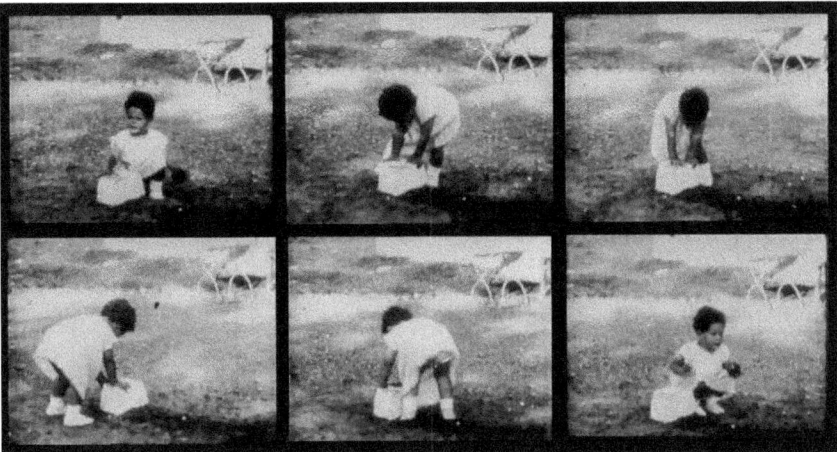

Figure 6.1 Frames from Kurt Lewin's film *Field Forces as Impediments for a Performance*, 1929

to sit down it is first necessary to turn around and thus to make a movement contrary to the direction of the goal.' Hannah does not succeed in quitting the 'visual direction' and multiplies her detours. Another short film shows Hans, age seven. Without hesitation, Hans sits down straight away, briefly turning his back to the stone. According to Lewin, the reason for Hannah's failure is her inability to restructure the field. 'The action of the older child is determined by the *functional* direction rather than by the *visual* direction. The "detour" no longer constitutes a difficulty.'[4]

The same year, Lewin (1929) commented on these experiments in a publication entitled *Die Entwicklung der experimentellen Willenspsychologie und die Psychotherapie* (The Development of Experimental Psychology of the Will and Psychotherapy).[5] The text contains incisive methodological arguments in favour of experimental psychology and addresses some psychoanalytic critiques regarding their simplicity. Lewin takes an empirical and comparative approach in studying a phenomenon that Freud conceptualised as repetition compulsion (*Wiederholungszwang*). In his book, Lewin juxtaposes frames that he has extracted from his film footage of children's actions with tracings children had made, directing his attention to the modulation of actions and gestures in time (Figure 6.2).

Observing such repetitive actions as the tracing of a pentagram or a game played with building blocks, Lewin became interested in the phenomenon of 'psychic saturation' (*psychische Sättigung*) (1929: 14; Figure 6.2). The moment in which psychic saturation occurs is

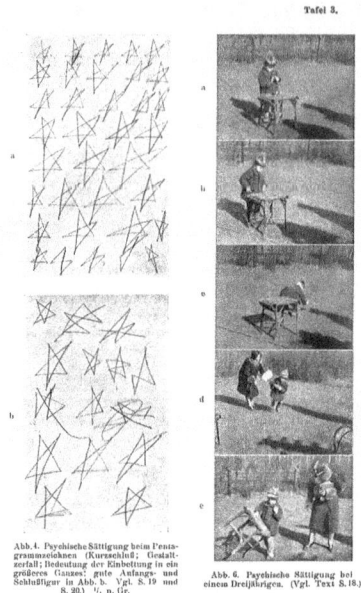

Figure 6.2 Plate from Kurt Lewin, *Die Entwicklung der experimentellen Willenspsychologie und die Psychotherapie*, 1929

crucial to gestalt theory, oriented as it is by shape construction. It is the moment when the repetition of the same action or gesture suddenly faces a conflict: a 'psychic saturation' resulting in an excess or denial of action. Lewin speaks of *Gestaltzerfall* – in German, the word *Zerfall* means decomposition, disintegration, or collapse – a decomposition of the shape occurring within the repetition of the gesture (1929: 17; Figure 6.2).[6] This happens not as a consequence of the child's exhaustion, Lewin underlines, but as a result of the exhaustion of the field in which the gesture operates. He gives an example of the repetitive recitation of a poem, which first unfolds a prolific variation of meaning, but soon leads to a decomposition of the entire poem into single words, '*forgetting, misspeaking, stutter*' (1929: 17). Analysing different situations of such decompositions of *Gestalt*, Lewin points to the insufficiency of a model which opposes 'causality' and 'finality', 'drive' and 'will', as pure tendencies outlined differently in the works of Alfred Adler, Sigmund Freud, or Ludwig Klages. Instead, he posits a complex entanglement of 'field forces' and 'psychic tension systems' (*seelische Spannungssysteme*) (1929: 22).

But more crucially for the present context, Lewin derives his observations of *Gestalt* and *Gestaltzerfall* from an acute attention to the field: a milieu of action carefully framed in his experiments, mediated through the camera lens or circumscribed by the surface of the page itself in the case of tracings. Gestalt psychologists point to the importance of this milieu not only for the mediation of the action, but above all for its development, conceptualising it as a 'field' in which the forces can unfold. In this case, the mediation isolates and frames the field in which the action takes place.

Tracing as Relational Inscription

In a similar way, one might be surprised to learn of the crucial role that the frame played in Janmari's tracings. Janmari was an 'autistic', mute child entrusted to Deligny in 1967 at the age of twelve. He lived in the care network that Deligny created in Monoblet, in the Cévennes region, for twenty-five years (Janmari and Durand 2013). As a child, he became one of the major figures in Deligny's theory and films. *Journal de Janmari* (2013) displays the tracings he produced between 2001 and 2002 during his weekly meetings with Gisèle Durand, a close presence who accompanied the children from the moment the network was created. The notebook reveals two different ways in which Janmari displayed shapes – small circles or waves – on the surface of a page. First, there are pages covered in shapes up to the margins; and second, there are those pages that contain a large figure – an ellipse or a rectangle – serving as a new frame for these circles or waves, and containing them. Gisèle Durand describes how she gave Janmari the first line for the frame, which was later replaced by a mere gesture completed by Janmari:

> Whenever I traced a vertical line from top to bottom, Janmari completed the rectangle by tracing the other three sides on his own. Soon I no longer needed to draw the line on the page. I just made the gesture in the air, and he drew all four sides. Then he set the pen down; I handed it back to him again, and he filled the frame with little circles and wavelets. (Janmari and Durand 2013: n.p.)

The frame given by the surface of the page, which served as a milieu for Janmari's tracings, is replaced by an artificially constructed frame in which the repetition of the waves and circles can take place (Figures 6.3–4). It is not only the traced line but also Durand's gesture that are active elements in milieu construction and mediation.

Ce Gamin, là (*That Kid, There*), a film made by Renaud Victor and Deligny in 1975, shows a close-up of Janmari's small circles traced repeatedly, one beside the other, on a large sheet of paper. These tracings are followed by maps produced by the close presences which

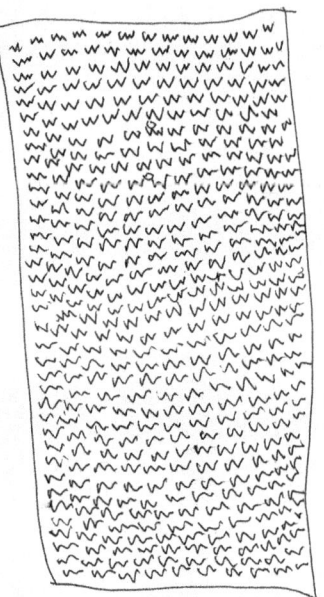

Figures 6.3 Lines traced on paper by Janmari (*Journal de Janmari*, 2013), courtesy Éditions L'Arachnéen

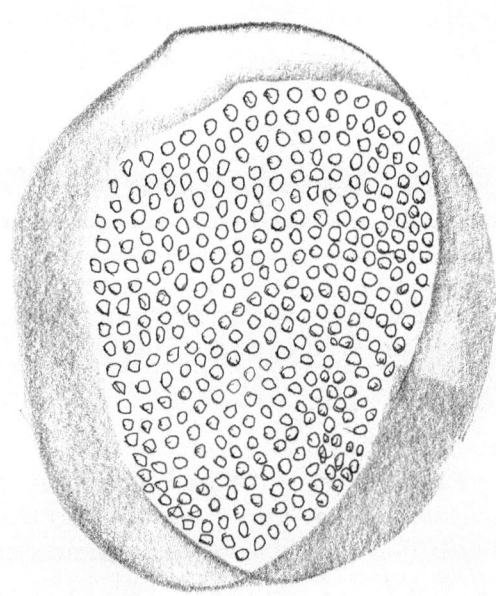

Figures 6.4 Lines traced on paper by Janmari (*Journal de Janmari*, 2013), courtesy Éditions L'Arachnéen

record Janmari's paths in a single day: 'He turns. He turns either around himself, the hands behind the back, one holding the other, or running.' Deligny's voiceover makes the transition from the elliptic figures on paper to Janmari's repetitive circular movements in the meadows of the Cévennes. Thus the film montage produces a relation between these different milieus: Janmari's circles on paper, his trajectories in the space, and his gestures. What the film's title suggests in the deictic, almost gestural mode of '*là*' reveals itself as a gesture of situating, an inscription of the milieu so important for Janmari.[7] In contrast to portraiture, this gesture inscribes a relation, a mediation that is not based on identification but rather subverts it as a principle. Moreover, the film itself establishes a common ground through montage, creating a visual and dynamic field – a milieu in which these different circles, these detours Janmari takes, coexist in their significant interrelation.

Janmari's tracings allude to one possible way in which mediation becomes part of milieu construction, a milieu in which the endless detours of a neurodiverse gesture can emerge and unfold. For Deligny, this mediation process was intimately linked to a theoretical reflection on such 'autistic' milieus and the practical camerawork in the Cévennes. One could even say that for him, media and milieus emerged simultaneously, enabling the actions and their detours. Thus media and milieus are closely related in their processual becoming, since mediation is a particular way of constructing the gaze. In this way, 'camering' can be seen as a means of entering the logic of the milieu, becoming part of it while simultaneously maintaining a distance and taking its images. Marlon Miguel (2022) insightfully points to the relation between camering and 'gathering (*recueillir*) or catching (*attraper*) images',[8] a process that resists the intentionality of filming in its traditional sense. This is how in 'Fossils Have a Hard Life: Apropos of the Image' Deligny abandons the notions of director or filmmaker in favour of the more impersonal and humble designation of 'image taker'. It is not a coincidence that the verb *camérer*, 'camering', resonates with *regarder*, 'looking', while replacing the authority of the subject with the accidental character of the milieu and its own temporality, envisioned by Deligny as camering 'the path of an iceberg and its thaw', as 'permanent cinema' (2021; 2022). Camering thus becomes an intransitive act involving the gaze in the process of uncovering a milieu.

Milieu and *moindre geste*

This becomes palpable in Deligny's work with the camera and his theory of the 'minor gesture'. *Le moindre geste* is one of the key concepts in Deligny's oeuvre. It serves as the title for the film *The Slightest Gesture*, produced collectively with Josée Manenti and Jean-Pierre Daniel, in collaboration with Aimé Agnel, Jean-Pierre Ruh, and Chris Marker between 1962 and 1971. It is also used in the title of a book: *Les detours de l'agir et le moindre geste* (The Detours of Acting and the Minor Gesture). The work is multidimensional – at once a complex theoretical essay, an empirical observation, and a political stance towards the present. Deligny refers to a scene projected on screen that shows neurodiverse children in their milieu of action. As if he were recovering the optical unconscious revealed by means of the camera, Deligny is far from reading these images as an immediate reflection of reality. For him (Deligny 2007: 1249), they instead bear traces of an irreducible singularity: *le reste* considered as 'residue' (*un résidu*), and more fundamentally as 'survival' (*une survivance*). But 'survival' of what, one could ask? Deligny answers this question dialectically: in this survival, relic, or 'atrophy', as he further describes the moment, he sees a fragment of a possible future, an outline or sketch (*l'ébauche*) of what could be 'human'.

Let us draw on the way Deligny constructs his gaze, the way he opens his own observations directed towards an interaction between two autistic children, two girls, Isabelle and Anne.

> I don't disregard the tableau effect (*l'effet du tableau*) of this video screen on which I see the puddle, the stones, the two girls and their gestures, and farther, in a close-up, Anne's hands and Isabelle's hands, the same hands, whereas the gestures aren't the same at all. (Deligny 2007: 1252)

The scene described by Deligny becomes a seminal point in his text – a situation from which further elements derive and unfold.

> On seeing Isabelle and Anne crouched down, facing each other, a puddle, or rather, a hollow full of water, between them, one might think both are playing, so to speak. Anne grasps the stones along the edge of the crater one by one; she rinses them in the water. Her gesture seems to wash each stone until there is no earth on it, and each stone washed is put on the other side of the puddle. Isabelle observes attentively.
>   Neither of them uses language. Isabelle hears, often understands, what is said. Anne is deaf to the meaning of words. (2007: 1251)

Deligny's attentive gaze uncovers in Isabelle's gestures a form of play, while Anne's actions are of a different nature (Figure 6.5). While Isabelle inhabits different roles, helping or disturbing Anne's actions, Anne's gestures 'stumble on this obstacle, attempting to take up their

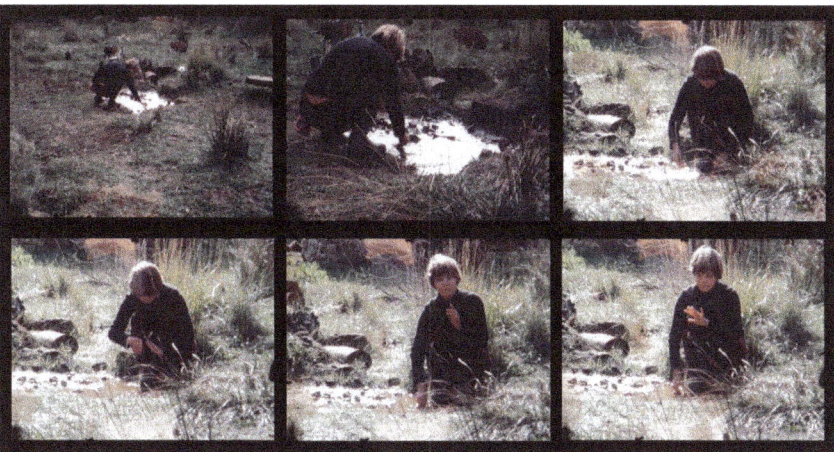

Figure 6.5 Anne in frames from super 8 rushes shot in the 1980s by Jacques Lin and Rose-Marie Ursenbacher, courtesy 'Ateliers de l'aire', Marina Vidal-Naquet and Martin Molina Gola

own line again', what Deligny refers to as *une ligne qui est ligne d'erre* – 'a line which is a wander line, a drift deriving from that *élan* where the other doesn't exist as other [. . .] Anne doesn't play' (2007: 1251). To discover the difference between the two girls' gestures, it is necessary to trace the line of demarcation within their apparent interaction. Deligny looks again and again; the scene reappears several times in his text, each time generating new insights.

The camera – crucially conceptualised by Deligny (2022) as a 'pedagogical tool' and thoroughly utilised in the Cévennes – returns virtually here, modelling Deligny's perspective on the scene, becoming part of his argument. In his text, it continues to serve as an analytical tool, providing a magnifying glass, a mediator of what Walter Benjamin (2002: 641) once called 'heightened vividness' (*erhöhte Anschaulichkeit*). The camera allowed Deligny to capture what otherwise remains imperceptible to the capacity of vision, and in so doing 'to discover in the analysis of the individual moment the crystal of the total event'. Repeatedly zooming into the scene, Deligny's text recovers a plurality of milieus within the same frame, the same scene, which coexist, one beside the other. 'Isabelle is very close to Anne', he writes. Theirs are the same gestures, but while Isabelle is able to sneak into different roles, Anne avoids the obstacles introduced by Isabelle; her 'automated but subtle gestures' make it difficult to say 'her gestures' (*ses gestes*), as Deligny (2007: 1252) puts it, in favour of an impersonal and intransitive mode: Anne's gestures are *those gestures* (*ces gestes*).

In *The Slightest Gesture*, several of these *minor gestures* appear. Indeed, they seem to be some sort of rite, as is the case, for example, with Yves's constant struggle to tie a knot. For Deligny, a gesture can be understood as a fundamentally intransitive act, an *infinitive* – that is, *to act* without finality or goal. What is the temporality of such acting, which necessarily revolves in endless detours? How to locate or inscribe its movement within the materially defined conditions? This question goes hand in hand with a genuine refusal of a *primal* or *authentic* gesture. Both image and gesture are a matter of construction, inasmuch as they participate in the act of their mediation, which becomes an infinite process, an intransitive *agir* rather than a teleological *faire* (Deligny 2007: 1252). Such is the premise for Deligny's associating the intransitive gestures of neurodiverse children with filming gestures, conceptualised via the French neologism *camérer*. Symptomatically, 'Mécréer', a text given the title of another such neologism – translated as 'Miscreating' – critically derives its origin from the verb *créer*, 'to create' (Deligny 2021: 76–95).[9] In it, Deligny analyses the parallels between 'autistic' gestures and filming gestures, revealing a crucial incommensurability between these and traditional forms of filmmaking, which also traverses *The Slightest Gesture* as a leitmotif. One of the film's central scenes can be read as a figuration for Deligny's understanding of neurodiversity or 'autism' and the use of film as an epistemic tool. Here the critique of the hero and his subordination of space and time, implied in the myth of Icarus, returns on the level of the cinematic plot. Deligny points out two events that happen simultaneously: two hands trying to knot a rope and a boy failing to climb out of a hole. Both scenes come to no end. While the tying of a knot stands for dramatic resolution, escaping from the hole delivers the matrix for a universal happy ending. But nothing happens. Instead, both actions idle in an infinite number of attempts. Deligny insists on the deceptive effect of such a scene, referring to his film's screening at the Cannes festival.

> Here one sees the difference between *camering* and making a film. The latter would be a question of providing the means with which to illuminate the pit so that one could follow the story and see the characters.
> Whereas with *camering*, the means are lacking, or nearly so [. . .]
> To show two hands that aren't able to tie a knot is, without fail, to disappoint. That is why one must first deprive oneself, if only of the intention of being successful, of fulfilling the audience. Those two hands fiddling with the two ends of rope don't mean much. (Deligny 2022)

Deligny alludes here not only to the interrelation between medium and milieu but also to that between medium and action: *minor gestures* are entangled with and require some sort of *minor media* able to follow them and their 'detours of acting'. Hence, following the gestures of the two boys, the process of filming cannot but participate in the logic of their movements. Deligny discovers here a double incommensurability: the length of the scene exceeds not only that of a classic drama, thereby deceiving the expectations of each potential viewer, but the boy's failing to tie a knot exceeds any economy of means, confronting Deligny with the sheer impossibility of filming the scene. At the same time, the excessive temporality of the action points to a stunning coexistence of *different milieus* within one frame, one field of vision. In the autistic person's 'wander line' or 'minor gesture', Deligny sees the necessity of filming, of making *those gestures* visible in their singularity. Here Deligny operates similarly to Soviet filmmakers such as Sergei Eisenstein, Esfir Shub, or Dziga Vertov, who worked with non-professional actors, the so-called *tipazh* (Figure 6.6), to reveal the irreducible marks of a particular social class.

In both cases, filming goes hand in hand with a crucial de-dramatisation and 'de-anecdotisation' of the action, to quote one of the key concepts that Eisenstein used in the 1920s to allude to this new mode of filmmaking. This cinema had to learn from the 'physiological quality of the detail', rather than from the shiny figure of the main actor. In this sense, Eisenstein argued for a general 'de-anecdotisation' of a particular case – a hero or a star – in favour of the intensity of a 'close-up', and 'the expression of the theme through a strong impact of the material'.[10] The material in Eisenstein's understanding can equally be opposed to the classical definition of portraiture and its exclusion of exteriority aiming at capturing an absolute subject. In contrast, *tipazh* inscribes a social

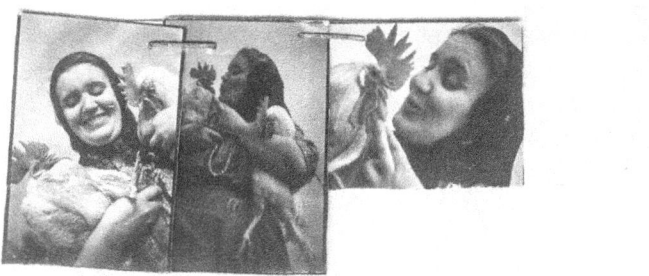

Figure 6.6 Casting card portraying non-professional actress (*tipazh*) for Sergei Eisenstein's film *Bezhin Meadow* (1935–37), Russian State Archive for Literature and Art, Moscow

relation emerging from the milieu, understood as a social environment on the one side, and from the singularity of expression of such type on the other. This is how Eisenstein argued for revealing the micro-drama of a gesture instead of the macro-drama of a happy ending, the singularity of a facial expression rather than the glamour of a character. This is a further meaning of *minor*, which comes close to Deligny's network in the Cévennes: a milieu where other – as yet non-visible – milieus can emerge.

In contrast to playing a role, such *acting* in and through film involves the milieu in a double sense: first, as a materially and historically produced *lieu*, a place with its particular structure, architecture, and temporality; and secondly, milieu as an extension of the intransitive action: as site of potentiality, a *lieu* of manifold coexisting *milieus* where Deligny sees a medium for new forms of collectivity. This understanding of cinema coincides with Eisenstein's claim for a cinema 'beyond the stars', a cinema operating with non-professional actors. Eisenstein's short text 'Beyond the Stars' (2002: 33), which ascribes its own meaning to the term *tipazh*, can be associated with Deligny's *minor gesture*. Eisenstein's ironically promotional text recommends releasing *Battleship Potemkin* in America, describing it as a 'film without stars'. 'The absence of "stars"', as Eisenstein writes, 'was a reason why attention within this work turned to countless cinematographic problems that ordinarily, under the conditions of the protagonists' "starlight" in other productions, invariably remain in the shadows' (2002: 33). That these 'cinematographic problems' need to be considered in terms of their political consequences – as problems of aesthetic figuration of a radical singularity – can likewise be understood as a central issue of Deligny's work.

The endless detours of the labyrinth addressed at the beginning of this chapter appear in this context not as the negative figure of an infinity to be overcome, but rather as a potentiality, a dialectical chance to recover the difference within the repetition. Detours of acting become synonymous with a mode of existence within a milieu and its simultaneous unity and multiplicity – a milieu of endless milieus.

Notes

1. I initiated this research on the role of *moindre geste* and milieu in Deligny's network and his theory of the image in the framework of a conference paper at ICI Berlin, presented together with Marlon Miguel. The present text takes up, reuses, and reframes ideas and arguments presented in Vogman 2022.

2. Slightly modified from the translation by Drew S. Burk and Catherine Porter (in Deligny 2015). In French Deligny makes use of two terms to allude to two different modalities of being: *l'humain* (the human) positively embraces the human in all its differences and singularities, including autism, while *l'homme-qui-nous-sommes* (the Man-that-we-are) refers rather critically to the humanist individual distinguished by rationality and carried by the teleology of progress.
3. This is how in his beautifully critical essay on surrealism Georges Bataille (1988: 38) relates the figure of Icarus with the project of the Enlightenment exempt of materialist inscription.
4. Quote taken from the intertitles to Lewin's film *Field Forces as Impediments for a Performance*, 1929.
5. Lewin first presented this research at the Third Medical Congress of Psychotherapy in 1929.
6. Lewin derives the term *Gestaltzerfall* from a study wherein repetition of a stimulus word induces its 'disintegration' (Weld and Don 1924).
7. In 'Mécréer' Deligny speaks of the adverb 'là' as referring to 'milieux et lieux repérables', a concrete locus of the network in Monoblet with its specific landscape and architecture.
8. See also 'Fossils Have a Hard Life: Apropos of the Image' in Deligny 2021 and 2022.
9. The text will be included in the English edition of *Camering*.
10. One of Eisenstein's answers to a questionnaire, published in a newspaper and later reprinted (Eisenstein 1968). See also Vogman 2019.

References

Bataille, Georges (1988), 'The "Old Mole" and the Prefix Sur in the Words *Surhomme* [Superman] and Surrealist', in Georges Bataille, *Visions of Excess: Selected Writings, 1927–39*, ed. Allan Stoekl, Minneapolis: University of Minnesota Press, pp. 32–44.

Benjamin, Walter (2002), *The Arcades Project*, ed. Rolf Tiedemann, Cambridge, MA: The Belknap Press of Harvard University Press.

Deligny, Fernand (2007), *Oeuvres*, Paris: L'Arachnéen.

Deligny, Fernand (2015), *The Arachnean and Other Texts*, Minneapolis, MN: Univocal Publishing.

Deligny, Fernand (2021), *Camérer. À propos d'images*, ed. Sandra Alvarez de Toledo, Anaïs Masson, Marlon Miguel, and Marina Vidal-Naquet, Paris: L'Arachnéen.

Deligny, Fernand (2022 forthcoming), *Camering: Fernand Deligny on Cinema and the Image*, ed. Marlon Miguel, trans. Sarah Moses, Leiden: Leiden University Press.

Eisenstein, Sergei (1968), 'Literatura i kino', in Sergei Eisenstein, *Izbrannye proizvedenia*, Vol. 5, Moscow: Isskustvo, pp. 525–9.

Eisenstein, Sergei (2002), *Metod*, vol. 1, ed. Naum Kleiman, Moscow: Muzei Kino.

Janmari, and Gisèle Durand (2013), *Journal de Janmari*, Paris: L'Arachnéen.

Johnstone, Fiona, and Kirstie Imber (2020), 'Introducing the Anti-Portrait', in Fiona Johnstone and Kirstie Imber (eds), *Anti-Portraiture: Challenging the Limits of the Portrait*, London: Bloomsbury, pp. 1–24.

Lewin, Kurt (1929), *Die Entwicklung der experimentellen Willenspsychologie und die Psychotherapie*, Leipzig: S. Hirzel.

Miguel, Marlon (2022), 'Introduction', in Fernand Deligny, *Camering: Fernand Deligny on Cinema and the Image*, ed. Marlon Miguel, trans. Sarah Moses, Leiden: Leiden University Press.

Nancy, Jean-Luc (2018), *Portrait*, trans. Sarah Clift and Simon Sparks, New York: Fordham University Press.

Vogman, Elena (2019), *Dance of Values. Sergei Eisenstein's Capital Project*, Zürich: Diaphanes.

Vogman, Elena (2022 forthcoming), 'Minor Gestures, Minor Media', in Fernand Deligny, *Camering: Fernand Deligny on Cinema and the Image*, ed. Marlon Miguel, trans. Sarah Moses, Leiden: Leiden University Press, pp. 239–50.

Weld, H. P., and V. J. Don (1924), 'Lapse of Meaning with Visual Fixation', *American Journal of Psychology*, 35(3): 446–50.

Woodall, Joanna (1997), 'Introduction: Facing the Subject', in Joanna Woodall (ed.), *Portraiture. Facing the Subject*, Manchester: Manchester University Press, pp. 1–32.

Chapter 7

Lifelike Portraits and 'Life Itself': Deepfakes through Gothic Horror

Nicole Morse

Offering a 'stark warning' about the dangers of false information (Rahim 2020), on Christmas Day 2020 the British public-service television network Channel 4 aired a speech purportedly by Queen Elizabeth II. The video begins relatively conventionally, only to culminate with the Queen on top of her desk as she records dance moves for the social networking site TikTok (Channel 4 2020a). Then the video glitches repeatedly to hint at the technical infrastructure that made this possible: digital face replacement facilitated by artificial intelligence. In other words, this video is a 'deepfake' – a neologism that describes the use of deep neural networks to create fake images. In behind-the-scenes videos released after the fact (Channel 4 2020b), the creators describe the project as top secret, reinforcing the idea (communicated by the video's narrative arc) that the video operated as a shocking exposé of technology's power to manipulate representation. Yet despite the video's structure and these assertions from the team who created it, the technological reveal at the video's conclusion did not actually expose the technical deceit. In fact, advance publicity about the video had described not only the technology employed but also each of the off-colour jokes about the royal family that the deepfake Queen would tell during the video's four-minute runtime (BBC 2020; Blackall 2020).[1] Perhaps the video's one remaining surprise might have been the close-up of the deepfake Queen's gyrating posterior, which was more titillating or laughable than revelatory. Instead of being startled, enlightened, and then chastened by this demonstration of technologically facilitated misinformation, spectators were experiencing something quite different: the delight of knowingly encountering new technology.

121

As a result, the video has a compromised status, for although it was supposedly intended as a warning about misinformation, it actually operates as a celebration of the technological apparatus that created it. In doing so, it is not unique – in the age of deepfakes, such celebrity-studded video warnings have proliferated. Some of the many examples of celebrities who have been featured in deepfake videos to warn about misinformation include Richard Nixon (Hall 2020), President Obama (BuzzFeedVideo 2018), and Mark Zuckerberg (bill_posters_uk 2019). By inviting audiences to appreciate false portraits that appear extremely realistic, they unintentionally reinforce the power and fascination of deepfakes. However, the deepfake Queen video not only cultivates awe in the face of technological advancements; simultaneously, it calms spectators' justifiable concerns through sexualised humour and objectification. The familiarity of misogynist humour shields the viewer from fully experiencing the disturbing possibilities of digital image manipulation.

Instead of being diffused through sexualised humour, the risks posed by new representational technologies require critical approaches that dwell with their potential for harm (in particular sexualised harm to feminised bodies) and demand accountability of spectators. Currently, the vast majority of deepfakes exist in online pornography, where the faces of female celebrities are combined with the bodies of female adult film actors. As media activist Sam Gregory notes (Blackall 2020), deepfakes are not yet common outside of pornography, and, as he put it in December 2020, responding to the deepfake Queen video, they have been primarily used 'to attack women'. In this way, most deepfakes are part of a larger troubling trend that legal scholars refer to as 'image-based sexual abuse'. The concept of image-based sexual abuse captures the wide range of image-based sexual harassment and violence that is often more colloquially described as 'revenge porn'. The basic definition of this form of sexual violence is 'the non-consensual creation and/or distribution of private sexual images' (McGlynn and Rackley 2017: 534), but it can be more broadly applied to 'a range of abusive behaviours beyond the familiar example of "revenge porn", such as "sexualised photoshopping", sexual extortion (often labelled as "sextortion"), "upskirting", voyeurism and many other similar forms of sexualised abuse' (McGlynn, Rackley, and Houghton 2017: 28). This broader definition captures the wide range of sexualised violence I discuss in this chapter, from portraits that kill the women they depict to deepfakes that use sexualisation to attack women.

To interrogate these dangers of deepfakes, I turn to fictional tales from the dawn of analogue photography and analyse how these

Gothic fictions about portraiture staged anxieties about lifelike representations of feminised bodies – long before artificial intelligence got involved in portraiture. In these nineteenth-century tales, the affective experience of horror is not merely an individually experienced emotion (Ahmed 2004), but instead a process of exchange between reader and text that deconstructs representational technologies in order to reveal how portraiture produces networked, intersubjective relationships between artists, models, images, viewers, and technology. Building on this framework, I develop a proposal for how discourse about the deepfake Queen could be rewritten as a Gothic horror story, one that grapples with deepfake technology as well as the spectator's responsibility in the face of its pleasures and harms.

Deepfake Gothic

The stories we tell about representational technologies are often about concerns over authorship, identity, subjectivity, knowledge, and representation – and portraiture intensifies all of these concerns. A portrait is manifestly not the person, and yet it may capture, contain, and re-present something of their personality, their weaknesses, even their fears. Indeed, this is the context for the infamous story of Graham Sutherland's portrait of Winston Churchill, which reportedly was so realistic in its depiction of the ageing statesman that it infuriated its model with its detailed revelations about his character and his health, and it was ultimately destroyed by his family (Black 2017: 154–70). A portrait is both object and, eerily, a separate body, threatening the subjecthood of the original. The image might know – and tell – something that the person does not fully acknowledge about themselves. This porous boundary between the thing and its image haunts stories about portraiture, especially lifelike portraits, threading them with a palpable mimetic anxiety. These discourses persist into the third decade of the twenty-first century, as many of our stories about digital technology are about how it threatens the distinction between reproduction and original. Open to apparently endless modifications and manipulations, digital technology does not merely offer human creators an immense power to transform images. Instead, artificial intelligence is poised to take over the act of image creation itself.

Deepfakes are photorealistic fictions that use digital face replacement, body compositing, and/or artificial intelligence to seamlessly combine and manipulate photographic originals in order to produce photorealistic images – often of people doing and saying things they did not actually do or say.[2] Obviously, that is the delight of the deep-fake Queen video, for it is impossible to imagine Queen Elizabeth openly discussing sex scandals involving the royal family or performing on TikTok, yet the image of her doing so is rather convincingly realistic. Instead of slipping into the 'uncanny valley', where digital representations of humans become stranger as they become increasingly realistic (Mori 1970), deepfakes produce a particular kind of pleasure by defying knowledgeable viewers to find such moments of failure. Deepfake portraits can be still images, but the deepfakes that are most fascinating – and threatening – are time-based media, particularly those that combine video and audio.

Since deepfakes are photorealistic representations that are not entirely dependent upon pro-filmic reality, they appear to sever the semiotic hierarchy that has long structured how we understand the relationship between image and referent. Yet this is not actually a new development; after all, older representational technologies do not necessarily transparently transmit the 'truths' of their referential objects either. Writing about the discourse around deepfakes for the non-profit research institute Data and Society, Britt Paris and Joan Donovan explain that 'what coverage of this deepfake phenomenon often misses is that the "truth" of audio-visual content has never been stable – truth is socially, politically, and culturally determined' (2019: 2). Nonetheless, discourse about deepfakes is often invested in presenting the problems they pose as wholly new.[3]

In doing so, such discourse emphasises technological achievement over the more mundane and persistent problem of image-based sexual abuse. As Gregory has pointed out on Twitter (2020), the discourse around the deepfake Queen focused on the popular idea that deepfake technology is overtaking reality, rather than truly interrogating the actual technical or political issues at stake, let alone how the video's sexualised humour relates to the sexual violence that deepfakes too often produce, such as in deepfake pornography. Yet this context shapes how Channel 4's representation of the Queen can be understood as well as its potential impact, for although the technology is new, portraiture's intimate relationship to the body and the gendered self is inflected by the stories we tell about the relationship between representation and real life. As John Berger writes (1977: 51), theories of portraiture have long been threaded through with male anxiety about controlling and containing female subjectivity. Portraiture entails confrontation; according to Linda Nochlin (2015: 86), portraiture 'demands the meeting of two subjectivities' of artist and subject, though I would contend that the viewer is also part of portraiture's intersubjective encounter. Thus, even when it seems to sidestep the issue of gender, discourse about deepfakes traverses long-standing gendered conceptions of how portraiture's fundamental intersubjectivity stages power and powerlessness, subjecthood and objecthood, the role of creator and the role of the image.

Since technological demonstrations such as the deepfake Queen reaffirm the power of technology, they produce an affective experience that is closer to amusement than horror, and as a result their critique of the technology is softened. By contrast, Gothic fictions about the power of lifelike photographic portraiture cultivate feelings of unease and fear while implicating the audience in the fictive horrors they depict – particularly through their treatment of patriarchal violence. From the eighteenth century to the present, Gothic fictions have interrogated the society out of which they emerge, rather than simply reproducing or remystifying social norms (Brown 2005: xii). Formal reflexivity contributes to the critical orientation of Gothic fiction (Smith 2000: 2). Indulging in the pleasures of horror, the Gothic explores tensions around fraught topics such as race, class, gender, and sexuality (Myrone and Frayling 2006: 18). According to Ellen Brinks (2003: 15), the central conflict of the Gothic occurs when male protagonists confront forces that strip those protagonists of phallic or patriarchal power. The theoretical or ideological implications of Gothic fiction are not necessarily unified or entirely coherent; Donna Heiland writes that 'Gothic fiction at its core is about transgressions of all sorts: across national boundaries, social boundaries, sexual boundaries, the boundaries of one's own identity' (2005: 11). As a result of this conjunction of themes, she argues that Gothic fictions are not necessarily feminist, but their exploration of the workings of patriarchy nonetheless analyses rather than naturalises misogyny. In these ways, Gothic stories about lifelike portraiture can provide a generic model that illuminates critical questions about deepfakes without reifying misogyny.

As analogue photography emerged in the nineteenth century, Edgar Allan Poe's 'The Oval Portrait' (1842) envisioned lifelike portraiture as vampiric, imagining that it consumed life itself. Other Gothic tales from the same period were similarly preoccupied by concerns about the way realistic portraiture might overtake reality. In these literary texts, Poe, Robert Browning, Nathaniel Hawthorne, and Oscar Wilde explored dark fantasies about portraiture's relationship to bodies, gender, sexuality, and control. Now in the twenty-first century, discourse about deepfakes must explore similar issues. The deepfake Queen does not fully realise its intended critique of misinformation, but it is possible to take it up as an invitation to examine urgent ethical, theoretical, and political questions about the portrayal of feminised bodies in digital representation.

First, it is critical to undo the mythologisation that positions digital image manipulation as entirely new, and instead to understand deepfakes as a dramatic acceleration of technological possibilities that were already available in analogue photography. It is a false dichotomy to imagine that analogue photography simply records the world, preserving the autonomy of its subjects, while digital photography presents the possibility of manipulating its referents. As Roland Barthes writes (2006: 80), analogue photography links its subjects and its viewers by transmitting light across time and space through technology, creating connections that he describes as one body reaching out to touch another. Metaphorically, then, photographic portraiture produces technologically mediated encounters that are as intimate as touch, and these encounters can make those represented in photographic portraiture vulnerable to image-based sexual abuse.[4] For Barthes, the medium that connects self to other in photography is light itself, which he describes as 'a skin I share with anyone who has been photographed' (2006: 80–1). Although it is anachronistic to apply Barthes's words to digital image-making, doing so supports an important corrective to the mythologisation of analogue photographic technology as uniquely bound to the intimate 'touch' of the indexical trace of light.[5] Following Barthes, then, I contend that across analogue and digital photographic portraiture, the 'shared skin' of technologically mediated light binds together the person represented, the photographer, and the viewer in a networked encounter that involves us in relationships that are open to harm, complicity, and accountability.

Second, it is important to recognise that the real risk posed by deepfakes is not merely that audiences will be duped, which is the explicit lesson of the deepfake Queen video and its ilk. Instead, one critical danger of deepfakes is that of image-based sexual abuse, which causes harm independently of, and in conjunction with, other forms of violence. With the deepfake Queen, the video actually reproduces this kind of violence when it uses sexualised humour to mock and undermine Queen Elizabeth; however worthy of critique she is, this particular mode reiterates misogynistic ideas about how power and control relate to bodies and sexuality. By contrast, the nineteenth-century fictions I analyse here provide a model of how to use genre tropes to interrogate these sexist dynamics (Hochberg 1991). In the video, sexualised objectification diffuses the real anxieties that viewers might otherwise experience, rather than actually allowing us to dwell within affects of fear and horrified awe. Conversely, Gothic horror produces an affective experience that compels us to confront the intimate, physical connection between lifelike portraiture, spectators, and reality. For these reasons, I contend that reading deepfakes through the genre of Gothic horror opens up a far more complex and rigorous critique than is available when viewers are merely tricked and/or titillated.

The Portrait as 'Life Itself'

The Gothic fictions I turn to as models for this critique were grappling with mimetic anxieties alongside the invention of analogue photography. Treating painting and proto-photographic processes as if they are photography, they explore concerns about the relationship between portraits and their referents. These tales trace our fascination with – and fear of – the dangerous connection between the representation of life and, as Poe writes, 'life itself' (2003: 204). In these works, including Poe's 'The Oval Portrait' (1842) and Hawthorne's 'The Birthmark' (1843), artists are able to control, manipulate, and/or transform the bodies of (feminised) others when they produce portraits that are so *lifelike* that they blur the distinction between the image of life and life itself. The two stories have such similar concerns about lifelike portraiture that Diane Price Herndl argues (1993: 87) that Hawthorne's tale was likely inspired by Poe's short story. Both writers were early adopters of daguerreotype technology, sitting for portraits in 1841 (Hawthorne) and 1843 (Poe) (Williams 2004: 15). Across fiction and non-fiction, the two authors' discussions of the technology 'helped to establish the terms in which those images [daguerreotypes/photographs] would be read' (Williams 2004: 16). In an 1839 letter, Hawthorne wrote that the advantage of the daguerreotype was its objective power to record, and added that 'such a record might also expose hidden truths' (Williams 2004: 17). Meanwhile, Poe wrote a short piece on daguerreotypes for *Alexander's Weekly Messenger* that was published on 15 January 1840, asserting that 'the consequences of any new scientific invention will, at the present day exceed, by very much, the wildest expectations of the most imaginative' (Ewer n.d.). In their stories, lifelike portraiture involves draining the light and colour from the original – evoking not only early photography's ability to transform the real world into black-and-white, but also the photographic process itself, wherein the rays of light that reflect off the photographed body do not only touch the spectator, as Barthes would have it, but are, in a sense, stolen away by the portrait, to then travel far beyond the portrait subject's control or even knowledge. Of course, it is important not to overlook the distinctions between painted portraiture, analogue photographic portraiture, digital portraiture, and portraiture created using artificial intelligence. Nonetheless, the haunting intimacy that allows us to sense that the 'real body, which was there' is connected somehow to the spectator, 'who [is] here' (Barthes 2006: 80) persists across these media – along with our felt sense that portraiture might make its subjects vulnerable.

In these nineteenth-century fictions that coincide with the emergence of analogue photography, lifelike portraiture does not merely represent living bodies, with the image remaining secondary to its referent. Instead, the lifelike portrait substitutes for or even destroys its subject in order to create visual pleasure for viewers – both for diegetic viewers within the fiction and for readers who identify with these fictive spectators. Thus, just as photography is being invented and popularised, these works imagine portraiture as an act of destruction instead of an act of creation. Through creating a portrait, an artist can control and alter the very body of another, with death instead of life as the ultimate result. Among their differences, each tale shares this broad narrative arc, culminating in the reader's uneasy dis/identification with the male protagonists. Through this fictional structure, these Gothic horror stories propel us to recognise how realistic portraiture produces the possibility for violence – within both representational and physical spheres. Nearly two centuries later, deepfakes demand a similarly rigorous examination of their relationship to violence and how this violence is intertwined with the kinds of spectatorial pleasure they produce. The genre tropes of Gothic fiction can construct an affective experience that supports such a reflexive critique of deepfakes. Ultimately, this critique requires spectators to interrogate how our pleasure is complicit with image-based sexual abuse.

The violent pleasures of the gaze are centred in Browning's Gothic dramatic monologue 'My Last Duchess' (1842), which aligns with other poems by Browning that explore the gendered power of photography to stop time and 'fix' or capture the image of a beautiful woman (Kreilkamp 2006: 420). The poem's speaker addresses an unnamed 'you' and invites the addressee to look at a painting that he rarely shows to others – a portrait of his late wife that is so excellently executed that 'There she stands / As if alive' (Browning 1994: 15). The lifelike quality of the portrait is central to the poem, which opens with the following introduction, including the first iteration of the description *as if* alive': 'That's my last Duchess painted on the wall, / Looking as if she were alive' (1994: 14). The fact that the image appears so lifelike is its appeal, for it offers the viewer access to the beauty of the late duchess without any of the vulnerability of actually relating to her. Through the dramatic monologue form, Browning constructs a seductively compelling yet duplicitous speaker whose bad faith and self-deception are slowly revealed to the reader (Shaw 1999: 439). The structure of the poem features interruptions that remind the reader of its interlocutory status (Maenhout 2007: 34), producing a complex experience of identification and disidentification (Gregory 2000: 498). As the speaker describes the circumstances of his last marriage, it becomes clear that he was jealous and suspicious of his late wife. Rather than ask her to behave differently, and to be less free with her smiles and her affection, he had her portrait painted and hung on the wall – and then he had her killed. Fixed in place, shrouded by a curtain that the speaker only occasionally withdraws, the duchess no longer threatens the speaker's masculinity and sense of pride now that she has been transformed into a lifelike portrait. As the speaker repeats, the painting presents the late duchess *as if* she were alive, with the distinction between life and representation, subject and object, reduced to this brief yet chilling phrase. Meanwhile, the poem's formal features implicate the reader in its violence. According to Melissa Valiska Gregory (2000: 496), the 'forced intimacy' of Browning's dramatic monologues interpolates an addressee who is unable to remain disinterested, since 'the rhetorical dynamics of his monologues, which metaphorically force themselves on their readers, parallel the dynamics of sexual violence'.

In Hawthorne's 'The Birthmark', the lifelike portrait functions as a kind of totemic substitute for the original, so that harm done to the image prefigures the demise of its subject. Rather than positioning the reader as an interlocutor through direct address, the third-person narration demands that the reader sit in judgement on the protagonist and weigh a variety of conflicting information. Critical opinion is sharply divided on the moral lesson of the story, pointing to its unresolved – and hence persistently troubling – depiction of intimate partner violence.[6] In Hawthorne's tale, female sexuality is threatening and signified by a birthmark on the otherwise perfect face of Georgiana, a young newlywed. An index of Georgiana's emotions, the birthmark blends into the rest of her skin when her face is flushed, and its power to evoke signs of arousal represents Georgiana's earthly imperfection. For her husband Aylmer, the birthmark is a sign of sin; although it attracts other, baser men, the birthmark so deeply disturbs the intellectual Aylmer that he becomes determined to remove it. Georgiana consents to this project because she can no longer bear to have her husband look at her face with such disgust. Over the course of extended scientific experimentation, which culminates when Aylmer serves Georgiana a chemical draught that removes the birthmark but simultaneously kills her, Aylmer amuses Georgiana with optical illusions and toys and then attempts to take a photographic portrait of her. However, Aylmer's scientific method of portraiture instead reproduces the blemishes of the original, and moreover, it is so 'blurred and indefinable' that Georgiana's birthmark is one of the few distinct features that are visible (Hawthorne 1954: 211). The lifelike portrait's fidelity to the original frustrates its creator, and his decision to destroy it foreshadows Georgiana's own death, encapsulating the ways that images operate as stand-ins for their referents. Dissolving the plate in acid, Aylmer turns to other methods to attempt to remove the birthmark from his wife's face, culminating with the chemical concoction that kills her. It is only when she is completely stilled in death, with all the colour – including the birthmark – drained from her face, that she finally embodies the perfection Aylmer desired. This ironic conclusion is open to multiple interpretations, including Judith Fetterley's reading that the story is hardly a tale of failure, but instead offers a 'demonstration of how to murder your wife and get away with it' (1978: 22). For Fetterley, the Gothic affect of horror is what invites the reader to understand that 'Hawthorne is writing a story about the sickness of men' (1978: 27).

Intimate partner violence is also central to Poe's 'The Oval Portrait', where the supernatural connection between the image of life and life itself exceeds the 'as if alive' of Browning's poem and the totemic substitution of Hawthorne's tale. Here, the portrait is linked to the body of the beloved through a reciprocal connection that is so strong that the portrait is able to absorb the life force of the woman it represents. As in 'The Birthmark', the flush of colour is drained from a young wife's face by her husband's attempt to perfect her – in this case, by transforming his beautiful bride, whose love and desire for him threaten his pure devotion to his art, into a painted portrait. Although it is possible to read the story as endorsing the artist's commitment to his art, Joan Dayan argues that Poe's use of irony, ambivalence, and exaggeration undercut such romantic idealisation and offer instead 'an exhumation of the lived, but disavowed or suppressed experiences of women in his society' (1993: 10). Along similar lines, Monika Elbert asserts that 'both Poe and Hawthorne [are] driven by a desire to get woman's story right, or at least to try to empower the hushed woman' (2004: 21). Although they ultimately use women's stories to examine their own concerns, 'Poe and Hawthorne were ahead of their time in deconstructing language' for feminist ends (Elbert 2004: 24).

Structured as a story-within-a-story, the wounded narrator of the framing story discovers an incredibly lifelike painting when he shelters in an abandoned chateau. This painting has a troubling history, and that story becomes the framed, central narrative. As recounted in a document that the narrator discovers near the portrait, this history involves a newlywed couple and the husband's desire to paint his bride, a desire to which she consents reluctantly. As the artist works on the portrait day after day, in a turret where 'the light dripped upon the pale canvas only from overhead' (Poe 2003: 203), his wife pines away, her life force being slowly transferred to the painting, a transformation that is signified by the draining of colour from her face to infuse the face in the image. Lost in his artistic reveries, the painter ultimately turns away from the portrait so rarely that he does not even notice his wife dying beside him as he works. Finally, as the painter puts the last touch to his work – which is, significantly, 'one tint upon the eye', a detail that suggests the threat of the look back – his wife dies. Crying out in sudden fear of his own creation, the painter exclaims, 'This is indeed Life itself!' (2003: 204). No longer merely 'as if alive', here the image achieves the 'ontological identity' between sign and referent that André Bazin (1967: 10) describes as central to the psychological and cultural impact of (early) photography.

'The Oval Portrait' is part of a larger body of Poe's work that is concerned with visual tricks and the act of seeing, work that was likely influenced by Poe's interest in optical illusions and developments in visual technology (Cantalupo 2005: 53). Meanwhile, through its narrative structure, 'The Oval Portrait' contributes to another dominant thread in Poe's stories: a thread that Debra Johanyak describes as a kind of proto-feminism that interrogates the gendered dynamics of intimate partner violence. By analysing the role of the narrator in several stories, Johanyak (1995: 63) shows how Poe's use of narrative structure produces a critique of misogynistic violence. Although Paula Kot notes that Poe leaves it up to the reader, who is implicitly male, to come to his own conclusions about how to interpret the pleasures of the story, she also argues that 'the structure of Poe's story undermines the very distinctions that the narrator and artist try to enforce' between 'subject and object, viewer and viewed, male and female, reality and art' (1995: 4). Reinforcing the importance of the story's formal structure, Robert N. Mollinger argues that '"The Oval Portrait" is set up in terms of a series that makes narrator, portrait, artist, and the author equivalent' (1979: 147). Responding to an emerging technology that creates remarkably lifelike representations, 'The Oval Portrait' challenges the reader to reflect on how this technology intersects with conceptions of control, authorship, and the gendered negotiation of power.

These fictions interrogate how lifelike portraits are imagined as granting their creators the power to contain and perfect the messiness of life through translating life itself into an image. Ultimately, these tales challenge the fantasy that lifelike image-making is the answer to the imperfections of life itself. Moreover, the moral resonance of each story is, in fact, a warning against attempting to use the image of life to control life itself. Critically, this moral message is possible *because* the tales depict lifelike portraiture as an ethically fraught project with tragic potential. Manifestly, however, this is not presented as a problem with the technology alone. As David Punter and Glennis Byron (2013: 278–9) note, Gothic horror often positions women as 'objectified victims' in order to explore themes of sexual violence and punish male protagonists for their transgressions. Thus, the men who use representational technology to control women and female sexuality seem to be the monsters or villains in these tales, and through the story-within-a-story structure, readers must engage 'multiple points of view' (Punter and Byron 2013: 278) and confront questions of our own complicity (2013: 289).

The Portrait as Network

Nearly fifty years after these three works were published, Oscar Wilde's *The Picture of Dorian Gray* (1890) explored the horror of the networked encounters that portraiture can produce by narrativising a bond between portrait and subject that is so intimate that energy, life force, violence, age, and sin can be exchanged fluidly between one and the other. Although this story is not about a heterosexual couple, the young, effeminate Dorian Gray is a feminised figure, controlled and harmed by more powerful men as he in turn visits harm on others who are more vulnerable than he. In Wilde's Faustian novel (Navarette 1997: 47), a portrait of Dorian is imbued with magical power. The portrait is able to capture and contain all of the signs of decadence, ageing, and sin that Dorian accumulates throughout a life perverted by the evil teachings of Lord Henry Wotton. As a result, Dorian himself appears never to age and seems unharmed by his degenerate and debauched lifestyle. After ruining many lives – and murdering Basil Hallward, the painter of his enchanted portrait – Dorian finally kills himself when he attempts to destroy the portrait with a knife. This narrative suggests that lifelike image-making might not only steal something from 'life itself', but that it directly puts the living body at risk through creating doubles[7] that could be exposed to harms that might recoil upon the portrait's original. Throughout the novel, the visible differences between Dorian and his portrait actually reveal the intimate connection – even the ontological identity – between the two, for everything that impacts Dorian's body leaves visible traces on the portrait. Moreover, since the painting constantly changes, it forces us to reconceive of the artwork as a process rather than an object, problematising any concept of 'passive reception' (Gillespie 1992: 20).

Inextricably linked to each other, Dorian and his portrait are also inescapably bound to the image's creator. In Wilde's novel, the vampiric relationship between the image of life and life itself is no longer confined to that dyad, but overtly involves the artist as well. Thus, in contrast to the earlier stories, the artist no longer assumes that he has the power to create without himself being transformed. When he refuses to exhibit the portrait, Basil explains that this decision is necessary because the painting reveals too much – not about Dorian, but about Basil. He tells Lord Henry (Wilde 2007: 9):

> Every portrait that is painted with feeling is a portrait of the artist, not of the sitter. The sitter is merely the accident, the occasion. It is not he who is revealed by the painter; it is rather the painter who, on the coloured canvas, reveals himself.

For Basil, it is not only that Dorian and the portrait share an ontological connection, but that he himself is also intertwined in this relation. There is a stark contrast here between the seemingly autonomous creators of Poe's and Hawthorne's stories and Basil's position, for he is explicitly affected by the web of intimate violence associated with the lifelike portrait.

In representing the permeable boundaries between the lifelike portrait and life itself, *The Picture of Dorian Gray* seems to anticipate how digital technology would accelerate the power of lifelike image-making to manipulate 'life itself'. Unlike the earlier literature, the portrait of Dorian Gray does not so much represent a double or doppelgänger but 'a more complex fragmentation of the subject' (Punter and Byron 2013: 41), an important theme within the Gothic as the genre explores the consequences of the scientific manipulation of human bodies (Punter and Byron 2013: 41–2). Where Poe and Hawthorne imagine a single (analogue) trajectory through which the lifelike image steals life force from life itself, in *The Picture of Dorian Gray* the fluid exchange between portrait and original makes possible continuous, infinitesimal alterations in the portrait. A telling example is the moment when the mouth changes so subtly that it is not even clear that the shape has been altered, but something is slightly – yet significantly – different (Wilde 2007: 76–7). This evokes the way that the digital image is uniquely characterised by the infinite separability of its elements, so that the kinds of control the digital image appears to make possible are similarly, seemingly infinite: 'All compositional elements', D. N. Rodowick writes, 'are discrete in a composite and, given the proper algorithm, can be changed or reversed at will: colours, angles, perspectives, positions of objects, and so on' (2007: 169). Obviously, this is part of what makes deep-fakes particularly threatening, since no element of pro-filmic reality seems to be able to resist the possibility of digital appropriation, modification, and transformation. Wilde's novel offers an imaginative account of this kind of networked vulnerability though its attention to the web of accumulated harm radiating outwards from (and recoiling back upon) the portrait. According to Gillespie (1992: 12), Wilde's novel 'eschews any move toward closure' through its structural reflexivity. In this way, it does not merely provide a myth that seems to reflect the reality we encounter today. Instead, through its meta-critical attention to spectatorship, *The Picture of Dorian Gray* reminds us that audiences, spectators, and witnesses are intimately bound up in the networked relationships that portraits produce.

The Picture of Dorian Gray is fundamentally concerned with the profound and violent effects people have on each other. The network of interpersonal violence generated by the portrait not only impacts its creator, but also appears in the dynamics of personal influence that the novel describes, and finally, in the way the spectator of the painting as well as the reader of the novel are also implicated in this web. For Basil, the influence Dorian has on him transforms his ability to create, such that the artist is no longer represented as autonomous and independent. Lord Henry describes his plan to exercise influence over Dorian through metaphors of music- and perfume-making; through these metaphors, Dorian himself 'becomes a piece of self-reflexive art' created by Lord Henry through the use of a dangerously compelling book (Robillard 1989: 33). Within the novel, then, literature is imagined as having the power to transform its reader, for good or ill. Thus, the web of influence implicitly extends outwards to ensnare audiences – both the spectators of the portrait of Dorian Gray and the readers of *The Picture of Dorian Gray*. Furthermore, in the preface, Wilde makes the work's investment in the spectator clear when he claims that 'it is the spectator, and not life, that art really mirrors' (Wilde 2007: 4).

The idea that art mirrors the spectator, and does not transparently capture 'life itself', is particularly provocative in the context of a novel that presents reflexivity as an intersubjective relationship involving influence, transformation, and violence. Wilde's preface suggests that the spectator does not merely observe the correspondence between portrait and subject, but that instead the spectatorial relationship is implicated in the boundary violations that emerge out of lifelike image-making. Highlighting spectatorial complicity, the novel offers a moral critique of the detached observer who can consume the pain of others as an aesthetic experience (Robillard 1989: 34–5). This interest in the spectator's role is not absent from the earlier works I described. Both Browning's poem and Poe's short story are stories nested within stories. As such, the framing devices draw attention to how the spectator is connected to the networks of intimacy, vulnerability, and permeable boundaries that lifelike portraiture seems to generate. Across these nineteenth-century works, lifelike portraiture breaks down the boundaries between the image, its referent, the creator, and the spectator, producing networks of interpersonal intimacy, vulnerability, and violence that do not merely speak to the mimetic anxieties generated by new representational technologies. Instead, they ask us to consider our own accountability to each other in the face of image-based sexual abuse.

The Deepfake Queen as Gothic Horror

Although photography has always been open to manipulation and modification, the accessibility of digital technologies puts spectators in a new relationship to the image. After all, the spectator is, in many senses, no longer in a purely spectatorial position, given that tools from television remotes to non-linear editing software grant spectators certain novel kinds of control over the image (Rodowick 2007: 166). Even the technology that makes deepfakes possible is increasingly accessible, with dozens of free programs and smartphone apps coming on the market in 2020, while the technology used to create so-called 'cheap fakes' was already widely available (Paris and Donovan 2019: 11–12). Nonetheless, discourse about deepfakes imagines that the spectator is subjected to a regime of deceit, constantly at risk of being fooled by the awesome power of artificial intelligence and image-manipulation technology. Ironically, in many cases these discourses are actually addressed to knowledgeable spectators, and part of the pleasure comes from imagining that someone else, but definitely not oneself, is being duped. The deepfake Queen is part of this discourse, one of many examples where deepfake celebrity parodies are used to encourage unwitting spectators to be more cautious and media-literate. But inviting spectators to be fooled – or, perhaps more accurately, amused and delighted – by the power of the technology obfuscates the harm it actually produces (Paris and Donovan 2019: 8).

Rewriting the discourse about the deepfake Queen video as a Gothic tale about human responsibility rather than technical wizardry would transform its critique and its impact – and its scope. After all, it was a full century and a half before deepfake pornography (and its particular kind of image-based sexual abuse) that these nineteenth-century literary texts imagined lifelike image-making technology being used by men seeking to control women, female sexuality, and feminised people. But in these tales that is not the end of the story. Implicating audiences, spectators, and witnesses, these tales feature narrative structures which address audiences and interlocutors in order to interrogate misogyny. A Gothic account of deepfake technology could explore the many ways sexism shapes the interactions between lifelike digital portraits and living bodies, including how digitally filtered selfies can trigger body dysmorphia (Rajanala, Maymone, and Vashi 2018).

Producing a reading of the deepfake Queen video that functions as a Gothic horror story would require a consideration of what motivated the scriptwriters, director, cast, and crew, but not simply in order to criticise their decisions. Instead, they would be tragically flawed characters, and the story would reveal how their hubristic effort to educate the public by transforming a standard celebrity impersonation into a seamlessly realistic digital puppet became instead a practice of sexist humiliation. The moral lesson of this tale might be how idealistic intentions can be thoroughly entangled within toxic ideologies. Even more crucially, the Gothic horror account of the deepfake Queen would demand more of spectators than a willingness to allow ourselves to be knowingly tricked. Instead, it would ask us to grapple with the way misogyny distorts and twists a necessary critique of the monarch and monarchy. It would confront us with our own complicity by interrogating our desire to see a photorealistic representation of the Queen humiliated, and it would ask us to consider how our pleasure is caught up in a system that disproportionately harms women and femmes with far less power than the Queen. Our myths and fictions have long made clear that there is something that seems frightening and dangerous about portraiture, especially realistic portraits. From haunting stories about doppelgängers to the Gothic fictions I have analysed here, lifelike images of real people are not simply eerie. They speak to our knowledge that image-based violence can be profoundly intertwined with other forms of harm.

It is not that the technology is absent from my Gothic retelling of the deepfake Queen. After all, it is important for us to understand how artificial intelligence is being used to create realistic images. However, the Gothic horror version of this tale does not venerate the technology, does not treat it as an autonomous agent, and does not imagine that the technology determines how humans will use it. Instead, Gothic genre tropes expose the all-too-human agency behind the ghosts, the spectres, and the seemingly magical technologies that haunt us. The affective experience of horror does not blunt our fear but solicits our engagement. In a vision of the world inflected by Gothic horror, human action and social structures are ultimately responsible for the harmful ways in which technologies are employed – and therefore, it is possible for us to develop strategies for living responsibly with these technologies.

Notes

1. Additionally, Channel 4 shared a 52-second clip of the video on Twitter on 23 December 2020 (https://twitter.com/Channel4/status/1341858620368142338).
2. As a term, 'deepfake' has quickly entered into discourse without always referring to media produced with these new, advanced technologies. Interestingly, and significantly, the deepfake Queen was not wholly created through deepfake techniques, for although deep neural networks can be used to construct realistic-sounding voices saying things that the original person would never say, in this case the voice is simply an imitation of the Queen by actor Debra Stephenson, who has used the same voice to impersonate the Queen in other contexts. It might seem that the video is a 'fake' deepfake, but this practice of using human impersonators' voices rather than voices produced by deep neural networks is common in celebrity deepfake videos (see, for example, Jordan Peele's performance as President Obama (BuzzFeedVideo 2018)).
3. Some examples of this kind of discourse of newness and danger include headlines such as 'Deepfakes are Going to Wreak Havoc on Society. We are not Prepared', subheadings like 'When Seeing is not Believing', and dramatic statements that describe deepfake technology as 'an important and dangerous new phenomenon' (Toews 2020). Another example features the headline 'Deepfakes are the most dangerous crime of the future, researchers say', positioning image manipulation as a futuristic phenomenon rather than as a long-standing practice with social and cultural implications (Smith 2020). Even in discussions of deepfake technology that acknowledge the long history of image manipulation, the emphasis is on the newness and danger of new technology rather than on how long-standing strategies to combat image manipulation

might be deployed in this moment (Eadicicco 2019). For more balanced discussion of methods for detecting deepfake videos, see Lyu 2020.

4. Tom Gunning (2001: 92) describes how the invention of instantaneous photography threatened the stability of the bourgeois self by exposing awkward and embarrassing chance poses and bodily movements unsuspected before the advent of the new technology.

5. Gunning (2008: 25) argues that the claim that digital technologies sever the indexical connection between sign and referent depends upon an inaccurate understanding of analogue photography as 'a transparent process', rather than its own form of technological mediation of light. Along related lines, Jose van Dijck (2008) writes that, although digital technologies shift the emphasis in photography's function from a technology of memory (in which the indexical connection between sign and referent is paramount) to a technology of communication (in which processes of circulation are central), this is a shift in the balance between these two tendencies, rather than a total transformation of photography.

6. For those critics who believe the story condemns the protagonist, some see its moral lesson as being focused on the error of obsessive hubris (Rucker 1987; Williams 2004: 17) while others identify violent misogyny as the protagonist's key transgression (Bromell 1990; Fetterley 1978). Across the texts cited here, references are made to a third approach which – far from condemning the protagonist – valorises his attempt to perfect nature and surpass the reproductive/creative capacities of women.

7. As Michael Patrick Gillespie (1992: 15) writes, there is not just one double of Dorian in the novel, for 'a number of pictures of Dorian Gray come to mind: composed by Basil Hallward, by Lord Henry, by Dorian himself, and by the reader'.

References

Ahmed, Sara (2004), 'Affective Economies', *Social Text*, 22(2): 119–39.

Barthes, Roland (2006), *Camera Lucida: Reflections on Photography*, trans. Richard Howard, New York: Hill and Wang.

Bazin, André (1967), *What is Cinema? I*, trans. Hugh Gray, Berkeley: University of California Press.

BBC (2020), 'Deepfake Queen to Deliver Channel 4 Christmas Message', 23 December, https://www.bbc.com/news/technology-55424730 (last accessed 8 March 2022).

Berger, John (1977), *Ways of Seeing*, London: Penguin.

bill_posters_uk (2019), Instagram post, https://www.instagram.com/p/BypkGIvFfGZ (last accessed 8 March 2022).

Black, Jonathan (2017), *Winston Churchill in British Art, 1900 to the Present Day: The Titan with Many Faces*, New York: Bloomsbury.

Blackall, Molly (2020), 'Channel 4 Under Fire for Deepfake Queen's Christmas Message', *The Guardian*, 24 December, https://www.theguardian.com/technology/2020/dec/24/channel-4-under-fire-for-deepfake-queen-christmas-message (last accessed 8 March 2022).

Brinks, Ellen (2003), *Gothic Masculinity: Effeminacy and the Supernatural in English and German Romanticism*, Lewisburg, PA: Bucknell University Press.

Bromell, Nicholas K. (1990), '"The Bloody Hand" of Labour: Work, Class, and Gender in Three Stories by Hawthorne', *American Quarterly*, 42(4): 542–64.

Brown, Marshall (2005), *The Gothic Text*, Stanford, CA: Stanford University Press.

Browning, Robert (1994), *Selected Poems*, New York: Gramercy Books.

BuzzFeedVideo (2018), 'You Won't Believe What Obama Says in This Video!', https://www.youtube.com/watch?v=cQ54GDm1eL0 (last accessed 8 March 2022).

Cantalupo, Barbara (2005), 'Poe's Visual Tricks', *Poe Studies/Dark Romanticism*, 38: 53–63.

Channel 4 (2020a), 'Deepfake Queen: 2020 Alternative Christmas Message', https://youtu.be/IvY-Abd2FfM (last accessed 8 March 2022).

Channel 4 (2020b), 'Deepfake Queen: The Making of our 2020 Christmas Message', https://youtu.be/alc6R_UfPkc (last accessed 8 March 2022).

Dayan, Joan (1993), 'Poe's Women: A Feminist Poe?', *Poe Studies/Dark Romanticism*, 26(1/2): 1–12.

Eadicicco, Lisa (2019), 'There's a Terrifying Trend on the Internet that Could be Used to Ruin Your Reputation, and No One Knows how to Stop It', *Business Insider*, 10 July, https://www.businessinsider.com/dangerous-deepfake-technology-spreading-cannot-be-stopped-2019-7 (last accessed 8 March 2022).

Elbert, Monika (2004), 'Poe and Hawthorne as Women's Amanuenses', *Poe Studies/Dark Romanticism*, 37: 21–7.

Ewer, Gary W. (ed.) (n.d.), *The Daguerreotype: An Archive of Source Texts, Graphics, and Ephemera*, http://www.daguerreotypearchive.org (last accessed 8 March 2022).

Fetterley, Judith (1978), 'Women Beware Science: "The Birthmark"', in Judith Fetterley, *The Resisting Reader: A Feminist Approach to American Fiction*, Bloomington: Indiana University Press, pp. 22–33.

Gillespie, Michael Patrick (1992), 'Picturing Dorian Gray: Resistant Readings in Wilde's Novel', *English Literature in Transition, 1880–1920*, 35(1): 7–25.

Gregory, Melissa Valiska (2000), 'Robert Browning and the Lure of the Violent Lyric Voice: Domestic Violence and the Dramatic Monologue', *Victorian Poetry*, 38(4): 491–510.

Gregory, Sam (2020), Twitter thread, https://twitter.com/SamGregory/status/134213661757481369> (last accessed 8 March 2022).

Gunning, Tom (2001), 'New Thresholds of Vision: Instantaneous Photography and the Early Cinema of Lumière', in Terry Smith (ed.), *Impossible Presence: Surface and Screen in the Photogenic Era*, Chicago: University of Chicago Press, pp. 71–100.

Gunning, Tom (2008), 'What's the Point of an Index? or, Faking Photographs', in Karen Beckman and Jean Ma (eds), *Still Moving: Between Cinema and Photography*, Durham, NC: Duke University Press, pp. 23–40.

Hall, Louise (2020), 'Deepfake Footage of Nixon Reading Apollo "Disaster" Speech Highlights Misinformation Dangers', *The Independent*, 20 July, http://www.independent.co.uk/news/world/americas/nixon-deepfake -moon-landing-footage-video-moon-disaster-media-misinformation- a9629376.html (last accessed 8 March 2022).

Hawthorne, Nathaniel (1954), *Selected Tales and Sketches*, New York: Rinehart.

Heiland, Donna (2005), *Gothic and Gender: An Introduction*, Malden, MA: Blackwell.

Herndl, Diana Price (1993), *Invalid Women: Figuring Feminine Illness in American Fiction and Culture, 1840–1940*, Chapel Hill: University of North Carolina Press.

Hochberg, Shifra (1991), 'Male Authority and Female Subversion in Browning's "My Last Duchess"', *Lit: Literature Interpretation Theory*, 3: 77–84.

Johanyak, Debra (1995), 'Poesian Feminism: Triumph or Tragedy', *CLA Journal*, 39(1): 62–70.

Kot, Paula (1995), 'Painful Erasures: Excising the Wild Eye from "The Oval Portrait"', *Poe Studies/Dark Romanticism*, 28(1–2): 1–6.

Kreilkamp, Ivan (2006), '"One More Picture": Robert Browning's Optical Unconscious', *ELH*, 73(2): 409–35.

Lyu, Siwei (2020), 'Deepfakes and the New AI-Generated Fake Media Creation-Detection Arms Race', *Scientific American*, 20 July, https://www.scientificamerican.com/article/detecting-deepfakes1 (last accessed 8 March 2022).

Maenhout, Freya (2007), 'Gender Relations in Robert Browning's Dramatic Monologues', dissertation, Ghent University.

McGlynn, Clare, and Erika Rackley (2017), 'Image-Based Sexual Abuse', *Oxford Journal of Legal Studies*, 37(3): 534–61.

McGlynn, Clare, Erika Rackley, and Ruth Houghton (2017), 'Beyond "Revenge Porn": The Continuum of Image-Based Sexual Abuse', *Feminist Legal Studies*, 25: 25–46.

Mollinger, Robert N. (1979), 'Edgar Allan Poe's "The Oval Portrait": Fusion of Multiple Identities', *American Imago*, 36(2): 147–53.

Mori, Masahiro (1970), 'The Uncanny Valley', *Energy* 7(4): 33–5, trans. Karl F. MacDorman and Norri Kageki, https://web.ics.purdue.edu/~drkelly/MoriTheUncannyValley1970.pdf (last accessed 30 March 2021).

Myrone, Martin, and Christopher Frayling (2006), *The Gothic Reader: A Critical Anthology*, London: Tate.

Navarette, Susan Jennifer (1997), *The Shape of Fear: Horror and the Fin de Siècle Culture of Decadence*, Lexington: University Press of Kentucky.

Nochlin, Linda (2015), 'Some Women Realists', in *Women Artists: The Linda Nochlin Reader*, ed. Maura Reilly, London: Thames and Hudson.

Paris, Britt, and Joan Donovan (2019), 'Deepfakes and Cheap Fakes', *Data & Society*, https://datasociety.net/library/deepfakes-and-cheap-fakes (last accessed 8 March 2022).

Poe, Edgar Allan (2003), *The Fall of the House of Usher*, New York: Penguin.

Punter, David, and Glennis Byron (2013), *The Gothic*, Malden, MA: Blackwell.

Rahim, Zamira (2020), '"Deepfake" Queen Delivers Alternative Christmas Speech, in Warning about Misinformation', https://www.cnn.com/2020/12/25/uk/deepfake-queen-speech-christmas-intl-gbr/index.html (last accessed 8 March 2022).

Rajanala, Susruthi, Mayra B. C. Maymone, and Neelam A. Vashi (2018), 'Selfies – Living in the Era of Filtered Photographs', *JAMA Facial Plastic Surgery*, 20(6): 443–4.

Robillard Jr, Douglas (1989), 'Self-Reflexive Art and Wilde's *The Picture of Dorian Gray*', *Essays in Arts and Sciences*, 18: 29–38.

Rodowick, D. N. (2007), *The Virtual Life of Film*, Cambridge, MA: Harvard University Press.

Rucker, Mary E. (1987), 'Science and Art in Hawthorne's "The Birth-Mark"', *Nineteenth-Century Literature*, 41(4): 445–61.

Shaw, W. David (1999), 'Masks of the Unconscious: Bad Faith and Casuistry in the Dramatic Monologue', *ELH*, 66(2): 439–60.

Smith, Adam (2020), 'Deepfakes are the Most Dangerous Crime of the Future, Researchers Say', *The Independent*, 5 August, https://www.independent.co.uk/life-style/gadgets-and-tech/news/deepfakes-dangerous-crime-artificial-intelligence-a9655821.html (last accessed 8 March 2022).

Smith, Andrew (2000), *Gothic Radicalism: Literature, Philosophy and Psychoanalysis in the 19th Century*, Basingstoke: Macmillan.

Toews, Rob (2020), 'Deepfakes are Going to Wreak Havoc on Society. We are Not Prepared', *Forbes*, 25 May, https://www.forbes.com/sites/robtoews/2020/05/25/deepfakes-are-going-to-wreak-havoc-on-society-we-are-not-prepared (last accessed 8 March 2022).

Van Dijck, Jose (2008), 'Digital Photography: Communication, Identity, Memory', *Visual Communication*, 7(1): 57–76.

Wilde, Oscar (2007 [1890]), *The Picture of Dorian Gray*, ed. Michael Patrick Gillespie, New York: W. W. Norton.

Williams, Susan S. (2004), 'Daguerreotyping Hawthorne and Poe', *Poe Studies*, 37(1/2): 13–20.

Chapter 8

Animal Portraits in Social Media: A Case Study Named Esther

Elisa Aaltola

Esther is a pig. In 2012 a Canadian couple, Steve Jenkins and Derek Walter, adopted her as a micro-pig. However, she grew to 650 pounds, clearly beyond the limits of the word 'micro'. Esther's aliveness is a form of defiance against the anthropocentric norms that tend to dictate the social status and treatment of non-human animals. That defiance stems both from her own agency (her moment-to-moment focus on living), and the agency of her caretakers, who have sought to use portraits of Esther as a method of contesting the above norms.

Jenkins and Walter decided to keep her regardless of her hefty size, and began recording their coexistence with Esther via social media. In just a couple of years, Esther had become a piggy celebrity, and she has been featured in major media outlets around the world – further, a handful of books detailing her life and constructing her story have appeared, including the bestseller *Esther the Wonder Pig: Changing the World One Heart at a Time* (2017).[1] Moreover, she has become a famed figure on social media. By early 2021 Esther had around 1.5 million followers on Facebook, and around 610,000 followers on Instagram. Esther's social media accounts usually consist of pictures of Esther, accompanied by captions. They comprise of daily portraits of Esther, which collectively form what I call *a meta-portrait* – each specific, daily portrait adds to a grander construction of a character called 'Esther the Wonderpig' (to be separated from the tangible, living pig called Esther). The aim of this chapter is to explore the following question: what do portraits of Esther tell us about cultural depictions of animals?

In answering this question, I approach Esther the Wonderpig as a human creation that expresses some and contests other cultural presumptions concerning other (that is, non-human) animals. More particularly, I will interrogate the tensions between humanisation and alterity, construction and essentialism, contact and distance, and humour and severity as the foundation on which Esther the Wonderpig unashamedly roams.

Esther in the Portrait Gallery

Portraits of non-human animals are not a novelty. Cave paintings stand as the classic example of animals in art, and arguably serve as the ancestors of animal portraiture. Another example of historical animal portraiture are the animal masks of indigenous cultures, which – along with the cave paintings – have been depicted as a route to making sense of animality (Toadvine 2014). Animal portraits have been present also in more recent history. In the West, animals frequently feature in human portraits (such as Leonardo da Vinci's *Lady with an Ermine* from 1490, and Jean-Baptiste Perronneau's *A Girl with a Kitten* from 1743). The early modern period became increasingly eager to include companion animals in particular in human portraits, usually as metaphors of obedience (Thomas 1983: 100–10). Moreover, portraits focused on individual animals without a human presence have made their way into the art world, with painters such as Edwin Landseer specialising in animal portraits. In sum, animal portraits are found in different cultures and historical periods – arguably, the urge to portray other animals is a relatively common feature of what it means to be a human animal.

Recent examples of animal portraiture can be found in photography books, including Andrew Zuckerman's *Creature* (2008), Sharon Montrose's *Menagerie* (2011), Mark Laita's *Sea* (2011), Randal Ford's *Animal Kingdom: A Collection of Portraits* (2018), Isa Leshko's *Allowed to Grow Old: Portraits of Elderly Animals from Farm Sanctuaries* (2019), and collections of undercover footage such as *We Animals* (2013) and *HIDDEN: Animals in the Anthropocene* (2020) featuring, among others, the photography of Jo-Anne McArthur. In the above works, portraits tend to fall into two broad categories: portraits of still animals often facing the camera (what I here call *humanising portraits*), and portraits of moving or aloof animals focused on doing their own thing (what I call *alterity portraits*). In the first category, textual references to human portraits are ample, as dogs and baboons seem to be posing for the camera, with often humanising results. In the second category, the animals' alterity and non-human specificity are more evident, as they jump, run, swim, fly, or simply stay still in ways inaccessible to humans, thereby manifesting their intricate agency.

I suggest that this duality, and the tension it contains, forms one pivotal aspect of the genre of animal portraiture.

How does Esther the Wonderpig fit into all of this? The oldest known cave painting dates back 45,000 years and was found in Indonesia – intriguingly, it is a depiction of a wild pig (Agence France-Presse 2021). Esther the Wonderpig can thus be viewed as nothing less than its descendant from the age of industrial agriculture and social media. With 45,000 years between them, one depiction consists of a wild pig painted on a cave wall, and the other consists of a farmed pig turned into a companion animal, whose images are posted on virtual platforms. Thus, Esther the Wonderpig brings cave painting to the contemporary era, and is arguably a product of the same human desire to make sense of the non-human realm via portraiture.

At first glance, portraits of Esther appear to follow the category of humanising portraits. She lives in a human environment and is placed in a human locale with props, edits, and backdrops, and thus she is separated from her natural environment and conspecifics (Figure 8.1). Moreover, she is often pictured from the front, with a focus on her face; she appears to speak in human language (and indeed to have mastered the art of writing her own captions); and she is frequently dressed in human clothes, which all come with a humanised effect. Yet Esther is also boisterous, and portraits of her highlight her alterity. Her body particularly often conflicts with humanising

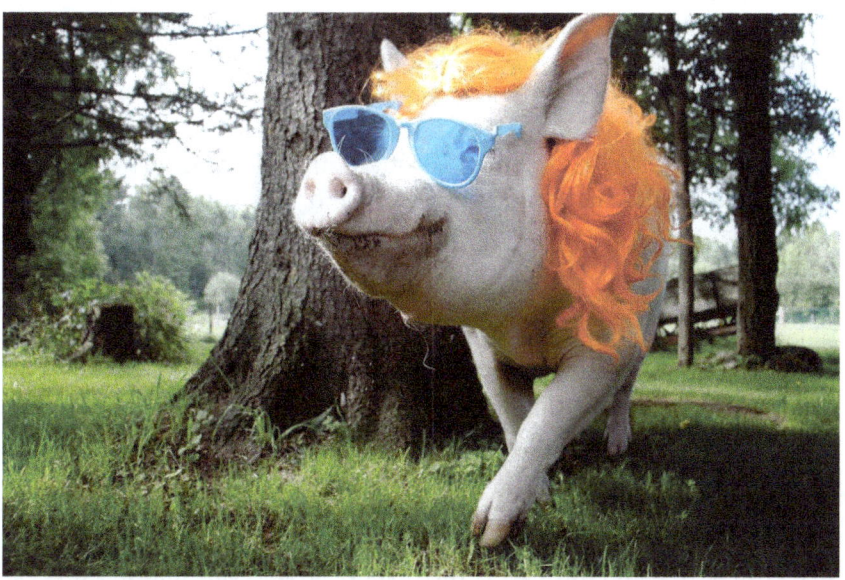

Figure 8.1 Esther, photograph courtesy of Derek Walter and Steve Jenkins

expectation. Polite society and human etiquette are chased away with images of Esther drooling without shame and eating with her mouth wide open, while keeping her striking, colossal, non-human body on full display. Suddenly, as she emerges as a non-human agent unwilling to submit to human rule, we witness her *susness*, her particularity as an animal other – although Esther the Wonderpig is an anthropogenic construction, its content can remind us of the distinctiveness of non-human existence. In such moments, Esther the Wonderpig is contesting the humanised standards of portraiture, and instead follows the category of alterity portraits by depicting a boisterous animal subject doing her own thing.[2]

Further, Esther the Wonderpig contests a given non-human identity, namely 'the cute animal' met in cat videos and social media snapshots of adorable critters (usually companion animals) doing 'funny things'. 'The cute animal' packages non-human creatures into the formula of neotenic appeal (Aaltola 2021), and thereby offers us passive, infant-like animals, which are safe in their apparent lack of mature agency. Cute, neotenic portrayals of animality often follow the rules of the anthropocentric order. Passive, cute, helpless animals doing clumsy things offer us an infantilised animal, with layers of humanised content and little trace of adult, non-human agency. Here, the hierarchies embedded in the anthropocentric worldview are fortified, as the non-human realm is reduced to a collective infant, which needs human beings as its adult ruler. It is because of this that anthropomorphic animal portraits, when they follow the standards of cuteness, can happily intertwine with anthropocentrism and the ruthlessness of animal industries. Thus, one can get a Bambi or a Babe toy with a McMeal, and kids learn to love cute piglets while eating their flesh. As a result, Western attitudes to animals struggle with what has been termed as 'the meat paradox' (Loughnan, Bastian, and Haslam 2014) – a dissonant state, in which one both loves and eats the objects of one's love. Portraits of cute animals are here to offer us positive affect and entertainment, not to contest our treatment of the cute animals' kin.

Esther the Wonderpig rebels against the expectations of cuteness placed on other animals. She is not cute nor adorable, but physically large, defiant, unexpected, and unruly. She is rebellious against human expectation – she does not obey the anthropocentric decree, which only affords space for animals who know their passive place, but instead bids her audiences to recognise adult animal agents with fully grown bodies and independent minds. Indeed, transgressing the identity-dichotomy usually forced upon domestic non-human animals (be cute or be unseen) is intrinsic to Esther the Wonderpig. She was the cute, pink piglet, a presumed micro-pig, who followed the neotenic conjecture. Then she grew into a rebellious adult pig, who despite her non-adorability fills social media spaces and lures audiences into witnessing her: Esther literally grew out of the cuteness-mould (she seems to tear and chew right through it) and yet portraits of her demand to be seen.

In sum, the contemporary cousin of the cave painting, Esther the Wonderpig, manifests the tension between humanised, pacified animality, which among domesticated animals often follows the formula of neotenic cuteness, and unruly non-human otherness. Indeed, portraits of Esther are built on this tension between humanisation and alterity.

The Non-human Face

The face is often presumed to act as a place of expression, wherein the individual reveals her inner nature. Here, the face communicates our emotions, needs, thoughts, and intentions – more broadly, it reveals our essence to others (Jirsa and Rosenberg 2019). This forms one path to making sense of Esther the Wonderpig. Can her face, and more broadly portraits of her, be read as a site that reveals her inner nature?

Studies show that, like many non-human animals, pigs are distinctly intelligent beings, capable of complex social behaviour, affective and emotive ability, conscious intent, memory, learning, grasping time (including the existence of future time), and even self-awareness (Marino and Colvin 2015). Following Thomas Nagel's depiction of consciousness, wherein the relevant factor is one's ability to feel one's existence *as* something (1974), that is, to have 'qualia', pigs are clearly conscious creatures. It is *like something* to be Esther, as she navigates through her world on the basis of numerous advanced cognitive abilities. If one ties phenomenal consciousness and subjectivity together (Midgley 1983), Esther is *a someone*, rather than a thing, a subject rather than a mere object, and from this perspective, her face and portraits of her appear as expressions of her internal realms, her subjectivity. Within this reading, when looking at images of Esther, one is glimpsing the mental landscape of one specific member of *Sus*. Here, 'the face' can include any bodily facets which communicate subjectivity. Of course, there are differences in how animal facial expressions are interpreted and the risk of projection is evident (Pico and Gadea 2021). Yet there is considerable evidence that animal expressions do communicate emotions and other mental states (Parr et al. 2007; Goossens et al. 2008; Wathan et al. 2016), and that animals can actively use them in order to enhance such communication in given contexts (Kaminski et al. 2017).[3]

Despite the rise of fields such as animal ethics and posthumanism, such a reading is still culturally stirring. When it comes to pigs, cows, pike, bees, and even dogs, the problem is usually not that we too readily presume to understand their subjectivity and read their faces or bodies as its direct manifestation, but rather that frequently their subjectivity is denied and the faces and bodily expressions ignored. René Descartes stands out as the notorious historical influence behind the denial of animal subjectivity, as he likened other animals to 'automatons' and machines (Descartes 1991: 366) and thereby gave rise to what is called *mechanomorphism* (Crist 1999). Yet even some more recent philosophers who are otherwise eager to question traditional humanistic philosophy have made the error of discounting non-human subjectivity and agency. Thus, for instance, Emmanuel Levinas famously asserted that non-human animals cannot have 'a face' in the morally relevant sense of the term (for discussion, see Atterton and Wright 2020). Mathew Calarco asserts that this refusal to recognise non-human 'faces' reveals that even radical thinkers often fail to question their own restrictively anthropocentric politics (Calarco 2008; Wolfe 2003).

Indeed, whereas essentialism of expression – where the face is reduced to a location that manifests one's internal character – is outdated when applied to human beings, it is fresh when it comes to non-human animals. Approaching portraits and faces of non-human animals as manifestations of their subjectivity is still a radical act, capable of questioning conservative species politics. Therefore, approaching Esther's face as expressive of her internal realms – for example, her intent, emotions, and agency – can contest anthropocentric, mechanomorphic norms, which in the Cartesian ethos condense farmed animals in particular into mechanisms void of subjectivity and vested only with instrumental value. This claim gains momentum when we acknowledge that even if 'the face' cannot be *reduced* to an expression of subjectivity, it nonetheless is often (albeit not always) *partly* engaged in such expression.

The face has also been defined as a construction, which does not express otherwise hidden interiors of a subject, but rather takes the form of a cultural object. In this vein, Tomáš Jirsa and Rebecca Rosenberg posit that the face is 'a cultural and media interface' (Jirsa and Rosenberg 2019: 4), which is layered with various subtexts. This take on 'the face' offers another advantage point to Esther the Wonderpig. The portraits of Esther are cultural sites that draw from differing narratives and meanings concerning humanity, animality, and the relation between the two. As a result, we get an object – a produced interface of often competing meanings – which replaces the real, biological animal used as a reference point of the portraits. In short, the portraits of Esther are not so much manifestations of subjectivity as objects with which that subjectivity is constructed. Here, portraits of Esther gain new significance, as they hold the promise of revealing, not the animal subject, but rather how human subjects conceptualise their non-human kin.

Therefore, although animal portraits can widen one's understanding of non-human subjectivity, they can also be approached as objects, which *construct* 'the animal'. I suggest that the balance between the two readings is dependent on how keenly the portrait in question focuses on the living animal as its concrete reference point. As pointed out by Carol Adams, living animals repeatedly remain 'absent referents' in cultural imagery concerning them (Adams 1990), whereby, for instance, a meat advert hides allusions to living fauna. The same logic can apply to any portrayals of non-human animality. In particular, if the constructive nature of the portrait is accentuated, there is an evident likelihood of the thinking, sensing, living animal becoming an absent referent. Esther as a specific, living pig can become partly or completely absent in the process of creating Esther the Wonderpig, and the degrees of her absence and presence deserve sustained attention.

If we understand the living face and the portrait to be intertwined rather than dichotomous (Belting 2017), we are bound to witness some degree of reference to living, minded animality in the more object-like portraits of Esther. Therefore, even when Esther the Wonderpig is approached as a cultural construct, Esther the living pig looms in the background as the obvious reference point – perhaps not wholly present, but not completely absent either. Here, 'the subject face' (face as a revelation of subjective realms) and 'the object face' (face as a constructed object) are not mutually exclusive categories, but rather participants in a constant negotiation concerning questions such as whether Esther the living pig can be known, how cultural discourses usually depict her kind, and who has the authority to speak on her behalf or to portray her with claims of accuracy. According to Hans Belting, portraits are masks, the historical purpose of which has been to represent one's character to others (Belting 2017: 25–6). Approaching Esther the Wonderpig as a mask allows us to combine 'the subject face' and 'the object face'. A mask is worn by someone, and thus implies a bearer, a subject – somebody is standing behind it. However, the mask cannot be reduced to that subject, and instead exists in a multifarious engagement with cultural meanings concerning 'humanity', 'non-humanity', and the relation between the two.

In his take on portraits, Jean-Luc Nancy (2018) underscores the tension between contact and opacity. Portraits both seem to bring the viewer closer to their subject, and remove that subject further away – they promise close encounters, yet constantly remind us of alterity and impenetrability. Esther the Wonderpig also manifests this tension. Like many social media influencers, she keeps speaking directly to her audiences, as if there was an intimate bond between her and them (she even frequently wishes her audiences 'good night' and 'good morning'), which suggests that she is personally accessible like a family member. We get to see thousands of images of her, which heightens the sense of proximity and contact, and which creates the impression that very little is left outside of view – that we can know Esther wholly. Yet Esther the Wonderpig also implies distance, imperviousness, lack of contact. We can only know the images and captions given to us, but have no physical contact – our relationship with Esther is virtual, edited, and manufactured, not visceral or embodied. By being our only portals to the specific living pig called Esther, the portraits epitomise distance from her (one example of this is her captions, which most of her adult audiences know were not actually written by her: distance is coded into even the most intimate moments). Therefore, Esther the Wonderpig is comprised of simultaneous, contradictory movements of going closer and further away – she signals both access and inaccessibility. The bearer of the mask, the reference point, is absent and present.

The above dualisms between the subject face and the object face, the mask and its bearer, and contact and opaqueness all point towards the limitations of fully knowing Esther through her portraits. Who is she, actually? The portraits invite me to think that I can gain a deeper understanding, if I just follow their cues, and open up new posts with yet more images and captions. However, the more posts I go through, the more exasperated I become, for it is obvious that I am no closer to knowing her. She invites emotional responses, which forms a contact between her and me – I feel for and with her. Yet portraits of her also invite apprehension, as one is continuously reminded of the fact that they are a construction, an object on to which various ironic elements are added (for example, a hefty pig is described as a skinny ballerina). This apprehension alienates me from the living pig, and makes me wonder whether the portraits offer even the slightest clue to who Esther is, what she thinks of the cameras, the clothes, and her companions. What is she feeling, thinking, intending, needing?

Anthropomorphic Ambivalence

The logic of the mask includes pretence: the mask is not the same as its bearer. If we approach Esther the Wonderpig as a mask, we are bound to accept that Esther is not whom she is portrayed to be, which forms one paradox of portraiture: it presumes its own unrealism. Esther's portrait will by necessity be unrealistic, even fantastical. Anthropomorphism is one manifestation of this unrealism. Humans are often decorated with animal masks, while in the portraits of Esther, a non-human animal is given a humanised mask.[4]

In many of the images and videos, Esther is dressed in human outfits, whether of a ballerina, a princess, a rocker, or a hippy. She is made to wear wigs, clothes, sunglasses, and other accessories. She also 'talks' in human language through captions to the portraits. The captions include the following: 'I remember going to my first ballet class like it was yesterday' or 'I went off-roading this morning because I'm a trailblazer'. As such, anthropomorphism is brashly present, and is accentuated by the way in which Esther the Wonderpig imitates the style of selfies. Although Esther the living pig does not take her own images or write her own captions, they are designed as if she did – her adopters are often visibly present, but their involvement in creating Esther the Wonderpig tends to remain allusive. The captions are often written in the first person, and the style of some of the images follows that of typical selfies. Here, anthropomorphism gains a new layer: Esther the Wonderpig is a self-conscious influencer, who seeks to engage with her audiences. She is the contemporary and hip anthropomorphic influencer, who promotes animal-friendly lifestyles in tune with cultural change.

What are we to make of humanised Esther? Anthropomorphism all too easily interlaces with anthropocentric dualism, which prioritises human beings while categorically differentiating them from the rest of nature. Such interlacing risks overemphasising humanity at the expense of non-humanity. Indeed, Steve Baker warns of 'disnification', whereby animals are drained of animality and reduced to empty forms on to which human content is projected (Baker 1993: 174). In my view, such anthropomorphism also re-establishes species boundaries. By projecting human characteristics into places where none can be found, the boundaries between 'human' and 'non-human' are paradoxically reaffirmed: anthropomorphic figures invite one to recall that mice, deer, and piglets don't actually speak in human tongue, and thus they redraw the dualistic species distinction. When designating Esther the Wonderpig as 'humanised' or 'anthropomorphic', I presume the category lines between 'humans' and 'pigs'. If these category lines become dualistic ('human'–'animal'), and if the animal becomes an empty bodily figure filled with human content, the humanised mask of Esther the Wonderpig is in danger of buttressing the anthropocentric worldview. Indeed, here the portraits of Esther risk becoming texts on human beings, telling us more about ourselves and very little about other animals.

One can also interpret the humanised mask more favourably. In his seminal text 'Why Look at Animals?', John Berger laments the loss of connection with our non-human kin. According to him, industrialism and capitalism have disconnected human beings from their animal others, paving the way for the alienated setting, in which human individuals stare at animals in zoos. Bars act as a concrete form of detachment, as does the gaze, which positions the animal as an object to be looked at from afar. Next to detachment, Berger criticises the species power-hierarchy entwined with modernity. By gazing at the animal in the zoo, the human animal asserts dominance and power by seeking the perfect vantage point and complete access to the non-human, while the animals are left in pacified misery that denies them even the most basic forms of well-being (Berger 1980).[5] Other theorists, such as Donna Haraway (1989) and Randy Malamud (1998), have offered similar critiques of the way in which the detached human gaze accentuated in institutions such as the zoo is a source of the species power-hierarchy; Adrian Franklin terms the phenomenon the 'zoological gaze' (Franklin 1999). By looking at and knowing the animal, who in turn has been rendered into a passive object, the human agent both takes distance from the non-human realm and exercises epistemic power in relation to it. At the same time, Berger adopts a rather positive perspective on anthropomorphism, as he posits that Disneyfied characters mark a profound longing for the animal world – indeed, they form a method of engaging with non-human realities, and as such hold the promise of counteracting detachment (Berger 1980: 22). Therefore, the anthropomorphic character of contemporary societies can at least on occasion be deemed as efforts to reconnect with the animal they have withdrawn from.

A curious contradiction, a paradox of anthropomorphism, is evident: anthropomorphism diminishes the portraits' animal content, and yet reminds human audiences of their own connections to the non-human realm. One might thus approach the humanising portrayal of Esther as an anchor that keeps us rooted in the non-human world, and indeed as a signal of a yearning for the non-human realm. Esther the Wonderpig does not invite the zoological gaze, detachment or power-hierarchies, but instead promises closeness and proximity. Farmed animals are particularly far removed from everyday urban realities, and Esther the Wonderpig arguably responds to a longing to gain contact with and access to these otherwise hidden and distant creatures. Here, instead of reaffirming the culturally constructed line between 'human' and 'non-human', the anthropomorphic portraits of Esther act as connectors between the two.

A third reading is that humanising Esther can act as an ironic way of manifesting the limits of knowing non-human alterity. The explicitly anthropomorphic dimensions of Esther the Wonderpig make it impossible to forget that we are not so much observing a pig as a humanised representation of one. As such, the anthropomorphism of the portraits of Esther can coax one to ask: who is the creature behind the mask?

Humour, Irony, and Performative Politics

Portraits of Esther mix two forms of aesthetics, the first of which is sleek and stereotypically attractive, and the second of which is raw, stereotypically unappealing, and even disconcerting. More specifically, Esther the Wonderpig combines the selfie-style, which generically goes together with beautiful, polished poses and 'wellness' lifestyles, with raw animality, which eats with its mouth open, has snot running down its face (we get to see many close-ups of both), has no consideration for polite society, and rejoices in gluttony and sloth. Therefore, while participating in the selfie-style, Esther the Wonderpig is also outrageously going against it, as she replaces the standard, high-achieving, skinny, and pretty influencer pictured by a pool in Dubai with a weighty, lazy lover of all food, who naps on her messy bed and has no regard for social expectation. As such, Esther the Wonderpig ironises a given human identity – that of the successful, healthy, wealthy, active go-getter, the epitome of the capitalist and consumerist dream, an individual who has managed to make herself into a sleek, purchasable, enviable product.

Also more generally, Esther the Wonderpig is soaked in comedy as she toys with identities and social norms. A hefty sow dressed as a hippy or a ballerina evokes easy humour, which rests on combining categories that are culturally deemed oppositional. Henry Bergson is among those who have argued that the combination of seemingly clashing categories produces humour (Bergson 2014) – the stereotypical if highly troubling example of which is (cis) men dressed as women in order to make their audiences roar with laughter.[6] Like gender, species have traditionally been presumed to be rigid and categorical. In the anthropocentric framework, species categories are not meant to interlace but rather clash, and the dualistic ethos in particular demands that 'humans' and 'animals' are oppositional. This means that combining 'the human' and 'the animal' can cause hilarity. When the otherwise dualistic categories are brought together, and the human acts like a non-human animal, or the animal is dressed as a human being, some (many?) find themselves giggling. As Bergson posited, by laughing at the coming together of clashing categories, we reproduce the notion that the categories do not belong together. Following this, I suggest that by laughing at the mixing of 'the human' and 'the animal', we all too easily reiterate the belief that these are mutually exclusive categories that should be kept separate. This brings us back to the above possibility that the portraits of Esther reaffirm the anthropocentric order – in this case, via humour.

However, approaching the comic dimensions of Esther the Wonderpig as forms of irony allows for a different conclusion. Here, the laughter is aimed at the superficiality of the species boundaries and the artificiality of many human and animal stereotypes, which in themselves become the target of an ironic gaze. When finding a pig dressed as a ballerina amusing, one's amusement may ultimately be aimed at the notion that any humans should dress in tutus instead of freely enjoying their animal bodies – it is aimed at the artificiality of the distinctions between 'civilisation' and 'nature', and 'human' and 'animal'. Here, humour and the apparent naivety of Disneyfication allow one to address an otherwise difficult topic – the fictiveness of the dualism that stands at the core of dominant, anthropocentric worldviews. The critique of dualism forms a threat to the anthropocentric order, and threatening things are best approached via humour, which may partly explain the popularity of funny, anthropomorphic characters. In sum, when Esther the Wonderpig is wearing sunglasses and a wig, she invites two contrary interpretations: either she is reinforcing dichotomies between humans and other animals, or exuberantly dismantling them.

The portraits of Esther engage with humour in other ways, interwoven with intra-human politics. One of these concerns bodily aesthetics. In many of the images, Esther is pictured from the front as she is sleeping or eating (Figure 8.2). Her large features and open mouth full of food are magnified, taking up a substantial portion of the picture. Moreover, Esther's weight and eagerness to eat are frequently underscored, with captions such as: 'I'm a really good nap snacker; I can do it with my eyes closed', 'My hobbies including eating and also thinking about the next time I will be eating', and (while ripping through a pillow) 'I was hoping it would be a jam-filled donut, but it wasn't.' Since Esther is portrayed anthropomorphically, her bodily

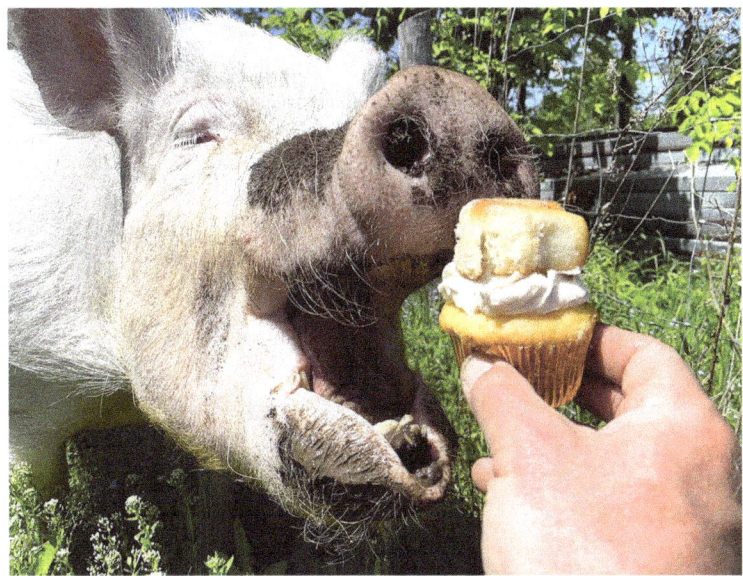

Figure 8.2 Esther, photograph courtesy of Derek Walter and Steve Jenkins

aesthetic is open to being judged via criteria usually applied to human beings. The portraits of Esther invite two quite different readings of the situation.

The captions typically represent Esther's aesthetics in a highly positive light. Examples include: 'I think you're beautiful, no matter what your mirror said' and 'Good morning, beautiful' (references to 'beautiful' are frequent). Judged by the beauty norms typical in Western cultures (for discussion, see Mills et al. 2018), Esther is over-sized and unappealing, and the captions use irony in order to highlight this while representing Esther as a challenge to those norms. In this sense, the portraits become politically rebellious performances akin to that offered by Miss Piggy of *The Muppet Show*. Esther the Wonderpig happily contests existing beauty norms, endorses body positivity, and invites her audiences to recognise that they, too, are ultimately salivating, chewing, sleeping, snoring, beautiful animals (see Pausé 2015). However, the body positivity included in the portraits of Esther is complicated by the dryness of the irony used, present in the caption that states that Esther's mirror might disagree with her beauty. These two readings leave recipients like myself confused as to whether some of the portraits are mocking 'ugly pigs' and fat people (categories that interlink in regrettable ways), or whether they partake in a more complicated critique, aimed at questioning the legitimacy of orthodox norms.

Gender considerations complicate the portraits of Esther even more. She is a sow, who is referred to with feminine pronouns. The uncomfortable question that emerges is whether the humour invited by the portraits of Esther is in fact humour usually directed at fat women (on fat-shaming and gender, see Gailey and Harjunen 2019). Can animal portraits act as an unfortunate outlet via which to engage in the sort of humour that is no longer socially acceptable in the human context? I leave the judgement open in Esther the Wonderpig's case.[7] However, on a broader level, the interconnections between animal portraits and human ethics and politics warrant more attention. The portrayal of non-human animals can entwine with and influence the portrayal of human animals, and vice versa (Baker 1993; Ritvo 1997; Adams 1990). This influence can be playfully constructive, as ironic connections make us question dualistic boundaries and cultural presumptions concerning both human and non-human beings. However, it can also work to deepen those boundaries and presumptions, whereby one can laugh once more at the fat ex-ballerinas and 'ugly pigs' in accordance with troubling stereotypes and standards.

There is one more dimension to consider. If we take note of Berger's suggestion that anthropomorphism reveals a sense of yearning for the non-human world, the comical effect of the portraits of Esther gains more nuance. What seems comical can in fact reveal collective sorrow over the loss of association with the non-human animal, and over the anthropogenic destruction of the animal world. Here, portraits of Esther participate in deeply dark yet well-meaning humour, webbed in sorrow, guilt, and loss. This interlinks the portraits of Esther with tragedy: while finding amusement in Esther the Wonderpig, many remain aware that Esther's kin do not live in houses but die *en masse* on farms and are hunted down in non-human nature. Esther's humanised, comical setting is outlandish enough to act as a reminder of its own unreality, which again turns one's attention to the unsettling reality of what happens to billions of Esther's kin each year, and what is happening to wild animals in the era of species extinction. In short, there is a gloomy, even terrifying, yet much-needed side to the comedy of Esther the Wonderpig, and it comes with a strong moral and political message.

The Chimeric Dismantling of Dualisms

Giorgio Agamben has spoken of the biopolitical desire to govern animality both externally and internally. Externally, animals are controlled on farms and other institutions, and internally human beings seek to govern the animal within themselves – their (our) animal biology (Agamben 2003). In the ethos of hierarchical dualism, the non-human is to be kept afar and in a subjugated position. In my reading, anthropomorphic animals can endorse this desire for governance by redrawing the boundaries between species in the manner mentioned earlier. Disneyfied characters can stir both fondness and unease, both of which are manifested in how the characters are positioned as appropriate only for children or other groups labelled as naive. Serious adults (the 'human norm') are not meant to engage with anthropomorphism, which reveals the socially dominant status of species dualism and the need to govern 'the animal' lest it contaminates 'the human'. However, by combining the human and the non-human, anthropomorphic animals can also form a challenge against this biopolitics: the animal and the human come together in the same body, thus defying the need for governance and replacing dichotomies with fusions.

Such a fusion forms one backdrop for making sense of Esther the Wonderpig. Portraits of a sow dressed as a hippy, aimed perhaps predominantly at adult audiences, defy dualism and the need for biopolitical governance. The external animal is no longer governed by the laws of anthropocentric consumerism, which would have chopped Esther's flesh into slivers of bacon long ago – moreover, she has come to inhabit the human home, thus transgressing the usual lines between farmed animals and humans. In sum, the external animal is suddenly living and closely engaging with human beings, and has become a member of their family, which challenges the biopolitical need to keep the animal detached from the human world. Internally, the body of Esther, the very livingness of which is an act of rebellion, combines the human and non-human in a carnivalesque fashion into a single flesh, thus questioning the biopolitical need to shield the human body from non-human contamination. Therefore, in portraits of Esther, the human and the animal come together on various levels, ranging from social engagement to inhabiting the same body. As such, those portraits not only speak of a longing for the non-human, but also of the viscerally wild reconnection between humans and other animals.

This leads us to the final stop: Esther the Wonderpig as a chimera, who illuminates the shared histories and bonds between humans and other animals. Donna Haraway has famously spoken of the intricate ways in which humans and other animals can entwine. 'A Cyborg Manifesto' (Haraway 1991) and *The Companion Species Manifesto* (Haraway 2003), both milestones in posthumanist theory, urge us to question the sort of essentialism that defines human–animal dualism, and which demands categorical distance from 'the other'. Esther the Wonderpig emerges as a Harawayan human–non-human cyborg, who brings together stereotypically human attributes and the genus of *Sus*, and explicates how species can cohabit. In this light, portraits of Esther form an 'Esther manifesto', which questions the essentialist dichotomy between humans and other animals, and which underscores the lived interconnections between human beings and other creatures.

Summing up, it is time to recall the distinction between the portrait and the reference point. Using a meeting with his cat as a famous example, Jacques Derrida (2008) sought to underscore how non-human creatures are unique agents, who cannot be lumped together under one, generic category 'animals' without doing them violence. Matthew Calarco (2008) has defined such encounters with specific animals as potential moments of madness that question anthropocentric presumptions, categories, and language. I suggest that Esther the Wonderpig (the meta-portrait) is ultimately such a moment of much-needed madness: in her multifarious humour, at times infuriating anthropomorphism, and rebellion against expectation, she exquisitely rumbles cultural presumptions about what it is to be 'an animal' or 'a human being'. Behind the portrait, dwells one, specific animal agent – a unique sow named Esther.

Notes

1. For more information, see https://www.estherthewonderpig.com/ (last accessed 15 May 2021).
2. Yet there is a danger here that Esther the Wonderpig also strengthens the dualism between humans and other animals, as the animal emerges as a literally brutish and primarily bodily creature, void of human sophistication.
3. On projection and both the challenges and possibilities of understanding non-human emotions on the basis of their bodily gestures, see Aaltola 2018.
4. Anthropomorphism refers to a projection of false similarities between humans and other animals, and should be separated from the presentation of actual similarities between species, of which there are many.
5. For a critical analysis, see, for instance, Burt 2005.
6. Contradiction has been underscored also in later analysis of humour (see Marteinson 2010).
7. Her caretakers appear well-meaning and politically aware, and belong themselves to a minority group. Yet their doubtlessly positive intent and the content of the portraits of Esther are, of course, separate phenomena.

References

Aaltola, Elisa (2018), *Varieties of Empathy: Moral Psychology and Animal Ethics*, London: Rowman and Littlefield.

Aaltola, Elisa (2019), 'The Meat Paradox, Omnivore's Akrasia, and Animal Ethics', *Animals*, 9(12): 1125.

Aaltola, Elisa (2021), 'Egoistic Love of the Nonhuman World? Biology and the Love Paradox', *Ethics, Policy & Environment*, 26(1): 86–105.

Adams, Carol (1990), *The Sexual Politics of Meat*, New York: Continuum.

Agamben, Giorgio (2003), *The Open Man and Animal*, Stanford, CA: Stanford University Press.

Agence France-Presse (2021), 'World's "Oldest Known Cave Painting" Found in Indonesia', *The Guardian*, 13 January, https://www.theguardian.com/science/2021/jan/13/worlds-oldest-known-cave-painting-found-in-indonesia (last accessed 15 May 2021).

Atterton, Peter, and Tamra Wright (eds) (2020), *Face to Face with Animals: Levinas and the Animal Question*, New York: SUNY Press.

Baker, Steve (1993), *Picturing the Beast*, Manchester: Manchester University Press.

Belting, Hans (2017), *Face and Mask: A Double History*, Princeton, NJ: Princeton University Press.

Berger, John (1980), 'Why Look at Animals?', in John Berger (ed.), *About Looking*, London: Writers' & Readers'.

Bergson, Henri (2014 [1900]), *Laughter: An Essay on the Meaning of the Comic*, trans. Cloudesley Brereton and Fred Rothwell, Eastford: Martino Fine Books.

Burt, Jonathan (2005), 'John Berger's "Why Look at Animals?": A Close Reading', *Worldviews*, 9(2): 203–18.

Calarco, Matthew (2008), *Zoographies: The Question of the Animal*, New York: Columbia University Press.

Crist, Eileen (1999), *Images of Animals: Anthropocentrism and Animal Mind*, Philadelphia, PA: Temple University Press.

Derrida, Jacques (2008 [2002]), *The Animal That Therefore I Am*, New York: Fordham University Press.

Descartes, Réne (1991), *The Philosophical Writings of Descartes: Volume III, The Correspondence*, trans. John Cottingham et al., Cambridge: Cambridge University Press.

Franklin, Adrian (1999), *Animals & Modern Cultures*, London: SAGE.

Gailey, Jeannine A., and Hannele Harjunen (2019), 'A Cross-Cultural Examination of Fat Women's Experiences: Stigma and Gender in North American and Finnish Culture', *Feminism & Psychology*, 29(3): 374–90.

Goossens, Brigitte M. A., Marusha Dekleva, Simon M. Reader, Elisabeth H. M. Sterck, and Johan J. Bolhuis (2008), 'Gaze Following in Monkeys is

Modulated by Observed Facial Expressions', *Animal Behaviour*, 75(5): 1673–81.

Haraway, Donna (1989), *Primate Visions: Gender, Race, and Nature in the World of Modern Science*, London: Routledge.

Haraway, Donna (1991), *Simians, Cyborgs and Women: The Reinvention of Nature*, New York: Routledge.

Haraway, Donna (2003), *The Companion Species Manifesto*, Chicago: University of Chicago Press.

Jirsa, Tomáš, and Rebecca Rosenberg (2019), '(Inter)Faces, or How to Think Faces in the Era of Cyberfaces', *World Literature Studies*, 4(11): 2–10.

Kaminski, Juliane, Jennifer Hynds, Paul Morris, and Bridget M. Waller (2017), 'Human Attention Affects Facial Expressions in Domestic Dogs', *Scientific Reports*, 7(1): 12914.

Loughnan, Steve, Brock Bastian, and Nick Haslam (2014), 'The Psychology of Eating Animals', *Current Directions in Psychological Science*, 23(2): 104–8.

Malamud, Randy (1998), *Reading Zoos: Representation of Animals and Captivity*, New York: New York University Press.

Marino, Lori, and Christina M. Colvin (2015), 'Thinking Pigs: A Comparative Review of Cognition, Emotion, and Personality in Sus Domesticus', *International Journal of Comparative Psychology*, 28: Article 23859.

Marteinson, Peter (2010), 'Thoughts on the Current State of Humour Theory', *Comedy Studies*, 1(2): 173–80.

Midgley, Mary (1983), *Animals and Why They Matter*, Athens, GA: University of Georgia Press.

Mills, J., A. Shannon, and Jacqueline Hogue (2018), 'Beauty, Body Image, and the Media', in Martha Peaslee Levine (ed.), *Perceptions of Beauty*, London: IntechOpen, pp. 145–70.

Nagel, Thomas (1974), 'What is it like to be a Bat?', *The Philosophical Review*, 83(4): 435–50.

Nancy, Jean-Luc (2018), *Portrait*, New York: Fordham University Press.

Parr, Lisa, Bridget Waller, Sarah-Jane Vick, and Kim Bard (2007), 'Classifying Chimpanzee Facial Expressions by Muscle Action', *Emotion*, 7 (February): 172–81.

Pausé, Cat (2015), 'Rebel Heart: Performing Fatness Wrong Online', *M/C Journal*, 18(3).

Pico, Alfonso, and Marien Gadea (2021), 'When Animals Cry: The Effect of Adding Tears to Animal Expressions on Human Judgment', *PLoS One*, 16(5).

Ritvo, Harriet (1997), *Platypus and the Mermaid, and Other Figments of the Classifying Imagination*, Cambridge, MA: Harvard University Press.

Thomas, Keith (1983), *Man and the Natural World*, London: Allen Lane.

Toadvine, Ted (2014), 'The Time of Animal Voices', *Environmental Philosophy*, 11(1): 109–24.

Wathan, J., L. Proops, K. Grounds, and K. McComb (2016), 'Horses Discriminate between Facial Expressions of Conspecifics', *Scientific Reports*, 6(1): 38322.

Wolfe, Cary (2003), 'In the Shadow of Wittgenstein's Lion: Language, Ethics, and the Question of the Animal', in Cary Wolfe (ed.), *Zoontologies: The Question of the Animal*, Minneapolis: University of Minnesota Press, pp. 145–62.

III Self-Constructions

Chapter 9

The Subject in the Frame: Aesthetic Opacity and the Reverberations of Race, Gender, and Sexuality through the Portrait

Sudeep Dasgupta

The genre of the portrait explicitly invites attention to an individual subject, the identity it embodies, and the form of its manifestation. Louis A. Waldman and Brenda Preyer, for example, describe the *Portrait of Giovanni di Paolo Rucellai* as 'an elaborate pictorial fiction' which illuminates 'the history of the Rucellai family at a critical moment, when the glowing artistic achievements of the early Renaissance were beginning to be exploited as social capital by the dominant families of the late Renaissance' (2012: 133). Rucellai's image in the portrait legitimates the sitter, while the artist is primarily the executor of an ascendant aesthetic style. Commissioned portraits intensify this legitimating dynamic between sitter and aesthetic form by extending it to the painter.[1] Hans Holbein's portrait of Henry VIII (c. 1537) and Rembrandt van Rijn's of Jan Six (1654) are examples where the mutually reinforcing relation between the patron and the artist manifested the former's identity and social standing while confirming the latter's form-giving talent.

The value of appropriate aesthetic form for the legitimation of individual identity is not certain, however, and perspectives critical of the genre of portraiture manifest this uncertainty. In Hegel's *Aesthetics* (1835), the narrative of art's relation to the Ideal begins with a consideration of the portrait, and its irrelevance. Hegel argues that art's 'harmony with its true Concept' must cast 'aside everything in appearance' which is 'contaminated by [. . .] chance and externality'

(1998: 155). He goes on: 'the portrait-painter, who has least of all to do with the Ideal of art, must flatter [. . .] all the externals in shape and expression, in form [. . .] he must [rather] let go, and grasp and reproduce the subject in his [*sic*] universal character and enduring personality' (1998: 155). Portraiture is furthest from the Ideal of art because its impulse to give accurate form to individuality, when 'let go', would destroy the very function of the genre of portraying the specificity of the sitter. Erasing the contaminating externality of representational form can take two aspects. For Hegel, the statues of classical Greece manifest ideal universality – 'Sculpture [. . .] is more abstract in its productions than painting' because 'the Ideal is still preserved in its strictness and [. . .] keeps every form in steady relation to the general meaning [abstract universality] which was to be given bodily shape' (1998: 167, 173).

While Hegel denigrates individual specificity in favour of universality in form, a far more radical option is offered by Leo Bersani's rejection of 'psychic density' for 'pure potentiality' rendered aesthetically through the expulsion of form itself (Bersani and Phillips 2008: 25). Bersani and Dutoit argue that, unlike the portrait, it is in the image where 'all subjects – human and narrative – are left behind' that 'aesthetics' figures the formlessness of 'subjectivity' in which 'nearly everything which would allow us to measure and to distinguish is gone' (2006: 69). From this perspective, given that individuality and a minimal clarity are intimately tied to portraiture, it could hardly qualify as the genre for a critical engagement with identity.

Both perspectives, one that stabilises identity (Hegel) and the other that erases it completely (Bersani), are based on understandings of aesthetic renderings of particularity that must be either surpassed or erased completely. This understanding of the aesthetic assumes that individual particularity and the identity it embodies, when given form, manifests either a stable identity stuck before its universalisation, or dissembles its actual dissolution through ideologically lending it form.

This chapter argues that the portrait is one site/surface where the real instabilities of identity, ignored in both formulations, are given aesthetic form by displaying the tension between conflictual appearances which reverberate through the subject that emerges in the image. The aesthetic play of forms, I argue, makes visible the unresolvable tensions that mark the 'psychic density' of the subject, bringing out the portrait's potential to register the reverberations of conflicting psychic, social, and historical relations manifested in identities. The historical reframing and visual translation of *existing* portraits, the production of non-commissioned portraits of ordinary subjects, the genre of self-portraiture to counter the social ordering of identities through phobic images, the focusing on the formal depictions of subjects portrayed rather than either their or the artist's privileged social status, technological shifts in the media through which portraits are produced – this chapter analyses these strategies in portraits of race, gender, and sexual identity, as they manifest the gaps between individual, identity, and social order in the image.

In 2013 the Royal Academy's retrospective *Manet: Portraying Life* exhibited Édouard Manet's portraits to give a collective face, not to a nation, but to the (art-)historical period of modernity and modernism. The curator Mary Anne Stevens argues that Manet, the 'father of modern art', makes 'particular use of the portrait to turn the sitters into actors in the paintings of modern life'.[2] Manet's modernity derives from the aesthetic form of portraiture, which is deployed to figure the historical experience of modernity itself. That is why Georg Simmel in 1900 insists that

> I believe that the secret agitation, the restless compulsion just below consciousness that drives the human being of today [. . .] from Bocklin to Impressionism [. . .] and back again is not simply a consequence of the external haste and excitement of modern life, but [. . .] is often the expression, the manifestation, the discharge of that most inner circumstance. (1989: 675, emphasis added)[3]

The portrait's form of manifesting subjective experience is intrinsically linked to the historical moment in which the latter is situated. That is also why Kobena Mercer, a century later, avers that

> to the extent that the building blocks of all signifying practice generate meaning on the basis of a relational process of differentiation, art's social dimension is never exterior to the moment of creation but is already inscribed in the multi-accentual character of semiotic resources that exist in a socially stratified condition of heteroglossia. (2016: 10)

The social dimensions of gender, race, and sexuality are intrinsic to questions of aesthetic form, while the formation of identities always involves transformations in the field of appearances.

Unnaming, Naming, Uncovering, Remodelling

Framing the portrait through the expansion from individual to social identity immediately exposes the gap between the two as a political opportunity for loosening the vexed relation between individual particularity and social totality at a specific historical moment. For example, the contraction of the importance attributed to the individual sitter is discernible in August Sander's *Face of Our Time: Sixty Portraits of Twentieth-century Germans*. First published in 1929 as *Antlitz der Seit: Sechzig Aufnahmen Deutscher Menschen des 20. Jahrhunderts*, Sander's photographs provide a composite chronotope of a place, Germany, and time, the twentieth century, by recording (*aufnahme*) different social types, including the secretary, the 'gypsy', the Jew, and the National Socialist. The shift from 'record' in German to 'portrait' in English obscures Sander's 'functional transformation' (Benjamin 1978: 228) of the camera from a device for portraying named individuals to the typological registration of the social diversity of the German people. That is why, in 1931, Walter Benjamin described the sixty published photographs as 'a training manual' whose 'topicality' resides in suggesting 'how to look at others', with direct political implications for both 'the Left or the Right' in the 'shifts of power now overdue in our society' (2005: 520). Further, the individual sitters do not portray social types in Germany but constitute German identity itself, pre-emptively calling the Third Reich's ideology of a homogeneous 'Aryan' German identity into question. In 1934 the Nazis confiscated and destroyed copies of the book, and then banned its future publication (Shaw 1991).

If portraits worked to register unpalatable truths about the reality of society, pictures generally have often operated precisely to hide them. What aesthetic strategies help give form to presences erased from history? Françoise Vergès organised *The Slave at the Louvre: An Invisible Humanity* during the Paris Triennial in 2016, taking visitors 'through the galleries in the search of an invisible humanity and the traces, fragments, and shadows of its ghostly presence' (2016: 10). Reading the existing and exhibited archive of art to recover seemingly insignificant renderings of commodities such as sugar and tobacco pipes takes on another significance from the perspective of an ambulatory remapping of the slave's presence in the Louvre. Readings of pictures tease out the significance of race locked up in the framing of objects and images as art. In October 2021 a discussion titled 'The Black Presence in Portraiture' was held under the auspices of London Art Week. Samuel Reilly, the presenter of the symposium, introduced the theme as 'a topic that arises when museums and art historians are increasingly turning with a renewed focus on the depictions of black subjects over the course of our history, many of which have often been overlooked'.[4] Rather than reading for ghostly presences in images, here the recovery of hidden presences focuses precisely on portraits whose existing framings erase race. Racial difference is signified directly on the body portrayed while its social significance is overlooked. The strategy of reframing existing portraits aims to elicit encounters with multiple forms of Black presence.

Alain LeRoy Locke's *The Negro in Art* (1940) provided the first articulate plea for what David Bindman and Henry Louis Gates Jr (2010: viii) understand as a 'study of European images of blacks' as 'an antidote to prejudice'. The subtitle of Locke's book – 'a pictorial record of the Negro artist and of the Negro theme in art' – shifted the focus from the Black subject *in* portraiture to Black artists as painters *of* portraits. Locke's intervention, and those of critics and artists afterwards, altered the framing of Black subjects and artists, in which the Black figure in the frame often functioned as adjunct/accessory to white subjects, their presence helping the latter accrue value and prestige. Modernist provocations, such as Manet's *Olympia* (1863) for example, re-cited the female nude's propriety in shocking painterly form while consigning the Black maid figure to the background. The Black presence also remains unnamed. Victorine Meurent, already famous as Manet's favourite model, posed as Olympia; the Black subject remains anonymous as model and subject in the image.

Catherine M. Soussloff contends that 'because the portrait more clearly than any other genre of representation elicits the question of who, it reinscribes more emphatically than any other kind of image a history that can do no more than name' (2006: 3). When racial difference is figured through the co-presence of a named and an anonymous subject, however, the potential of the portrait does not just pose the question of naming. It transforms the portrait's social significance by forming identity through the conversion of the human form into a named individual with their own history.

Addressing the anonymity of Black figures in portraits, Michael Ohajuru describes how National Trust properties in the UK reinscribed the inventory of some portraits by converting anonymous Black figures into individuals through naming. When John Martin's portrait *Lady Elizabeth Finch-Hatton* (1778) in Scone Palace, Perthshire, was entered into the inventory, the Black sitter was described as 'the negro attendant'. Historical research later showed the figure to be 'the cousin of the white sitter', and the painting was retitled *Lady Elizabeth Finch-Hatton and her cousin Dido Elizabeth Belle*. Naming as a strategy does not just register the individuality of the Black subject, it exposes the structurally unstable relations across racial difference which give form to identity's contingent emergence through history in the image.

The Wallach Gallery at Columbia University in New York and the Musée d'Orsay in Paris partnered to stage exhibitions in 2019 on the Black subject in portraiture. The exhibition in New York was titled *Posing Modernity: The Black Model from Manet and Matisse to Today*, referring both to the practice of modelling and a particular staging, a giving form to a historical period, through the figure of the Black model. *Le modèle noir de Géricault à Matisse*, the title of the Paris exhibition, avoids the term 'modernity' while situating the Black model in the more limited frame of the names of particular artists. By focusing on the Black model, the exhibitions exemplified how the genre of portraiture can work to erase the presence of Black bodies, while simultaneously disturbing understandings of modernity.

In Paris, the name of Théodore Géricault, a crucial figure in the rise of the Romantic movement, linked the exhibition to an art-historical moment, while the focus on the 'Black model' paradoxically erases his role in the anti-slavery movement. Géricault's most famous painting, *The Raft of the Medusa* (1819), was originally titled *Scène de naufrage* (Scene of a Shipwreck) – it shows the aftermath of the wrecking of the French Navy frigate *Méduse* as it ferried French officials to Saint Louis in Senegal, West Africa, in 1816. The painting confronted its audience in the Salon of 1819 with this recent, controversial moment in French naval (and colonial) history, whose details – the ineptitude of the *Medusa*'s captain, the raft on which some survivors fled the shipwreck, and the horrific circumstances leading to their death, including drowning and cannibalism – provoked outrage at the Salon. The Black figure at the apex of the triangle of writhing bodies on the raft could clue a viewer to the location, and occasion, of the shipwreck off Senegal in 1816. Alhadeff argues that 'for most Frenchmen, the colonies were too far away, an ocean parting them from the mainland, for them to care or see what was happening abroad', yet 'lack of visibility and distance [. . .] hardly deterred Géricault from picturing the Other' (2020: 2). The significance of the Black figure could have coloured the self-congratulatory image of Napoleonic France while reorienting art history's focus on Gericault's formally striking composition. However, the painting did not feature in the exhibition because it did not include a 'model' – its genre was uncertain: history painting, tableau? – and since the exhibition's focus on Blackness was framed by the names of famous painters rather than 'modernity' as in New York, the meaning of 'painting Black bodies' beyond portraiture did not arise in 2019. The name of the painter evokes his controversial masterpiece, yet the context of slavery and Gericault's motives were whitewashed both by the work's initial reception and its absence from the exhibition more than a century later. This is where the focus on 'le modèle noir' in Gericault's portraits elides the crucial relation between unnamed and ignored painted Black bodies and *another* understanding of modernity in which slavery is centrally implicated (Falola 2013; Grüner 2020).

Race and Sexuality through the Body in the Image

The discursive construction of the visibility of racial difference through naming the subject in the image loosened the link between blackness as mere bodily presence and biology as the evidential basis of racial identity. Stuart Hall therefore asked, 'should we not dispense with the problematic trappings introduced by the term's [race] references to the biological and take the plunge – take culture seriously?' (2017: 80). Anthony Appiah, for example, argues that 'What exists "out there" in the world – communities of meaning, shading variously into each other in the rich structure of the social world – is the province not of biology but of hermeneutic understanding' (1985: 36). Answering his question, while Hall rejects biology for understanding the significance of racial difference, he goes on to argue that 'we cannot get rid of the biological trace and eliminate the specificity of the racialized discourse just like that' (2017: 60).

In the relationship between sexual identity, visual culture, and biology – biomedical discourse in particular – the politics of naming takes on politically contradictory dimensions during what Simon Watney (1987: 71) called 'the Spectacle of AIDS'. First, gay activists convincingly argued that state biomedical discourses refused to name the group most affected by the virus, while media discourses sensationalised homosexual practices. Watney observed that 'The British government's AIDS information campaign, which has been widely admired overseas, dutifully exhorted the "general public" not to die of "ignorance" yet was unable to address one single word to British gay men, who constitute almost ninety percent of people with AIDS in Britain' (1987: 72–3). In the United States, the formation of the Gay Men's Health Crisis (GMHC) in 1982 turned the focus from the general public to gay men, explicitly naming a group which biomedical (state) discourses were ignoring. Secondly, the 'Founding Statement of People with AIDS/ARC (The Denver Principles)' extended the focus on gay identity and sexuality, demanding access to 'quality medical treatment [. . .] without discrimination of any form, including sexual orientation, gender, diagnosis, economic status, age, or race' (Navarre 1989: 149). Thirdly, this discursive expansion was accompanied by a move from the label 'victim' to 'people with AIDS', reframing them beyond sensationalist renderings of sexual abandon and medical misery. For example, Jane Rosett's (1989: 155) photograph of PWA Coalition member Joseph Foulon, with his lover Mark Senak leaning against him, portrays the life of intimacy and care between a gay couple. Rosett's photograph of 'two lesbian PWAs' (1989: 154), Carol LaFavor and Allyson Hunter, smiling broadly as they hug each other at a demonstration, extends the representation of coupledom to a broader community extending beyond same-sex desire. Commissioned by the GMHC, Jean Carlomusto produced a cable TV series *Living with AIDS* (1984–87), picturing the health crisis from the varied perspectives of the diversity of people living with rather than only dying from the disease. Commissioned portraiture's visual manifestation of the alignment between individual sitter and social identity counters phobic renderings of sexual identity while illustrating human sexuality's expansive potential to connect with non-homosexual others.

An exhibition by Autograph, the Association of Black Photographers, *Autoportraits* (1989–90), curated by Canadian-Indian British resident Sunil Gupta, manifested the intersection of race and sexuality within a largely white media discourse and gay visual culture. Gupta and queer arts activist Tessa Boffin went on to curate the groundbreaking exhibition *Ecstatic Antibodies: Resisting the AIDS Mythology*, which travelled across the UK from 1988 to 1990. The exhibition challenged the phobic discourse of AIDS-carriers through the portrayal of queer, Black, and diasporic subjects as 'antibodies'. Manifesting what Finley and Willis (2016: 6–7) call the 'appropriation and varied performances of sexuality across racial lines', the exhibition helped pioneer the work of now-established artists including Pratibha Parmar, Isaac Julien, Allan deSouza, and Rotimi Fani-Kayode. Robert Mapplethorpe's now-famous *Self-Portrait* (1978), first exhibited in an alternative art space in San Francisco in 1978, countered the voyeuristic gaze on homosexual subjects by deviating the viewer's line of focus from the body to the portrayed subject's returning gaze. None of the other 18 black-and-white photographs picturing sadomasochistic practices were self-portraits. Dressed in chaps and a leather vest, Mapplethorpe is turned away from the camera and bent over, exposing his rear into which a bullwhip whose tail he clasps is inserted. Mapplethorpe's *self*-portrait converts the portrait from a snapshot of a deviant culture into a portrayal of sexual and photographic agency in two ways. Mapplethorpe situates himself within the S/M culture which his other photographs portray, while objectifying himself from the position of the self-recording subject. The subjective agency of the camera-operating subject is further extended within the frame of the portrait itself. Mapplethorpe turns round to face the camera and meet the viewer's gaze, foregrounding the play between his exhibited body and the agency of one look countering another. The multiple positions of participant, object, and subject are constructed through the play between the backward pose of the body and the frontal direction of the gaze. Meyer (1993: 360) argues that by making explicit 'the power games [. . .] conventionally, though usually more discreetly, played between photographer and subject', aesthetic play destabilises the objectification of the 'deviant' body and its practices by the theatrical *self*-presentation of sexual identity as it counters the look of the viewer at the portrayed subject.

Engendering History

How might history be reviewed by reproducing portraits of historical figures to open a gap between race and nation? Further, how can portraiture aesthetically stage hegemonic images of gender in visual culture to critically interrogate them through form? This section reads specific portraits as they conflictually configure race, gender, nation, and history through the play of appearances that subjects in the image manifest. Identity is given form despite or rather through the subject's changing location within the power relations that co-constitute it and manifest its uncertain form in portraiture.

Senegalese artist Omar Victor Diop's portrait photograph *Jean Baptiste Belley* (2014) reproduces and transforms Anne-Louis Girodet's *Portrait of Jean-Baptiste Belley* (1797), restaging the portrait by posing himself as the historical figure.[5] Girodet's *Belley* was completed in 1797 to mark a momentous event in French history – the appearance in the Convention after the French Revolution of the first Black Deputy, an ex-slave from Saint Domingue, where slavery was abolished in 1793. Girodet portrayed a new role and identity for diasporic Black citizens of post-Revolutionary France, one later compromised by Napoleon's reinstatement of slavery in 1802 after its 1794 abolition. Diop's portrait restages that ambivalent historical marker of the racial transformation of national identity to portray France's contemporary inability to integrate this difference into the nation's imaginary.

Girodet's *Belley* rests his right elbow against the base of a bust of the French abolitionist Guillaume Thomas Raynal. Diop's *Belley* assumes the exact same pose, but Raynal's bust goes missing, with a football under the right arm keeping the elbow in position instead. The empty left hand now holds a goalkeeper's glove. Beth Buggenhagen observes that 'Diop uses footballs and other sports props that seem anachronistic' in the historical frame of eighteenth-century portraiture (2017: 39). Buggenhagen rightly argues that 'Diop's use of football props points to dislocations of migrants in space and time, separated from the contexts in which certain objects of value make sense' (2017: 40). Diop displaces the social position of the body portraying Black emancipation and the conflictual history it bears – Belley was later jailed, slavery was re-established, a football replaces Raynal, and the Deputy is re-embodied by staging him as a young African/French footballer. The anachronistic, multilayered subject in the portrait registers the significance of one image and extends its configuration of race and nation to picture another narrative of diaspora in which the opportunities that football clubs today offer African migrants wishing to make a life in France are given form. The transformations between the two images configure a previous conjunction of race (slavery) and national identity (Parliament) with a contemporary manifestation of this conjunction in which racial difference in the national football team precipitates competing discourses of identity embodied by the subject.

By portraying a sitter 'enclosed in [an uneasy] individuality and intertwined with a determinate existent' (Hegel 1998: 156), the portraits fail to fulfil art's potential to materialise 'reason in history' (Hegel 1997). Instead, the second portrait reasons with history, configuring a play of forms 'through a profusion of [anachronistic] details and [planned] accidents' (Hegel 1998: 153). This image makes no pretence to faithfully portray a specific individual and their history, giving form through a play between appearances to a multilayered and dissonant subject in the image as a lever to prise open history's closed narrative of linear progression towards the 'Ideal as such' (Hegel 1998: 153). The aesthetic play of forms across both portraits registers the psychic density of the subjects whose tense embodiment of irreconcilable ideals is made manifest through the donning of multiple, conflictually related identities. The display of Diop's *Belley* in the Victoria and Albert Museum's *Fashioning Masculinities: The Art of Menswear* exhibition centralises the transformation of masculinity in the uneasy historical overlap of race and nation. Fashion, as making or fabricating and as sartorial elaboration of the body, takes on multiple meanings when manifested through Diop's *Belley*. Refashioning the Black body within a contentious national identity, Diop's *Belley* queers French identity while denaturalising the portrayal of masculinity.[6]

'A feminism concerned with the question of looking', argues Jacqueline Rose (2005a: 232), 'can stress the particular and limiting opposition of male and female which any image seen to be flawless is serving to hold in place.' Moving from gendered configurations of specific historical events in Diop to the 1970s works of Cindy Sherman turns attention now to contemporary feminist restagings of historical forms of looking at women. The collection of seventy photographs titled *Untitled Film Stills* (1977–80) are often described as self-portraits of Sherman, though the uneasy relation between self and the subject is manifested in the image through a subtle commentary on the history of mediated stereotypes of women, including in American film noir and 1950s melodrama, and post-war Italian neo-realism.

In *Untitled Film Still #35*, Sherman extracts Sophia Loren's performance in Vittorio de Sica's *Two Women* (1960), arresting the narrative of the two women based on Alberto Moravia's novel and transformed by Cesare Zavattini and de Sica's screenplay through a self-portrait.[7] The woman in the 'film still' comprises a gendered configuration of social class by altering the filmic representation through the details of gaze, pose, and clothing. The young woman, wearing an apron and headscarf, in her oddly shiny heels, stares somewhat defiantly and apprehensively upward, her hand poised on her hip, disrupting stereotypical expectations mediated by the film of working-class women among the ruins of post-war Italy. *Untitled Film Still #14* (1978) stages Sherman as a 'domesticated sex kitten' (Galassi 1997) sporting a pearl necklace and a lacy black dress and clutching a dustpan, while the mirror behind her reveals a man's jacket hanging on the back of a chair by a table on which a full cocktail glass rests.[8] The possible presence of a man in the scene is signalled through the jacket, while the woman's apprehensive look away from the camera suggests her indeterminate subjective and physical relation to his absent gaze. The three looks configured by the jacket visible in the mirror, the woman's eyes, and the image itself portray an anxiety manifested in the expression on her face as she faces the camera but looks away at an object outside the frame. The staged, visually available, and sexually appealing female body gives form to what 'is seen [. . .] from the side of the man', yet the disturbing configuration of gazes registers the instability of 'the sexual relation' implied in the desiring look as if to say that the gender distinction it implies 'comes down to fantasy' (Lacan 1982: 157). In both images, and many of Sherman's other self-portraits, the woman looks away from the camera, upward and to the side, with an expression moving between apprehension and slight defiance, giving form to the unstable gender relations in the activity of looking through a critical restaging of femininity.

Sherman, I argue, is also tapping into a larger history of women's portraits in painting, including the unreadability that Manet's portraits provoked in the Salon of 1869, *The Balcony* in particular. The active/

passive, male/female distinctions of looking at women's faces in Sherman's images are undermined by the 'facingness' (Fried 1996: 297) of the portraits, which convert the 'unreadability' in Manet's faces into the registration of the instability of the gendered look. For Michael Fried, the subject–object relation of looking in Manet's portraits is destabilised because the image invites absorption while simultaneously pulling the viewer out of it through its theatrical presentation. Presenting the woman as object to be looked at while averting the viewer's gaze by looking apprehensively at something outside the frame, the women in the images produce a 'presentational theatricality of facingness' which 'eschews theatricality traditionally associated with excess, rhetorical or gestural overkill of the sort often called melodramatic' (Fried 1996: 297).[9]

The history of images of women in portraiture and their unreadability refuses the 'pretension to a narcissistic perfection of form' (Rose 2005a: 232). Rather, they exhibit what J. M. Bernstein (2006: 266) terms the 'anxiety of narcissism', which structures the subject and its inability to give an unambiguous form to gender norms. Can gender, or indeed any identity, be given form without ambiguity? Or do such images run the risk of unreadability through the under-determination of meaning on their faces, thereby exposing a paradoxical 'brilliance of invisibility' (Foucault 2009: 71)? Can a desired alternative be given form to counter the historical norms that legislate good from bad identities?

Responding to a question about how one might 'recognize [. . .] the "good image" of the people', Jacques Rancière insists that there are no aesthetic criteria for the 'adequation of political, social and fictional figures' (2017: 157). Instead, setting into play the forms through which identities (are made to) appear can provide 'representations that try [. . .] to make us feel this gap with regard to every simple identity of the people' (2017: 157). The history of cinematic and media culture's attempts at adequating political and social identities is indexed by staging subjects in self-portraits whose forms make explicit 'the composition of the trajectory that passes through them' (2017: 158). The subject in the image is given form through the unstable gendering of the look, by citing its manifestations in the art history of the genre of portraiture and the history of mass culture.

The Colour of Modernity

Sherman's self-portraits delink posed body and social identity through a feminist politics of quotation and critical transformation within a specific Western modernity. Rather than the subject's unstable image in modernity, what insights could the portrait yield as the instrumental constructor of modernity itself? If modernity emerges through the image rather than in it, how might modernity's spatial framings be rethought when they emerge beyond the West? MoMA's controversial 1984–85 exhibition *'Primitivism' in 20th Century Art: Affinity of the Tribal and the Modern* distinguished the 'tribal' objects of the non-West from the modern artworks they inspired in the West. 'Primitivism' as an art movement warranted scare quotes, but the tribal did not. 'Tribal', one might surmise, describes cultures outside the West whose objects do not qualify as objects of art in themselves. West African studio portraiture, for example, in which the modern medium of photography from the 1950s onwards pictured carefully staged subjects of decolonising nations, would have disturbed the geographical coordinates of art history manifested at MoMA.[10]

The now-famous Malinese photographer Seydou Keïta's portraits explicitly invite attention to the visually arresting presentation of human subjects, including the highly styled composition of images, light design, and placement of props.[11] Posed often singly, or in twos, the photographed subjects were often provided the option of 'accessories' including watches, pens, radios, and even a scooter.[12] If, for Simmel, aesthetic forms such as Impressionism registered the inner substance of modernity, Keïta's stagings register through form a peculiar kind of African modernism in the transition to Senegalese independence, connecting with, yet different from, the form of facingness Fried identifies in Manet's late nineteenth-century Parisian modernity. In a photograph from 1956/7, a young woman leans over a radio set while facing the camera, the gown and headdress she wears framed conspicuously by a delicately patterned cloth covering the wall behind her. Her gaze solicits the viewer's look while the staging simultaneously draws attention to the setting. In an earlier photograph (1949), a young man wearing a suit poses against a far more dramatically designed cloth backdrop, the elaborate tassels of which fall to the ground above a striking black-and-white, diamond-tiled floor into which his carefully placed feet in black and white shoes disappear. The overall effect of this patterned, composite surface seemingly lifts the model above the ground. The attention to patterning, especially on backdrops in the studio set, and the elaborate printed material of the subject's clothing in Keïta's portraits eschews the construction of perspectival depth. Further, the portrayal of psychological depth is avoided by turning the sitter into one of the many forms in the image.

Christopher Pinney rightly claims that in Keïta's oeuvre 'photographic surfacism [. . .] engages with texture, where everything springs out of the photograph toward the viewer, rather than a field of spatio-temporal certainty receding within the image' (2003: 216). The 'refusal of external verification' (2003: 216) through the rejection of perspectival depth makes Keïta's portraits operate like many modernist artworks, though they manifest no particular affinity with 'Primitivism'. The indeterminate position occupied by the studio portraits, neither 'tribal', nor 'tribal'-inspired modernism, nor something in between, displaces modernism itself and the spatialisation of modernity underpinning art history. Manthia Diawara forcefully states that 'To go before Keïta's lens is to pass the test of modernity, to be transformed as an urbane subject even if one has no power in the market or at the train station' (1998: 67). Non-Western studio photography exploits the potential of portraits to disrupt the spatial organisation of modernism by passing the test of modernity in spaces that confound its Western provenance.

The deracinated understanding of modernism that subtends art-historical typologies typically meant that the reception of non-Western artists, whether, for example, in Africa or even in the West, was framed by and focused on their origins and racial and cultural identities. Rasheed Araeen observes that

> Some Afro-Asian artists were successful and institutionally cele-brated in the late 1950s and early 1960s in Britain. But underlying their success was a fascination with their racial differences or cultural backgrounds, by which they were separated from the mainstream discourse and excluded from the narratives of British art history. (2008: 127)

Araeen's critique of institutional culturalism towards non-Western/non-white artists is compelling. Pinney and Diawara's reframing of studio portraiture, however, suggests less the need for inclusion in official art history than the disruption of the spatial frames of art history, and history itself.

Subjectivity and/as the Dissolution of Form

How do the disruptive, relational dynamics of the portraits analysed above for thinking and picturing identity relate to far more radical arguments around the dissolution of both subjectivity and modes for expressing it broached in the introduction to this chapter? Leo Bersani suggests that a 'foundational approach to the question of relationality' might begin at 'a certain threshold of the relational [. . .] one at which each human subject [. . .] might have the option of *not* moving, of *not* connecting' (2001: 352). Bersani introduces a specific, psychoanalytic understanding of 'desire' as the 'foundational motor' for 'the invisible rhythms of appearance and disappearance in all being' (2001: 353). His reading of sexual desire, emphasising the 'depsychologizing of desire', is crucial, since this formulation absents the subject from an understanding of sexual desire for figuring relational identity which gets 'grounded in loss [. . .] of being itself' (2001: 358). As Christopher Lane rightly observes, 'the perceptual emptying out of desire from identification [. . .] Bersani turns into an all-out critique of sociality' (2001: 149).

The paradoxical conjunction of relationality and non-connection is given form for Bersani precisely in art, and the non-figurative representation of identity, or 'the erasure of figurality' (2001: 353). The aesthetic production of perception and the negation of possible subjectivity through the failure of identification make formlessness the only correct form to picture the subject. Bersani argues that 'If art is the principal site/sight (both place and view) of being as emergence into connectedness, then the metaphysical dimensions of the aesthetic [. . .] is an erosion of aesthetic form' (2001: 353). The absence of clear outlines delineating discrete objects in the paintings of J. M. W. Turner and Mark Rothko, Bersani avers, invites an immersive experience into formlessness through colour rather than grasping discrete presences through stable form. He insists that 'emphatically present forms designate nonaesthetic functions and registers of being. Brutally authoritative interventions in space [the picture surface] – presences secure in their legitimation – violate the ecological ethic for which art trains us' (2001: 353). The erosion of figurality by 'the rubbing out of formal relations' (2001: 353) manifests the ontology of the 'aesthetic' – which form violates. The argument for dissolution of form throws up problems for thinking the portrait's political potential, since the gap that portraits invite one to aesthetically explore between 'political, social and fictional figures' (Rancière 2017: 157) is closed down by rejecting figuration itself through the rubbing out of formal relations. Aesthetic form becomes an oxymoron.

Analysing the transition in Sherman's oeuvre from the self-portraits in *Untitled Film Stills* (1978–80) to her 'sex pictures' of 'sexual and/or excretory body parts', Hal Foster contends that 'the impulse to erode the subject and tear at the screen has driven Sherman from the early work where the subject is caught in the gaze [. . .] to [. . .] where it is obliterated by the gaze' (1996: 113). His reading resonates partially with Bersani's (2001: 353) argument against 'emphatically present forms'. In the 1990s photographs, Foster observes that 'the images pass beyond the abject [. . .] towards the *informe*, a condition described by

Bataille where significant form dissolves because the fundamental distinction between figure and ground, self and other, is lost' (1996: 112). Extreme close-up figurations of organs, viscera, and bodily fluids obliterate the signifying and significant coherence of the gendered subject's identity.[13]

Arguments about the dissolution of sexual identity, in their desire to escape the restrictive normalisation of subjectivity, fail to adequately acknowledge the troubling, intractably contradictory sources and effects of desire grounding the contingent (in)stability of identity.[14] Sherman's self-portraits do not figure 'subjects caught in the gaze' (Foster 1996: 112) but configure this capture and its deflection by registering its anxiety-producing effects in the ambivalent form the woman's body takes on. The portraits analysed above exploit the tensions between political, social, and fictional identities by giving them aesthetic forms, *contra* Bersani's understanding of the aesthetic, which blur the distinctions between self and other, man and woman, ground and figure, human and nature, subject and object.

Psychoanalysis 'enters the political field', Jacqueline Rose argues, precisely because the 'question of identity – how it is constituted and maintained' focuses on the 'problem of identification and its laws, in all their force and impossibility' (2005b: 5). The valorisation of non-conflictual negativity, absolute loss, and the move from 'psychic density' to formless 'pure potentiality' fail to register the tension produced by 'splitting, denegation, foreclosure, denial, or even repression [. . .] the insignia of how we *struggle* with our inner world' and 'the shifting forms of identity and loss of identity whereby we try, and fail, to exert psychic and sexual mastery over ourselves' (Rose 2017: 393).

In Sherman and Diop, the sighting and re-citing of the fantasy of gender, race, and nation (Theweleit 1987) destabilise individuality through the play of forms which make visible both the uncertain identity of the subject in the image, and the persistence of fantasy in any relation between the desiring look and the object it fastens on. The psychoanalytic understanding of fantasy ('phantasy') blurs the distinction between the desiring male gaze and the female as the passive object of the gaze (Lacan 1982; Stern 1982: 60). Rose (1982: 33) argues that 'the difficulty of sexuality instantly disappears . . . when the categories "male and female" are seen to represent an absolute and complementary division', and 'the fantasy on which this notion rests' should be exposed. Sherman's self-portraits cite normative forms of femininity while registering the 'anxiety of narcissism' provoked by the life of fantasy, which both structures and destabilises how women relate to the norms of the gender binary through the gaze. By exposing the instability of complementary male/female distinctions through the non-reciprocal alignment of gazes, her self-portraits reveal how sexual 'fantasy' can yield 'key insights into the structure and dynamic of historically constituted organizations of power and violence' located in the look (Butler 2021: 36).

Lewis R. Gordon argues that the continuous splitting of the (Black) subject between phobic social constitution and the self's inability to successfully embody it accurately explains the 'lived realities of mixture [. . .] since reality (is) relations of living negations of purity [. . .] negations of and for being' (2022: 130). In other words, the lived relations of negations do not simply precipitate loss of being; instead, they both negate being and produce *for* being forms that register this conflictual dynamic. Diop's *Belley* converts the already compromised historical agency of the Black/French Deputy, the loss of which through the 1804 re-establishment of slavery is transformed through the contemporary embodiment of the dis/empowered Black/French footballer.

The formal (com)posing of the subjects reveals the gap in the appearances of 'social, political, and fictional figures', rather than stabilising 'brutally present' identities. For Bersani and Dutoit, the appearance of formlessness in the image matches the reality of identity it represents. For Rancière, however, 'appearance does not oppose itself to the real, it opposes itself to another appearance, just as one reality opposes itself to another reality' (2019: 75).[15] Diop's *Belley* and Sherman's *Untitled Film Stills* play with appearances to expose the gap in racial, gender, and national identity. They exploit the potential of the self-portrait's picturing of self as other by rendering the subject's recognition of the split between self-consciousness and social perception as it is played out in the field of appearances.

Desire connects being to other beings and nature, and this open relationality is precisely the cause of the struggles of the subject's inner world manifested in its dispersion into the world through gaps in identity. Rachel Stein, for example, argues that 'the revolutionary belief in social and sexual justice' takes form and place precisely by 'situating lesbian desire out in the social/natural world' (2010: 290). Here too, rather than precipitating loss of being and 'impersonal narcissism' (Bersani 2015: 5), the movement of desire out into the 'social/natural world' relates identities to each other and the world (land, nation).[16] How can the subject's displacement from itself and into a changing world be captured by the figuration of this dynamic relationship through a play of forms?

Opacity and the Reverberations of Identity-in-motion

By way of concluding, I will analyse how identity manifests through the reverberations produced by a specific play of forms in Maria Magdalena Pons's 2002 work *Elevata*.[17] In the reading of the portrait below, literal and metaphorical displacement of identity is given form through the presence of a persistent opacity in/of the subject in the image figured through the irreconcilable play between opposite aesthetic strategies. Pons, a Black, Cuban-born, American artist, manifests her identity in the self-portrait, which situates and relates herself to a changing history and geography of displacement. *Elevata* comprises 16 polaroid film prints arranged to form a single rectangular surface gridded by the black frames of each print. The connotations of submersion in water are produced by the upside-down and back-to-front self-portrait of Pons at the top-left edge, from which her tendril-like hair seems to waver in the aquamarine environment around her. The arrangement of each of the 16 separate framed prints, however, forms a continuity on the picture plane's surface. Pons's head and hair, and the bluish spheres suspended in the multiple shades of blue, are not broken up into fragments by the gridded surface but spread out across/under it as if the grid had been superimposed after the whole image was constructed, rather than the other way around. Unity and separation are co-formed within and on the surface of the picture frame. Further, the rich, blue, horizon-less colour invites the viewer into an immersive visual experience, while the grid simultaneously frames viewing as a mediated experience of looking through to look at the self-portrait and the objects around it. The play of proximity and distance continues through a perspective limited only to the back of Pons's head, making her present to the viewer while she also turns her face away from them. The fluidity of the (marine) blue environment is further dynamised by the upside-down self-portrait, suggesting a submersion in, and movement about, the water. Is this movement up – the title of the artwork – towards the water's invisible surface or perhaps heading down to the ocean floor?

Elevata deploys the picture surface to portray a dynamic yet clearly outlined presence of the human subject in its shifting relation to a fluid environment. The portrayal of human presence yet absence of face, presence as movement rather than stasis, immersion in and separation from, unified surface and fragmented form – the rhythms of this dynamic figuration manifest the tense interplay between opposing strategies whose aesthetic forms render the scenography of the subject without dissipating into formlessness. The inevitable losses and gains marking the displacement of identity are given form in the present through a composite portrait comprising photographic snapshots in which the moment is the time for registering their historically shifting relation through dispersion in the present.

Bersani and Dutoit argue that 'When subjects and objects are eliminated, the exaggerations of expressiveness lose their seductive appeal' (2006: 70). Rather than opacity produced through only partial transparency, the absence of form is valued in registering the presence of the subject. Cutting against this notion of presence-in-absence, Pons's *Elevata* instantiates what Édouard Glissant (1997: 111) calls the 'right to opacity' produced by the experience of displacement, and the historical, social, and psychic complexity which confounds a transparent rendition of subjectivity. Glissant's invocation of opacity is contingently grounded in 'the Black Beach' (1997: 121) as way point in the abyssal journeys through which displaced subjects are formed and give chaotic form to the world in turn. The abysses encountered in physical displacement, the epistemological uncertainties they produce for knowledge, and the indeterminacy of aesthetic forms are linked. Glissant argues that

> Every time an individual or community attempts to define its place in it [the *chaos-monde*] [. . .] [relation] helps blow the usual way of thinking off course [. . .] By rediscovering the abysses of art or the interplay of various aesthetics, scientific knowledge thus develops one of the ways poetics is expressed, reconnecting with poetry's earlier ambition to establish itself as knowledge. (1997: 137–8)

Poesis as the play of forms registers the abysses of art's desire to accurately produce knowledge. Opacity does not mean the complete absence of knowledge through the dissolution of form and the elimination of subjects from the image; rather, it lends form to figurations of transforming subjects through their partly non-transparent and changing relations to themselves, others, and nature. The subjects in the image also instantiate opacity through the configuration of non-aligned/confronting looks between viewer and sitter. By making the portrayed subject's gaze unavailable (Pons), ignoring the look of the viewer (Sherman/Belley), and gazing back to counter the look (Mapplethorpe), the ocular desire for transparency is thwarted by the opacity generated through the unresolved play between looks.

For Bersani, psychic density grounds unacceptable 'modern notions of individualism', which are exemplified in 'national, ethnic and racial identities' (Bersani and Phillips 2008: 85). These identities, he rightly argues, are not 'monolithic identitarian blocks', yet their 'diffused presence' is often expressed in 'imaginary yet powerfully operative borders outside of which lies everything that is essentially different from them' (2008: 85). Hence the equation between psychic density, critique of identitarian thinking, and the aesthetic of diffusion imaging formlessness. Portraiture, I have argued, manifests an interrogation of 'individualism' precisely by giving form to the crossing of the borders that mark non-separatist figurations of identities. The portrait manifests the subject in the image by undoing the stabilisation of homogeneous identities, deploying the play of forms which simultaneously cite, set into relation, and reframe the spurious borders secured by histories of discursive and visual normalisation. The subject emerges in the image through the reverberations in and across race, gender, and sexuality produced by the non-resolvable social, psychic, and historical relations manifested in the forms lent by aesthetic strategies in portraiture.

Notes

1. See Baxandall 1988. He observes, for example, that 'in the fifteenth century, painting was still too important to be left to the painters' (1988: 3), the power of patrons being crucial to the practice of the art of painting. His focus on the 'Conditions of Trade' (1988: 1–28) emphasises this broad patron–artist relationship, though it is not limited solely to portraiture.
2. *Manet: Portraying Life*, https://www.royalacademy.org.uk/exhibition/manet (last accessed 10 May 2022).
3. See Goodstein 2002 for a detailed engagement with Simmel's phenomenology of culture.
4. Available at https://www.youtube.com/watch?v=z8aR9lSIQBs (last accessed 8 May 2022).
5. For the politics of transformation between painting and photography, see Garb 2020: esp. 592–3.
6. Diop's *Belley* sports a sartorial excess that gives a particular form to the queer figure of the 'black dandy'. See Miller 2009.
7. Available at https://www.moma.org/collection/works/56722 (last accessed 6 May 2022).
8. Available at https://www.moma.org/collection/works/56581 (last accessed 6 May 2022).
9. Looking as a visual epistemology of perfection is disturbed in a far more dramatic fashion in Hans Holbein's *The Ambassadors* (1533). Further, the at-first unrecognisable figure in the foreground takes on form and meaning only when the viewer's look emerges by moving the body. See Lacan 1977: esp. 85–90. In Sherman's stills, it is the direction of her gaze in the image, rather than the displaced look of the viewer, that subtly destabilises the portrait's meaning.

10. See Araeen 2005. Araeen focuses primarily on painting, though his nuanced understanding of both post-coloniality in Africa and the vexed relationship through the former between modernity and modernism is directly relevant for my broader argument about Western art history's provinciality. My shift in focus to African studio photography emphasises the shift in the configurations of colonial power-relations when the camera as tool for fixing, controlling, and exoticising the colonised subject is taken back by the latter.

11. The Seydou Keïta Photogaphy Estate Advisor Corporation (SKPEAC) is the official website of the late photographer: http://www.seydoukeitaphotographer.com (last accessed 9 May 2022).

12. Available at http://www.seydoukeitaphotographer.com (last accessed 9 May 2022).

13. My analysis of Sherman's self-portraits emphasises the figuration of woman as embodied gendered subject without dissipating the images into disembodied and ungendered forms of textual *différance*. This point is important given Derrida's (1972) influential formulation of 'woman' as a figure of textuality. See Gayatri Spivak's (1984) critique of the disappearance of 'woman' as identity through Derrida's formulation of *différance*.

14. Bersani's depsychologised understanding of desire is central to his psychoanalytic understanding of homosexual identity, developed in *Homos* (1995) and elaborated on further in *Intimacies* (2008) with Adam Phillips. See Lane 2001: 148–9, 151 for Bersani's theorisation of sociality from homosexual desire.

15. 'L'apparence ne s'oppose pas au réel, elle s'oppose à un autre apparence, comme un réel s'oppose à un autre réel.' My translation. *Réel* is literally 'real' in French. I have chosen 'reality' (*réalité*) because it signifies the relation between appearance and reality in the interview, and it avoids a psychoanalytic misreading of the term with the Lacanian 'Real'.

16. Stein's reading of Adrienne Rich's 'Yom Kippur 1984' brings out the intersection of multiple gendered, sexual, and raced identities which form a 'we' through the paradoxical desire for 'solitude', and the threat of violence this desire poses for marginalised identities. Desire isolates, connects, and threatens the subjects it brings together into a 'we'. See Stein 2020: 292–4.

17. For a brief, largely thematic analysis of *Elevata*, see Mercer 2016: 16.

References

Alhadeff, Albert (2020), *Théodore Géricault, Painting Black Bodies: Confrontations and Contradictions*, Abingdon: Routledge.

Appiah, Anthony (1985), 'The Uncompleted Argument: Du Bois and the Illusion of Race', *Critical Inquiry*, 12(1): 21–37.

Araeen, Rasheed (2005), 'Modernity, Modernism, and Africa's Place in the History of Art of Our Age', *Third Text*, 19(4): 411–17.

Araeen, Rasheed (2008), 'A Very Special *British* Issue? Modernity, Art History and the Crisis of Art Today', *Third Text*, 22(2): 125–44.

Baxandall, Michael (1988), *Painting and Experience in Fifteenth Century Italy: A Primer in the Social History of Pictorial Style*, Oxford. Oxford University Press.

Benjamin, Walter (1978 [1934]), 'Author as Producer', in *Reflections: Essays, Aphorisms, Autobiographical Writings*, New York: Schocken Books, pp. 220–38.

Benjamin, Walter (2005 [1931]), 'Little History of Photography', in *Selected Writings, Volume 2, Part 2, 1931–1934*, ed. Michael W. Jennings, Howard Eiland, and Gary Smith, Cambridge, MA: The Belknap Press of Harvard University Press, pp. 507–30.

Bernstein, J. M. (2006), *Against Voluptuous Bodies: Late Modernism and the Meaning of Painting*, Stanford, CA: Stanford University Press.

Bersani, Leo (1995), *Homos*, Cambridge, MA: Harvard University Press.

Bersani, Leo (2001), 'Genital Chastity', in Tim Dean and Christopher Lane (eds), *Homosexuality and Psychoanalysis*, Chicago: University of Chicago Press, pp. 351–66.

Bersani, Leo (2015), *Thoughts and Things*, Chicago: University of Chicago Press.

Bersani, Leo, and Ulysse Dutoit (2006), *Forms of Being: Cinema, Aesthetics, Subjectivity*, London: British Film Institute.

Bersani, Leo, and Adam Phillips (2008), *Intimacies*, Chicago: University of Chicago Press.

Bindman, David, and Henry Louis Gates Jr (2010), *The Image of the Black in Western Art: From the 'Age of Discovery' to the Age of Abolition, Artists of the Renaissance and Baroque*, Cambridge, MA: Harvard University Press.

Buggenhagen, Beth (2017), 'If You Were in My Sneakers: Migration Stories in the Studio Photography of Dakar-Based Omar Victor Diop', *Visual Anthropology Review*, 33(1): 38–50.

Butler, Judith (2021), *The Force of Non-Violence: An Ethico-Political Bind*, London: Verso.

Derrida, Jacques (1972), 'Freud and the Scene of Writing', *Yale French Studies*, 48: 74–117.

Diawara, Manthia (1998), 'Talk of the Town', *Artforum* 36(6): 64–71.

Falola, Toyin (2013), *The African Diaspora: Slavery, Modernity, and Globalization*, Rochester, NY: University of Rochester Press.

Finley, Cheryl, and Deborah Willis (2016), 'Black Portraiture(s)', *NKA: Journal of Contemporary African Art*, 38/39: 6–7.

Foster, Hal (1996), 'Obscene, Abject, Traumatic', *October*, 78: 106–24.

Foucault, Michel (2009), *Manet and the Object of Painting*, London: Tate Publishing.

Fried, Michael (1996), *Manet's Modernism, or the Face of Painting in the 1860s*, Chicago: University of Chicago Press.

Galassi, Peter (1997), 'Cindy Sherman's Complete *Untitled Film Stills*', https://www.moma.org/interactives/exhibitions/1997/sherman/index.html (last accessed 6 May 2022).

Garb, Tamar (2020), 'Painting/Politics/Photography: Marlene Dumas, Mme Lumumba and the Image of the African Woman', *Art History*, 43(3): 588–611.

Glissant, Édouard (1997), *Poetics of Relation*, Ann Arbor: University of Michigan Press.

Goodstein, Elizabeth (2002), 'Style as Substance: Georg Simmel's Phenomenology of Culture', *Cultural Critique*, 52: 209–34.

Gordon, Lewis R. (2022), *The Fear of Black Consciousness*, London: Penguin.

Grüner, Eduardo (2020), *The Haitian Revolution: Capitalism, Slavery and Counter Modernity*, Cambridge: Polity.

Hall, Stuart (2017), *The Fateful Triangle: Race, Ethnicity, Nation*, Cambridge, MA: Harvard University Press.

Hegel, G. W. F. (1997 [1837]), *Reason in History: A General Introduction to the Philosophy of History*, London: Macmillan.

Hegel, G. W. F. (1998 [1835]), *Aesthetics: Lectures on Fine Art, Volume 1*, Oxford: Clarendon Press.

Lacan, Jacques (1977), *The Four Fundamental Concepts of Psychoanalysis*, London: Hogarth, 1977.

Lacan, Jacques (1982), 'A Love Letter (*Une Lettre d'Âmour)*', in *Feminine Sexuality: Jacques Lacan and the* École Freudienne, ed. Juliet Mitchell and Jacqueline Rose, Basingstoke: Macmillan, pp. 149–61.

Lane, Christopher (2001), 'Freud on Group Psychology: Shattering the Dream of a Common Culture', in Tim Dean and Christopher Lane (eds), *Homosexuality and Psychoanalysis*, Chicago: University of Chicago Press, pp. 147–67.

Locke, Alain LeRoy (1971), *The Negro in Art: A Pictorial Record of the Negro Artist and of the Negro Theme in Art*, New York: Hacker Art Books.

Mercer, Kobena (2016), *Travel & See: Black Diaspora Art Practices since the 1980s*, Durham, NC: Duke University Press.

Meyer, Richard (1993), 'Robert Mapplethorpe and the Discipline of Photography', in Henry Abelove, Michele Anna Barale, and David Halperin (eds), *Lesbian and Gay Studies Reader*, London: Routledge, pp. 260–380.

Miller, Monica L. (2009), *Slaves to Fashion: Black Dandyism and the Styling of Black Diasporic Identity*, Durham, NC: Duke University Press.

Navarre, Max (1989), 'Fighting the Victim Label', in Douglas Crimp (ed.), *AIDS: Cultural Analysis, Cultural Criticism*, Cambridge, MA: MIT Press, pp. 143–51.

Pinney, Christopher (2003), 'Notes from the Surface of the Image: Photography, Postcolonialism, and Vernacular Modernism', in Christopher Pinney and Nicolas Peterson (eds), *Photography's Other Histories*, Durham, NC: Duke University Press, pp. 202–20.

Rancière, Jacques (2017), 'Identifications of the People: With Diane Arnaud and Stéphane Bou', in Emiliano Battista (ed.), *Dissenting Words: Interviews with Jacques Rancière*, London: Bloomsbury, pp. 153–72.

Rancière, Jacques (2019), 'Langage et images', in Jacques Rancière, *Les mots et les torts: Dialogue avec Javier Bassas*, Paris: La Fabrique, pp. 73–96.

Rose, Jacqueline (1982), 'Introduction – II', in Jacques Lacan, *Feminine Sexuality: Jacques Lacan and the* École Freudienne, ed. Juliet Mitchell and Jacqueline Rose, Basingstoke: Macmillan, pp. 27–57.

Rose, Jacqueline (2005a), 'Sexuality in the Field of Vision', in Jacqueline Rose, *Sexuality in the Field of Vision*, London: Verso, pp. 225–33.

Rose, Jacqueline (2005b), 'Introduction: Feminism and the Psychic', in Jacqueline Rose, *Sexuality in the Field of Vision*, London: Verso, pp. 1–23.

Rose, Jacqueline (2017), 'Something Amiss', in Eve Watson and Noreen Giffney (eds), *Clinical Encounters in Sexuality: Psychoanalytical Practice and Queer Theory*, New York: Punctum Books, pp. 391–6.

Rosset, Jane (1989), 'Photographs by Jane Rosett', in Douglas Crimp (ed.), *AIDS: Cultural Analysis, Cultural Criticism*, Cambridge, MA: MIT Press, pp: 151–60.

Sander, August (1994), *Face of Our Time: Sixty Portraits of Twentieth-century Germans*, Munich: Schirmer.

Shaw, Hannah (1991), 'The Trouble with the Censorship of August Sander's *Antlitz der Zeit*', *PhotoResearcher: ESHPh, European Society for the History of Photography*, 31: 193–220.

Simmel, Georg (1989 [1900]), *Philosophie des Geldes*, Gesamtausgabe, *Volume 6*, Frankfurt: Suhrkamp.

Soussloff, Catherine M. (2006), *The Subject in Art: Portraiture and the Birth of the Modern*, Durham, NC: Duke University Press.

Spivak, Gayatri (1984), 'Love Me, Love My Ombre, Elle', *Diacritics*, 14(4): 19–36.

Stein, Rachel (2010), '"The Place, Promised, That Has Not Yet Been": The Nature of Dislocation and Desire in Adrienne Rich's *Your Native Land/Your Life* and Minnie Bruce Pratt's *Crime Against Nature*', in Catriona Mortimer-Sandilands and Bruce Erickson (eds), *Queer Ecologies: Sex, Nature, Politics, Desire*, Bloomington: Indiana University Press, pp. 285–308.

Stern, Leslie (1982), 'The Body as Evidence', *Screen*, 23(5): 39–60.

Theweleit, Klaus (1987), *Male Fantasies: Volume 1, Women, Floods, Bodies, History*, Minneapolis: University of Minnesota Press.

Vergès, Françoise (2016), 'The Slave at the Louvre: An Invisible Humanity', *NKA: Journal of Contemporary African Art*, 38–39: 8–13.

Waldman, Louis A., and Brenda Preyer (2012), 'The Rise of the Patronage Portrait in Late Renaissance Florence: An Enigmatic Portrait of Giovanni di Paolo Rucellai and its Role in Family Commemoration', *Mitteilungen des Kunsthistorischen Institutes in Florenz*, 54(1): 133–54.

Watney, Simon (1987), 'The Spectacle of AIDS', *October*, 43: 71–86.

Chapter 10

The Avatarisation of the (Self-)Portrait: Notes Towards a Theological Genealogy of the Virtual Self

Andrea Pinotti

Avatāra: The Theological Background

In recent decades, a major transformation in the representation of personal identity has occurred in the contemporary iconosphere: the advent of 'avatars', digital pictures operating as proxies, allowing users of the Web, of social networks, of cyber-communities, or of video games to interact with synthetic objects or with other avatars in the virtual world, thus pushing the traditional representational function of the portrait towards an interrelational and interactive agency (Schroeder 2002; Cooper et al. 2007; Amato and Perény 2013). In terms of medium, style, and genre, the spectrum of avatars is vast and varied, ranging from simple drawings or photographic (self-)portraits to elaborate figures produced by CGI (computer-generated imagery).

As a surrogate or representative of the subject's identity, the practice of the avatar is at the same time old and new. The very term 'avatar' belongs to the ancient Hindu tradition: the Sanskrit word *avatāra* designates the terrestrial descent of a divinity, usually Vishnu, who decides to temporarily interfere with earthly affairs when these perturb the cosmic order and so takes on an appearance visible to humans. The specific forms which the deity can embody vary according to the circumstances: for instance, Vishnu can appear as a fish, a tortoise, a boar, a man-lion, a dwarf, the Buddha. Every single *avatāra* constitutes a partial manifestation of the deity it renders visible. Once the assigned task is accomplished, the *avatāra* merges back into its deity (Hacker 1960; Kinsley 1987). As studies in the comparative history of religions have shown, far from being an exclusively Hinduist doctrine, the essential process performed by the *avatāra* (making visible and perceptible the invisible divinity) can be found in various creeds: suffice it to think of the 'incarnation' of God in Christ (Parrinder 1997; Sheth 2002).

In Western languages, the occurrence of the term 'avatar' can be traced back to the end of the eighteenth century.[1] Théophile Gautier employed the word as the title of a short novel published in 1856 (Gautier 2011), and Samuel J. Macknight published a poem under the title 'The Avatar of Peace' in 1896 (Macknight 1896). The preacher and 'prophet' Thomas Lake Harris, who founded the Californian 'Brotherhood of the New Life' in 1851, was defined as an 'avatar' in one of his hagiographic biographies (Respiro 1897). At the beginning of the twentieth century, the homeopath Jirah Dewey Buck fused theosophy and empirical psychology, acknowledging 'our indebtedness to ancient India' and invoking the arrival of a new Avatar or Revealer (Buck 1911). In the 1920s Gandhi's disciple Vengal Chakkarai spoke of Jesus as an avatar in an attempt to prove the convergence of Christianity and Hinduism (Chakkarai 1926). In the 1940s Indian spiritual master Meher Baba claimed to be the human form or avatar of God, and was recognised as such in the biography written by his American disciple Jean Adriel (1947).

In subsequent decades, the term has been employed far beyond the domain of religious and esoteric writings: its widespread use has been determined by its extensive diffusion in the context of popular culture, especially video games (the eponymous *Avatar* was produced in 1979), chatrooms, social networks, and more generally in digital communication. The worldwide success of James Cameron's movie *Avatar*, released in 2009, definitively contributed to its planetary fame (Depraz 2012). The theological line of descent can also be reconstructed for another key term in the vocabulary of contemporary digital culture: 'icon' (from the Greek *eikon*: picture): this term, long before designating a pictogram or ideogram displayed on a computer screen so as to offer the user an interface for navigating a computer system, was a central notion in semiotics (suffice it to think of Peirce's tripartition of the sign into 'icon – index – symbol'), and much earlier it identified the painted wooden panel of Christ and the saints in the Byzantine tradition of sacred images (Belting 1994).

Presence vs. Representation

As I will try to show in what follows, the theological pedigree of the notions of 'avatar' and 'icon', far from being a cyber-curiosity, forms the historical background to a central issue in the phenomenology and ontology of contemporary digital pictures, namely the oscillation between two opposite poles: *presence* and *representation*. The polarisation between real presence and mere representation constitutes a deep tension in the Western conceptualisation of the image experience which has a very *longue durée* and seems to resurface nowadays with particular strength, albeit reformulated, in the contemporary debate on digital images in general, and on digital images representing the self (avatars) in particular.

The oscillation between presence and representation corresponds to the very same polarisation that, *mutatis mutandis*, characterised the excruciating Byzantine debates between iconophiles and iconoclasts back in the eighth century, culminating (although not conclusively) in the Second Council of Nicaea (787 CE). The *horos* (definition) of the Holy, Great, Ecumenical Synod established the preservation and defence of the 'reproduction in painted images' of Christ, the Virgin Mary, the angels and saints, decreeing that 'venerable and holy images, made in colours or mosaic or other fitting materials, in the same way as the figure of the honourable and life-giving cross, are to be dedicated in the holy churches of God, on sacred vessels and vestments, on walls and panels, in houses and in the streets' (Price 2018: 564–5).

The justification for *representing* such subject matters was based on a specific Christological line of argument: Christ himself as the Son is the image of God the Father, and looking at him means looking at the Father himself incarnate and thus made visible to human eyes, that is, put into image. The main authorities on this point are John and Paul. As John puts it, 'no one has ever seen [*heoraken*] God. The only Son, God, who is at the Father's side, has revealed him' (John 1:18). Adopting the profoundly Greek identification of knowledge and vision, his Jesus affirms: 'If you know me, then you will also know my Father. From now on you do know him and have seen him [*ginoskete auton kai heorakate auton*]' (John 14:7). Paul is even more explicit, declaring that Christ 'is the image of God [*eikon tou Theou*]' (II Corinthians 4:4); 'He is the image of the invisible God [*eikon tou Theou tou aoratou*]' (Colossians 1:15).

Nevertheless, this Christological foundation introduces a crucial hierarchy in the iconic system; as fully promulgated in 451 at the Council of Chalcedon, Jesus is one person with two natures, divine and human (dyophysitism), which is explicitly recalled in the Second Nicene *horos*: 'We acknowledge the two natures of the one who was incarnate for our sake from the immaculate Theotokos and ever-virgin Mary, recognising him to be perfect God and perfect man' (Price 2018: 563). Therefore, Christ is at the same time the direct presence of God and his *eikon*. The sacred *eikones* made by human hand, on the contrary, are merely pictures devoid of divine presence (if they possessed this, they would be divine in themselves, thus fostering a polytheistic multiplication of divinities). In this respect, they can be the object of reverence and veneration (*proskynesis*) as merely transitive representations referring to the divine prototypes, but not the object of true adoration (*latreia*), which is exclusively reserved for the divine prototypes (including the 'special', as it were, *eikon* which is Christ himself): 'The honour paid to the image passes over to the prototype, and whoever venerates the image venerates in it the hypostasis of the one who is represented' (Price 2018: 565).

While overcoming the aniconic prohibition expressed in the Old Testament ('You shall not make to yourself an idol [*eidolon*], nor any representation [*omoioma*]': Exodus 20:4) and the traumatic event of Aaron's golden calf (Exodus 32) by introducing a rigorous separation between veneration/representation on the one hand and adoration/presence on the other, the creed expressed as a conclusion of the Second Nicene Council did not succeed in eliminating presence from Christian ritual. According to the Catholic Church and other Christian confessions, during the consecration the rite of the Eucharist performs the 'transubstantiation' (a term introduced by the 1215 Fourth Lateran Council), that is the transformation of the substances of bread and wine into the body and blood of Christ, which are considered to be not just symbolically or metaphorically or representationally, but 'really' present in the flesh.

Despite this polarisation between representational icon and presential Eucharist, popular Christian faith has tended to restore presence in various ways: suffice it to think of prayer cards – *santjes* in the Netherlands, *santini* in Italy, *kleine Andachtsbilder* in Germany – miniaturised icons of sorts which have been so often fetishised as objects in themselves miraculously powerful, namely by virtue of their sheer talismanic presence and not just of their being representational (Freedberg 1989: 126–8).

The Resurgence of Archaic Idols

Why this theological excursus on the tension between real presence and representation? Because I argue that the 'representationalist' model, which was established at Nicaea and was subsequently the foundation of mainstream Western theories of the image as well as the popular account of what an image is ('Hollywood vient de là', as Régis Debray (1992: 77) puts it), is being challenged by a 'presentationalist' paradigm promoted by recent developments in image-making techniques which significantly impact on (self-)portraiture strategies. Presentness, often referred to with the formula 'being there', is one of the most salient properties of immersive virtual environments, which in their unframed and seamless continuity surround users with a 360-degree iconic world, arousing in them the feeling of being present within an *Umwelt* rather than standing in front of a picture. I feel present in the environment, and the digital objects populating the environment seem present to me, in the flesh as it were, and not just as mere iconic representations of objects.

A specific disciplinary domain, namely 'presence studies', has developed in order to address the manifold issues related to (tele-) presence – a term coined by Marvin Minsky back in 1980 – and has institutionalised its research activities through an MIT journal (*Presence: Virtual and Augmented Reality*, founded in 1992) and a scientific society (The International Society for Presence Research, founded in 2002). Remarkably, this specific research domain in VR and AR seems to belong to a much broader scholarly resurgence of interest in the notion of 'presence', as paradigmatically attested to by Hans Gumbrecht's seminal 2004 book *Production of Presence*. Although addressing a very ample domain ('"production of presence" points to all kinds of events and processes in which the impact that "present" objects can have on human bodies is being initiated or intensified'), the author does not neglect the particular context of our media environment, whose paradoxical condition is highlighted as follows: 'It has alienated us from the things of the world and their present – but at the same time, it has the potential for bringing back some of the things of the world to us' (Gumbrecht 2004: xiii, 140).

If, extending this argument, we also include, among the 'things' we relate to, other human subjects, we can see that avatars (both as total-body simulacra and as partial substitutes of our bodily image, namely as faces, half-length self-portraits, or even just hands in the case of virtual gloves) perform precisely the function pointed out by Gumbrecht. When I wear a VR HMD (head-mounted display), I lose the visual perception of my own body and become, so to speak, blind to myself, perceptually distanced and alienated from myself; but at the same time I regain a kind of self-perception via the embodiment in my own avatar: that is to say, via a self-portrait of a sort, which can, but need not, be imitative, and mostly is not so. At the same time, when my avatar interacts with other avatars in virtual space, it intersubjectively mirrors the embodied presence of the others, similarly incarnated in their own avatarised self.

This phenomenon of avatarisation of the (self-)portrait in the contemporary scenario of digital communication promotes a resurgence of archaic presential traits which goes hand in hand with the most advanced technology. This uncanny coupling had been already described by Walter Benjamin (1999: 461) in his explorations of the imaginary in nineteenth-century Baudelairean Paris (but also in Kafka's world):[2] 'Only a thoughtless observer can deny that correspondences come into play between the world of modern technology and the archaic symbol-world of mythology.'

In this regard, in addition to the discussion of presence and representation concerning Byzantine icons, we could consider even more archaic iconic artefacts, such as those investigated by Jean-Pierre Vernant in his thought-provoking research into the production and reception of pre-Platonic Greek images. Vernant has convincingly shown that the usual (presumed) starting point of Western aesthetics, namely Plato's theory of mimesis, should be deemed a late point of arrival if considered from the perspective of more archaic ways of experiencing the image, in which concern for a realistic and imitative representation of the perceptible model had as yet no place, to the advantage of an immediate presence of the invisible (either the god or the dead) in the idol carved in wood or stone. Vernant notes that the many Greek expressions to designate the 'divine idol' in the various forms it can take – *baitulos, dokana, kiōn, herma, bretas, xoanon, palladion, kouroi* and *korai, hedos, agalma, eikōn* and *mimēma* – do not entail the implication of mimesis: 'Of all these terms, excluding the last two, there is no single one that has any relation whatsoever to the idea of resemblance or imitation, of figural representation in the strict sense' (Vernant 2006b: 334; see also Vernant 2006a). Instead, it is a question of visualisation, in the literal sense of making visible the invisible: 'Whatever the *avatars* of the image may have been, this impossible quest is one that perhaps continues to remain valid to a large degree – that of evoking absence in presence, revealing the else-where in what is given to view' (Vernant 2006b: 336, emphasis mine). Although Vernant employs here the term 'avatars' in the generic sense of the multifarious transformations and inflections of image experience, we could apply his insight to the avatar as it is signified in contemporary cyberspace, namely as a 'presentification' (rather than a representation) of the absent self operating in tele-presence.

Performative and Operational Images

Digital avatars, archaic idols, and religious icons seem all to belong to the broad class of 'performative' images, whose functional meaning is triggered only in the context of a performative action, namely a ritual. *Proskynesis*, the veneration reserved for Byzantine icons, consisted not just in a motionless optical contemplation but rather in the prostration of the whole body of the devotee and in kisses that progressively wore out the material support of the image. Commenting on the *xoanon* (a wooden idol succinctly carved with no mimetic intention), Vernant observes: 'When a *xoanon* is involved, the plastic representation can never be wholly separated from ritual action. The idol is made in order to be shown and hidden, led forth and fixed in place, dressed and undressed, and given a bath' (2006b: 338).

Similarly, we dress and undress our own avatars, display them in certain circumstances and hide them most of the time, as happens with the entire iconosphere of digital pictures, which pass most of their obscure lives secluded, concealed, and sheltered in their invisible nature as bytes, to which they return every time we pause our smartphone or shut the screen of our laptop, ready to reappear, that is, to resurface to visibility, every time we need to retrieve them: 'What's truly revolutionary about the advent of digital images' – Trevor Paglen (2016) argues – 'is the fact that they are fundamentally machine-readable: they can only be seen by humans in special circumstances and for short periods of time [. . .] However, the image doesn't need to be turned into human-readable form in order for a machine to do something with it' (see Somaini 2020).

In his reflection on machine-readable images, Paglen draws on Harun Farocki's notion of 'operative Bilder', as presented in his 2001 video installation *Eye/Machine*: 'operative' or 'operational' images that are 'made neither to entertain nor to inform [. . .] images that do not represent an object, but rather are part of an operation' (Farocki 2004: 17).[3] Although the primary examples are drawn from the military application of such images (for example, the cameras installed on bombs offering a subjective point of view from the weapon; see Beck and Bishop 2020), warfare does not exhaust the applicative domains of such images. Their main functional property is the 'visualisation' of data and algorithmic processes that are not in themselves perceptible to the human eye and that determine and govern operations and interventions in the transformation of reality. In this sense, operational images, while eschewing the representational function in favour of the performative, maintain a privileged relationship with invisibility.

Visualisation as the procedure of making visible the invisible and its powers, as we have seen, was also the function performed by archaic Greek idols and (in their mediated way, passing through the visible person of Christ) Byzantine icons. Occult transactions can take place between the invisible god and its avatar secluded in the *sancta sanctorum* of the temple, regardless of its being perceived or not by a human eye. And yet, once retrieved from invisibility to visibility, such images do exert deep transformative effects on those who look at them.

The performative effectiveness of contemporary avatars is confirmed by the fact that they do not merely grant the user access from the real into the digital world, but also empower a two-way relation, enabling transformations from the digital to the real: despite their being low-level bodily representations, these mediators are effectively employed in the context of applicative approaches in empirical psychology because they are capable of modifying high-level attitudes and beliefs, such as gender and racial biases, via an illusion of full-body ownership: the assumption of an avatar of a different gender or skin colour, as has been demonstrated through experiments, can successfully contribute to amending stereotypes and prejudices (Seinfeld et al. 2018; Hasler et al. 2017; Peck et al. 2013). Avatar therapy is also commonly used in VR healthcare and rehabilitation, for the treatment of anxiety, PTSD, and many other clinically relevant syndromes in order to provide an ecological setting which is at the same time safe for the patient – because it is simulated – and convincingly embodied – because of its presentness effect (Freeman et al. 2017; Park et al. 2019).

The Subject(s) at Stake

Embodiment in one's own avatar is enhanced via a mirror-like self-recognition that implies a relationship to a frontal face or, more generally, figure. This is a feature that suggests that a further link between digital avatars and ancient religious icons and idols is frontality, as opposed to profile. As Meyer Schapiro remarked in a brilliant essay:

> The profile face is detached from the viewer and belongs with the body in action (or in an intransitive state) in a space shared with other profiles on the surface of the image. It is, broadly speaking, like the grammatical form of the third person, the impersonal 'he' or 'she' with its concordantly inflected verb; while the face turned outwards is credited with intentness, a latent or potential glance directed to the observer, and corresponds to the role of 'I' in speech, with its complementary 'you'. It seems to exist both for us and for itself in a space virtually continuous with our own, and is therefore appropriate to the figure as symbol or as carrier of a message. (Schapiro 1973: 38–9)

In this regard, frontality also applies more broadly to the wider class of (self-)portraits. In order to institute an avatarial relationship with its iconic surrogate, the 'I' outside the image must address the other

'I' within the image in an 'I–You' connection so as to trigger a mirror-like self-recognition. This requisite has most probably contributed to the statistically higher number of frontal or semi-profile portraits and self-portraits compared to those in profile.

The first-person address embedded in frontality engages the 'self' implied both in portraiture and in self-portraiture, determining its avatarial status, its 'mineness': avatars necessarily need the reflection of their own identity as a condition of possibility, its doubling, enabling both the separation between the self and its depiction on the one hand, and their embodied identification on the other (once again, the polarisation between representation and presence). 'Mineness' as a constitutive property of avatars differentiates them from the domain of post-photographic digital simulacra that Hans Belting (2017: 239–46) has conceived of as 'cyberfaces': whereas cyberfaces are digital constructs that look like realistic photographic portraits but do not actually refer to any real person (one might call them pseudo-photographs), avatars (be they realistic or not) necessarily maintain a constitutive anchorage to their masters.

However, 'mineness' is not exclusively attained through frontality. A remarkable counterpoint to the frontal avatar is offered by its 180-degree rotation, the so-called *Rückenfigur* (Prange 2010): the figure seen from behind, a representational scheme that dates back to ancient mosaics, frescoes, and vase paintings (Koch 1965). The *Rücken-avatar*, so frequently employed in video games, seems to suggest the possibility of traversing the threshold separating the real world from the iconic world, inviting the user to embody her own proxy from the back, assuming as it were its perspective and visual angle on the digital world.[4] The specific case of shooter games calls for a further distinction between the *full-body* avatar (which can be perceived by its master in the third-person view and is typically found in multi-player games) and the *partial* avatar (e.g. floating hands holding a gun, mostly employed in first-person shooters; see Walters 2019).

'Mineness', moreover, should not be intended as 'my singularity'. This aspect contrasts with influential accounts of traditional (self-)portraiture. If we consider, for instance, Georg Simmel's reflections on the representation of the self, we find a polarisation between the 'classical portrait' and Rembrandt's (self-)portrait: the former 'captures us in the moment of its present, but this is not a point in a series of comings and goings, but designates a timeless idea beyond such a series: the trans-historical form of the spiritual-physical existence' (Simmel 2005: 9). The latter contains 'the movement of the inner life by way of, or as, this accumulation' (2005: 11), so that the entire existence as a constant flow comes to be synthesised in the picture. But in both cases what is at stake is the core of subjectivity as *in*dividuality.

On the contrary, *di*viduality, as it were, seems to constitute the nucleus of our avatar experience.[5] From the point of view of their relation to personal identity, avatars cover a wide range of possibilities, whose extremes are determined on the one hand by the faithful and realistic (self-)portrait, and on the other hand by the mask, thus allowing their masters to negotiate an ideally infinite variation of fluid selfhood and its display. This characteristic is, of course, not new in the history of (self-)portraiture: we might think of role-playing self-portraits, such as Rembrandt depicting himself as the apostle Paul in the 1661 painting in the Rijksmuseum in Amsterdam (not surprisingly neglected in Simmel's account) or, in more recent times, the *Untitled Film Stills* realised by Cindy Sherman between 1977 and 1980 and the appropriative re-enactments by Yasumasa Morimura (for instance, his series *An Inner Dialogue with Frida Kahlo*, 2001). But the phenomenon of avatarisation pushes this process to its climax.

Revealing and Concealing

In its dialectical function of revealing and concealing the physiognomic traits of the subject's face or body, the avatar mobilises two opposite semantic implications of traditional (self-)portraiture. In fact, if we consider and compare how the depiction of the sitter is designated in European languages, we find a polarisation between an inward and an outward direction: the Italian 'ritratto' and the Spanish 'retrato' derive from the Latin verb *retraho* (to hold, safeguard, protect), whereas the English and French 'portrait' and in the German 'Porträt' stem from *protraho* (to pull out, to let out, to reveal).[6] Offering the possibility of assuming multiple personalities in different cyberspaces (swapping gender, race, age, profession etc.), avatars –like Vishnu with his different incarnations – also allow a multifaceted perspective-taking on the world in relation to the 'others-in-me', thus admitting various trends of self-identification and 'auto-empathy' (Tordo and Binkley 2013).

As in the above-mentioned case of the use of avatars in clinical and therapeutic settings, such avatarised perspective-taking can be put into practice, for instance with educational goals: 'A lesson about identity' is what the *Avatar Drawing – Identity Art Project* promises to offer. Teacher Stacey Peters invites students to draw their own avatar: 'A choice we make based on our identity; what we prefer and what we want others to know about us. Many of these choices come from our culture and the groups we belong to.'[7] This possibility of communicative preferences entails inclusion and exclusion, revelation and secrecy: a decision which can change in time, thus documenting the historical development of self-narration. The archive of all our avatars in their progressive accumulation testifies to the self-understanding of subjectivity as a becoming rather than as a being.

However, individual freedom in expressing one's own dividual natures through an avatar or multiple avatars is not absolute, but rather conditioned by a series of specific morphological constraints. This is particularly evident when the user is invited to 'choose' his/her own avatar among a series of ready-to-wear digital figures that have been generated with no regard to the subject's physiognomic traits or personality. In this circumstance, the avatar rather resembles other typologies, such as the *objet trouvé*, the *readymade*, the *found footage*. And its ability to represent the self consists in a 'becoming-portrait' of a picture that was not originally conceived as such by virtue of a process of appropriation and assumption decided by the users themselves.

A hybrid case is constituted by 'make your own avatar' apps and websites (such as https://avatarmaker.com or https://getavataaars.com), in which you are 'free' to compose your own avatarial self-portrait, choosing among a predetermined set of hair, eyes, noses, etc. This is a condition of liberty on parole, as it were, which is the standard situation of the user operating in digital interactive environments, where the subject's freedom to choose and to express self-determination is always and inherently limited by a predetermined range of options, however numerous they might be. In this respect, the avatarisation of the self is not dissimilar to the practice of (self-)portraiture, which obeys in different times and schools various formal and genre conventions that operate as veritable pre-structures conditioning the representation of subjectivity.

Should we, then, conclude on this basis that avatars simply constitute the latest chapter in the long history of the representation of the self, which can be traced back to the hand stencils of the Upper Palaeolithic? On the one hand, they surely belong to that history and epitomise how in present times we deal with issues of (self-)portraiture according to the specific possibilities allowed by digital immersive technologies. On the other hand, precisely by virtue of the shift from the representationalist to the presentationalist paradigm, which I have described above by addressing the re-emergence of archaic traits in their operational agency, avatars expose to full light and explicitly make clear that property of (self-)portraiture which traditionally was reserved for the domain of legends, anecdotes, tales of the supernatural (*par vivo vivo*, it seems truly alive, is the eulogistic refrain in Vasari's *Lives*, when referring, for instance, to Mantegna, to Raphael, to Rosso Fiorentino, to Giulio Romano (Vasari 1991: 248, 318, 355, 368)), and nineteenth-century fantasy literature (Gogol's *The Portrait*, 1835; Poe's 'The Oval Portrait', 1842; Wilde's *The Picture of Dorian Gray*, 1891): the property of harbouring a real presence in the image or, to put it better, of making us experience the image as a real presence. A real presence that as such is not offered as an object of aesthetic contemplation, but rather plays a transformative role in the field of intersubjective interactions.

Acknowledgements

This chapter was written within the framework of the research project 'AN-ICON. An-Iconology: History, Theory, and Practices of Environmental Images'. The project has received funding from the European Research Council (ERC) under the European Union's Horizon 2020 research and innovation programme (grant agreement No. 834033 AN-ICON), and is hosted by the Department of Philosophy 'Piero Martinetti' at the University of Milan (Project 'Departments of Excellence 2023–2027' awarded by the Italian Ministry of University and Research).

Notes

1. In his comparative study 'written in 1784, and since revised', the British orientalist W. Jones writes about 'the ten Avatárs, or Descents, of the deity' (Jones 1799: 234).
2. See Benjamin's remarks on the archaic and forgotten 'swamp world' stage in Kafka's work: 'The fact that this stage is now forgotten does not mean that it does not extend into the present. On the contrary: it is present by virtue of this very oblivion' (2005: 809).
3. On the notion of 'operative' or 'operational' image, see Paglen 2014; Pantenburg 2016. See also the ongoing research project directed by Jussi Parikka, 'Operational Images and Visual Culture: Media Archaeological Investigations': https://www.famu.cz/cs/vyzkum-a-zahranici/granty-famu/operational-images/ (last accessed 20 March 2022).
4. On the iconographic lineage of the *Rückenfigur* in video games, see Beil 2012: 131–70.
5. In a similar way, Lomas (1997: 167) underlines with reference to psychoanalysis that 'the subject is divided – is not, in other words, *in-dividual*'.

6. On *ritratto* in the sense of the 'withdrawn', see Nancy 2018.
7. https://expressivemonkey.com/avatar-drawing-identity-art-proje/ (last accessed 20 March 2022).

References

Adriel, Jean (1947), *Avatar. The Life Story of the Perfect Master, Meher Baba*, Santa Barbara, CA: J. F. Rowny Press.

Amato, Etienne-Armand, and Etienne Perény (eds) (2013), *Les avatars jouables des mondes numériques. Théories, terrains et témoignages de pratiques interactives*, Paris: Lavoisier.

Beck, John, and Ryan Bishop (2020), *Technocrats of the Imagination: Art, Technology and the Military-Industrial Avant-garde*, Durham, NC: Duke University Press.

Beil, Benjamin (2012), *Avatarbilder. Zur Bildlichkeit des zeitgenössischen Computerspiels*, Bielefeld: transcript.

Belting, Hans (1994), *Likeness and Presence: A History of the Image Before the Era of Art*, Chicago: University of Chicago Press.

Belting, Hans (2017), *Face and Mask: A Double History*, Princeton, NJ: Princeton University Press.

Benjamin, Walter (1999), *The Arcades Project*, Cambridge, MA: The Belknap Press of Harvard University Press.

Benjamin, Walter (2005), 'Franz Kafka. On the Tenth Anniversary of His Death', in *Selected Writings, Volume 2, Part 2, 1931–1934*, ed. Michael W. Jennings, Howard Eiland, and Gary Smith, Cambridge, MA: The Belknap Press of Harvard University Press, pp. 794–818.

Buck, Jirah D. (1911), *The New Avatar and the Destiny of the Soul*, Cincinnati: The Robert Clarke Company.

Chakkarai, Vengal (1926), *Jesus the Avatār*, Madras: Christian Literature Society for India.

Cooper, Robbie, Julian Dibbell, and Tracy Spaight (2007), *Alter Ego: Avatars and their Creators*, London: Chris Boot, 2007.

Debray, Régis (1992), *Vie et mort de l'image. Une histoire du regard en Occident*, Paris: Gallimard.

Depraz, Natalie (2012), *Avatar: 'je te vois': une expérience philosophique*, Paris: Ellipses.

Farocki, Harun (2004), 'Phantom Images', *Public*, 29: 12–24.

Freedberg, David (1989), *The Power of Images: Studies in the History and Theory of Response*, Chicago: University of Chicago Press.

Freeman, Daniel, Suzanne Reeve, Amanda E. Robinson, Anke Ehlers, David Clark, Bernhard Spanlang, and Mel Slater (2017), 'Virtual Reality in the Assessment, Understanding, and Treatment of Mental Health Disorders', *Psychological Medicine*, 47(14): 2393–400.

Gautier, Théophile (2011), 'Avatar', in *Clarimonde and Other Stories*, Leyburn: Tartarus Press.

Gumbrecht, Hans Ulrich (2004), *Production of Presence: What Meaning Cannot Convey*, Stanford, CA: Stanford University Press.

Hacker, Paul (1960), 'Zur Entwicklung der Avatāralehre', *Wiener Zeitschrift für die Kunde Süd- und Ostasiens*, 4: 47–70.

Hasler, Béatrice S., Bernhard Spanlang, and Mel Slater (2017), 'Virtual Race Transformation Reverses Racial In-Group Bias', *PLoS One*, 12(4), https://journals.plos.org/plosone/article?id=10.1371/journal.pone.0174965 (last accessed 20 March 2022).

Jones, William (1799), 'On the Gods of Greece, Italy, and India', *Asiatic Researches*, 1: 221–75.

Kinsley, David (1987), 'Avatāra', in Lindsay Jones (ed.), *Encyclopedia of Religion, Volume 2*, Farmington Hills, MI: Thomson Gale, pp. 707–8.

Koch, Margarete (1965), *Die Rückenfigur im Bild von der Antike bis zu Giotto*, Recklinghausen: Bongers.

Lomas, David (1997), 'Inscribing Alterity: Transactions of Self and Other in Miró Self-Portraits', in Joanna Woodall (ed.), *Portraiture: Facing the Subject*, Manchester: Manchester University Press, pp. 167–88.

Macknight, Samuel J. (1896), *The Avatar of Peace, and Other Poems*, Boston: Shawmut.

Minsky, Marvin (1980), 'Telepresence', *Omni Magazine*, June: 45–51.

Nancy, Jean-Luc (2018), *Portrait*, New York: Fordham University Press.

Paglen, Trevor (2014), 'Operational Images', *e-flux journal*, 59, https://www.e-flux.com/journal/59/61130/operational-images/ (last accessed 20 March 2022).

Paglen, Trevor (2016), 'Invisible Images (Your Pictures Are Looking at You)', *The New Inquiry*, 8 December, https://thenewinquiry.com/invisible-images-your-pictures-are-looking-at-you (last accessed 20 March 2022).

Pantenburg, Volker (2016), 'Working Images. Harun Farocki and the Operational Image', in Jens Eder and Charlotte Klonk (eds), *Image Operations: Visual Media and Political Conflict*, Manchester: Manchester University Press, pp. 49–62.

Park, Mi Jin, Dong Jun Kim, Unjoo Lee, Eun Jin Na, and Hong Jin Jeon (2019), 'A Literature Overview of Virtual Reality (VR) in Treatment of Psychiatric Disorders: Recent Advances and Limitations', *Frontiers in Psychiatry*, 10(505), https://www.frontiersin.org/articles/10.3389/fpsyt.2019.00505/full (last accessed 20 March 2022).

Parrinder, Edward G. (1997), *Avatar and Incarnation: The Divine in Human Form in the World's Religions*, Oxford: Oneworld.

Peck, Tabitha C., Sofia Seinfeld, Salvatore M. Aglioti, and Mel Slater (2013), 'Putting Yourself in the Skin of a Black Avatar Reduces Implicit Racial Bias', *Consciousness and Cognition*, 22(3): 779–87.

Prange, Regine (2010), 'Sinnoffenheit und Sinnverneinung als metapic-turale Prinzipien. Zur Historizität bildlicher Selbstreferenz am Beispiel der Rückenfigur', in Verena Krieger and Rachel Mader (eds), *Ambigu-ität in der Kunst. Typen und Funktionen eines ästhetischen Paradigmas*, Cologne: Böhlau, pp. 125–67.

Price, Richard (ed.) (2018), *The Acts of the Second Council of Nicaea*, Liverpool: Liverpool University Press.

Respiro (1897), *The Man, the Seer, the Adept, the Avatar; or, T.L. Harris the Inspired Messenger of the Cycle*, London: E. W. Allen.

Schapiro, Meyer (1973), 'Frontal and Profile as Symbolic Forms', in Meyer Schapiro, *Words and Pictures: On the Literal and the Symbolic in the Illustration of a Text*, The Hague: Mouton, pp. 37–49.

Schroeder, Ralph (ed.) (2002), *The Social Life of Avatars. Presence and Interaction in Shared Virtual Environments*, London: Springer.

Seinfeld, Sofia, Jorge Arroyo Palacios, Guillermo Iruretagoyena, Ruud Hortensius, Lenin Zapata, David Borland, Beatrice de Gelder, Mel Slater, and Maria V. Sanchez-Vives (2018), 'Offenders Become the Victim in Virtual Reality: Impact of Changing Perspective in Domestic Violence', *Scientific Reports*, 8(2692): 1–11.

Sheth, Noel (2002), 'Hindu Avatāra and Christian Incarnation: A Compari-son', *Philosophy East and West*, 52(1): 98–125.

Simmel, Georg (2005 [1916]), *Rembrandt: An Essay in the Philosophy of Art*, New York: Routledge.

Somaini, Antonio (2020), '"Unlearning to See Like Humans": Trevor Paglen on Machine Vision', in Greta Plaitano, Simone Venturini, and Paolo Villa (eds), *Moving Pictures, Living Machines: Automation, Animation and the Imitation of Life in Cinema and Media*, Milan: Mimesis, pp. 63–8.

Tordo, Frédéric, and Caroline Binkley (2013), 'L'auto-empathie médiati-sée par l'avatar, une subjectivation de soi', in Etienne-Armand Amato and Etienne Perény (eds), *Les avatars jouables des mondes numéri-ques. Théories, terrains et témoignages de pratiques interactives*, Paris: Lavoisier, pp. 91–109.

Vasari, Giorgio (1991 [1568]), *The Lives of the Artists*, Oxford: Oxford University Press.

Vernant, Jean-Pierre (2006a), 'From the "Presentification" of the Invis-ible to the Imitation of Appearance', in Jean-Pierre Vernant, *Myth and Thought Among the Greeks*, New York: Zone Books, pp. 333–49.

Vernant, Jean-Pierre (2006b), 'The Figuration of the Invisible and the Psycho-logical Category of the Double: The Kolossos', in Jean-Pierre Vernant, *Myth and Thought Among the Greeks*, New York: Zone Books, pp. 321–32.

Walters, Michael (2019), 'FPS Avatars: Floating Arms vs Full-Bodied Models', *The Gamer*, 4 August, https://www.thegamer.com/fps-avatars-floating-arms-vs-full-bodied-models/ (last accessed 20 March 2020).

Chapter 11

Iiu Susiraja: Self-shooting as Playful Practice

Kaisu Hynnä-Granberg and Susanna Paasonen

If there is one recurrent characteristic associated with selfies in public debate, it is their allegedly frivolous banality (see Tiidenberg 2018; Saltz 2014). Associated with a culture of shallowness and self-obsessed narcissism, selfies are, in most analyses, set apart from their more established visual predecessor, the self-portrait. As parts of quotidian digital snapshot culture, selfies are used socially to communicate mood, atmosphere, location, context, and appearance, and to document mundane happenings as part of an ever-growing series, some of which are selected to be shared on social media platforms. In their personal and social functions, selfies seem to share little of the cultural codes of portraiture premised on broader and more permanent sense of likeness, or even character, as interpreted through an artist's brush or the lens of their camera.

This chapter focuses on the photographic work of the Finnish artist Iiu Susiraja, analyses of which variously frame it as 'redefining portrait photography' (Nielsen 2016), 'playing with the selfie phenomenon' (Fogelholm 2014), and challenging 'our definition of the selfie' (Frank 2014; see also Orpana 2015; Sandell 2016). For her part, Susiraja simply explains that 'selfie is a nice word. I don't want to set limits to what people say about my pictures' (Mäntymaa 2014). Some identify her photos as selfies, others as self-portraits and yet others more broadly as works of contemporary art. Starting from the premise that her work is simultaneously all of the above, we argue that while selfies and self-portraits fill diverse and differing social, cultural, and personal functions, the boundaries between them are highly fluid. Rather than interpreting Susiraja's work as critical commentary on selfie culture within or from the realm of high art, we explore it in terms of ludic, creative visual practice that broadens understandings of what self-shooting is, what it can be, and what it can do. Addressing Susiraja's Instagram presence, this chapter contributes to expanding notions of selfies as visual practice (see also Gómez Cruz and Thornham 2015; Frosh 2015; Hynnä-Granberg 2021). Taking seriously the presumed frivolousness and banality of self-shooting, we consider playfulness as key to the creative practice and seek less antagonistic ways of exploring the interconnections between selfies and self-portraits.

Playful Anarchism

Whether understood as selfies or anti-selfies, Iiu Susiraja's self-portraiture continues the tradition of female artists using their own bodies as the key foci of photographic work, of which the performative self-portraits of Claude Calhoun and Cindy Sherman remain probably the best-known and the most broadly discussed examples (Guimond 1994; Jones 2002; Burton 2006). Susiraja works in photography and video, and uses her own body as the main visual theme and prop, creatively combined with mundane household objects and foodstuffs in domestic spaces. She is the only person to appear in her work, which she chooses not to explain or analyse beyond describing it as 'playful anarchism' (Frank 2014; Nielsen 2016).

On the one hand, Susiraja states that she wants to be herself in the photos she takes, without any posing involved (Friman 2011). On the other hand, she identifies her figure in them as a fictitious character, 'a burnt-out stay-at-home mom whose husband cheats when traveling for work and whose children have left home and abandoned their mother' and who then 'loses it' and starts to do odd things (Mäntymaa 2014). The particular visual mode of Susiraja's work is both laconic and absurd: repurposing sausages, loaves of bread, fish, clothes hangers, tights, bananas, plastic buckets, and inflatable toys as accessories, often to refashion, reframe, and reshape her body, she poses deadpan, without a hint of smile. Her works are both playful and ambiguous about what they signify (Skregelid 2021) – 'as mundane as they are bizarre' and 'both jarring and intoxicating' in the impressions they make (Frank 2014).

While Susiraja distances her work from the interpretative frameworks of both feminism and body positivity (Lehmusvesi 2019), these remain key to analyses of her art produced within art critique and research, journalism, and thesis work, most of which focus on the uses of Susiraja's body, its size, look, and 'shameless' display (e.g., Friman 2011; Lalja 2017; Snider 2018; 2019). For some commentators, her work involves an aesthetic of ugliness, whereas for others it comprises a critique of gendered body norms, as supported by social media (Halkosaari 2015; Malmberg 2019). For yet others, it entails more ambiguous displays aiming to affect the viewer through discomfort (Skregelid 2021). Bringing such approaches together through a feminist disability studies and fat studies lens, Stephanie Snider argues that Susiraja's work 'embodies absurdity and abjection in ways that make her imagery especially compelling examples of unflattering, even ugly, self-portraits' (2019: n.p.).

Susiraja's Instagram presence (@iiu.susiraja) merges her artistic work with other photos of the artist, some of which are taken by professional photographers for journalistic outlets, others of which are credited to her mother, and yet others of which date back to her childhood and teenage years. Explaining her aesthetic principles, Susiraja states that she tries to look 'beautiful and attractive' in regular photos whereas in artistic shots she can 'look like anything' (Lehmusvesi 2019). As a publishing platform, Instagram offers visibility for artistic work, while the horizontality of its image galleries effaces contextual differences among images created for a range of purposes. It is to a degree tempting to identify artistic self-portraits published on Instagram as comments on the platform's visual ecology, as encapsulated in the cultural form of the selfie. This is certainly the case with Cindy Sherman who broadly rejects the interpretation of her work as selfies (Blasberg 2019), yet whose self-portraits posted on a public Instagram account have been recurrently interpreted as both comments on and reworkings of selfie culture (Becker 2017; Harrison 2018). In this context, Susiraja's work can be read as involving a 'politics of ugliness' and as helping 'to make fatness, strangeness, ugliness, and awkwardness visually and conceptually compelling' (Snider 2019). We nevertheless suggest that the horizontality of Susiraja's Instagram presence offers more dynamic understandings of visual practice and interpretation than those simply positioning it as commentary on and critique of the selfie.

Selfies and Self-portraits

Although selfie research often refers to images as 'digital self-portraits' (e.g., Iqani and Schroeder 2016; Lasén 2015), the relationship between the portrait and the selfie has not been thoroughly analysed. When selfies have been discussed in relation to their 'artistic predecessor', analyses have focused on the differences between the two, especially with regard to their social roles and functions. While the artistic portrait has been reserved for the elites, selfies are 'folk art' (Saltz 2014) that virtually anyone can create. Several scholarly and cultural analyses of selfies (e.g., Gómez Cruz and Thornham 2015; Saltz 2014) suggest that selfies and portraits are further different in their aesthetics: whereas traditional portraits are celebratory depictions of their subject, selfies are everyday images with a specific composition and camera angle.

Despite the differing social roles of selfies and portraits, the meaning of selfies to marginalised groups is often similar to that of self-portraits. Sociologist Kath Woodward (2015: 52–6) argues that women have always had a particular relation to self-portraiture. At the same time, as women have been largely excluded from the arena of portraiture, both as artists and as objects of formal portraits, some have used self-portraiture to actively challenge their own silencing. Woodward suggests that the self-portraits of such artists as Käthe Kollwitz and Frida Kahlo show how self-portraiture enables female artists to envision themselves outside patriarchal conventions and to actively 'look back' at both themselves and the viewer (see also Betterton 1987; Pollock 1988).

Several fat studies scholars (e.g., Sastre 2014; Afful and Ricciardelli 2015) similarly suggest that body-positive selfies claim space from normatively sized bodies on social media and challenge common fatphobic understandings of fatness, thus sharing the understanding of self-portraits' liberatory possibilities. Susiraja's work has been interpreted in this framework as an intentional reshaping and redefinition of fat identity, so that her self-portraiture becomes transgressive and liberating for the fat subject. Yet as we argue in more detail below, there is ambiguity at play that affords Susiraja's work a critical edge irreducible to any singular interpretative framework. As a playful practice, self-shooting can be tinted with shame, or even disgust, just as it can be laced with laughter or fuelled by enjoyment. The ambiguity of self-shooting practices, resonant with the ambiguity of the photos produced and the affective encounters that they allow for, can be seen as key to their appeal.

In her analysis of a Japanese photography practice that can be seen as a kind of sister genre of the selfie, *purikura* (a series of photograph stickers taken at a photo booth), Mette Sandbye (2018) argues that selfies and *purikura* are about idealisation. The photographing subject, often thought to be a teenage girl, tries to mimic a pose that she has seen in magazines or social media. For their part, Susiraja's photographs play with cultural codes of femininity (both idealised and not) in rather complex ways – for example, by mimicking bodily poses familiar from men's magazines. In *Baseball Lover* (2019) (Figure 11.1), Susiraja is seen sitting on a bed in a

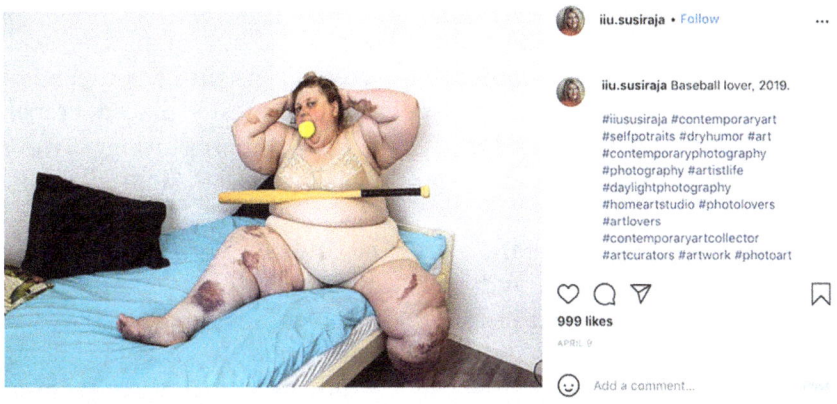

iiu.susiraja • Follow   ...

iiu.susiraja Baseball lover, 2019.

#iiususiraja #contemporaryart
#selfpotraits #dryhumor #art
#contemporaryphotography
#photography #artistlife
#daylightphotography
#homeartstudio #photolovers
#artlovers
#contemporaryartcollector
#artcurators #artwork #photoart

999 likes
APRIL 9

Add a comment...

Figure 11.1 Iiu Susiraja, *Baseball Lover*, 2019, by permission of the artist

slightly backwards leaning position, with her arms crossed behind her head and her legs spread wide across the mattress. She is wearing nude-coloured underwear and her arms and legs are covered in bruises. She holds a tennis ball in her mouth and has firmly placed a baseball bat between her breasts and stomach. The pose itself can be understood as formulaically seductive in allowing for visual access to the body displayed (hands behind the back, legs ajar, seated on a bed), yet the photo's background with wrinkly turquoise sheets and squashed black pillows, Susiraja's body type, choice of underwear and stern, unsmiling stare, combined with the bizarreness of the baseball and bat in the composition, contrast with the conventions of mainstream erotic pictures, giving it an off-kilter, humorous, and vaguely violent tone.

While *Baseball Lover* can be interpreted as a critique of body and beauty norms and forms of gendered display, it simultaneously repeats gestures associated with commercially produced sexual images. As such, it can be seen as idealising the visual genre of a pornographic pose by playing with its conventions. Idealisation here refers to an appreciation of a certain ideal while critiquing it, a wish to be similar while wanting to be different, and an act of mimicking cultural codes while simultaneously deconstructing them (Sandbye 2018: 313–19). Building on Kaja Silverman (1996), Sandbye argues that idealisation is closely affiliated with identification, since one cannot idealise something without identifying with it. Although many selfie- and *purikura*-takers appear to automatically take on poses familiarised by models and celebrities when faced with a camera, posing is also 'an active procedure of becoming an "other" and in the end a "self"' (Sandbye 2018: 316; see also Gómez Cruz and Thornham 2015: 1–2). Susiraja's *Baseball Lover* mimics as well as deconstructs, and the other way around – as do her other photographs combining erotic poses with strategically placed French loaves, plastic horses, and raw fish, or her poses using various household objects and beauty products in unusual, unpredictable, and playful ways.

Sandbye (2018) compares the selfie and the *purikura* to Cindy Sherman's self-portraits, and specifically to her *Untitled Film Stills* from the late 1970s and early 1980s, which Silverman (1996) has also analysed. While these have been criticised for reproducing objectifying Hollywood visual culture, Silverman discusses them as examples of 'good enough' ways of being, and as the simultaneous living and deconstruction of ideals. Sherman's later work has a more marked playful tone, not least in her heavily filtered and modified self-portraits published on Instagram. Susiraja's work is much less concerned with fashioning her body to a different likeness than with using it to experiment and play to absurd effect. The ample fleshiness of Susiraja's body further positions her photographs as being farther away from the idealised, explaining why her work has not been interpreted as mimicry so much as visual activism. At the same time, Susiraja's stern stare communicates a blank non-apology, inviting the viewer to an open-ended conversation.

If, in selfies taken with a front-facing camera, the photographer's visible, outstretched arm works a gesture that 'invite[s] the viewer to infer and adopt a physical position in relation to the photographer' (Frosh 2015: 1617), in Susiraja's art, it is often this unblinking, expressionless stare that draws the viewer into interaction with the image. Simultaneously, other constituents of the portraits, such as the bruises on Susiraja's body, her size, and the bizarre positioning of household objects in the images, seem to induce a stare while chasing it away. Many of the elements further invite questions, such as whether or not there is a causal relation between the bruises and the bat in *Baseball Lover*, and if so, of what kind; are these self-inflicted; does the tennis ball function as a gag; is she preparing to grab the bat herself? Such ambiguity is key to Susiraja's work in general, yet becomes particularly pertinent when analysing the image separately from the context of her Instagram presence or that afforded by art shows featuring series of her work. Since bruises are a recurrent element in Susiraja's other work, their existence may well be accepted as just another element of strangeness, or of the aesthetics of ugliness (Snider 2019; 2018). The viewer's interaction with Susiraja's work goes far beyond the dynamics of looking, as discussed in several analyses (e.g., Sandell 2016; Orpana 2015):

in their absurdity unfolding in the familiar surroundings of kitchens, bedrooms and living rooms, and their homely object-worlds, the photographs ask the viewer not to question their internal logic of topsy-turvy but to play along and to revel in their absurdity.

Many scholars and cultural critics (Murray 2015; Saltz 2014) see selfies as differing from artistic portraits in their sociability and shareability. Yet portraits too have always been shared with others, whether through display in homes, galleries, or museums, or through circulating reprints in books, cards, and posters. Whereas during previous centuries a portrait constituted an affirmation of a person's social position and status, in the contemporary world digital images function as mechanisms for securing and making identity in a more processual and reiterative vein (Woodward 2015: 100–1). If portraits 'exist at the interface between art and social life' and are motivated by an desire 'to think about oneself, of oneself in relation to others, and of others in apparent relation to themselves and to others' (Brilliant 1991: 11, 14), the same can be said of both Susiraja's work and selfies as tools for self-reflection, self-presentation, and social exchange. Selfies and portraits, both in general and on social media platforms, ask the viewer to do more than look: they require conspicuously communicative, gestural responses. They invite 'sensorimotor mirroring' (Frosh 2015: 1621–2), sometimes by taking one's own selfie, sometimes by liking or commenting, and sometimes through the viewer's fingers moving on the touchscreen.

Playing with Stuff

Susiraja's work can be broadly seen as premised on play, in that she 'plays with everyday, seemingly random objects, and places them on, within, and next to her own body in unexpected, but calculated, ways' (Snider 2019: n.p.). Play, as theorised in studies of games and play, refers to autotelic practices where the activity is an end in itself. Play can happen within the fixed rules of a game and in specific spaces designated for the purpose, but it can also unfold as open-ended improvisation, exploration, and experimentation where the rules and logic of everyday life are momentarily reimagined (see Stenros 2015). Playfulness can be understood as a mode, capacity, and orientation of openness, curiosity, and zest for variation that precipitates improvisation in acts of play (Paasonen 2018: 2). Describing her creative practice as starting from the feelings raised by mundane objects and leading to experiments in repurposing them, Susiraja foregrounds the mode of playfulness and acts of play as being key to how her photographic and video work comes about.

We suggest that the notion of play offers analytical avenues for understanding self-shooting practices more generally. Previous scholarship has analysed how social media platforms, apps, and devices invite their users to play with selfies, yet the broader connections between selfie culture and play remain in need of further exploration. Media scholars James Katz and Elizabeth Crocker (2015: 1862, 1867–8), for example, connect play to Snapchat's design, arguing that since pictures disappear from view after a limited timeframe, users feel free to experiment with different kinds of selfies than those they would normally share on social media. For their part, Gaby David and Carolina Cambre (2016: 5–8; also Garda and Karhulahti 2021) address Tinder's videogame-like affordances, which make looking for a partner and sharing selfies feel increasingly like play. Our take on playfulness and experimentation, again, is not connected to particular affordances of social media platforms, mobile devices, or apps. While some platforms and devices are, by default, more common arenas and vehicles for play than others in their gamified designs and the interactions they invite, it remains the case that play can take place almost anywhere, and with anything (Sicart 2014: 1–7). Susiraja's photos, taken with a system camera rather than a smartphone, and shown in art galleries and museums in addition to Instagram, speak of the multifacetedness of playful self-shooting and the spaces in which it is viewed.

Play, much like selfies, is often regarded as a spontaneous leisure activity specific to children and teenagers before they mature and 'grow out of it'. Yet ethnographic research on selfies reveals that they are a form of play that can be both time-consuming and laborious (e.g., Abidin 2014; 2016; Warfield 2016). Play and selfies can unfold in an unplanned fashion, just as they can be simultaneously thoughtful and spontaneous. Susiraja describes her working method as of the latter kind (Snider 2019). Many of her works are parts of series involving experiments with objects, locations, and props in different variations, the photographs and videos representing the end result selected for public view. Since selfies are often taken in a serial manner (Rettberg 2014: 33, 35), again and again, one after another, something in the activity seems to arouse pleasure and lead to repetition. This does not mean, however, that selfies are necessarily simply an enjoyable practice: the activity can come embedded in feelings of discomfort, the results are not necessarily pleasing, and there is an inevitable risk of vulnerability involved in posting the outcome on social media (Hynnä-Granberg 2021).

While play is routinely associated with fun, game studies scholar Miguel Sicart foregrounds its complex connections with pleasure that can be dark and uncomfortable in its hues. The pleasures of play 'are not always submissive to enjoyment, happiness, or positive traits. Play can be pleasurable when it hurts, offends, challenges us and teases us, and even when we are not playing' (Sicart 2014: 3). That is, pleasure is embedded in complex affective textures where positive and negative intensities intermesh so that the resulting patterns are not reducible to either (Paasonen 2021: 71, 95–6, 160). It is our argument that affective ambiguity is central to many acts of play, just as it is key to selfies and the appeal of Susiraja's work.

Understanding play as pleasurable activities rife with complexity and affective ambiguity is a helpful way of framing Susiraja's work, much of which centres and foregrounds her own body, with much carnal thickness and humour. Since humour and comedy are default modes of a fat-phobic culture (Kyrölä 2014; Braziel and LeBesco 2001), representing a fat body in a playful fashion involves connotations with marginalisation. Extant analyses of Susiraja's work do not, however, see its playfulness as being in contrast with its political character, or potentiality. On the contrary, its humour and strangeness are understood to interrogate 'normative assumptions about bodies and their various configurations' (Snider 2019: n.p.) and to deny any outside-originated shaming of fat bodies (Lalja 2017: 15–17). Since humour is 'frequently part of digital culture and social media imagery' (Snider 2019: n.p.), playfulness makes Susiraja's photographs easily adaptable to Instagram. She further accentuates this connection with her use of hashtags adding contextual metadata to the photos, such as #dryhumor, #funphotography, and #humorart, as well as #selfportraits, #contemporaryart, and #artistsoninstagram. Through hashtags, Susiraja invites a lightness of interpretation regardless of any dualistic divide separating seriousness from play, or contemporary art from selfie culture.

It has been argued that seriousness and formal stillness are key to the cultural form of the portrait, so that its facial expressions become sanitised and formulaic, conveying 'looks' (of pensiveness, intelligence, assertiveness, or affection) characteristic of personality over expression of feeling (Brilliant 1991: 11, 112). Susiraja's serious and notably blank stare throughout her work falls outside both emotional expression and the more formal emoting of character through mood. It is equally resistant to interpretations of self-portraits as intimate in their self-reflection (Brilliant 1991: 164). There is no penetrating Susiraja's stare nor reading her expression for signs of personality, for the reason that she is posing in character (the 'burnt-out stay-at-home mom'), the expressive register of which is drastically different from those in other photos of the artist posted on her Instagram account. She is simultaneously the work's subject and object, artist and character, yet there is more than twoness to the outcome. Susiraja's figure appears blank while also being the work's main theme and focus: her self-portraits are simultaneously repetitively serial and rife with playful discovery and surprise. Susiraja plays with the cultural forms of self-portraits and selfies just as she plays with her own body and the object-worlds of which her photos are composed.

In *Pollo Mona* (2020) (Figure 11.2), Susiraja poses in a kitchen with a large poster of Leonardo da Vinci's early sixteenth-century portrait *Mona Lisa*, with her hands holding two raw chicken carcasses pushed through holes in the poster. Looking directly at the camera without much expression, Susiraja seems as if stuck in the painting while fluids from the chickens run down the poster's surface, *Mona Lisa*'s hands almost meeting Susiraja's bare legs in a bizarre assemblage and the pink chickens looming above *Mona Lisa*'s covered breasts. The idealised renaissance landscape behind *Mona Lisa* is framed by the cupboards and utensils of a kitchen space, while the painting itself frames the bodies of the chickens. Considered to be a portrait of Lisa Gherardini, *Mona Lisa* has also been interpreted as da Vinci's disguised, gender-fluid self-portrait, so

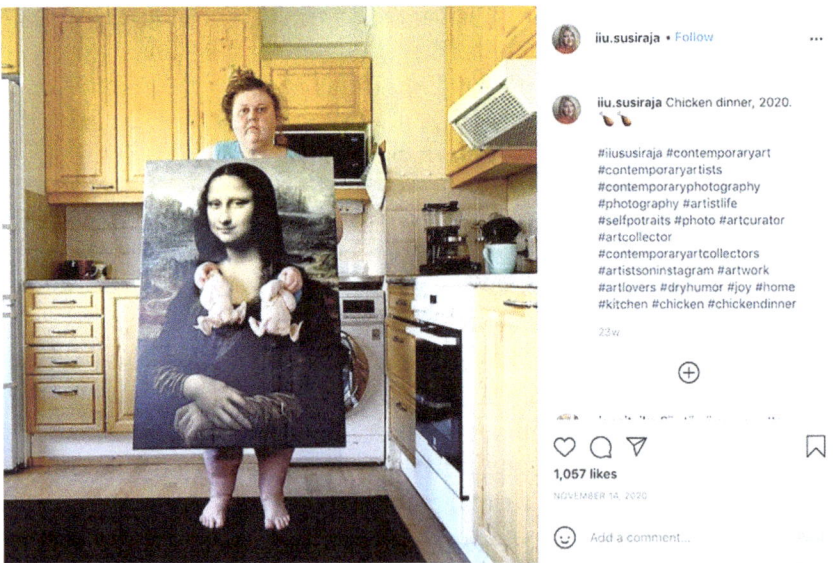

Figure 11.2 Iiu Susiraja, *Pollo Mona*, 2019, formerly titled *Chicken Dinner*, by permission of the artist

that there are degrees of obscurity as to what or whom the painting depicts, and why. In Susiraja's treatment, marked on Instagram with hashtags including #selfportraits, #joy, #kitchen, and #chicken, *Pollo Mona* displays a portrait within a self-portrait, transforming one of the world's best-known paintings into a surface for domestic object experimentation and, in reframing and renaming *Mona Lisa*'s fabled mysterious smile through the proximity of raw chicken, landing firmly within the absurd.

The photograph is simultaneously light and disturbing, playful and stern in ways that allow for ambiguity of meaning, intention, interpretation, and experience. It is precisely such playfulness, which both amplifies and is key to Susiraja's refusal to pin down the meanings of her work, that opens up routes for ambiguity so that joy and discomfort, tenderness and cruelty, can simultaneously coexist, without one trumping the other, in the affective encounters that her photographic and video work give rise to.

References

Abidin, Crystal (2014), '#In$tagLam: Instagram as a Repository of Taste, a Burgeoning Marketplace, a War of Eyeballs', in Marsha Berry and Max Schleser (eds), *Mobile Media Making in the Age of Smartphones*, Basingstoke: Palgrave Pivot, pp. 119–28.

Abidin, Crystal (2016), '"Aren't These Just Young, Rich Women Doing Vain Things Online?": Influencer Selfies as Subversive Frivolity', *Social Media + Society*, April–June: 1–17.

Afful, Adwoa A., and Rose Ricciardelli (2015), 'Shaping the Online Fat Acceptance Movement: Talking about Body Image and Beauty Standards', *Journal of Gender Studies*, 24(4): 453–72.

Becker, Noah (2017), 'How Cindy Sherman's Instagram Selfies are Changing the Face of Photography', *The Guardian*, 9 August, https://www.theguardian.com/artanddesign/2017/aug/09/cindy-sherman-instagram-selfies-filtering-life (last accessed 7 March 2022).

Betterton, Rosemary (ed.) (1987), *Looking on: Images of Femininity in the Visual Art and Media*, London: Pandora.

Blasberg, Derek (2019), 'Why Cindy Sherman Thinks Selfies are a Cry for Help', *WSJ Magazine*, 29 October, https://www.wsj.com/articles/why-cindy-sherman-thinks-selfies-are-a-cry-for-help-11572352378 (last accessed 7 March 2022).

Braziel, Jana Evans, and Kathleen LeBesco (eds) (2001), *Bodies out of Bounds: Fatness and Transgression*, Berkeley: University of California Press.

Brilliant, Richard (1991), *Portraiture*, Cambridge, MA: Harvard University Press.

Burton, Johanna (ed.) (2006), *Cindy Sherman*, Cambridge, MA: MIT Press.

David, Gaby, and Carolina Cambre (2016), 'Screened Intimacies: Tinder and the Swipe Logic', *Social Media + Society*, April–June: 1–11.

Fogelholm, Sonja (2014), 'Iiu Susirajan kuvissa leikitään ruoalla ja selfie-ilmiöllä', *Yle elävä arkisto*, 5 November, https://yle.fi/aihe/artikkeli/2014/11/05/iiu-susirajan-kuvissa-leikitaan-ruualla-ja-selfie-ilmiolla (last accessed 7 March 2022).

Frank, Priscilla (2014), 'Artist's Strange and Beautiful Images Challenge our Definition of the Selfie', *Huffington Post*, 20 October, https://www.huffpost.com/entry/iiu-susiraja_n_6004232 (last accessed 7 March 2022).

Friman, Laura (2011), 'Muoto ja kuva', *Helsingin Sanomat*, 27 January.

Frosh, Paul (2015), 'The Gestural Image: The Selfie, Photography Theory, and Kinesthetic Sociability', *International Journal of Communication*, 9: 1607–28.

Garda, Maria B., and Veli-Matti Karhulahti (2021), 'Let's Play Tinder! The Aesthetics of a Dating App', *Games and Culture*, 16(2): 248–61.

Gómez Cruz, Edgar, and Helen Thornham (2015), 'Selfies Beyond Self-Representation: The (Theoretical) F(r)ictions of a Practice', *Journal of Aesthetics & Culture*, 7(1): 1–10.

Guimond, James (1994), 'Auteurs as Autobiographers: Images by Jo Spence and Cindy Sherman', *MFS Modern Fiction Studies*, 40(3): 573–91.

Halkosaari, Eeva (2015), 'Perinnepirkot huomio: Iiu Susirajan omakuvat sosiaalisen median ylläpitämän perinteisen naiskuvan haastajina', BA dissertation in Art Education, University of Jyväskylä, https://jyx.jyu.fi/bitstream/handle/123456789/47153/1/URN:NBN:fi:jyu-201509213219.pdf (last accessed 7 March 2022).

Harrison, Jess (2018), 'How Cindy Sherman's Photography Predicted Our Selfie-Obsessed Generation', *Fineartmultiple*, https://fineartmultiple.com/blog/cindy-sherman-photography-selfie-generation/ (last accessed 7 March 2022).

Hynnä-Granberg, Kaisu (2021), '"Why can't I take a full-shot of myself? Of course I can!": Studying Selfies as Socio-Technological Affective Practices', *Feminist Media Studies*, 22(6): 1363–78.

Iqani, Mehita, and Jonathan E. Schroeder (2016), '#Selfie: Digital Self-Portraits as Commodity Form and Consumption Practice', *Consumption Markets & Culture*, 19(5): 405–15.

Jones, Amelia (2002), 'The "Eternal Return": Self-Portrait Photography as a Technology of Embodiment', *Signs: Journal of Women in Culture and Society*, 27(4): 947–78.

Katz, James, and Elizabeth Crocker (2015), 'Selfies and Photo Messaging as Visual Conversation: Reports from the United States, United Kingdom and China', *International Journal of Communication*, 9(1): 1861–72.

Kyrölä, Katariina (2014), *The Weight of Images: Affect, Body Image, and Fat in the Media*, Burlington, VT: Ashgate.

Lalja, Roosa (2017), 'Positiivisen kehonkuvan representaatiot nykytaiteessa', BA thesis in Visual Arts, Tampere University of Applied Sciences, https://www.theseus.fi/bitstream/handle/10024/127285/Lalja_Roosa.pdf?sequence=2 (last accessed 7 March 2022).

Lasén, Amparo (2015), 'Digital Self-Portraits, Exposure and the Modulation of Intimacy', in José Ricardo Carvalheiro and Ana Serrano Telleria (eds), *Mobile and Digital Communication: Approaches to Public and Private*, Covilhã: LabCom Books, pp. 61–78.

Lehmusvesi, Jussi (2019), 'Joku raja', *Helsingin Sanomat*, 14 March.

Malmberg, Katarina (2019), 'Ei mitään hävettävää', *Helsingin Sanomat*, 12 September.

Mäntymaa, Marjut (2014), 'Susirajan selfiet haastavat katsojat', *Yle uutiset*, 4 November, https://yle.fi/uutiset/3-7598350 (last accessed 7 March 2022).

Murray, Derek Conrad (2015), 'Notes to Self: The Visual Culture of Selfies in the Age of Social Media', *Consumption Markets & Culture*, 18(6): 490–516.

Nielsen, Joacim (2016), 'Iiu Susiraja on Redefining Portrait Photography', *Culture Trip*, 22 December, https://theculturetrip.com/europe/finland/articles/iiu-susiraja-redefining-portrait-photography/ (last accessed 7 March 2022).

Orpana, Essi (2015), 'Katseen edestä ja takaa', BA thesis in Photography, Turku University of Applied Sciences, https://www.theseus.fi/bitstream/handle/10024/98836/Katseen_edesta_ja_takaa_Essi_Orpana.pdf?sequence=1 (last accessed 7 March 2022).

Paasonen, Susanna (2018), *Many Splendored Things: Thinking Sex and Play*, London: Goldsmiths Press.

Paasonen, Susanna (2021), *Dependent, Distracted, Bored: Affective Formations in Networked Media*, Cambridge, MA: MIT Press.

Pollock, Griselda (1988), *Vision and Difference: Feminism, Femininity and Histories of Art*, London: Routledge.

Rettberg, Jill Walker (2014), *Seeing Ourselves through Technology: How We Use Selfies, Blogs and Wearable Devices to See and Shape Ourselves*, Basingstoke: Palgrave Macmillan.

Saltz, Jerry (2014), 'Art at Arm's Length: A History of the Selfie', *Vulture*, 26 January, https://www.vulture.com/2014/01/history-of-the-selfie.html (last accessed 7 March 2022).

Sandbye, Mette (2018), 'Selfies and Perikura as Affective, Aesthetic Labor', in Julia Eckel, Jens Ruchatz, and Sabine Wirth (eds), *Exploring the*

Selfie: Historical, Theoretical, and Analytical Approaches to Digital Self-Photography, Copenhagen: Copenhagen University Press, pp. 305–77.

Sandell, Inari (2016), 'Selfie katsoo takaisin', BA thesis in Photography, Turku University of Applied Sciences, https://www.theseus.fi/bitstream/handle/10024/118674/Sandell_Inari.pdf?sequence=1 (last accessed 7 March 2022).

Sastre, Alexandra (2014), 'Towards a Radical Body Positive. Reading the Online Body Positive Movement', *Feminist Media Studies*, 14(6): 929–43.

Sicart, Miguel (2014), *Play Matters*, Cambridge, MA: MIT Press.

Silverman, Kaja (1996), *The Threshold of the Visible World*, London: Routledge.

Skregelid, Lisbet (2021), 'Zoom in on Dry Joy—Dissensus, Agonism and Democracy in Art Education', *Education Sciences*, 11(1): 28.

Snider, Stefanie (2018), 'On the Limitations of the Rhetoric of Beauty: Embracing Ugliness in Contemporary Fat Visual Representations', in Sara Rodriquez and Ela Przybylo (eds), *On the Politics of Ugliness*, London: Palgrave Macmillan, pp. 337–65.

Snider, Stefanie (2019), 'Staring Back, Deadpan: Ugliness and Abjection in Iiu Susiraja's Self-Portraits', *ASAP Journal*, 26 March, http://asapjournal.com/staring-back-deadpan-ugliness-and-abjection-in-iiu-susirajas-self-portraits-stefanie-snider/ (last accessed 7 March 2022).

Stenros, Jaakko (2015), *Playfulness, Play, and Games: A Constructionist Ludology Approach*, Tampere: Tampere University Press.

Tiidenberg, Katrin (2018), *Selfies: Why We Love (and Hate) Them*, Bingley: Emerald.

Warfield, Katie (2016), 'Making the Cut: An Agential Realist Examination of Selfies and Touch', *Social Media + Society*, April–June: 1–10.

Woodward, Kath (2015), *The Politics of In/Visibility: Being There*, London: Palgrave Macmillan.

Chapter 12

The Quantification Trilogy's Loss-of-Self Portraits, or Mediating the Technologies of the Self

Kate Rennebohm

This chapter approaches the portrait and the self-portrait through the lens of the 'technologies of the self', a concept of Michel Foucault's that names activities by which individuals labour to affect their own current and future states of being (Foucault 1997a). In positioning self-portraiture as a practice of such technologies, and portraits and self-portraits as (potential) material agents within the same, this chapter thus aligns itself with other re-evaluations of portraiture following what might be phrased as the non-representational turn. Here, thinkers including Ernst van Alphen, Hans Belting, Jean-Luc Nancy, and Sigrid Weigel have developed alternatives to the traditional mode of analysing portraits for their likeness to their represented subjects or their resulting ability to bestow authority through such representation (van Alphen 2005; Belting 2017; Nancy 2018; Weigel 2017). As Tomáš Jirsa has noted, these thinkers do not take mimetic depictions as guaranteeing identity, but instead 'understand the portrait as a generative work of the subject's transformation, absence, and disappearing' (2019: 67). Approaching portraiture as a kind of self-technology or practice similarly emphasises such modalities and effects of the portrait, positioning them as elements in the processes and operations of self-focus and self-materialisation that recursively transform, constitute, and maintain what we call the human self.

Bringing the portrait into conjunction with Foucault's framework does something else as well, which is to foreground questions about the broader role of media in the technologies of the self. Here, I take the (self-)portrait as one example of media's influential presence in these self-focused activities – a notion Foucault hinted at but left unexplored (1997a: 232–3). While I turn to different media theorists below to address the mediation of technologies of the self, I also find a prompt for thinking about these questions in Canadian artist Jeremy Shaw's 'Quantification Trilogy' films (2014–18). These films centralise the varied roles that media play in self-focused or spiritual technologies, as, in each film, individuals use such mediated practices in order to *lose* or transcend themselves – ultimately aiming to produce or spur a new or different phase of human existence. As such, the films reveal experiences of transcendence to be both dependent on and (unavoidably) understood through historically differentiated media. In other words, they both maintain the conceptual space and value of transcendence while denying its purported escape from materiality. Shaw's films, then, finally reveal themselves as a unique kind of portrait; that is, a 'loss-of-self' portrait. In other words, they become portraits of the media landscapes framing both the finding of the self and the losing of the self.

The Quantification Trilogy and Technologies of the Self

Over the course of artist Jeremy Shaw's Quantification Trilogy – a series of three films screened both theatrically and in gallery installations – a somewhat oblique science-fiction narrative unfolds. Fifty years into humanity's future a singularity event sees all human experience quantified. In its wake, humans begin to merge with the 'Hive' – a computational medium that houses this quantified information and provides, as a character explains, a 'unitive consciousness and perception of all things'. Through this process, humans eventually disappear in favour of the resulting, newly evolved 'quantum humans', beings who have lost the ability to experience transcendence, belief, and other affective states associated with spirituality. The films recount this narrative in reverse chronological order, with the first film, *Quickeners* (2014), set one hundred years after the quantification event. A group of quantum humans has started to develop 'Human Atavistic Syndrome' – a name for the weakening of their connection with the Hive, as well as a renewal of their desire for spiritual experience – and the film follows a group of these HAS sufferers as they participate in the antiquated scenario of a Pentecostal revival. They give testimonials (one character: 'I felt the need to believe in something that is not of the Hive'), sing, dance, shriek, play musical instruments, handle snakes, and speak in tongues, all with the aim of experiencing a 'quickening', or a state of ecstatic, transcendent loss of self.

Similarly, the second film, *Liminals* (2016), follows a particular 'periphery altruistic culture', or group of individuals who, facing the human species' looming extinction in the wake of joining the Hive, begin attempts to access a transcendent 'paraspace'. They do so through the use of various techniques of self-alteration, with the group using rapid and forced breathing, spinning, stasis, repetitive and rocking motions, dancing, as well as external mediating aids to help provoke the desired ecstatic experience and loss of self-awareness. This project to reactivate the capacity for belief will, the audience is meant to understand, produce the next phase of human evolution, or the quantum humans of the third film (the group also inject machine DNA into their brains during these activities). The final film, *I Can See Forever* (2018), is set only forty years in the future, and follows the sole survivor of a government experiment dedicated to producing humans with machine DNA biology. Now a young man, the character avoids using the recently developed proto-Hive and instead devotes himself to dance, a self-affecting practice whereby he can 'see forever', or access a 'digital plane of total unity'.

The films each invoke different historical and media-aesthetic reference points – *Quickeners* is an example of 1960s direct cinema or observational documentary, *Liminals* is a 1970s educational documentary, and *I Can See Forever* a videotaped film for 1980s television – presenting themselves as 'documentaries' about these fictional groups or individuals and their use of self-focused practices. Each film has a 'voice of God' narrator addressing itself to the 'normal' audience of the film's time period, and explaining the strange practices of the documented groups. In other words, Shaw manufactures an ethnographic distance on the various self-focused activities shown in the films, estranging practices that would be otherwise recognisable (and perhaps personally familiar) to many viewers. These impulses, to compare such practices across different historical moments as well as to estrange them, bring the films into contact with Foucault's approach to such self-focused practices. Later in his career, the philosopher would home in on these activities as sites for analysing the historically shifting relations between – as well as conceptualisations of – the subject, on the one hand, and truth, on the other. To his thinking, the technologies of the self consist of actions that

> permit individuals to effect by their own means, or with the help of others, a certain number of operations on their own bodies and souls, thoughts, conduct, and way of being, so as to transform themselves in order to attain a certain state of happiness, purity, wisdom, perfection, or immortality. (Foucault 1997a: 225)

In other words, these activities materialise a particular period's 'practical reason' concerning what the self is, what the truth is, and how the subject can access, speak, or engage the truth (Foucault 1997a: 225). Here, for example, Foucault compares shifts in such practical reason across the Hellenistic and Roman cultural paradigms of the 'care of the self' through the early Christian period. In the pre-Christian period, individuals undertook various practices of the self (often in concert with a guide or companion) in order to build the kind of self considered necessary for ethical and political life. These included various activities of focusing on oneself: meditation, memorisation of the past, examination of conscience, checking representations that appear in one's mind, and recording and reporting on one's daily activities and diet. In the Christian period, by comparison, the self-technology of confession would express a different understanding – one in which the subject's now-secreted (and already obtained) self is in need of investigation and analysis in order to attain purification and absolution.

The picture of the subject Foucault provides with this framework strikes a particular balance. On the one hand, the subject or self becomes an iterative product of the technologies of the self and the epistemic discursive frameworks they materialise. Here, any notion of the self as autonomous, self-identical, or wholly self-driven is undermined by this scenario, in which the self is always to-come, and is produced through the combined influence of the material scenes, other individuals, and 'practical reason' guiding these activities. However, in contrast to this, Foucault was also drawn to the technologies of the self – particularly the constellation of technologies and reason comprising the care of the self – because he felt they might offer models of self-concern and self-building that could challenge the infiltration of external, authoritarian, or disciplinary control of the self through that self (a phenomenon Foucault refers to as 'governmentality') (1997b: 260; 1997a: 225). In this, even as he denies the possibility of a wholly self-determining individual, Foucault finds ethical and political necessity in the *picture* of self-building. The practical enactments of the (past) self's relation to the (arriving) self, as a component of one's *ethos*, here support the potential of ethics to be, in Foucault's words, 'a very strong structure of existence, without any relation with the juridical per se, with an authoritarian system, with a disciplinary system' (1997b: 260). Indeed, in their invocations of self-focused technologies, the Quantification films play this conception out, as each film finds such practices supporting and enabling unpredictable departures from the reigning (diegetic) paradigms of life and social existence.

With their centralising of specific media in their respective depictions of self-technologies (and, as I will discuss in the final section, the effects of those technologies), Shaw's films also point to a question that Foucault opens but leaves largely unexplored in his theorisations. This is the question of media's role in the technologies of the self, and, by extension, the broader shifts in subjectivity they bring about and evince.[1] In Foucault's framing, discourse or epistemic frameworks play the predominant role in grounding and determining subjectivity and its technologies, but he does also briefly point towards the effects of media in this regard. He notes, for example, that letter writing, scrolls, and administrative notebooks participated in both opening up and reifying a particular sense of self in the first century CE. He states, 'a relation developed between writing and vigilance. Attention was paid to nuances of life, mood, and reading, and the experience of self was intensified and widened by virtue of this act of writing. A whole field of experience opened which earlier was absent' (Foucault 1997a: 232–3). In other words, Foucault hints here at the ways in which media and their varied material frameworks affect, modify, or induce different self-technologies, and how, in this way, such media influence the nature of the 'selves' that can be conceptualised, enacted, and produced in their wake. As I will explore in the final section of this chapter, Shaw's films insist on this latter point. As such, they also open the door to questions of what comes of framing portraiture as a form of mediating and mediated self-practice, questions that will guide the next section.

(Self-)Portraiture and the Mediated, Cultural Techniques of the Self

By drawing attention to portraiture's existence within the dynamics that Foucault has called the technologies of the self, a picture comes into focus. This picture has individuals creating self-portraits in order to know, affect, encounter, remake, or perhaps renounce or even destroy themselves; that is, the working of the media of sculpture, pigment, canvas, photographic chemicals, or digital pixels houses and materialises such activities. Here, these individuals produce an object inscribed in a material substrate, an object that then itself becomes a potential participant in or prompt for such (ongoing) technologies. In other words, portraits and self-portraits alike become incitements towards any number of potential forms of self-operation – offering themselves as points of focus, incitements to self-examination or concern, recordings or memorialisations of aspects of the self for future attention, etc. I will address some of the implications of this framing below, first discussing the questions of the kinds of truths and self-work at play in these dynamics, before turning to questions of figuring the (self-)portrait as one instance (among others) of the mediation operative within the technologies of the self. Here, for example, it will become clear that understanding portraiture through the lens of self-technologies emphasises its placement within different scales of temporal unfolding – those of the ongoing processes constitutive of selves as well as the longer histories in which the concepts comprising the human take shape.

Foucault's technologies of the self involve individuals conducting 'operations on their own body' (1997a: 225). Individuals and artists composing self-portraits do this as well, whether in creating a single selfie or an extended multi-part self-portrait – as in the sometimes years-long photographic projects of artists such as Tehching Hsieh, Nancy Floyd, and Nan Goldin. As these individuals pose, or draw on bodily knowledges to work with different materials, they use prior, culturally inflected training and physical knowledge, enacting what Marcel Mauss (1992) named as 'techniques of the body'. But, for Foucault, the technologies of the self involve more than individuals conducting operations on their bodies. Rather, these operations are distinguished by efforts to attain those states that Foucault lists – knowledge, perfection, immortality, or, indeed, self-renunciation or destruction – and, additionally, the invoking or accessing of 'truth'. To put that point differently, the claim that self-knowledge (or truths about the self, or certain kinds of self-presentation) is invoked in the activities of self-portraiture is easy enough to accept, but one should be careful not to mistake the truths of self-technologies for solipsistic or private revelations. Foucault has something else in mind here. After all, truth would not be truth without a wider reach.

To Foucault's thinking, self-technologies engage truths available *only through* a subject putting their being at stake. This is what he calls a 'spiritual' rather than empirical knowledge: a form of truth that 'is only given to the subject at a price that brings the subject's being into play'. In other words, this truth cannot be accessed without a 'conversion or transformation of the subject' – without the work accomplished (at least in part) by the technologies of the self (Foucault 2005: 15). For an example of this kind of truth, one could look to Tehching Hsieh's *Time Clock Piece (One Year Performance 1980–81)*, in which the artist punched a time clock every hour for a year and photographed himself doing so. In this piece, Hsieh is able to engage truths concerning the detrimental effects of contemporary systems and understandings of 'productivity', or productive and measured time. These are truths that take shape – that can only be accessed and given – through Hsieh's extended techniques of self-portraiture and the accompanying gruelling effects on his body and self. The fact of Hsieh's piece instantiating a critical truth speaks in turn to Foucault's hope that these self-technologies might open space for departures from predominant models of power.

Indeed, in his analysis of self-technologies in the Hellenistic, Roman, and early Christian periods, Foucault contends that this spiritual model of truth took self-conversion and transformation as being necessary for the achievement of knowledge (he contrasts this with the understanding that prevails in the modern age, where, independently of any change in or prescription for the subject, 'knowledge alone gives access to the truth' (2005: 17–18)). This claim speaks to the presence of another conceptual figure at play in these scenarios, a figure that again links self-portraiture and the technologies of the self. This is that of the imagined 'self-image' – a term whose expansiveness, or perhaps vagueness, usefully foregrounds the difficulties in (or even impossibility of) separating visual and conceptual modes of self-understanding. In producing a self-portrait, the maker calls up and aims to manifest (or elide) some visual or conceptual characterisation of themselves – some aspect of their self-image. Self-portraiture thus becomes a material nexus for one's self-image; a space for creation, location, and intercession. Indeed, work on one's self-image is a distinguishing and necessary feature of the technologies of the self more broadly. The act of affecting one's self or one's psychological state – say, by drinking alcohol or imbibing drugs – does not alone make a technology of the self. Rather, one must be aiming to affect one's state in order to alter one's self-understanding and shift one's future possibilities for selfhood. In the context of those technologies linked to the cultural paradigm of the 'care of the self', Foucault goes so far as to note that this care, which involves 'a certain way of attending to what we think and what takes place in our thought', is predicated on the activities of turning one's attention and 'looking' away from the outside and 'toward oneself' (2005: 10–11). In other words, the technologies of the self, as in self-portraiture, constitute an intervention into (or discovery or renunciation of) one's self-image.

In Foucault's discussions of the kinds of self-work specific to the care of the self, many of these activities even call for focusing on the self as a kind of image; here, this 'image' and the act of turning one's attention to it serve the goal of building and affecting one's future self. Shaw's *Quickeners* provides an instance of such a scenario. During the film's spiritual 'revival', a woman delivers her testimonial regarding her experiences with HAS. She describes her efforts to 'quicken', noting that these both involve and depend on her ability to 'meet' her self-image. She tells the crowd,

> I come here and imagine that this is where everything I've lost was born. I tell myself that if I wait long enough then a blurry figure will appear on the horizon and gradually get larger until I'd see I was looking at my own image. I'd wave and maybe call out to myself.

As she continues, it becomes clear that this other self, this image on the horizon, is who she wants to become, and she sermonises to the others present that doing so will require moving further away from their prior lives as 'quantum humans' and toward their unknown future selves. The film here exemplifies this act or technique of self-envisioning that is central to technologies of the self, revealing it to be a kind of virtual self-portraiture – a mode in which the lived self becomes the medium worked in service of affecting the (future) self-image.

Acknowledging the self-image's centrality to the technologies of the self does not, however, necessitate a picture of such self-work as discrete or superfluous instances of solipsistic activity. Foucault's conceptualising of the technologies of the self as both producing and reproducing epistemic reason already positions such activities as nodes for broader historical shifts – as indexing and influencing that which makes subjects perceivable as ontological actors. One finds a similar approach in the frameworks of German media theory's 'cultural techniques', though these take media and mediation as a constitutive focus. Here, media are reconceptualised away from the 'technical *a priori*' of earlier Kittlerian media theory into inextricable components of the processes and operations that produce or enable culture (Siegert 2015: 3, 11). As Bernhard Siegert writes, such processes operationalise 'distinctions in the real' – distinctions such as those between human and animal, inside and outside, and nature and culture. The enactment of these techniques then works to unify and concretise the terms on either side of the division: there are not humans, time, and space *as such*, but rather techniques of hominisation, time measurement, and spatial control (2015: 14, 9). In understanding technologies of the self as cultural techniques, the act of producing and viewing (self-)portraits, then, becomes a process involving both the territorialising and deterritorialising of certain grounding distinctions – say, those of the 'inside' and 'outside' of the subject. Such works, for example, project and materialise the notion of subjectivity as coinciding with the physical border of the body, with the lines around photographed, painted, drawn, or sculpted bodies entrenching the cultural divisions between body and not-body, subjectivity and not-subjectivity. They also, at a somewhat deeper register, provide a picture of subjectivity as *like* matter: as something capable of having an inside and an outside, as persisting in time and space, as something that can be 'discovered', 'built', 'lost', etc.

Cultural historian and philosopher Thomas Macho has gone so far as to claim not only self-portraits but cultural techniques more broadly as technologies of the self, noting that cultural techniques 'have always been practiced as' self-technologies (2013: 31). However, in making this claim, Macho operates with a rather idiosyncratic reading of both of these terms. He advocates for limiting cultural techniques to 'second-order techniques', or symbolic technologies that allow for recursive self-reference – writing about writing, painting depicting painting, etc. (a circumscription that other theorists have taken issue with) (Macho 2013: 30–1; Siegert 2015: 11–12). More pressingly for this chapter, he also excludes aspects of Foucault's concept without explicitly acknowledging these exclusions. Renaming Foucault's self-technologies as 'techniques of identity', Macho focuses on histories of material forms of authentication, registration, and identification of subjects; taking portraits as one example of these, he places them in conjunction with cave markings, personal seals and signets, fingerprints, and signatures (2013: 44). As such, Macho somewhat conflates the technologies of the self with two other of Foucault's technologies: technologies of signs, or communication, and technologies of power, or domination (Foucault 1997a: 225). While Foucault claims no hard and fast boundaries between these categories, noting that each routinely crosses into and underwrites the others to different degrees in practice, Macho's account ultimately avoids what Foucault centralised in his conceptualisation of the technologies of the self – that is, subjects' concern with affecting themselves. In other words, while Macho is undoubtedly correct that the possibilities of conceiving of a self lie in and are indivisible from forms of material, other-facing authentication, the technologies of the self nevertheless involve more than these identity-bestowing grounds for conceiving or recognising the subject as a being. They also name that 'mode of action that an individual exercises upon himself' to the end of intervening into and affecting that self (Foucault 1997a: 225).[2]

With these self-affecting goals in mind, another set of media, operative in the technologies of the self but different from those Macho explores, and to which we can append (self-)portraits, comes to the fore. Rather than media framing the legibility, location, and authentication of the subject, these would include media provoking or supporting attitudes of self-focus, self-examination, remembering, etc. Foucault's aforementioned means of self-writing – letters, diaries, scrolls, notebooks – provide an example of such

media. The crystals or semi-precious stones used in both historical and contemporary spiritual practices for 'centring' or affecting individuals' states of being would offer another instance. The
materials of augury, with their provision of structures for self-
attention and deliberation on one's actions, would provide yet
another example: tarot cards, the yarrow stalks of I Ching divination, the organic materials of tasseography (tea leaf reading), coins
to be flipped, or animal entrails to be read.[3] Finally, one could
include here the open-ended set of objects (or locations, or spatial configurations) that can become cathected with familiarity and
affective associations; French filmmaker and theorist Jean Epstein
gives the examples of a book or 'perhaps a very banal and somewhat ugly trinket' in which individuals see the 'memories and emotions, plans or regrets' that they had attached to them.[4] Positioned
now within this list, self-portraits and portraits, no less than the
media involved in producing them, take up a mediating position
within the chain of operations underwriting the self – those cultural techniques that set the physical and conceptual stage for the
self's affecting of the self.

Marshall McLuhan, in his *Understanding Media: The Extensions
of Man* (1964), takes a related (if characteristically idiosyncratic)
approach to these questions. There, he argues for acknowledging
what he considers to be the self-relation at the heart of individuals' engagements with media, taking this as key to moving past the
narcissism associated with such engagements. He finds the myth
of Narcissus – wherein the eponymous figure falls in love with his
reflected but unrecognised image – to emblematise humans' relation to their media landscape, as humans 'at once become fascinated
by any extension of themselves in material other than themselves'.
To his thinking, such extensions include everything from horses to
clocks to electrical media (McLuhan 1964: 51). Importantly though,
this fascination rests for McLuhan, like Narcissus's, on individuals'
inability to recognise such media as self-extension, or what he calls
'images of ourselves'; that is, it rests on their failure to see media
as 'idols' that, in being beheld, conform the beholder to that media
(1964: 55). Indeed, individuals 'auto-amputate' this awareness of
their manifestation in the media they use – a measure of protection
for an over-extended nervous system, in McLuhan's estimation –
and in turn block the possibility of seeing the self-relation latent in
such material (1964: 52). What is left *instead* is narcissism, or the
fending off of that which would affect, alter, change, or otherwise
threaten the self-as-it-is – those outcomes that the technologies of
the self promise.

As this narcissism involves adapting to a 'closed system', McLuhan finally claims that the age of electronic media would open the possibility of awareness of humans' extensions, enabling self-recognition and a potential escape from 'individual separateness' into 'total social involvement' – an optimism that would, of course, be refuted (1964: 51, 56). In response, we might make the more modest claim that technologies of the self involve, to different degrees, the act of finding or recognising oneself in media – in McLuhan's 'images of ourselves', as well as in actual images of ourselves. But the refutation of McLuhan's hopes for the broader possibilities of media-historical shifts casts light on a related point, which is the proneness of mediated technologies of the self to failure or co-optation, or to simply not taking place at all. To put it differently, it may be that Macho's techniques of identity are more prevalent than ever, but that technologies of the self, with their need not just to maintain but to affect a self in service of creating a self, are much rarer events indeed.

In departing from Macho's characterisation of self-technologies as techniques of identity, one further aspect of Foucault's original concept returns to the fore. While technologies of the self may be put to service in overt or conscious forms of self-building – forms that may emphasise continuities or identity between the self in past, present, and future forms – Foucault's self-technologies also encompass the possibilities of *breaks* or ruptures in identity (a key element in Foucault's sense that ethics, with their technologies of the self, may allow for breaks with reigning paradigms and institutional power). Indeed, a number of the technologies of the self that Foucault explores are concerned with the destruction or abandonment of identity. The self-renouncing activities comprising Christian penance provide Foucault with one such example: as he writes, penance does not have 'as its target the establishing of an identity but, instead, serves to mark the refusal of the self, the breaking away from self'; 'it represents a break with one's past identity'; or, again, 'self-revelation is [here] at the same time self-destruction' (1997a: 245). In these kinds of technologies of the self, then, the escape or overcoming of the past self becomes necessary to achieving the desired possibilities of acquiring or building a new self. As these are the kinds of self-technologies that Shaw's films organise themselves around, I turn back to these now. In the Quantification Trilogy, such self-transcending activities can escape mediation, or what Sybille Krämer (2015) has called the conditions of 'mediality', no more than the other technologies of the self explored thus far. Ultimately, the films will reveal themselves to be, first, portraits of the mediations that make self-loss possible and, secondly, mediators in their spectators' (potential) experiences of self-escape.

The Quantification Trilogy's Loss-of-Self Portraits

Characters endeavour to lose themselves and achieve transcendence in all of Shaw's Quantification films, utilising self-affecting practices that feature media as conspicuous and ubiquitous components. In *Liminals*, for example, characters' self-affecting techniques of movement and breathing involve what the film's sceptical narrator comically names as 'antiquated effects devices used by catharsis-seeking hedonistic twentieth century secular cultures'; in other words, mirror balls, stroboscopic lights, and 'dream machines', or flickering light devices designed to affect the optical nerve and resulting brain waves. In the third film, *I Can See Forever*, the mediating force would seem primarily to be the character Roderick Dale's physical body, but even this cannot be extricated from technological mediation, as Roderick's abilities to both dance and transcend human experience are imputed to his 'machine DNA biology'. And if various media feature in the films' diegetic depictions of self-technologies, the formal and aesthetic structures of the films further foreground the particularities of different mediating processes. While *Liminals* fashions itself as a celluloid-shot 1970s-era documentary, and *I Can See Forever* a 1980s video-shot television broadcast, *Quickeners* actually consists of reworked footage from the 1967 observational documentary *Holy Ghost People*, directed by Peter Adair and shot in Scrabble Creek, Virginia. (Shaw and his collaborators ingeniously insert their new fiction into this footage by garbling the original, recorded voices and then 'translating' them via added subtitles.) With these formal codings – drawing attention in *Quickeners*, for example, to the qualities of the period's black-and-white, fast-photographing, 16mm film stock – the films activate a tension between the irreal narratives on offer and the documentary modes and media being invoked to deliver them. In other words, if the Quantification Trilogy draws on the historicity and documentary value regularly ascribed to film and other audiovisual media, they also already, at this point, hint at the fact that these media may have a relationship to historicity that exceeds the simple recording of quotidian, real events.

At a certain point in each of the films, an affective crescendo takes hold: trance-evoking music or drones swell on the soundtrack, footage is slowed while the editing pace picks up, and bodies in the frame begin to move rhythmically. This is the rise to the transcendent space that the characters seek – their 'quickening', or 'paraspace', or 'seeing forever' – but it is not the space itself. These spaces arrive instead in clear breaks at the apex of the crescendo, breaks that irrupt into the frame as colours, forms, and sounds unpredicted by what the film has shown thus far: aesthetic rupture as rapture. In *Quickeners*, this takes the form of coloured auras appearing around certain figures as they shake and seize in slow motion (Figure 12.1), while the accompanying sounds deepen and noticeably expand into other speakers through a now multi-channel mix (something the other films will employ in their breaks as well). In *Liminals*, on the other hand, the black-and-white filmed images of dancing characters are violently torn through by digitally datamoshed images of their own bodies, now in garish colour and morphing in and out of recognisable figuration, while distorted and overtly synthetic sounds simultaneously screech and rumble on the soundtrack. Finally, *I Can See Forever*'s break with reality also employs glitching and datamoshing, though now with a kind of algorithmic animation that generates liquid neon lines around the dissolving bodies.

Here and elsewhere, Shaw is interested in questions of the representation of esoteric experience and the different media and aesthetic forms that have been in service of such representation. And while one

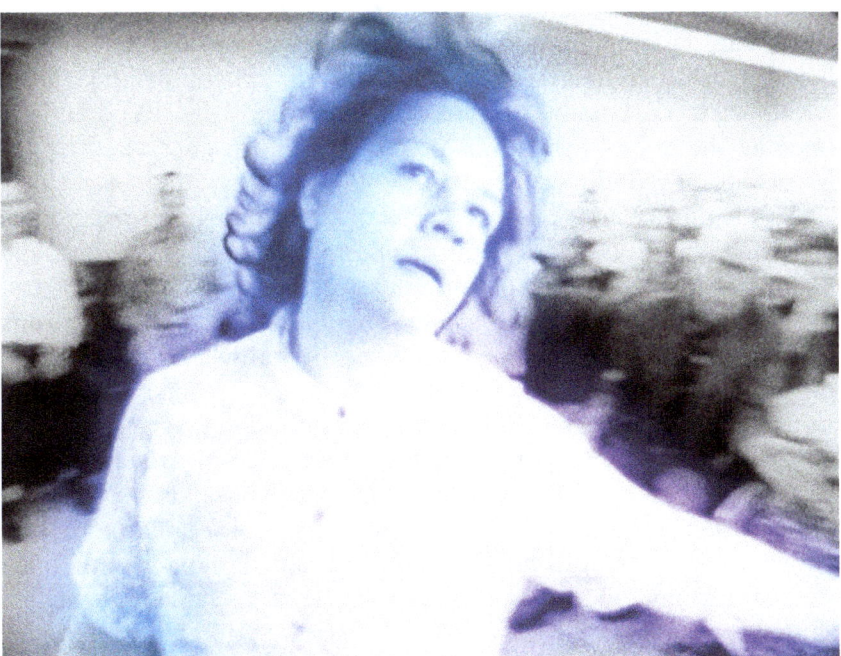

Figure 12.1 Jeremy Shaw, *Quickeners*, 2014, courtesy of Jeremy Shaw Studio

understanding of such endeavours would have rapturous or ecstatic experience necessarily escaping any such 'capture' – lamenting that the representation of the superphysical in physical form will always be inadequate or adulterating – the Quantification films do not share this view. Rather than framing media's relation to these kinds of experiences as one of (reductive) representation, and thus as always and only coming after the fact, the films instead approach mediation as a constitutive aspect of moments of self-loss. The use of media in the various depicted self-technologies already speaks to this, but such an emphasis appears again in the films' final, post-rupture sections. Here, through the formal presentation of these rapturous spaces, the films fashion and offer themselves *as* media that might prompt transcendent or sublime experiences. The various combinations of sound, colour, rhythm, and movement turn the films into what, with a nod to filmmaker Peter Tscherkassky, we might call light and sound machines; something that differs in degree, but not in kind, from the light and sound machines that the films' diegetic characters use in service of their own technologies of (loss of) self. Indeed, while all three films employ a richer and more physically affecting soundscape in these final sections, the latter two also shift their aspect ratios, transitioning from the 4:3 frame common to 16mm and early video footage to the widescreen (and peripheral-vision filling) format associated with the projection of large-format film and digital cinema. The Quantification films, then, become, like other examples of media listed in the previous section, prompts for and influential agents within viewers' possible self-loss or altered experience, potentially opening the door to the kinds of self-technologies activated by the 'return' to or refinding of a self at the films' close.

If the films enact a latent scene of a mediated self-technology in their exhibition and spectatorship, so too do they explore and expound on mediations of esoteric states that have come previously, and that have informed the possibilities for conceptualising and experiencing transcendence. Here, the films 'feel' the ecstasies of self-escape through – or in and as – recognisably mediated forms. In *Quickeners*, for example, the applied auras call up the slight misalignments of colour print roller technologies, with their tell-tale, off-colour borders around illustrated figures. They also invoke hand-painted silent films, a format that saw waves of fluctuating colour added after the fact to bodies and objects filmed in black and white. In the next film, the mediated conceptions of transcendence have first shifted forward in time, as *Liminals*' break into glitch art references the irruption of digital audiovisual media into an analogue world (Figure 12.2). However, these glitching pixels eventually settle into

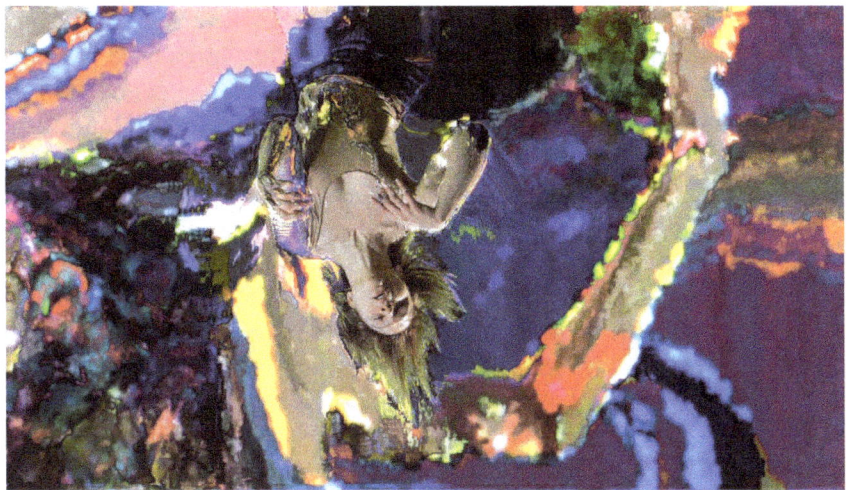

Figure 12.2 Jeremy Shaw, *Liminals*, 2016, courtesy of Jeremy Shaw Studio

soft colour washes on the screen – a seeming nod to early and mid-twentieth-century 'Lumia' or light art. Finally, over the course of its ecstatic section, *I Can See Forever* similarly moves chronologically backward from the more contemporary datamoshing into a series of non-objective animations of multicoloured geometric patterns, conjuring early computer art in its produced sense of 'movement through' these shifting lines and squares.[5] Throughout then, with their foregrounding of comparisons between different historically situated media, the Quantification films point to the fact of transcendence as conceptualised and experienced differently in different periods, or as emerging from and within particular landscapes of mediation and mediated self-technologies.

And so, if the Quantification films are not particularly concerned with mystical or apophatic claims about the impossibility of representing transcendent states, they are instead intent on drawing out the ways that media mark any possible conception of what transcendence is, or the ways in which they frame what Ludwig Wittgenstein would have called the 'grammar' underwriting these experiences.[6] Here, the sonic, visual, and phenomenal qualities offered by different media shape the possible and various senses of transcendence, and self-technologies become a site for the iteration of such senses: as mirror balls and strobe lights become available to individuals endeavouring to escape themselves, for example, transcendence now becomes a softness of coloured light – an atmospheric, dynamic weightlessness. For the films, then, the media in play in these scenarios become their own kinds of portraits, recalling McLuhan's 'images of ourselves'. They are portraits of any self that might be conceived and produced through such self-technologies, as well as portraits of what the produced *loss* of those selves might look, feel, and sound like. Here, the Quantification films' depiction or 'documentation' of the effects of self-shedding practices offer what we might call 'loss-of-self' portraits.

In broaching the notion of a loss-of-self portrait, I have in mind something different from what van Alphen has noted as modern portraiture's turn towards depicting a 'loss of self'. This turn, as van Alphen (2005: 25) writes, followed from the modernist recognition of an 'irreconcilable split between signifier and signified', or the failure of the signifier – the portrait – to provide the signified – the self – with the unity and wholeness it seems to offer. As van Alphen describes, a tension then arises between subjectivity and representation. Roland Barthes, for example, characterises images as providing the self with an illusion of wholeness only at the contradictory cost of subjecting oneself to the impersonal conventions of representation, while Francis Bacon's portraits conjure a battle between the subject and representation, with the latter mortifying self-experience and embodying a destructive will to 'nail the subject down' (van Alphen 2005: 31–2, 35). In other words, in the way of thinking van Alphen describes here, subjectivity and representation are set in opposition, and the referenced 'loss of self' is the loss of self-as-representation, or the loss of a self purportedly unified by representation.

But Shaw's films, no less than this chapter's broader argument for conceiving of (self-)portraiture as an example of mediated technologies of the self, sidestep this impasse of framing subjectivity and aesthetic representation as locked in a zero-sum game. The picture of subjectivity at play in the films is one set against unity, completion, or wholeness – the selves here are always-to-come or in the process of being produced, maintained, or abandoned. This resonates in turn with the frameworks of the mediated technologies of the self: where the representational model has mimetic portraiture freezing and threatening the self by purporting to capture it, here mimetic visual representations are instead one part of a landscape of media objects – all waiting to be put to use or already participating in those techniques that build and produce the self, and which, in some instances, already bear the marks of prior activities of self-inscription and self-externalisation. In other words, in this way of thinking, mediating images of the human body do not impinge on, replace, or authorise selfhood but, instead, belong to its recursive constitution.

This conception is emblematised in the Quantification Trilogy's loss-of-self portraits. Rather than invoking the inimical relation between subjectivity and representation, these speak instead to the inevitable mediations of the self-image, that conceptual figure at play in the technologies of the self. Self-images are products of longer chains of mediated scenes of self-relation, wherein the media of mirrors, reflective surfaces, photographs, portraits, film, and video have made their marks on the pictures of the self they present; as Hagi Kenaan notes, 'a visual self-relation is not part of our in-born capacities' (2019: 119). Shaw's films conjure this reality by presenting their final sections as its converse. In other words, they show that just as an operative or quotidian self-image follows from and takes shape in prior instances of mediated self-relation, so too does any imagination of the self's denaturing, dissolution, or escape. Here, for example, *Liminals* and *I Can See Forever*'s use of digital media and algorithmic art 'document' these forms' remaking of conceptions of what it means to lose oneself, or one's self-image.

To put that differently, the films show how media and related aesthetic forms have furnished transcendence with new experiences and new pictures: Now, losing oneself finds its feeling shaped, for example, by the mediated, aesthetic possibilities of the glitch – by its picture of the ways in which bodies might disintegrate and reintegrate in and through one another, or its picture of spaces where perceived ontological boundaries give way to a shared plane of pixels with no boundaries, where concepts of depth and surface retain no more hold than concepts of up and down. The films' loss-of-self portraits, then, are portraits of the channels and routes available for the finding and losing of selves in certain moments. The loss of self portrayed here is not a threat to a subject's wholeness, but the material and mediations that have made this loss possible. Here, as individuals endeavour to escape themselves, hastening the passing of the self and the human into what will come after, the Quantification films stubbornly remain – portraits of media landscapes that, in their proffering of transcendence, finally cannot be transcended.

Notes

1. For an extended discussion of Foucault's reception by (and promise for) media scholarship, see Hansen 2012.
2. Macho's discussion of cultural 'techniques of solitude' in a recently translated essay (Macho and Rashof 2021) falls more in line with this aspect of Foucault's concept, though here Macho is not discussing self-portraits or related art forms.
3. As regards the question of the cultural techniques contributing to and unifying distinctions between the 'inner' and the 'outer' of the subject,

one could reference here Julian Jaynes's claims (2000: 239–42) about the material scenes of augury as forms of 'exo-psychic thought' that both pre-date human consciousness – understood as an analogic metaphorical space occupied by an analogue 'I' – and as helping to shape the picture of 'inner' consciousness that would emerge, a picture built on a forgetting of its 'outer' origins.

4. In full, Epstein (2012: 304) writes, 'Each of us, I assume, may possess some object which he holds onto for personal reasons: for some it's a book; for some, perhaps a very banal and somewhat ugly trinket [. . .] We do not look at them as they really are. To tell the truth, we are incapable of seeing them as objects. What we see in them, through them, are the memories and emotions, plans or regrets that we had attached to these things for a more or less lengthy period of time, sometimes forever.'

5. This section's allusion to Stanley Kubrick's *2001: A Space Odyssey*'s (1968) 'stargate sequence' – in that this sequence was similarly inspired by the early computer-graphic-containing films of Jordan Belson – then becomes, with the stargate sequence's oft-remarked uptake by adherents of the period's culture of drug use and 'mind expansion', a doubled reference to film's history as a medium for self-technologies.

6. For further discussion of the connection between media and grammar in Wittgenstein's thought, see Rennebohm 2021.

References

Belting, Hans (2017), *Face and Mask: A Double History*, trans. Thomas S. Hansen and Abby J. Hansen, Princeton, NJ: Princeton University Press.

Epstein, Jean (2012), *Jean Epstein: Critical Essays and New Translations*, ed. Sarah Keller and Jason N. Paul, Amsterdam: Amsterdam University Press.

Foucault, Michel (1997a), 'Technologies of the Self', in Michel Foucault, *Ethics: Subjectivity and Truth*, ed. Paul Rabinow, trans. Robert Hurley et al., New York: The New Press, pp. 223–49.

Foucault, Michel (1997b), 'On the Genealogy of Ethics', in Michel Foucault, *Ethics: Subjectivity and Truth*, ed. Paul Rabinow, trans. Robert Hurley et al., New York: The New Press, pp. 253–80.

Foucault, Michel (2005), *The Hermeneutics of the Subject: Lectures at the Collège de France, 1981–82*, ed. Frédéric Gros, François Ewald, and Alessandro Fontana, trans. Graham Burchell, New York: Palgrave Macmillan.

Hansen, Mark B. N. (2012), 'Foucault and Media: A Missed Encounter?', *South Atlantic Quarterly*, 111(3): 497–528.

Jaynes, Julian (2000 [1976]), *The Origin of Consciousness in the Breakdown of the Bicameral Mind*, New York: First Mariner Books.

Jirsa, Tomáš (2019), 'Faces without Interiority: Music Video's Reinvention of the Portrait', *World Literature Studies*, 4(11): 55–68.

Kenaan, Hagi (2019), 'The Selfie and the Face', in Julia Eckel, Jens Ruchatz, and Sabine Wirth (eds), *Exploring the Selfie: Historical, Theoretical, and Analytic Approaches to Digital Self-Photography*, Cham: Palgrave Macmillan, pp. 113–27.

Krämer, Sybille (2015), *Medium, Messenger, Transmission: An Approach to Media Philosophy*, trans. Anthony Enns, Amsterdam: Amsterdam University Press.

Macho, Thomas (2013), 'Second Order Animals: Cultural Techniques of Identity and Identification', *Theory, Culture & Society*, 30(6), special issue: 30–47.

Macho, Thomas, and Sascha Rashof (2021), 'Alone with Oneself: Solitude as Cultural Technique', *Angelaki: Journal of the Theoretical Humanities*, 26(1): 9–21.

Mauss, Marcel (1992), 'Techniques of the Body', in Jonathan Crary and Sanford Kwinter (eds), *Incorporations*, New York: Zone Books, pp. 454–77.

McLuhan, Marshall (1964), *Understanding Media: The Extensions of Man*, New York: Signet Books.

Nancy, Jean-Luc (2018), *Portrait*, trans. Sarah Clift and Simon Sparks, New York: Fordham University Press.

Rennebohm, Kate (2021), 'The "Cinema Remarks": Wittgenstein on Moving Image Media and the Ethics of Re-Viewing', *October*, 171 (winter): 47–76.

Siegert, Bernhard (2015), *Cultural Techniques: Grids, Filters, Doors, and Other Articulations of the Real*, trans. Geoffrey Winthrop-Young, New York: Fordham University Press.

van Alphen, Ernst (2005), 'The Portrait's Dispersal', in Ernst van Alphen, *Art in Mind: How Contemporary Images Shape Thought*, Chicago: University of Chicago Press, pp. 21–47.

Weigel, Sigrid (ed.) (2017), *Das Gesicht*. Dresden: Wallstein.

IV Afterlives

Chapter 13

As if to Say Nothing: On Balthus's Portraits

Brian Price

The paintings of Balthus are as admired as they are reviled, as cel-
ebrated for their beauty as they are condemned for their alleged
transgressions, so much so that the moral challenge of the work, for
many, is difficult to disentangle from the aesthetic logic of the com-
positions. At the heart of what can only be described as an ongoing
disturbance created by the paintings – a strong moral objection to
Balthus's work that has followed his paintings unabated since at least
the late 1930s – are the portraits he made of 'pubescent' girls in a
state of repose, often with their underwear showing. The paintings
I have in mind include *Girl with a Cat* (1937), *Thérèse Dreaming*
(1938), and *Les Beaux Jours* (1944), as the most typical instances;
portraits, as they are, of the young girl alone, or alone before the
painter, as we regularly take to be the condition of any portrait's production. And I should say at the outset that I will only use the word
'pubescent' in quotes, since what I am dealing with here, before all
else, is a problem of naming. Most simply put, the problem of naming that concerns me is how difficult it can be, especially where moral
judgement is concerned, to say whether our description of an object
follows from the object or begins elsewhere, prior to our encounter
with any object in particular – as, for instance, when we remark on
the subject *of* or *in* a painting, as if it were the only object, or only
part of the object, before us. As if an object remains impervious, in
every instance, to mediation. In that way, the name is free of every
object in particular, despite the fact that words feel as though they
are bound to things the more often we use them, as if by nature or
moral law.

As a description of Balthus's early-teenage sitters, 'pubescent' is
used nearly everywhere the paintings are described, in sources both
hostile *and* reverential. For instance, it was a central term in the

headline of a petition generated by Mia Merrill in New York in 2017
against the Metropolitan Museum of Art for continuing to display
Thérèse Dreaming in its collection: 'Metropolitan Museum of Art:
Remove Balthus's Suggestive Painting of a Pubescent Girl, *Thérèse
Dreaming*' (quoted in Kinsella 2017). But it is also used by the Gagosian Gallery in their biography of Balthus: 'Casting viewers as voy-
eurs of brooding pubescent female subjects, he scandalized audiences
with his first gallery exhibition, at Galerie Pierre, in 1934' (Gagosian
Gallery n.d.). That is to say, the difficulty of Balthus's work may
have less, or at least as much, to do with the paintings he made as
with those who have described them, as if the many who describe the
painting do so in agreement about what is at stake in the work even
though one critic may be at radical odds with another who nevertheless employs the same concept and attendant mode of description.
The hostile response can be said to agree, at least at root, with the
favourable one, no matter how benign the description may seem,
and despite the fact that description both follows from and remains
subject to the limits of the concept at hand, such as 'pubescent'. In
short, what we identify as transgressive stands as a better description
of ourselves than of what we see.

Related to the question of naming – of the seemingly unselfconscious use of the word 'pubescent' to describe Balthus's subjects, in terms both favourable and condemnatory – is also a problem of mores, context, and, thus, time. Despite the obvious fact that
Balthus's paintings have been exhibited in a wide variety of contexts
for nearly a century now, the moral outrage that regularly follows
the public exhibition of his portraits of 'pubescent' girls in states of
repose seems to have changed rather little, so much so that one might
have reason to wonder what it means to say – as we commonly do –
that mores change in time. Or, for that matter, what it means to think
that mores can be distinguished from contexts. Or else, we might
wonder how mores – as essential characteristics of what a society at
a distinct period of time deems acceptable – can be accounted for in
ways that do not rely upon abstractions about social relations that
are predicated on moral claims, to begin with.

I want to consider, then, what it might mean that Balthus's portraits provoke the same grief and grievance in time. My suggestion,
I will say at the outset, is that the moral response to Balthus's work,
the anxiety it so consistently stokes, has less to do with the record of
flesh than it does with the presence of stone. It has more to do with
what remains the same across time rather than with what is young
and, thus, premature – as if not yet in the form that stone will keep.
And if what we confront in Balthus's portraits is what remains the

same across time, as I will ultimately suggest that it is, then we will find ourselves before the eternal and thus speechless, or else with always the wrong words to describe what we think we are seeing anew.

Ideas in Search of Objects

Since what we are ultimately dealing with in Balthus's portraits is the relation between painting and words, I want to begin by presenting two descriptions of one of Balthus's most notorious portraits, *Thérèse Dreaming*: one from an art critic who objects to the work, even though he also seems not to want to, and one from Balthus's biographer, who likewise appears to be on Balthus's side – supposing, of course, that we can say what that side is.

In 2018 the influential American art critic Peter Schjeldahl published an essay about Balthus in response to Merrill's petition to have Balthus's *Thérèse Dreaming* removed from public display in the Metropolitan Museum of Art in New York. Schjeldahl's response is representative of the mixed reception that Balthus's work has received, and he says it all with remarkable economy in the opening paragraph of his essay, 'Moral Conundrums and Political Passions'.

> I both like and dislike 'Thérèse Dreaming' (1938), the Balthus painting that thousands of people have petitioned the Metropolitan Museum to remove from view because it brazens the artist's letch for pubescent girls – which he always haughtily denied, but come on! The man was a creep. The subject sits with head turned, eyes closed, and a knee raised to expose her panties. On the floor, a cat – a personal totem for Balthus – laps milk from a dish. The picture is strongly painted, with a dusky tonality in which colors smolder. There is a sense of time run aground on a day – in the afternoon, you somehow know – without end. (Schjeldahl 2018: n.p.)

How to account for a response that moves from moral condemnation to aesthetic celebration in the same paragraph? Schjeldahl begins with what he takes to be the obvious moral problem of the image: that it is the work of a creep, that Balthus's denials that the paintings are erotic are absurd. While it is true that Balthus, on many occasions, denied that there was an erotic dimension to his portraits of 'pubescent' girls, one might do better to simply note that refusal, and regard, instead, what else he says of them. For instance, in his memoir, Balthus says of *Thérèse Dreaming*: '*Thérèse Dreaming* and *The Mirrored Room* shouldn't be seen as erotic acts where anatomy and libido unite indecently, but rather as the need to expose and capture something that must be termed elusive and inscrutable, yet which vibrates and resonates, belonging to what Camus called "the world's beating heart"' (2002: 116). Schjeldahl reaches a similar assessment of the work's elusiveness at the end of the paragraph, when he speaks of smouldering colours and a 'sense of time run aground – in the afternoon, somehow you know – without end'. I take it that in saying 'somehow you know', Schjeldahl wants to indicate that either we don't really know, otherwise we would say so, or that the painting evokes a sense of what remains elusive in time, or about time, as when we feel nearly thoughtless and without purpose in the midst of a hot, languorous day.

But that is definitely not how he begins. Rather, in the sentence that immediately follows Schjeldahl's statement of what he takes to be obvious – that Balthus was a creep – he describes Thérèse, Balthus's sitter, this way: 'The subject sits with head turned, eyes closed, and a knee raised to expose her panties.' In putting it this way, it seems to me that Schjeldahl means to indicate one of two possibilities, though many other things are possible too: that Thérèse, the model before the canvas, has raised her knee with the intention of showing her underwear as a deliberate act of sexual provocation; or else, that Balthus has posed her this way, *as if* she were intending to be seductive, so as to paint her this way – so as to mould this being to a fiction for the sake of a real desire. Balthus loses in either case, since he has either painted what is not meant to be seen, even if, while sitting, Thérèse acted according to her own desires; or else, and possibly worse, he posed her this way so as to paint her this way, in which case what matters is not only the implied index between painting and girl, but also what the index (if we can really speak of painting as an indexical sign) points to, even though it is not what we see: Balthus touching, moulding the girl so that she can appear as she does. In other words, what shows is bad, and what does not show but 'had' to have happened is even worse.

And yet, if the portrait can be said to be an indexical sign, what is indexed is not the real Thérèse but the imagination of the viewer. These two options appear as the only options, however, if one precedes the description of the painting with the assertion that *Balthus was a creep*. If we think we know that Balthus was a creep – maybe he was, maybe he wasn't – then how will we avoid describing the painting itself in creepy terms? If what we think we know is that Balthus was a creep, then do we not ask, prior to looking and prior to describing, what might be creepy about what we see? After all, we do not see movement in the painting – there is no record, as there would be in cinema, of how that leg got there, what else the face showed, what else hands did, whether those of Thérèse or Balthus or both. Rather, all we see in the painting is a teenage girl sitting in a room in daylight, leaning slightly back with her eyes closed, with one leg on the floor and one perched on a stool, such that her skirt falls closer to her waist than to her knees. If Thérèse is dreaming, we do not know of what. If Thérèse is sitting seductively, who, exactly, decides that? On what grounds does one say so?

For instance, when asked about the eroticism of Balthus's paintings, Sabine Rewald, curator of *Cats and Girls*, the 2013 show on Balthus at the Met, voiced an opinion that is rather different from Schjeldahl's: 'Very young girls sit like that – awkwardly, with their legs askew or open, exposing themselves. I see it on the city bus all the time; it is totally unselfconscious' (quoted in Hansen 2013: n.p.). Rewald goes on to say, as if the identification of an untoward eroticism were a matter of mores, Anglo-American ones specifically: 'It's so funny how people get offended or outraged by him, personally. Perhaps it's because I'm German, but I have never found him offensive.'

The second description of *Thérèse Dreaming* that I want to discuss comes from Nicholas Fox Weber, Balthus's biographer, a passage that needs to be quoted at length, even though we will arrive at more or less the same place we were with Schjeldahl.

A signature Balthus, exquisitely crafted, tasteful to a fault, *Thérèse Dreaming* presents the nubile schoolgirl exposing herself coyly but shamelessly. Because of the girl's age, her clothing, and her apparent indifference to the effect of her fierce sexuality, the image is more laden with libido than Titian's Venuses, Goya's Mayas, or Ingres's bordello scenes. Thérèse emanates eroticism while looking blithely unaware of that fact.

Balthus poses the young adolescent with her legs spread and her skirt and petticoats thrust back. Her crotch, scantily clad in white underpants, faces us in full view. The lack of modesty or embarrassment is completely out of character for a young woman at this point in her maturation, when she has just begun to develop breasts. Her attitude suits either a mature seductress or a younger child who does not know any better. Or perhaps she is asleep and is not aware that we are seeing her in this indecent way. In any event, either out of his allegedly deliberate attempt to shock or, more likely, because of a desire to satisfy his own longings, the thirty-year old artist has not just been risqué in having Thérèse display herself this way; he has been remarkably salacious. Thérèse's sexuality may be dormant for her, but it is rampant for us. (2014: 389–90)

There are a number of things to observe here, very little of which has to do with the painting itself. First, Weber begins his description of this painting, 'tasteful to a fault', as an image of a 'nubile schoolgirl exposing herself coyly but shamelessly'. To describe Thérèse as nubile is, of course, to describe her as both newly sexually mature *and* erotically attractive, not just attracted. In this respect, Weber's exuberant response obviates what the more common adjective 'pubescent' seems, for most of its users, to imply: that this is an image of becoming sexually mature, and in that way, a sign of both Thérèse's arousal and ours, as if both things can only ever be the same, and as if the onset of puberty necessitates erotic thought and erotic feeling at every moment, such that we can feel confident that this one moment painted was one of those moments, whether she was moulded into shape or shaped herself.

Weber also tells us that Thérèse exposes herself, 'coyly but shamelessly'. But how can we know this from one still image? I note only that, in the painting, Thérèse's head falls slightly to the left side of the canvas with her eyes closed, mouth shut, hands on her head, as if she were cooling off on a warm day and drifting off to sleep. Her eyes and mouth both run in straight, horizontal lines. Should we not require more than one pose, frozen in time, to describe someone as coy? Such judgements are easier to justify in a narrative painting instead of a portrait, which indicates, graphically, a relation between one figure or figures and another. Why can't Thérèse just be sitting this way, doing what the title suggests? Dreaming.

I presume that in ascribing an erotic intention to Balthus's sitter, writers such as Weber are ultimately describing what they take to be the unseemly intention of a painter as that is expressed, deceptively, as the will of the subject painted. That Balthus is the one dreaming, and hopefully nothing more. But it is more difficult, in my view, not to notice how quickly judgement piles on in ways that seem to depart as much from the subject of the painting as the painter. After all, having just told us that Thérèse is acting coy and shameless, Weber immediately adds that 'Thérèse emanates eroticism while looking blithely unaware of that fact.' Surely she cannot be blithely unaware and coy at once, the improbability of which speaks more to the way that the painting unnerves Weber than it does to the portrait. Indeed, if one were asked to paint a picture of what Weber describes, I strongly suspect that it would look different from what we see in *Thérèse Dreaming*. Much like Schjeldahl's description – what is meant to stand as mere description of the image and not as comment – Weber's description of the painting is clearly motivated less by what the painting shows than by an idea of Balthus's lecherousness, if not the becoming public of his own. Can one really take seriously, for instance, the idea that 'Her crotch, scantily clad in white underpants, faces us in full view'? Does it? I confess that I don't know how to understand Thérèse's underpants as scanty, when they simply appear to be rather conventional white cotton underpants that cover all but her legs. It is equally difficult to agree that her 'petticoats' are 'thrust back'. In the end, Weber would seem to admit that this has more to do with his own concerns than anything the painting depicts, when he concludes: 'Thérèse's sexuality may be dormant for her, but it is rampant for us.' Having said, first, that Thérèse is 'exposing herself coyly but shamelessly', then 'blithely unaware', and then that her sexuality is dormant for her (can one be coy about what remains dormant?), Weber arrives at a statement that seems most germane: that Thérèse's sexuality is rampant *for us*. It is rampant for us only if what we are speaking about is not Thérèse's sexuality, but the viewer's. Or to be more precise, Weber's. One is not obliged to see it this way.

To be clear, in noticing the ways in which Schjeldahl and Weber both exceed mere description – insofar as their least outrageous-seeming claims come wrapped in judgement (in the case of Schjeldahl) or lusty and conflicted enthusiasm (in the case of Weber) – I am not simply trying to defend Balthus against his critics. In fact, I do not wish to make any claim at all about his intentions or his moral character. Rather, what I want to suggest is how most descriptions of Balthus's portraits operate on an idea about Balthus that is based on what gets said about the paintings. And what gets said about the paintings seems to have only to do with what the critic wishes to see, more than what is definitively, or even just obviously, there. As Balthus's biographer, Weber does not hesitate to make projections about Balthus's supposed licentiousness, even though this does not in any way appear to emanate from anything Balthus said. Weber tells, us for instance,

> That Balthus could, on every occasion when I ever saw him, be shocked and appalled that anyone might call his work erotic – and that his campaign against the notion of eroticism in his art has been the rallying cry of all of his recent interviews – at times seem laughable, and at other moments odd and pathetic. (2014: 390)

Such an assumption appears to guide the evidence that Weber summons from two of Balthus's other sitters:

> In *Thérèse Dreaming*, Balthus spread his nubile subject's legs in a way that threw them open for imaginary penetration and took it further with that perfectly angled foot. Balthus's often repeated claim to me

that he simply painted teenagers the way they sit in their usual poses is about as likely as Lord Byron being his grandfather. Dolores Miró and Jane Cooley confirmed that Balthus situated his models solely to suit his very precise goals – with scant concern for his subjects' comfort or the issue of naturalness. Thérèse sits the way Balthus wants to see her. (2014: 391)

How to set aside Weber's idea of 'imaginary penetration' when we arrive at the testimony of two sitters, who remain unquoted but are said to confirm, merely, that Balthus posed them in the way he wanted to? This, it seems to me, simply confirms what is likely true of most portraitists: that they arrange their models as they want them. The evidence is damning only if we assume that Balthus was indeed interested in soliciting spectatorial acts of 'imaginary penetration'. But whose intention are we actually documenting at that point? Is not 'imaginary penetration' a way of stating the fantasy of a very particular beholder? Would the critic care to have his writing on Balthus read in the way that he reads Balthus? It seems to me that the critic would be correct in asserting – and surely would do so in the face of such an accusation – that one cannot index a fantasy, or mere consciousness. Why, then, is it more reasonable to assume that we know the mind of Thérèse?

Context

If we take seriously the fact that what gets said about Balthus's portraits would seem to significantly exceed what the portrait shows – moreover, that what gets said has become very difficult to dislodge as a way of seeing the paintings in the first place, since what gets said seems always the same – then we are in a slightly different place than we normally are when asking after the moral character of portraiture. For, on the one hand, Balthus's critics and detractors appear to agree that the paintings are erotic renderings of 'pubescent' girls, and then simply seem to slide in one direction or the other of moral permissibility in placing the adjective or its synonym, nubile, as the organisational concept that precedes and anchors every description. In this way, the critic proceeds from the most basic assumption that we make, when considering the moral valence of a work of art, and also the claim that is often the most difficult to demonstrate: namely, if the one who produced the work is known to be immoral in his personal life then the work will necessarily be immoral, too. And yet, in the case of Balthus, the judgement stems more from what has been said previously about the painting than what is actually known about the conduct of the painter, on the idea that anyone who would paint a 'pubescent' girl in a state of repose is necessarily immoral. But why, exactly, must one describe Thérèse as 'pubescent' and not teenage, early adolescent, or simply as a girl? What exactly does sexual maturation have to do with *this* image? Is that all that one must or can say about a girl at an age that roughly coincides with the onset of sexual maturation? How did it become so important in the first place to describe Thérèse as 'pubescent'? There is at least one explanation why this has been the case, though it will not explain why it should be.

In 1995 the Penguin Classics edition of Nabokov's *Lolita* appeared with Balthus's 1937 portrait of Thérèse, *Girl with a Cat*, as its cover image. The gesture has not gone unnoticed. For instance, in a 2014 article in *Artnet* entitled 'Lolita Book Covers are a Tad Oversexed', Sarah Cascone writes that 'The French-Polish artist Balthus also gets in on the act. One of his "girls and cats" portraits of a reclining young girl, her underwear provocatively visible, appears on the cover of a 1995 edition published by Penguin.' However, Balthus did not 'get in on the act', as the writer suggests, and with a phrase that implies something like gang rape. On the contrary, Balthus refused to have his paintings used for book covers at all. Penguin merely went behind his back, as Weber (2014: 399) noted, and got permission from the Design and Artists Copyright Society, which controlled the reproduction rights for Balthus's work, and so did not require his permission.

The conflation of Balthus's painting and Nabokov's text is not insignificant and it happens in a variety of ways. The Oxford English Dictionary, for example, identifies the publication of *Lolita* in 1955 as one of the primary sources for the word 'pubescent' – one of two examples given for twentieth-century usage of the term. The notorious narrator of Nabokov's novel, Humbert Humbert, tells us that 'The median age of pubescence for girls has been found to be thirteen years and nine months in New York and Chicago' (Nabokov 1989: 43). Likewise, in a later passage, once Lolita and Humbert have hit the road, our unreliable narrator describes Lolita in a way that might be said to graphically resemble the way that Thérèse appears to sit in Balthus's paintings of her in the late 1930s:

> Most often, in the slouching, bored way she cultivated, Lo would fall prostrate and abominably desirable into a red springchair or a green chaise lounge, or a streamer chair of striped canvas with footrest and canopy, or a sling chair, or any other lawn chair under a garden umbrella on the patio, and it would take hours of blandishments, threats and promises to make her lend me for a few seconds her brown limbs in the seclusion of the five-dollar room before undertaking anything she might prefer to my joy. (1989: 147)

The differences between Balthus's reclining figures and Humbert Humbert's description of Lolita are, of course, important and depend entirely on what Humbert says about her posture, her interest in being in a state of recline, rather than on the position Lolita's body takes. Namely, Humbert – to be distinguished from Nabokov – describes her in such instances as 'abominably desirable'. He also tells us at the end of the passage quoted about the work it took to get Lolita to tend to his joy rather than hers, since her joy would seem to have nothing to do with his. That is to say, one of the things we might note about this passage from Nabokov's novel is that it self-consciously indicates the interested character of description itself. Humbert Humbert, in other words, cannot separate his descriptions of how Lolita sits from his volatile desire for her, which includes an admission of coercion that Humbert feels he must exert in order to get her to tend to his joy and not hers. One way of reading *Lolita*, then, is as a book that describes, in critical terms, the gulf between what men say and think and feel about teenage girls and what teen-age girls actually think or do, or think about what they do, which is nowhere indicated.

Thus, it is tempting to say that Balthus's critics and admirers regard the paintings as Humbert regards Lolita, insofar as they cannot separate what they think, desire, or detest from what they expect before or as they see the object that interests them. In one sense, at least, they have described the paintings this way, insofar as the language critics have used to describe Balthus's work from 1955 onwards – especially the use of the adjective 'pubescent' – stems from the notoriety of Nabokov's novel. The discourse about 'pubescence', in addition to Humbert's descriptions of the character Lolita – and including the visualisation of a posture that may very likely have been influenced by Balthus's paintings of Thérèse – has, somehow, remained tethered to the paintings as a critical resource for both detractors and celebrants of the work itself. In this respect, what we think we know or see about Balthus's portraits is in place before we ever look at them, or might as well be, and regardless of whatever else might be different about my place, my time – or simply, the context in which I 'experience' them.

The constellation of words and images that comprise the *Lolita* discourse emerges for most, however unconsciously – I imagine – as a response to a sense of panic that befalls both the moral critic of the work and also its admirers, and does so as a way of explaining and containing what one takes to be the volatility of the work. And yet that volatility, as I have suggested, owes less to the painting than to the discourse or context that one relies on to explain or condemn the work in the first place. That is to say, what one accesses first is the discourse of 'pubescence'. This is where fear begins – either as moral panic about transgression or as a panic about what might read as transgressive in us, and thus slip and begin to show. And it does so as an orientation towards a real object that cannot be seen independently of what one feared, discursively, in the first place. Most striking of all, in my view, is how this discourse – which supposes, always, that the work is erotic for everyone – suggests that the portraits effect a sense of fleshy immediacy that is temporally at odds with the iterability of the language used, decade to decade, to respond to it. That is to say, 'pubescent', sometimes 'nubile', continue to appear as the words used to characterise the portraits, even though the words we use to describe sex and sexuality change, in many instances, rather dramatically across time.

If I am correct about this, then the case of Balthus's portraits is an especially curious one, since what aspires to the condition of the eternal – as that which persists in and across time as the same, and as a force of attraction – is context, which many would regard as its opposite. Or to be more precise, context cannot be distinguished from discourse precisely because what any given context is assumed to reveal is what remains particular about either the origin of the painting or else the situations in which the work is viewed across time and place. And yet, across contexts and time, the discourse remains the same, and in that sense expresses always the same hurt, even though the conditions under which the paintings have been seen over the last century vary considerably. For this reason, among many others, one might do well to ask to what extent historicism, which begins and ends with an appeal to context, can be properly distinguished from a moral discourse that always exceeds what it describes. One might also do well to wonder whether historicism is itself a perverse discourse, one that blocks our access to what we might see for ourselves in favour of what one takes pleasure in both imagining and condemning; or imagining and condemning so as to say what one really wants to see without really saying it.

Silence

In many respects, the response to Balthus's portraits that I am tracking here can simply be referred to a generalised fear of abstraction, even where the response of the art critic is concerned, in that what is often the most abstract is nested in figuration; or, whatever resists immediate comprehension, even though one feels what one sees immediately, if not precipitously. *What if I say the wrong thing? What are the chances that I don't?* And yet, in the case of Balthus's portraits of teenage girls, I want to suggest that it is more than the ordinary fear of abstraction, and the subsequent feeling of being without the right words and afraid of the ones that come to the tongue that so often follows one's experience of abstraction. Added to the fear of abstraction is a generalised fear of the silence of girls. That is to say, the moral discourse about Balthus's portraits does not stem from the obvious eros of the portrait, so much as it does from the pensive silence of its sitters. What the paintings ask of us is not to say what we take Thérèse to be thinking or doing (which one rarely asks of a portrait, since the subject is typically seated), but that we recognise, in fact, that we have no access to what she thinks or dreams, only to what we think about her.

For many philosophers of the portrait, the pensive silence of the figure is a constituent feature of the genre. In *Portrait*, for example, Jean-Luc Nancy notes that the subject of a portrait is always shown to be at least partially clothed. For, 'The portrait makes a break with nudity (without repressing it) because it exposes another sort of nudity altogether, that of the subject' (2018: 15). The nudity of the subject is not something that we see, like skin beneath clothes; rather, in Nancy's formulation, the portrait marks the external limit of the self of the sitter. The subject is nude because uncorrelated to signs of the social that ask that we see the sitter in terms of something external to her. What shows in the portrait – the face, and what else appears of the body – is an image of the self withdrawing from itself. Or, as Nancy puts it, the portrait marks the relation of 'being-to-itself', and the only access we have to that relation comes by way of the image of the sitter before us: what would stand for the sitter as merely one image of the self among many others (2018: 20).

Despite the fact that the portrait, in Nancy's assessment, describes the withdrawal of the self from the self, that process is understood to be an important expression and experience of the social, just not in the way that we have come to expect it. Nancy defines the social dimension of the portrait in two related but conflicting ways – one that moves outwards towards the social, and one that reaches inwards for it.

   1. When the portrait moves in the direction of social position, when it becomes referential and descriptive (when it becomes a portrait designed for the recognition, in every sense of the word, of posterity, of the people, of the family, even of the police, as has sometimes been the case) the identity of the person lies outside it, and pictorial identity, by conforming to referential identity, is lost.

2. Painting gives its own 'social' position; it engages its own civility or sociality, and it is perhaps only through it and in it, moreover, that subjects enter a relation between *subjects* and not of identificatory objects. In other words, the horizon of our questions is in no sense solipsistic; on the contrary, it is one in which the portrait is always the portrait of another in which, however, the value of the face as the *sense* of the other is truly only given in the portrait (in art). (Nancy 2018: 16–17)

In the first instance, Nancy addresses what we take to be a common function of the portrait – that the sitter becomes emblematic of a particular period and a social discourse. Moreover, Nancy understands the referential dimension (or, the historical discourse) – to which the painting both appeals and attests – as what negates the pictorial specificity of the work in the first place. Another way of saying this is that the more the portrait painter refers to a historical context that cannot be easily indicated in the painting, the more completely does the subject of the painting, properly speaking, disappear. If context overwhelms the pictorial specificity of the portrait, it does so precisely because a sociohistorical context can only become legible, and thus instrumental, once it has reached a level of generality that defies the specificity of any given instance or possible sitter. In order for history to work, it must work for no one in particular. If historically concerned, the portrait can be of anyone, since what we will say of *this* sitter we will say of every other, and yet no one at all.

In the first social instance of the portrait identified by Nancy, the referential dimension of the portrait severs the subject from what it is related to; the subject, we might say, is the cause of a history to which it, paradoxically, cannot belong, or be seen independently of what it 'belongs' to. In the second, the subject of the painting relates only to itself. What is social in the portrait is neither referential nor discursive. If the self is always withdrawing from itself, there is always more than one self, all of which – and as a function of thought – relate to one another in what continues, however contingently and varied, as subject. Moreover, if the portrait is always a portrait of another, as Nancy suggests, it is not in the usual art-historical sense of what it means to demonstrate influence across or between two or more artists. Rather, in Nancy's example, what comes to sense in and as the portrait is an aesthetic effect of the work which gives us the sense that there are more selves indexed by this version of the self before us, but none that we will see.

Nancy's conception of the social dimension of the interiority of the portrait chimes in important ways with Hannah Arendt's claim about the social dimension of thought: 'Only someone who has had the experience of talking to himself is capable of being a friend, of acquiring another self' (2005: 20). For what Arendt is describing here is not only the capacity for friendship – which emerges as the self multiplies, recedes, and, most importantly, continues – but also for politics. We can only represent another, which I take to be the most basic feature of politics, if we have the capacity to acknowledge the difference between a self and itself; if we can see how difference begets continuity by defying sameness, by not insisting on it at the expense of what the senses perceive otherwise. It is not a difference that implies a choice between one self and another, one way of being and another, but of seeing the self as multiple, however unevenly so.

Perhaps we have reason to say, then, that one explanation for what one fears in Balthus's portraits, and everywhere else, is that what lies behind the silence of a young girl is a social world to come, the logics and spacing of which she alone can access. What if we take seriously the idea that *Thérèse Dreaming* is a portrait of a young girl reimagining the social, thinking about what better social relations might look like? Such fears, should one have them, no doubt compel a turn to historical discourse, to the way we think things have been, and thus are, as if to think historically is simply to understand yesterday as the cause of today, such that it is not easy, conceptually and practically speaking, to distinguish yesterday from today. This is also one of the reasons, in my view, why 'pubescent' remains the dominant adjective that follows Balthus's paintings of reclining girls. In grounding the sitters' age in their bodies, 'pubescent' has the whiff of objectivity about it, of science, even though in my estimation it is more likely that one only ever started to employ the terms because of *Lolita*, in which it is used by Nabokov in an ironic way, as if to indicate that the discourse of 'pubescence' has less to do with the development of the body in normative terms than it does with the non-normative response that Humbert Humbert has to the process of that development. It may be that the adjective 'pubescence' has been retained across the years on the basis of a formally insensitive reading of an ironic novel.

The silence of the sitter figures even more strongly in Jacques Rancière's conception of the portrait and 'the pensive image' in *The Emancipated Spectator*, and what he says there only amplifies the social and historical problems noted by Nancy. Rancière is drawn in particular to Rineke Dijkstra's *Beach Portraits* (1992–94), a series of photographic portraits of teenagers in bathing suits standing beachside, posing, largely deadpan, for the camera. At the centre of Rancière's discussion is Dijkstra's well-known photograph of a Polish adolescent girl, *Kolobrzeg, Poland, July 26, 1992*.

On the one hand, she belongs to a series that represents beings of the same kind: adolescents who rather fluctuate in their bodies, individuals who represent identities in transition – between ages, social statuses and lifestyles. Many of these images were taken in former communist countries. On the one hand, then, these photographs characterize ways of being; they testify to the problems of identity that affect individuals belonging to social groups and age groups that are in transition. On the other hand, however, they impose on us raw presences, beings of whom we do not know either what made them decide to pose for an artist or what they intended to show and express in front of the lens. Faced with them, we are therefore in the same position as when confronted with paintings from the past that represent Florentine or Venetian nobles: we no longer know who they are or what thoughts informed the gaze captured by the painter. (Rancière 2009: 115–16)

In one sense, what Rancière indicates here is rather straightforward: that Dijkstra's portraits document, and freeze in time, the being of bodies that are in a heightened state of flux because they are becoming, but are not yet, adult. They are also bodies and beings shaped by cultural norms, particular expressions of what can be said or done at a particular time in a particular place, and in that sense of what is shared cross-culturally, and what is different in what is shared. But, as Rancière says, they are beings for whom we will never know the reasons for appearing as they have, or what they were thinking, in which case any reference we make to historical discourse about what was sayable or doable at the time can only be made without reference to what the subject of that history thought about it. The image is pensive, for Rancière – just as for Nancy, and just as I want to suggest for Balthus – because what remains before us is a record of thinking and not of what was thought, including the thought of the photographer. If the photograph is of historical interest, that interest is likely of a despairing kind, in that what the portrait documents is that we do not know how or what the subject of the portrait thought of the historical conditions that we nevertheless believe to have constituted, or at least limited, that subject in one way or another. For this reason, Rancière says of the image:

It is what I shall call a dis-appropriate similarity. It does not refer us to any real being with which we could compare the image. But nor is it the presence of the unique being spoken of by Barthes [as the effect of the punctum]. It is that of the ordinary being, whose identity is unimportant, and who hides her thoughts in offering up her face. (2009: 116)

Bearing Nancy's conception of the interior movement of the social in mind, along with Rancière's provocation, we can say that the similarity of the teenage Polish girl in Dijkstra's portrait is 'dis-appropriate' in at least two senses. First, the portrait marks the withdrawal of the self from itself, in which case every instance of withdrawal is a dis-appropriate similarity by virtue of the fact that it cannot help differ in what nevertheless bears a resemblance to something else. And second, the subject of Dijkstra's portrait is dis-appropriately similar to itself in that what she thinks – and as an experience of the social dimension of self-reflection, if not simply time – cannot but be at odds with a histori-cal discourse about what can be said, done, or simply appear, at the moment in which the photograph is taken. Moreover, as Nancy sug-gests, the historical discourse – even when the subject of the portrait is also understood as the agent of a historical event or the author of the logic of social spacing at a particular moment in time – diminishes the pictorial specificity of the portrait. In which case, the practice of history has to be understood as the eradication of thought and the imagination of social relations that will never come to be. The reason for this is not that the subject is peculiar or exemplary, but, as Ran-cière suggests, ordinary. To be ordinary is not to be something like the ontological mean of all social possibilities: rather, it is to be elevated from time within time at the very moment in which the photograph is taken, or the painting finished. Where painting is concerned, the atemporal fate of the portrait is rehearsed in the time of production, insofar as the sitter is asked to remain still across hours and days, as if neither time was passing, nor the body moving: as if all too alive and yet as set as stone.

Perhaps the problem with *Thérèse Dreaming*, and with Balthus's portraits of reclining girls in general, is that they are ordinary. If ordi-nary, then not in the sense that 'pubescent' indicates, as an inescapable biological fact of the body at a roughly particular moment in time, and *thus* as the dawning of a sexual desire so encompassing, so self-defining that it assimilates every gesture made to a gaze that is always prepared for it. Construed that way, ordinary would come to describe a norm more than what eludes or cannot be defined by a norm. If we confuse a norm with the ordinary, we might believe we have good reason to condemn the painter for his desire, since we take ourselves to have access to what everyone else knows, and thus knows what to think. What else could the painter be doing in painting a being in such a state? Or else, we try and restrain our own desires as we attempt to say what we see in relation to a norm, which likely we knew, as an image, before we ever saw the portrait that we will describe.

In one sense, both Nancy and Rancière describe the formal con-ditions of the portrait in terms that should – or at least could – pre-clude such a response, insofar as both regard the portrait as a scene of thought, and thus of social relations, to which we have no access. But as my own brief account of responses to Balthus's *Thérèse Dreaming* should suggest, the barred access is only one part of the problem. Or perhaps it is better to say that the formal features of the portrait, by which the image we see is also a limit to what we can know, even though we sense it, is only amplified when what we see in the painting is a girl thinking, or, in this case, dreaming. If this is an ordinary experience, and I don't know how to say that it is not, then we can also say that the eternal, as that which persists across time, in time, is likewise a constituent feature of Balthus's portraits of Thérèse. Balthus's critics and admirers may very well take themselves to be agitated by flesh, when in fact what hurts, or challenges, is stone; or what will appear always as same, and always as a reminder of what we do not, and in many cases cannot, know.

Another way of describing this problem, or the logic of my argument for that matter, is that we have seen critics, favourable and unfavourable, saying too much about portraits that ultimately honour silence, portraits that make no claim on what is being thought, just that something is. The trouble is not that there is too much speech, but too much of the same speech, which is better understood, as I've argued, as a problem of context and discourse, or a way of understanding context as discourse and discourse as always atemporal, because always aggregating its descriptive resources across time in order to say the same thing, as if no time has passed, and as if no place is different from any other place where social mores are concerned. In this respect, the context that a portrait summons and is often negated by is – just like the painting that compelled the search for context in the first place – always out of time. This would seem to be the joke (even though Rancière himself doesn't actually make one) that follows from the title of Dijkstra's photograph of the teenage Polish girl: *Kolobrzeg, Poland, July 26, 1992*, as if the name can hold time, and not merely mark the instant in which it is extinguished. Derrida, for instance, described the problem of the date in precisely these terms, as something that is meant to articulate and honour a singularity that it cannot help but destroy. 'A date', Derrida asks, 'cannot be secret, can it? Once it is read, whether it makes reference to the calendar or not, it is immediately repeated and, consequently, in this iterability that makes readable, it loses the singularity that it keeps. It loses what it wants to keep' (1995: 378).

This is, of course, what 'pubescent' does as well, at least when one does not bother to wonder, in the first place, why it is used so often. Or as Wittgenstein puts it in *On Certainty*:

When a child learns a language it learns at the same time what is to be investigated and what not. When it learns that there is a cupboard in the room, it isn't taught to doubt whether what it sees later on is still a cupboard or only a kind of stage set. (1969: 62e)

If the learning of language is understood to imply the eradication of doubt about what one sees, then one is less likely to wonder about what other words one might find or use to describe the same thing and turn instead to different objects for different words, or different feelings.

References

Arendt, Hannah (2005), 'Socrates', in Hannah Arendt, *The Promise of Politics*, ed. Jerome Kohn, New York: Schocken Books.

Balthus (2002), *Vanished Splendors: A Memoir*, trans. Benjamin Ivry, New York: Ecco Books.

Cascone, Sarah (2014), 'Lolita Book Covers are a Tad Oversexed', *Artnet*, 23 April, https://news.artnet.com/art-world/balthus-retrospective-vienna-432860 (last accessed 27 May 2021).

Derrida, Jacques (1995), 'Passages – from Traumatism to Promise', in Jacques Derrida, *Points. . .: Interviews, 1974–1994*, ed. Elisabeth Weber, trans. Peggy Kamuf et al., Stanford, CA: Stanford University Press.

Fox Weber, Nicholas (2014), *Balthus: A Biography*, Dallas, TX: Dalkey Archive Press.

Gagosian Gallery (n.d.), https://gagosian.com/artists/balthus/ (last accessed 25 May 2021).

Hansen, Nadja (2013), '*Cats and Girls* – Interview with Sabine Rewald', *The Met*, https://www.metmuseum.org/blogs/now-at-the-met/features/2013/sabine-rewald-interview (last accessed May 27, 2021).

Kinsella, Eileen (2017), 'The Met Says "Suggestive" Balthus Painting Will Stay After Petition for Its Removal is Signed by Thousands', *Art World*, 5 December 2017, https://news.artnet.com/art-world/met-museum-responds-to-petition-calling-for-removal-of-balthus-painting-1169105 (last accessed 15 March 2022).

Nabokov, Vladimir (1989 [1955]), *Lolita*, New York: Vintage.

Nancy, Jean-Luc (2018), *Portrait*, trans. Sarah Clift and Simon Sparks, New York: Fordham University Press.

Rancière, Jacques (2009), *The Emancipated Spectator*, trans. Gregory Elliot, London: Verso.

Schjeldahl, Peter (2018), 'Moral Conundrums and Political Passions', *The New Yorker*, 1 January, https://www.newyorker.com/magazine/2018/01/01/moral-conundrums-and-political-passions (last accessed 25 May 2021).

Wittgenstein, Ludwig (1969), *On Certainty*, ed. G. E. M. Anscombe and G. H. von Wright, New York: Harper Torchbooks.

Chapter 14

Speaking, through the Eyes, with the Dead

Georges Didi-Huberman (translated by Shane Lillis)

The dead look at us, yet they have no eyes left to see with. They talk to us, yet they do so without uttering a single distinct word. The mouths of the dead are full of dust; no more are their words in their mouths; no more, since we buried them, is there a sparkle in their eyes. Yet we talk to them so that they will continue to talk to us in return, and we imagine them so that they can look at us in return. This is how we see them still, how we speak with them even though they have vanished from our world, and from our living space.

I

Melina Balcázar's book *Aquí no mueren los muertos* (2020) deals with different ways – ways that are private or institutionalised, religious or profane, spiritual or corporeal – to speak with the dead. The author's own split genealogy shows through the different ways that she was able, when she was a child, to see adults make 'their dead' intervene in everyday life: to 'communicate' with them. We discover, in this book, a whole spectrum of aspects – often unexpected, neither quite 'Christian' nor 'Indian' – of this culture of the dead in which Mexico, especially, is remarkable.

Here I discovered the importance of Juan Rulfo's *Cuadernos*, written between 1944 and 1955, and in which Balcázar begins with the following extract which clarifies, in a way, her own research: 'In Mexico no one ever dies, we never let the dead die' (*en México nunca muera nadie, nunca dejamos morir a los muertos*) (1994b: 169).[1] It should be noted that Juan Rulfo's great novel *Pedro Páramo*, published in 1955, dealt with the confusion between the world of the living and the world of the dead. As Balcázar does today, Rulfo opened his story with the death of his mother, in a way, perhaps, to posit *death as the mother* of our own lives, our own quests and questions, our own desires.

II

Everything begins, in *Pedro Páramo*, when Juan Preciado, the narrator, 'pulled [his] hands free of her death grip' (Rulfo 1994a: 3), meaning the grip of his mother who has just closed her eyes forever. But he pulled himself free from the body of his dead mother, only to start out on a quest – as she made him promise just before she died – for a father who had been gone for a long time, dead. 'Don't ask him for anything. Just what's ours. What he should have given me but never did . . . Make him pay, my son, for all those years he put us out of his mind. – I will, Mother' (1994a: 3).

Can we keep such a promise? Do we want to keep it? No, thinks the narrator, when 'my head began to swim with dreams and my imagination took flight' (1994a: 3). What dreams? The kinds of dreams that change the course of our lives. The kinds of images or visual phrases that seemingly extend their bidding to us – with one word murmured before the silence, or a sparkle in the eye as it closes – by our loved ones at the moment of their death. And so, it was necessary to set off on the road towards whatever such dreams demanded. A road, as Rulfo wrote, that 'rose and fell', from the possible to the impossible, and from the living to the afterlife. 'It rises or falls depending on whether you're coming or going [. . .] I had come in her place. I was seeing through her eyes, as she had seen them' (1994a: 4). And that is how we inherit the gaze of our dead mother.

Here, in any case, the wanderer in that rugged Mexican terrain has arrived in a place called Los Encuentros, at a 'crossroads'. One road leads to Comala. '"And why are you going to Comala, if you don't mind my asking?" I heard the man say. "I've come to see my father," I replied. "Umh! That so?" he said [. . .] After a while he added: "Whoever you are, they'll be glad to see you"' (1994a: 5). It happens that the speaker he met by chance turns out to be his brother: '"Pedro Páramo is my father, too"' (1994a: 5). And as Juan Preciado learns, it happens too that '"Pedro Páramo died years ago"' (1994a: 7). Yet why must this road be followed? Because the dead person – or death – beckons, in spite of all. Because a dead person has always gone before us and shows us the way. Soon Juan Preciado finds himself in the house of an old woman who, mysteriously, recognises him, claiming to have been 'told' by his dead mother, from beyond (1994a: 10).

III

This is a story about an interregnum, a story where the living speak with the dead, see with the eyes of the dead who are no longer quite underneath the ground, nor quite in the heavens. In the interval opened by this strange spectrality there appears, significantly, from the very beginning of the novel, a simple plan, a page, an interface. It is a little piece of photographic paper:

> The picture of my mother I was carrying in my pocket felt hot against my heart, as if she herself were sweating. It was an old photograph, worn around the edges, but it was the only one I had ever seen of her. I had found it in the kitchen safe, inside a clay pot, filled with herbs: dried lemon balm, castilla blossoms, sprigs of rue. I had kept it with me ever since. It was all I had. My mother always hated having her picture taken. She said photographs were a tool of witchcraft. And that may have been so, because hers was riddled with pinpricks, and at the location of the heart there was a hole you could stick your middle finger through. I had brought the photograph with me, thinking it might help my father to recognize who I was. (Rulfo 1994a: 6)

Photography, then, is the ideal *medium*: the space or the material – even if it is reduced to a surface, a thin film of visibility – of the interregnum, of the communication with the dead. It happens that Juan Rulfo also practised photography, admirably in fact, as though there were a link with such an encounter or confusion between reigns (see Fuentes et al. 2001; Tatard 1994). In 1961, for example, he created an image of a poor cemetery in the Jalisco region, where he had spent his childhood in an orphanage in Guadalajara, following the murder of his father and a number of his family members in 1923 (Figure 14.1). In this image we see very scanty wooden crosses, planted, here and there, in the bush and arid land. It is as though the dead are very close, lying in the ground just beneath the surface. We imagine that a breath would be enough to call them, or a song, or a word, to make them rise up again, if only to voice a grievance, once again, to the court of history – there are so many unjust deaths in these areas, in this history of endless terrors, yet from which the desperate gestures of uprising and emancipation arise before disappearing once again.

Once, yet not once and for all. Photography would be the ideal *medium* for the time of survivals, of a *possible next time*. As though each of our dead projected their shadow before us, to show us the road to follow. Like that other photograph by Juan Rulfo in which

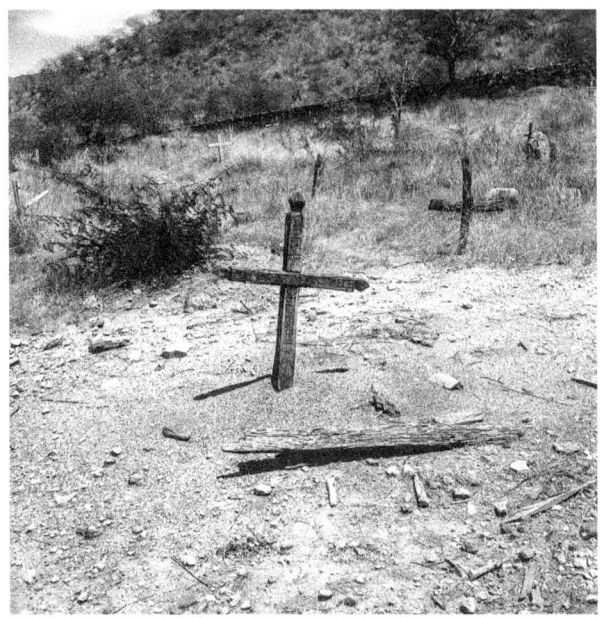

Figure 14.1 Juan Rulfo, *Cemetery in the south of Jalisco*, 1961, gelatin silver print. Mexico, Fundación Juan Rulfo

we see two women from Jalisco at a distance – in a harsh, mineral, craggy landscape – in front of the shadow of a cross, a deified sign of a death and of a sacrifice that claims to show them, from the Catholic *credo*, the road that must be followed (Figure 14.2).

IV

In all cultures, perhaps, the living speak to their dead – in one way or another, and beyond the fear that the dead might create in them – so that the dead can speak to them once again.[2] Sometimes the living even imagine they are witnessing, between somewhere below the ground and the heavens above, the dialogues of the dead with their God or creator. A famous European example is that of the *Grandes Heures de Rohan*, an illuminated manuscript from around 1430–35, in which we see an emaciated corpse, naked in its shroud – and surrounded by many human bones scattered on the ground – who addresses God with the following words: *In manus tuas, Domine, commendo spiritum meum* ('Into your hands, O Lord, I commend my spirit') (see Avril and Reynaud 1993: 26–7). To which the Creator replies, in French (which might seem strange from a certain

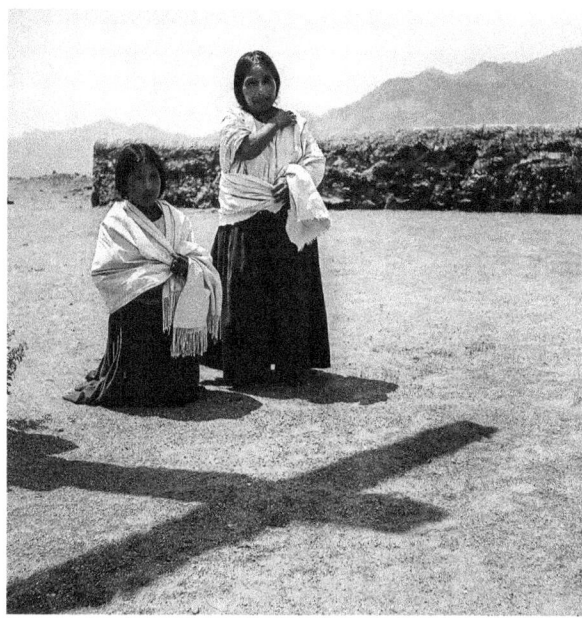

Figure 14.2 Juan Rulfo, *Women from Ayutla, Oaxaca*, 1955, gelatin silver print. Mexico, Fundación Juan Rulfo

viewpoint): *Pour tes pechiez pénitence feras. Au jour du Jugement avec moi seras* ('Do penitence for thy sins. On Judgment Day thou shalt be with me') (Figure 14.3). To create an image of such a dialogue – or to turn it into a *visual medium of speech* – the medieval painter employed a multi-secular convention by using phylacteries: bands of text written in black against a white background (like a ribbon of paper or cloth) which 'come out' of the mouths of the characters shown. If indeed *to speak with the dead* is a matter of belief, above all of the unconscious, of dreams, and of desire, it should be no surprise that the visual and linguistic tool of phylacteries should have appeared in Freud's thoughts (1997: 194) on what he called, in *Traumdeutung*, 'the means of representation in dreams' (*die Darstellungsmittel des Traums*). In the reign of conscious time and language, we have at our disposal all kinds of tools – that are both semantic and syntactic – to express temporal and logical relations. But what about the interregnum of dreams?

Freud asked: 'what representation do "if", "because", "as though", "although", "either–or", and all the other conjunctions, without which we cannot understand a phrase or a sentence, receive in our dreams?' Dream expression seems to suffer from a structural handicap, does it not? He continued:

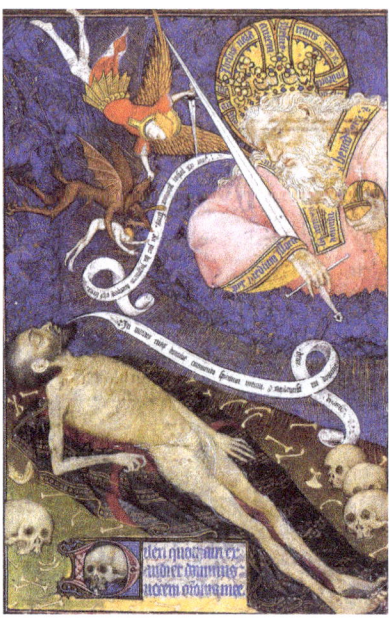

Figure 14.3 Anonymous, French (Maître de Rohan), *Le mort devant son Juge*, 1430–35, illuminated manuscript of *Grandes Heures de Rohan*, fol. 159. Paris, Bibliothèque nationale de France, ms. Lat. 9471. Photo DR

> To begin with, we must answer that the dream has at its disposal no means for representing these logical relations between the dream-thoughts. In most cases it disregards all these conjunctions, and undertakes the elaboration only of the material content of the dream-thoughts. It is left to the interpretation of the dream to restore the coherence which the activity of the dream has destroyed. (1997: 194)

And this is where Freud recalls the old use of phylacteries in the history of visual representation:

> If dreams lack the ability to express these relations, the psychic material of which the dream is wrought must be responsible for this defect. As a matter of fact, the representative arts – painting and sculpture – are similarly restricted, as compared with poetry, which is able to employ speech; and here again the reason for this limitation lies in the material by the treatment of which the two plastic arts endeavor to express something. Before the art of painting arrived at an understanding of the laws of expression by which it is bound, it attempted to make up for this deficiency. In old paintings little labels hung out of the mouths of the persons represented, giving in writing the speech which the artist despaired of expressing in the picture. (1997: 196)

V

In what material, in what *medium* does the interregnum appear and call to us, express itself, and respond to us? Melina Balcázar cites at the beginning of her book the following two lines by Victor Hugo from his poetry collection *Les Contemplations*:

> Crois-tu que le tombeau, d'herbe et de nuit vêtu,
> Ne soit rien qu'un silence. . . (Hugo 1985: 534)
> [Do you think that the tomb, dressed in grass and night
> Is nothing but a silence. . .]

Entitled 'Ce que dit la bouche d'ombre' ('What the mouth of shadow says'), Hugo's poem is a profound approach to the interregnum between the dead and the living. It was directly inspired by the words emitted during a spirit séance on 24 April 1854, when 'the table' had urged Hugo to compose lines of pity for the souls of the dead. The poet's response is an abyss of words that turns around a single image, that of the *mouth of shadow*. The shadow is black, indistinct, abyssal. Before all language? No, because the hole that it forms is a mouth that speaks, that expresses, that exhales. Abyss and language become one. No more is there any need for phylacteries it would seem: for here,

> Everything speaks; the air that passes and the kingfisher that navigates
> The blade of grass, the flower, the bud, the element.
> [. . .]
> No, everything is a voice and everything is a perfume;
> Everything says in the infinite something to someone;
> A thought fills the superb tumult (1985: 534–5)

As Hugo wrote, 'everything is full of souls'. This comes out of everywhere, crosses everything, and fills everything. It does not mean there are no more phylacteries, but rather that there are only phylacteries. The world rises up, then, full of messages from the grave which double the air – the air that we breathe to live – with the breaths of the deceased, and that invade our visible world with powerful *spectral draperies*. We can recall the diagnosis offered by Walter Benjamin in his 1935 essay on 'The Work of Art in the Age of its Technological Reproducibility':

> In the cult of remembrance of dead or absent loved ones, the cult value of the image finds its last refuge. In the fleeting expression of a human face, the aura beckons from early photographs for the last time [*die Aura zum letzten Mal*]. This is what gives them their melancholy and incomparable beauty. (2008: 27)

VI

Actually, the human countenance sometimes produces – exhales, spits, or vomits – its own aura. In the age that Benjamin wrote of, photography acted as the privileged medium for *seeing the dead speak*, or for *speaking to them with the eyes*. A remarkable example of this is found in the book by Albert von Schrenk-Notzing – who was at the same time a psychotherapist, parapsychologist, and photographer – on 'phenomena of materialization' that appeared at the end of 1913. It involved recording the visual traces of the presence of the dead through numerous experimental protocols carried out on Eva C. and Stanisl-awa P., two women, two 'mediums' from the time (Schrenck-Notzing 1914). The extraordinary photographs from these sessions render visible a sort of formless phylactery that comes out of the mouth of the 'medium', somewhere between an aerial drapery and a liquid vomit from somewhere unknown (see Fischer 2004) (Figure 14.4).

We can think too of the Mexican woman photographed by Romualdo García Torres in 1905, her dead child in her arms and a great white kerchief that seems to come out of her mouth – this woman takes on, in front of our eyes (and, first, those of

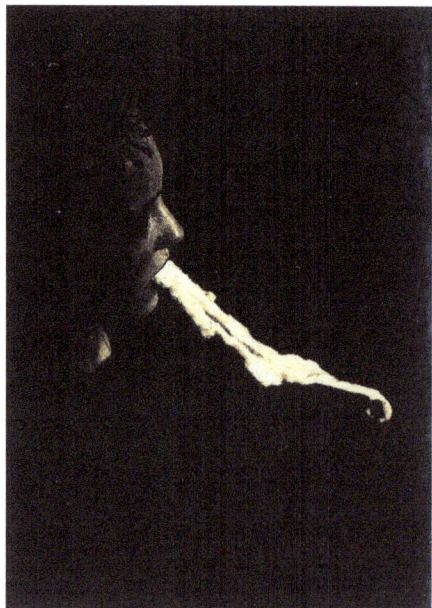

Figure 14.4 Albert von Schrenck-Notzing, *Le médium Stanislawa P. avec un voile ectoplasmique*, 1913, silver gelatin print. Freiburg im Breisgau, Institut für Grenzgebiete der Psychologie und Psychohygiene

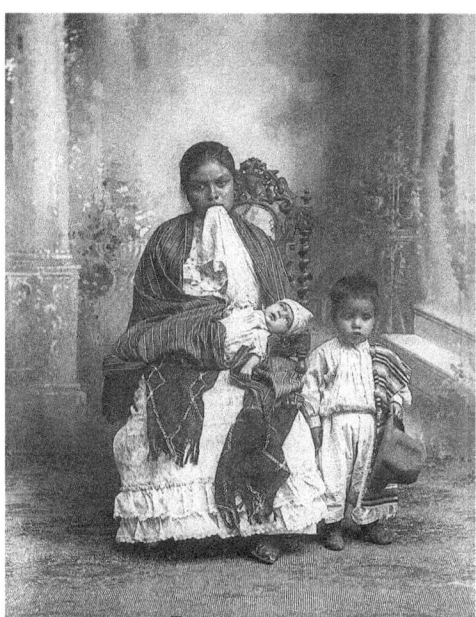

Figure 14.5 Romualdo García Torres, *Mujer y su hijo mayor rodeando a un bebé murto*, c. 1905, gelatin silver print. Mexico, Instituto Nacional de Antropología y Historia

Melina Balcázar) the stature or the status of a moving 'intercessor' between the world of the living and that of the dead, the world of closed eyes and that of sealed eyes, the world of visible aspects and that of definitive shadows (Balcázar 2020: 87) (Figure 14.5). What then can be said of that *intercession* that passes from the subject in mourning to the photographic object itself, and finally, to our own gaze on images?

To answer this question, we must certainly keep in mind Walter Benjamin's own viewpoint, but also link it to the viewpoint that Marcel Mauss (1992), in exactly the same period, intended to develop on the anthropological level: in every case this has to do with techniques. *Spiritual techniques* set to the imaginative exercise of dialogue with deceased beings; *visual techniques* made possible by the photographic dramaturgy of shadow and light; techniques of the body, then, as when the 'medium' lets a piece of cloth come out of her mouth, a cloth that was oiled and ingested earlier (a well-known method among magicians and circus performers). If we wish to follow the anthropological lines developed by Marcel Mauss, *speaking with the dead* or *speaking with the eyes* would be no less 'technical' than adopting a rhythm when we dance, a position when we make love or when we give birth.

VII

It would be possible then to speak, through the eyes, with the dead. An image could then be looked at as an interjection addressed to the dead, 'offered to the innumerable people of the dead', as Jean Genet (1979: 43) wrote regarding the work of art in general. And he added, with regard to Alberto Giacometti:

> His statues seem to belong to a defunct age, and to have been discovered after time and night – which worked away at them intelligently – corroded them to give them that appearance which is both soft and harsh of *eternity passing*. Or they come out of an oven, residues of a dreadful cooking: with the flames extinguished, no more would remain but that. But what flames! Giacometti tells me that he once had the idea of modelling a statue and of burying it. (You soon imagine: 'Let the earth be light there upon'.) Not so that it might be discovered there, or found much later, when it and the memory of its name even would have disappeared. To bury it, was it to offer it to the dead? (1979: 55–6)

Around ten years ago, Melina Balcázar published a wonderful book on Jean Genet, entitled *Travailler pour les morts* (2010). It is not surprising that Genet and Juan Rulfo appear in the same chapter in Balcázar's *Aquí no mueren los muertos* (2020: 30). This appears in a perspective that is nothing short of a *politics of memory* whose central issue is the transformation of our world by means of a complete reconfiguration – an inversion of standard values – regarding *relations of the visible and what is finished*. Evoking the practices of funeral photography in Mexico made sense for Melina Balcázar only insofar as it reversed the commonly accepted idea of our *link with loss* in what we call 'mourning-work' (2020: 28). This is generally thought of as a process by which, little by little, we manage to detach ourselves from whatever 'object of attachment', so that, as Freud put it, 'the ego is left free and uninhibited once again after the mourning-work is completed' (2005: 205), by assuming the reality of the loss. Free of its dead inasmuch as they are dead and buried: *finished*.

What appears in the anthropological context of Mexico – in Juan Rulfo's writing for example – is, on the contrary, that we are totally unfinished without our dead. That it is with them that our freedom itself is built (we might think of Emiliano Zapata and his importance as a figure in the contemporary Chiapas uprisings). Consequently, the dead are understood as our own *survivals*, surviving us, we who 'survive' them inasmuch as we are made of the *body of their very absence* (see Fédida 1978: 69–78). Here, as always, visual techniques accompany the techniques of the body. All Mexican anthropology – which fascinated so many Western thinkers and artists engaged in the poetic or political work of 'overturning values', from Antonin Artaud to D. H. Lawrence or Sergei Eisenstein – seem to give great importance to these visual, even spectacular potentialities of the body of absence (as is done in Greece, for example, where the fact of unearthing the dead to show their bones in wooden caskets creates a very unusual relation to the commonly shared 'mourning-work') (see Danforth 1982).

It is necessary then to *overturn what is finished* of the dead and, consequently, the very meaning of mourning-work as a definitive separation. It is necessary to overturn the elegiac genre as an inconsolable lamenting for something forever lost. For *all is not lost*, as we should say with those who wish to transform the world. All is not lost if we succeed in making what is lost a body once again, a body incorporated into our own body but which can also be expressed, a body capable of animating our gestures and our images (see Abraham and Torok 1987: 203–51). Is this not what Warburg's concept of *Nachleben*, 'after-life', was linked to? And is it not true that the world of images comes fundamentally from this very potential, this *dynamis* of survivals, whose concept was moulded in 1856 by Edward B. Tylor, on a market in Mexico City (see Didi-Huberman 2002)?

All is not lost to those who make something of the loss. For are we not already able to *dream* of what is finished? To *see it again*? To *reactivate* it? To imagine it, whereby our spectres would come to aid our present, push us to make time rise up, to start everything over? That is the 'politics of memory' which is the aim of the book *Aquí no mueren los muertos*: a movement that soars from the *finished* to the assuming of a *revolt* or *revolution*. That which is finished, which has accomplished 'full circle' in life, finds itself, if we take charge of its memory, at the point of departure of a new cycle. We can agree with Laurent Jenny who said recently that 'the age of photography' – of silver gelatin photography – is 'finished' (Jenny 2019: 9–12, 134–8). And we should add that it enters into its *Nachleben*, into its age of survival, which is no less *revolutionary* – albeit in a very different way – than it was in the nineteenth century. It is true that, for this reason, we should have the courage to *reimagine* all things as at once an anamnesis and as a vivacious desire, outstretched towards what is to happen, what is to come.

Notes

1. Unless otherwise indicated, all translations from Spanish are by the author.
2. For more on this, see Frazer 1933 and Thomas 1975. On the Mexican case specifically, see Butterwick 1999 and Barranco 2001.

References

Abraham, Nicolas, and Maria Torok (1987), *L'Écorce et le noyau*, Paris: Flammarion.

Avril, François, and Nicole Reynaud (1993), *Les Manuscrits à peintures en France, 1440–1520*, Paris: Flammarion; Bibliothèque Nationale.

Balcázar Moreno, Melina (2010), *Travailler pour les morts. Politiques de la mémoire dans l'œuvre de Jean Genet*, Paris: Presses Sorbonne Nouvelle.

Balcázar Moreno, Melina (2020), *Aquí no mueren los muertos. Duelo y fotografía en México*, Mexico-Monterrey: Argonáutica.

Barranco, María E. Jurado (2001), *Xantolo. El retorno de los muertos*, Mexico: Jaiser.

Benjamin, Walter (2008 [1935–36]), 'The Work of Art in the Age of Its Technological Reproducibility', in *The Work of Art in the Age of Its Technological Reproducibility and Other Writings on Media*, ed. Michael W. Jennings, Brigid Doherty, and Thomas Y. Levin, Cambridge, MA: The Belknap Press of Harvard University Press, pp. 19–55.

Butterwick, Kristi (1999), 'Days of the Dead: Ritual Consumption and Ancestor Worship in the Ancient West Mexican Society', PhD dissertation. University of Colorado Boulder.

Danforth, Loring M. (1982), *The Death Rituals of Rural Greece*, Princeton, NJ: Princeton University Press.

Didi-Huberman, Georges (2002), *L'Image survivante. Histoire de l'art et temps des fantômes selon Aby Warburg*, Paris: Les Éditions de Minuit.

Fédida, Pierre (1978), *L'Absence*, Paris: Gallimard.

Fischer, Andreas (2004), '"L'adaptation réciproque de l'optique et des phénomènes". L'enregistrement photographique des matérialisations', in Clément Chéroux and Andreas Fischer (eds), *Le Troisième Œil. La photographie et l'occulte*, Paris: Gallimard, pp. 171–215.

Frazer, James G. (1933), *The Fear of the Dead in Primitive Religion*, New York: Biblio and Tannen.

Freud, Sigmund (1997 [1899]), *The Interpretation of Dreams*, trans. Abraham Arden Brill, Hertfordshire: Wordsworth Classics.

Freud, Sigmund (2005 [1915]), 'Mourning and Melancholia', in Sigmund Freud, *On Murder, Mourning and Melancholia*, trans. Shaun Whiteside, London: Penguin, pp. 201–18.

Fuentes, Carlos, Marco Glantz, Jorge Alberto Lozoya, et al. (2001), *México: Juan Rulfo Fotógrafo*, Barcelona: Lunwerg Editores.

Genet, Jean (1979), 'L'atelier d'Alberto Giacometti', in *Œuvres complètes, Vol. 5*, Paris: Gallimard.

Hugo, Victor (1985), *Œuvres complètes. Poésie, II*, ed. Jean Gaudon, Paris: Robert Laffont.

Jenny, Laurent (2019), *La Brûlure de l'image. L'imaginaire esthétique à l'âge photographique*, Sesto San Giovanni–Paris: Éditions Mimésis

Mauss, Marcel (1992), 'Techniques of the Body', in Jonathan Crary and Sanford Kwinter (eds), *Incorporations*, New York: Zone Books, pp. 454–77.

Rulfo, Juan (1994a [1955]), *Pedro Páramo*, trans. Margaret Sayers Peden, New York: Grove Press.

Rulfo, Juan (1994b), *Los cuadernos*, ed. Y. Jiménez Báes, Mexico: Era.

Schrenck-Notzing, Albert von (1914), *Materialisations-Phänomene. Ein Beitrag zur Erforschung der mediumistischen Teleplastie*, Munich: Ernst Reinhardt.

Tatard, Béatrice (1994), *Juan Rulfo, photographe: esthétique du royaume des âmes*, Paris: L'Harmattan.

Thomas, Louis-Vincent (1975), *Anthropologie de la mort*, Paris: Payot.

Tylor, Edward Burnett (1861), *Anahuac: Or Mexico and the Mexicans, Ancient and Modern*, London: Green, Longman & Roberts.

Chapter 15

Revenants: On the Animation of Dead People's Portraits in Contemporary Technoculture

Pietro Conte

Hunting Apollinaire's Ghosts

In a little-known science fiction tale titled 'The Moon King' (1916), Guillaume Apollinaire imagines a traveller losing his way in a storm and seeking refuge from the weather and the dark in the entrance of a Tyrolean cavern. On perceiving a distant sound of music, he goes further in and discovers a labyrinthine network of shelters, which, as we learn later, is the subterranean realm of the dead King Ludwig II of Bavaria. In a vast hall at the heart of the lair with marble walls and shells in the half-light, a banquet with about fifty guests is taking place. Once the meal is over, the young people move to a different room where inflatable furniture seems to magically dance about, rising little by little until it changes into ordinary armchairs and divans.

After a bridge game, the lights are turned off and everyone leaves again. Following their voices, the protagonist comes to a stairway at the bottom of which a door opens on to a corridor carved into the rock. A series of obscene graffiti with pierced hearts, phalluses, and winged Cupids makes up 'an indecent and whimsical heraldry' (Apollinaire 1988: 75), and enigmatic inscriptions all over the etchings evoke anachronistic orgies, one phrase reading 'I must have Madame de Pompadour', while another claims that Michelangelo 'really turned on' a certain Hans von Jagow. Elsewhere, someone boasts that, in one night, he had 'the same pretty Tyrolean of the seventeenth century when she was 16, 21 and 23' (1988: 74).

Disconcerted by such senseless obscenities, the narrator continues down the corridor until he gets to a room where he spots the guests lying down on the floor, each of them equipped with a wooden box and completely absorbed in looking through several albums of nude photographs. After becoming aroused by the pictures, they shamelessly take their clothes off and start some mysterious machines inside the boxes, which begin to turn slowly 'like phonograph cylinders' (1988: 76). Connected to the devices by a sort of belt, these men rapidly turn into a college of priapic maniacs:

> Their hands strayed in front of them as if over supple, beloved bodies, and they gave the air amorous kisses. Soon they became more irrepressible and lascivious and wedded themselves to the emptiness [. . .] Sounds escaped from their lips, words of love, voluptuous gasps, very ancient names [. . .] I listened more attentively to the licentious language and witnessed the performance of every desire of these libertines, who were finding sexuality in the arms of death. 'The boxes', I told myself, 'are cemeteries where these necrophiles dig up amorous corpses.' (Apollinaire 1988: 76)

Intrigued by the scene and eager to plunge into the same exciting experience as the cave dwellers, the traveller quickly seizes one of the boxes near the door without anyone noticing. Immediately upon starting the machine, a naked woman materialises before his eyes who he imagines to be Leda warding off Zeus in the form of a swan. He thus finds himself able 'to look at, feel, and, in a word, work at the body' within his grasp, whereas the latter has no notion of his presence, 'having itself no actual reality' (1988: 77). After the machine stops and the woman disappears, he tiptoes away, but before leaving, feels compelled to add to the vulgar graffiti by writing: 'I cuckolded the swan.'

What Apollinaire imagined back in 1916 is a sophisticated apparatus enabling its users to make love with any person from any century by holding and resuming frozen moments in time. On the one hand, the device records and abstracts a certain event from the past, while on the other hand, it brings its contents back to life by making the individuals involved once again visible and palpable. Importantly, such special technology allows its wearer to interact with ghostly presences that, however, seem to have no consciousness of themselves being abused.

Two points of Apollinaire's tale are particularly salient for the purposes of the present chapter: first, the connection established between image and death, epitomised by a fantastic device that makes it possible to conjure dead people from anytime and anywhere; and second, the highly illusionistic quality of those 'living' pictures, one that goes so far as to make the experiencers seemingly forget (if only momentarily) the true nature of what they are confronted with.

These two aspects, closely intertwined throughout Apollinaire's text, have recently moved from science fiction to techno-mediated reality, where individuals are given the possibility to meet (and in some cases even to interact with) the animated portraits of their deceased loved ones. Here, in the contemporary mediascape of immersive virtual environments, a polarity resurfaces that has haunted the history of portraiture since its mythical origins, giving rise to two very distinct – not to say opposite – theories, one based on the notion of *presentification*, the other anchored in the concept of *representation*.

Blending Substitution with Portrayal

Apollinaire's story is patently reminiscent of Plato's allegory of the cave, which famously describes the condition of people imprisoned from childhood in a chamber underground, initially unable to distinguish between the shadows cast by objects passing in front of a fire behind them and the real things in themselves. Both in 'The Moon King' and in the very first part of the ancient narrative, the images are not taken merely to depict their referents: in fact, they replace them. They *are* (ontologically) images, yet they are not *perceived* (phenomenologically) as such. In other words, they do not simply *represent* the objects that they embody, but rather *make* them *present*.

This contrast between representation and presentification lies at the very core of portraiture since its mythical origins. According to Pliny the Elder, a potter of Sicyon named Butades was the first to discover the art of modelling portraits in clay, and he owed the invention to his daughter, who was in love with a young man. Since the latter was about to travel abroad, she traced his profile around the shadow cast on the wall by the light of a lantern. Her father saw the outline, pressed clay onto it and made a relief, which he then hardened by exposure to fire. The story is well known, but little mention is made of how Pliny's text unfolds. Immediately after describing Butades's discovery, the author of the *Naturalis Historia* (77–78 CE) argues that it was left to another man from Sicyon, the sculptor Lysistratus of the fourth century BCE, to introduce 'the practice of giving likenesses' (1938: 35, 44). A clear-cut distinction is traced here between two kinds of picture-making, one aimed at presentifying the absent without pursuing mimetic realism, the other intended to replicate the individual's physiognomic traits.

This dichotomy was the subject of Jean-Pierre Vernant's scientific investigations since the publication of his 1960 essay 'Some Aspects of Personal Identity in Greek Religion', followed two years later by

'The Figuration of the Invisible and the Psychological Category of the Double: The *Kolossos*'. Within the theoretical context of historical psychology, the French scholar identified a radical change in the understanding of image-making, a shift that took place in ancient Greece between the sixth and fourth centuries BCE and led 'from the presentification of the invisible to the imitation of appearance' (Vernant 2006c: 335). The image as we usually understand it, that is, an imitation of the outer form, cannot be conceived of as an ahistorical, let alone 'innocent', notion. On the contrary, it resulted from a cultural process which tended to obliterate a previous conception where images had been considered more as doubles than as representations whose validity comes solely from their outward resemblance to the represented subject.

Vernant's notion of the double characterises the image object not in terms of a likeness of an absent entity but rather as its (explicitly paradoxical) real presence. The archaic *eidolon* is a substitute for the invisible and inaccessible, and it serves as a medium to give visual presence to sacred agencies which do not belong to the worldly space: 'Whatever the avatars of the image may have been, this impossible quest is one that perhaps continues to remain valid to a large degree – that of evoking absence in presence, revealing the elsewhere in what is given to view' (Vernant 2006c: 335–6).

A physical object can take on the role of the double if – and only if – it becomes part of a ritual context that frames it into a whole system of symbolic meanings and cultic references. Thus, the *eidolon* acts as a surrogate body for either a god(dess) or a dead person, both being crucial cases of absent, invisible, and intangible entities:

> Figure of the gods, figure of the dead. In each case, the problem is the same: by means of localization in an exact form and a well-determined place, how is it possible to give visual presence to those powers that come from the invisible and do not belong to the space here below on earth? The task is to make the invisible visible, to assign a place in our world to entities from the other world. (Vernant 2006c: 335)

From this perspective, as Vernant liked to emphasise, 'the idol is not a portrait' (2006a: 361), given that gods and the dead have no bodies that might be mimetically represented. Their most intrinsic essence is to be invisible, ungraspable, always beyond any form whatsoever in which they might manifest themselves or in which they are made present through the performative act of the ritual.

A few years after Vernant, Alfred Gell would use much the same notion in claiming that 'idols are not depictions, not portraits, but (artefactual) *bodies*' (1998: 98). The image-substitute is not meant to portray or represent an absent body; rather, it stands in for a divine being or a deceased person, manifesting in even one single visible trait the role and power of the absent agency. In order to acquire such functional identity with the substituted, the *eidolon* does not need to mimic the visual features of the presentified entity. In this sense, making direct reference to Vernant's work, Hans Belting too (2011: 108) has insisted upon the difference between the image as an ersatz body (*Medium der Verkörperung*) and the image as a mimetic medium of remembrance (*Medium der Erinnerung*), or in other words, a portrait.

In light of these findings from the field of the so-called anthropology of the image, it might be tempting 1) to describe the relationship between doubles and portraits merely in terms of the opposition between presentification and representation, or between substituting and depicting; and 2) to conflate such opposition with the contrast between schematic and mimetic images. The double would then be a schematised, abstract, or non-representational picture whereas the portrait would rest upon lifelikeness and representational adherence to the individual's outward appearance.

Yet one need only refer to such an emblematic episode of Greek mythology as the ghostly apparition of the dead Patroclus to Achilles to realise that both assumptions would be highly misleading and that the notion of the double cannot be equated simplistically with non-mimetic images. On the one side, the *eidolon* of Patroclus unquestionably provides a powerful instantiation of the category of the double, for it commands authority on behalf of the real Patroclus's absent agency. On the other side, however, it is an image that perfectly resembles the deceased, reproducing the physical traits of the once living hero down to the last detail, but lacking the substance of his body: as soon as Achilles attempts to grasp his friend, he sees the spirit fly away like a thin smoke. The *psyche* of Patroclus *is* Patroclus, not just a portrait resembling him. At the same time, and although it achieves 'complete similarity [*similitude complète*]' (Vernant 2007: 2026) to the substituted entity, it still remains markedly different from it, so that an unbridgeable incommensurability between the sacred agency and its apparition is made manifest. The likeness of the double is more a matter of contiguity than of just similarity with respect to the outward appearance:

> It is not a question of a more or less accurate reproduction: this portrait *is* the other person's very existence, this representation embodies his very being. Like the shadow, the portrait is debilitated and mute: but it is that person. It means, somehow, that the person is still here. (Bettini 1999: 47)

Two conclusions can be drawn from the considerations above. First, presentification is not incompatible with the mimetic stance. While it is true that to act as a substitute an artefact *does not necessarily need* to pursue physiognomic resemblance, this does not mean that a substitute *cannot* employ figurative means to convey a veridical appearance of its subject. Put another way, substitution may also imply portrayal. Accordingly, as argued by Jakub Stejskal (2019: 60–1), the domain of substitution by the image should be split into two subcategories: besides non-portraying, 'schematic' substitution, one should also acknowledge substitution by portrayal, as in the case of 'the two most paradigmatic accounts of substitution by image handed down through centuries in the West', that is, the Mandylion (or the *vera icon*) and the story of Pygmalion and Galatea, which both involve presentification and representational lifelikeness simultaneously.

The second conclusion is that despite all the overlap, a difference between the image and its referent must still be there. Patroclus's apparition is, and at the same time is not, the same person as the once living Patroclus. The *eidolon* should be regarded as only a partial representation of the hero for it lacks the completeness of genuine bodily interaction with his friend Achilles – and this lack is the very mark of death itself. While repeatedly calling attention to the crucial role played by the experience of loss and death in the genesis of image-making and to the essentially human act of seeking to extend life through (mostly visual) representations, Vernant has repeatedly insisted on the immeasurable difference between the sacred agency of the dead and its visible manifestation. In its operative and effective function, the *eidolon* of the departed 'seeks to establish real contact with the beyond and to bring about its presence in this earthly world. Yet in the very attempt to do this it emphasizes all the elements of the inaccessible, the mysterious, and the fundamentally foreign that the world beyond death holds for the living' (Vernant 2006b: 332).

To sum up, substitution by image does not need to, but can, indeed, coexist with representation in the sense of a likeness of the substituted subject. After all, the possibility of coupling presentification with similarity to outer appearances – and this with special reference to depicting dead people – is a long-standing commonplace in conceptions of the portrait in the history, mythology, and critique of art. The examples are uncountable, and range, just to name a few, from the story of Laodamia consoling herself with a waxen simulacrum of her husband Protesilaus, who was killed during the Trojan war, to the role played by hyper-realistic effigies in the Roman rites of imperial *consecratio* or in the royal funerary and burial ceremonies in France and England (Kantorowicz 1957; Giesey 1960; Marin 1988; Ginzburg 2001; Marek 2009); from Leon Battista Alberti's famous statement that portraiture contains a divine force 'which makes the dead seem almost alive' (1966: 63), or Francesco Lancilotti's claim that painting has the power to 'make a dead thing appear alive' (1885: 4), to Nikolai Gogol's Mephistophelian moneylender who, in order to survive death, asks an artist to paint his portrait (or rather his double) 'as if it were perfectly alive' (1998: 384).

In all these cases, the emphasis is on the extraordinary lifelikeness of cultural products construed to act as placeholders for dead people who, thanks to images, are made once again alive, or rather, more precisely, *almost* alive: an irremediable distance of the living from the departed is at any rate retained in that the deceased does not appear as present in person but is only presentified through a clearly perceivable medium. This mediateness is what characterises all images qua images, hence what makes all the difference between the pictures and the depicted subjects in the flesh. Regardless of how convincingly similar the image may be to its referent, a distance between the two needs to be noticeable. As pointed out by Edmund Husserl (2005: 22) in relation to his son's photographic portrait, depending on the kinds of depiction, the differences between representing image and represented subject may vary a great deal, but they must always be there: 'The appearing object is not just taken by itself, but as the representant of another object like it or resembling it.'

Yet what happens when a picture does not allow the beholder to distinguish clearly between representing object and represented subject? What if the image comes so close to its referent that the differences between the two become obliterated?

Holographic Resurrections

If we go back with these questions in mind to the phantom lovers of 'The Moon King' and compare them with Patroclus's apparition, a striking similarity emerges. In both cases, the simulacrum reproduces in every single detail the features of the deceased person, but cannot be considered as simply a mimetically accurate portrait, for it does not merely looks like that person; rather, it implies the presence – not (solely) the representation – of the referent. At the same time, however, Homer's description differs drastically from Apollinaire's in one significant respect, that is, bodily interaction. While the *eidolon* of Patroclus is ethereal and disembodied, the virtual images in

'The Moon King' possess concrete and tangible presence. The magic machines used by Ludwig II and his court accord them the ability to physically (and sexually) interact with the uncanny apparitions, thus undermining the image-character of those people brought back from the past.

Still, undermining is not the same as eliminating. No matter how vivid the cave dwellers' experience, a distance of the ghostly apparitions from their once living counterparts is clearly maintained. Apollinaire (1988: 76) lingers in describing the technical limitations of the priapic devices, which, 'being not very powerful', allow the users to bring back the dead for a few minutes only. Furthermore, and most crucially, even during such a short time the interaction between the real human beings and the images of people from the past only goes one way. As François Albera (2012) has pointed out, genuine communication proves impossible, since the simulacra of the dead are unable to utter words, and even less to answer questions; they can be kissed, but they can neither refuse kisses nor actively kiss back; and they seem completely unaware of themselves and of the fact that they are used as sexual objects. In short, the situation imagined by Apollinaire might be defined as a sort of virtual necrophilia, where the discrepancy between the once living human beings and their ghostly replicas is all but overcome. While in the case of Patroclus's apparition to Achilles, interacting with the dead agent is possible only on the condition of immateriality (the *psyche* having no corporeality), the converse is true in Apollinaire's story, where the dead agent is, indeed, provided with a body, but at the same time it is also reduced to that mere body. In both narratives, the empty presence of the simulacrum accords representation an ambiguous status, for it simultaneously poses, and assumes the absence of, its referent.

Thus, even in a science-fiction tale such as 'The Moon King', the dream (or perhaps the nightmare) of resuscitating the dead and interacting with them seems far from coming true. Nowadays, however, the rush towards more and more sophisticated technological apparatuses is bringing about a whole arsenal of rhetorical strategies used to suggest the possibility of finally finding a way to escape death. In what follows, I focus on some of the most recent methods used to 'reanimate' dead people by means of hyper-realistic artefacts that ambiguously waver between the physical and the virtual. In so doing, I find myself on the same page as Tom Gunning in calling for a new understanding of the notion of phantasm:

Although a discredited and untimely concept in both philosophy and science, the phantasm provides a tool for thinking through

modern – including 'new' – media [. . .] In the new media environment based in the proliferation of virtual images, the concept
of the phantasm gains a new valency as an element of the cultural imaginary. The ghost has emerged as a powerful metaphor in
recent literary studies, cultural history, and even political theory.
An examination of their history of representation, including the
newly emerging visual devices can sharpen and renew these metaphors. (Gunning 2007: 98)

The contemporary mediascape offers plenty of examples of such
'ghostification'. Late in October 2020, Kanye West astounded his
wife Kim Kardashian with a hologram of her late father Robert, a
lawyer best known for representing O. J. Simpson during the infamous trial in 1995. A recording of the woman's teary reaction to that
'special surprise from heaven', as she described the uncanny present
on Twitter, was immediately posted on social media. Needless to say,
the video went viral and sparked fierce debate about the appropriate-
ness of both the gift and its public sharing.

Besides any ethical concerns, what is most striking about the
whole thing is the impressively lifelike quality of the portrait (if it can
still be called so: I shall return to this shortly), which is not limited to
remarkable visual detail but also includes motion and a reasonably
well-matched voice. The holographic resurrection was made possible
by a complex combination of physical choreography, visual effects,
machine-learning algorithms, and sound synthesis. The first step was
to recruit an actor for motion capture who resembled the deceased
and was good enough at imitating his movements, facial expressions,
and the way he expressed himself. Once the footage was captured, a
team of visual effects artists employed machine learning to manipulate it by merging the actor's body (especially his face) with that of
Robert Kardashian as it appeared in some original video recordings.
After that, a compositor fine-tuned the algorithm-generated image
and made it turn into the person to be resurrected by bringing up
the hairline, adjusting the skin tone of the face and making sure it
matched with that of the hands and neck. A similar mimetic strategy
was used for the voice: the artificial intelligence generated a sort of
flat, unemotional version of the person's voice, which the sound engineer modified and modulated in order to achieve the right inflection,
accent, and intonation.

However astonishingly realistic the end product, one crucial
aspect needs to be highlighted, namely Kim Kardashian's inability to enjoy even the most minimal interaction with the image of
her late father. The reality-effect of the two-minute-long illusion
was considerably undermined by the fact that the TV star could

not do anything but watch, and passively listen to, the animated portrait. After all, Robert Kardashian's ghostly figure was only a sophisticated and far more expensive version of other similar products released into the consumer market, such as the Looking Glass Portrait, a device that allows users to convert photographic portraits containing depth information into lifelike three-dimensional holograms. It is therefore no wonder that hologram technology has found its widest application in contexts where genuine interaction between the speaker or performer and the audience is limited, unbalanced, if not completely absent, as in the case of the growing number of exhibitions of long-dead singers (Maria Callas, Frank Sinatra, Whitney Houston, Amy Winehouse, Tupac Shakur, Dio and others) playing 'live' in concert. The same goes for the digital cloning of dead movie stars (such as James Dean, Peter Cushing, or Carrie Fisher) via computer-generated imagery, thanks to which virtual actors, also known as synthespians, appear on screen who are barely distinguishable from their once living counterparts.

Meanwhile, a different technology is becoming increasingly mainstream and promises to be a game-changer in the field of digital resurrections. Virtual reality has made it possible to produce immersive environments where the user experiences a strong feeling of 'being there', either alone or in the company of avatars driven by real other humans and/or artificial intelligence. These 'environmental images' tend to conceal their mediateness (their resting upon a material support), their referentiality (their pointing to an extra-iconic dimension), and their separateness (usually ensured by some sort of framing device), hence paradoxically challenging their status as images, as icons: they are veritable 'an-icons' (Pinotti 2020). As such, they appear to be the best candidates to eventually replace representation with presentification. A concrete example may help us understand why this new iconoscape is more and more triumphally hailed as opening up the possibility of turning what has so far been confined to the realm of *utopian* or *dystopian* science fiction into reality.

From Portraiture to Spectrality

In February 2020 a documentary was aired in which a South Korean woman named Jang Ji-sung met a virtual recreation of her daughter Nayeon, who died at the age of seven in 2016. As in the above-mentioned cases, the avatar was created using real photographs and footage of the child. The hyper-realistic portrait was then animated with the aid of an actor equipped with motion-capture gear, and machine-learning algorithms were fed with original audio recordings to give Nayeon her voice back. Wearing a virtual reality headset and touch-sensitive gloves, Jang Ji-sung was seen racked with emotion when her 'daughter' emerged from an elaborate park scene (Nayeon's favourite playground until she passed away) and asked: 'Mum, where have you been? Did you think about me?' The video went on to show the two picking flowers together and celebrating Nayeon's birthday, the mother resting on a virtual bench overlaid onto a physical seat in a cross-reality environment. At the end of the simulation, after asking Jang Ji-sung to stay with her beside the bed, the virtual child turned into a butterfly and floated away.

One might be tempted to argue that the ancient quest for a way to ensure some sort of after-death communication is almost over. Not coincidentally, a few significant terms recur over and over again in the innumerable descriptions of the Korean show which can be found online in newspapers and blogs: the mother would have once more 'seen', 'met', or 'visited' her daughter, and the two would have been finally 'reunited' thanks to the power of immersive media. Debunking the rhetoric behind the use of these verbs and, more generally, behind the narrative of absolute immediateness and perfect transparency that is the hallmark of virtual reality is certainly an urgent scholarly goal that can be achieved through attention to underlining aspects such as the lack of credible eye movement of the little girl's avatar, its inability to honestly react to the mother's grief and to answer her questions, or the absence of any genuine interaction as a consequence of the technical constraints peculiar to all existing versions of the haptic gloves. And the situation is made even more tragic by the fact that, should the woman wish to meet her 'daughter' again in the future, she could only return again and again to that tricked-out simulation, where the child will never grow up, change, or surprise her. Despite all the rhetoric, a death-like stasis still permeates this technology of 'animation'.

Nevertheless, what counts most is that the astonishingly rapid pace of technological progress is changing the traditional idea of portraiture as representation by corroding it from the inside, that is, by pushing it to the point where representation tends to negate itself and turns into presentation. After all, the use of rhetorical strategies such as those just mentioned is in itself meaningful. These words seem to indicate that the South Korean mother, when wearing the virtual reality headset, felt as though she was actually there in front of her daughter. This feeling is the definition of presence in immersive virtual environments: one finds oneself transported or, to put it with Gordon Calleja (2011), incorporated into a quasi-real world where the virtual meets the physical, and where a human being of flesh and blood is for the first time given the possibility to see, touch, and talk to a digitally animated hyper-realistic portrait.

The technical limitations that currently affect the quality of the simulation and anything that can be done within virtual environments are all too evident, resulting in the impression that convincing digital resurrections such as the one depicted in the *Black Mirror* episode 'Be Right Back' will never be more than a pipe dream. However, we should remind ourselves of Walter Benjamin's idea that the history of every art form – and, we might add, of every image-making – points towards creating 'a demand whose hour of full satisfaction has not yet come', straining after effects that can be achieved 'only with a changed technical standard' (2008: 38). Indeed, it looks as though the advance of new imaging techniques is bringing the finish line of virtual immortality through animated portraits of the deceased closer than ever.

In order to realise, at least partially, the potential of such technological progress, one only has to think about how easy it is nowadays to model a personal, unbelievably realistic, and fully customisable avatar from a 3D body scan or, even more simply, from a single input photo taken with a smartphone and transformed into a perfect replica of the individual thanks to machine-learning frameworks such as GANs, generative adversarial networks (Li et al. 2021). This digital portrait can subsequently be animated using deepfake technology, which allows users to modify their facial expressions, body movements, and voice even in real time.

Following this path, over the last years innovative start-ups have been working intensively to produce digital 'selves' that can live on forever in the form of chatbots. In 2016, for instance, James Vlahos, the CEO of HereAfter, created an interactive chatbot dubbed 'Dadbot' that mimicked his late father's speech patterns, trying to replicate conversational attributes such as style, tone, and accent. That very same year, Eugenia Kuyda, co-founder of technology company Luka, digitally recreated her late best friend Roman Mazurenko using text messages he had sent her before his death in a car accident (on this and other similar examples, see Sisto 2020).

To be sure, these digital doubles still suffer from imperfections of all sorts and respond clumsily to even the most basic questions. And yet they have already attracted the attention of tech giants such as Microsoft, which filed a patent in December 2020 that envisions a system for creating a chatbot modelled after a 'past or present entity [. . .] such as a friend, a relative, an acquaintance, a celebrity, a fictional character, a historical figure' by using their social data. Images, voice recordings, electronic messages, written letters and posts might be collected, as the patent explicitly suggests, to revive a dead loved one through the creation of a model able to converse and interact 'in the personality of [that] specific person'.

The outcome of processes such as this depends on the available amount and quality of data on the dead, but in the light of the impressive advances in machine learning, and given that our everyday lives have moved online so much that a new term 'phygital' was coined to indicate the increasing blending of digital experiences with physical ones, it is a safe bet that we are not so far any more from being able to convincingly animate the photo-portrait of a deceased individual so that it no longer looks like a picture but like the real person. Innovative enterprises such as TheIncLab (https://www.theinclab.com/work/avatarAI.html) provide a glimpse into where technology is headed. Among the many interesting projects advertised on the company's website, one promises to capture 'somebody's mind, memories and soul' in order to create a 'virtually immortalised' three-dimensional version of the individual that can move, express, and generate new sentences just like the model. At this stage, one could barely tell the difference between the animated portrait and its referent, between the replicant and the real person. And we would perhaps be reminded of Jacques Derrida's statement that 'if there is something like spectrality, there are reasons to doubt the border between the present, the actual or present reality of the present, and everything that can be opposed to it: absence, non-presence, non-effectivity, inactuality, virtuality, or even the simulacrum in general, and so forth' (1994: 48).

And yet, despite techno-optimistic expectations and enthusiastic forecasts, the historical and theoretical genealogy that we have sketched out from Homer to the contemporary iconoscape demonstrates that the distance between the portrait and the portrayed can never be completely overcome. This distance is inherent to the very notion of the portrait, and more generally of the image. After all, even in Apollinaire's imaginary story, or in the virtual meeting between the South Korean mother and her 'daughter', or in all the other cases analysed here, the subjects involved remained well aware of being confronted with a simulation. This awareness provides a perceptual and cognitive frame to *all* image experiences, and this, in turn, is precisely what makes and will make it impossible to completely bridge the gap between the image world – no matter how realistic it might be – and actual reality.

Acknowledgements

This chapter was written within the framework of the research project 'AN-ICON. An-Iconology: History, Theory, and Practices of Environmental Images'. The project has received funding from the European Research Council (ERC) under the European Union's Horizon 2020 research and innovation programme (grant agreement No. 834033 AN-ICON), and is hosted by the Department of Philosophy 'Piero Martinetti' at the University of Milan (Project 'Departments of Excellence 2023–2027' awarded by the Italian Ministry of University and Research).

References

Albera, François (2012), 'Le cinéma projeté', *Intermédialités/Intermediality*, 20 (autumn), https://www.erudit.org/fr/revues/im/2012-n20-im0528/1015084ar/ (last accessed 15 February 2021).

Alberti, Leon Battista (1966 [1435]), *On Painting*, New Haven, CT: Yale University Press.

Apollinaire, Guillaume (1988 [1916]), 'The Moon King', in Guillaume Apollinaire, *The Poet Assassinated and Other Stories*, London: Grafton, pp. 70–83.

Belting, Hans (2011 [2001]), *An Anthropology of Images*, Princeton, NJ: Princeton University Press.

Benjamin, Walter (2008 [1935–36]), 'The Work of Art in the Age of Its Technological Reproducibility', in *The Work of Art in the Age of Its Technological Reproducibility and Other Writings on Media*, ed. Michael W. Jennings, Brigid Doherty, and Thomas Y. Levin, Cambridge, MA: The Belknap Press of Harvard University Press, pp. 19–55.

Bettini, Maurizio (1999 [1992]), *The Portrait of the Lover*, Berkeley: University of California Press.

Calleja, Gordon (2011), *In-Game: From Immersion to Incorporation*, Cambridge, MA: MIT Press.

Derrida, Jacques (1994 [1993]), *Specters of Marx: The State of the Debt, the Work of Mourning and the New International*, London: Routledge.

Gell, Alfred (1998), *Art and Agency: An Anthropological Theory*, Oxford: Oxford University Press.

Giesey, Ralph E. (1960), *The Royal Funeral Ceremony in Renaissance France*, Geneva: Droz.

Ginzburg, Carlo (2001 [1998]), *Wooden Eyes: Nine Reflections on Distance*, New York: Columbia University Press.

Gogol, Nikolai V. (1998 [1835]), 'The Portrait', in *The Collected Tales of Nikolai Gogol*, ed. Richard Pevear and Larissa Volokhonsky, New York: Pantheon, pp. 340–93.

Gunning, Tom (2007), 'To Scan a Ghost: The Ontology of Mediated Vision', *Grey Room*, 26: 94–127.

Husserl, Edmund (2005 [1904–05]), 'Phantasy and Image Consciousness', in *Phantasy, Image Consciousness, and Memory (1898–1925)*, ed. John B. Brough, Dordrecht: Springer, pp. 1–115.

Kantorowicz, Ernst (1957), *The King's Two Bodies: A Study in Mediaeval Political Theology*, Princeton, NJ: Princeton University Press.

Lancilotti, Francesco (1885 [1509]), *Trattato di pittura*, Recanati: Simboli.

Li, Zhong, Lele Chen, Celong Liu, Fuyao Zhang, Zekun Li, Yu Gao, Yuanzhou Ha, Chenliang Xu, Shuxue Quan, and Yi Xu (2021), 'Animated 3D Human Avatars from a Single Image with GAN-based Texture Inference', *Computers & Graphics*, 95: 81–91.

Marek, Kristin (2009), *Die Körper des Königs*, Munich: Fink.

Marin, Louis (1988 [1981]), *Portrait of the King*, Minneapolis: University of Minnesota Press.

Pinotti, Andrea (2020), 'Towards An-Iconology: The Image as Environment', *Screen*, 61(4): 594–603.

Pliny the Elder (1938 [77–78 CE]), *Naturalis Historia*, Cambridge, MA: Harvard University Press.

Sisto, Davide (2020 [2018]), *Online Afterlives: Immortality, Memory, and Grief in Digital Culture*, Cambridge, MA: MIT Press.

Stejskal, Jakub (2019), 'Substitution by Image: The Very Idea', *The Journal of Aesthetics and Art Criticism*, 77(1): 55–66.

Vernant, Jean-Pierre (2006a [1960]), 'Some Aspects of Personal Identity in Greek Religion', in Jean-Pierre Vernant, *Myth and Thought among the Greeks*, New York: Zone Books, pp. 353–67.

Vernant, Jean-Pierre (2006b [1962]), 'The Figuration of the Invisible and the Psychological Category of the Double: The *Kolossos*', in Jean-Pierre Vernant, *Myth and Thought among the Greeks*, New York: Zone Books, pp. 321–32.

Vernant, Jean-Pierre (2006c [1983]), 'From the Presentification of the Invisible to the Imitation of Appearance', in Jean-Pierre Vernant, *Myth and Thought among the Greeks*, New York: Zone Books, pp. 333–49.

Vernant, Jean-Pierre (2007 [1990]), 'Figuration et image', in *Oeuvres. Religion, rationalités, politique*, vol. 2, Paris: Seuil, pp. 2019–31.

Index

EU representative:
Easy Access System Europe
Mustamäe tee 50, 10621 Tallinn, Estonia
Gpsr.requests@easproject.com

www.ingramcontent.com/pod-product-compliance
Lightning Source LLC
Chambersburg PA
CBHW071711170526
45165CB00005B/1967